Private Wrongs

PRIVATE WRONGS

ARTHUR RIPSTEIN

Harvard University Press

Cambridge, Massachusetts

London, England

2016

Library of Congress Cataloging-in-Publication Data

Names: Ripstein, Arthur, author.
Title: Private wrongs / Arthur Ripstein.
Description: Cambridge, Massachusetts : Harvard University Press, 2016. |
Includes bibliographical references and index.
Identifiers: LCCN 2015034402 | ISBN 9780674659803 (alk. paper)
Subjects: LCSH: Torts—Philosophy. | Torts—Moral and ethical aspects. |
Torts. | Damages. | Liability (Law) | Personality (Law)
Classification: LCC K923 .R57 2016 | DDC 346.03—dc23

For Karen, Aviva, and Noah

Contents

Preface

Tort law addresses two of the most familiar and most pressing questions of social life: How should people treat each other? Whose problem is it when things go wrong? Other normative systems seek to answer one or the other of these questions. Criminal law and administrative regulation restrict the ways in which people are allowed to treat each other, as do informal social norms and the demands of morality. Schemes of social insurance and disaster relief address unwelcome consequences in one way, private charity in another, and indifference in a third. Tort law is distinctive because it answers both by treating them as a single question, articulating norms of conduct by specifying rights, and fashioning remedies to give effect to those very rights.

The central claim of this book will be that the unity of right and remedy is the key to understanding tort law. In the service of this central claim I will develop a systematic account of the rights to person and property that private persons have against each other. I will both characterize and explain the distinctiveness of those rights in terms of the thought that no person is in charge of any other person. This idea, I will contend, explains both the structuring features of the rights to bodies, reputations, and property to which the law of tort affords protection, and also why the form of that protection must be specifically remedial—why rights, so understood, survive their violation, and so must be given effect, however imperfectly, through remedies.

At various points in the book, I contrast my view with prominent accounts that treat tort law as an instrument for achieving results—accounts that do not focus on the relations between the parties or the idea that rights survive their own violation. Many of these grow out of Oliver Wendell Holmes's confident announcement that the "moral phraseology" of the law of torts is a façade behind which policy decisions are hidden. For Holmes (at least when he was writing as a scholar rather than a judge) there is no place for the idea that one person is entitled to constrain the conduct of another, nor for the idea that a right survives its own violation. Generations of scholars have followed this approach. Others accept the idea that the norms of tort law focus on rights, but regard remedies as a tool for, or expression of, other social purposes. I do not purport to show that no instrumental account could be made to work, only that a rights-based account can overcome all of the familiar objections to it. In some cases I suggest that something close to the converse of Holmes's claim is true: Arguments cast in the language of interests and balancing actually presuppose rights-based analyses. Because my aim is to show not that instrumentalism is impossible, only that it is not necessary, I focus on showing how tort law could be something other than an instrument of policy. I want to demonstrate that the "moral phraseology" is not a façade: Tort law gives effect to moral ideas that look very similar to the doctrines that give effect to them.

I am not the first person—not even the first person in my hallway—to argue for a noninstrumental understanding of tort law. Beginning with Ernest Weinrib's groundbreaking works, especially *The Idea of Private Law,* noninstrumentalist accounts of tort law have arisen from their Holmesian ashes. The argument of this book builds on Weinrib's arguments. Weinrib's use of the Aristotelian vocabulary of corrective justice and correlativity somehow led some readers to mistakenly suppose that his analysis applies only to cases in which a defendant gains at the plaintiff's expense, that his concern was exclusively with the after-the-fact allocation of losses that had already occurred, that corrective justice could be paired with any specification of rights, or that a noninstrumental account must presuppose that tort law has intrinsic value of a sort that is to be added to the catalogue of socially desirable outcomes that the modern state should pursue. I hope to avoid these misunderstandings by beginning with an account of the morality of interpersonal interaction, and showing how it manifests itself in the law of private wrongs. This approach may, I realize, invite other misunderstandings. My work also builds on that of other writers who have contributed to rights-based accounts of tort law. Because my central ambition is to articulate a systematic account of the rights tort law protects, I do not engage in extended discussions of many of those contributions.

Much of my other writing in recent years has focused on Kant's legal and political philosophy, and my understanding of private wrongs has been shaped by my engagement with his arguments. A number of people have asked, either in person or in print, about the viability of "turning Kant into a common lawyer." Students of the history of the common law often note its antitheoretical orientation, its practice of developing one case at a time, and some writers have thought it important to point out the great common law judges of earlier centuries did not read Kant. No doubt they did not, but any felt need to point this out betrays a misconception of Kant's, and indeed any, philosophical project of understanding an area of legal doctrine. In a casuistical system such as the common law, doctrine develops as judges decide cases, drawing on precedents and learned authors. I do not put forward a historical hypothesis according to which moral principles invented in Kant's writings are the secret source of the common law of tort, and as yet undisclosed source of judicial authority. Nor do I think citizens need to read Kant to figure out what the law is demanding of them, or that judges must do so in order to resolve cases. To the contrary, I take seriously Kant's own insistence that he would not presume to invent a new moral principle. The point of providing an account of the form of thought in an area of legal doctrine is not to invent that area, or give someone else credit for inventing it. Instead, it is to make it intelligible, to show how the characteristic modes of reasoning, the questions asked, and the inferences permitted or refused fit into an integrated pattern. That pattern is composed of conceptual and normative structures rather than causes and effects. The pattern of reasoning on which I focus is itself an articulation of simple but powerful moral ideas about each person's independence from others. Kant articulates this idea of independence, but it is not to be confused with the idea of autonomy that figures elsewhere in Kant's moral writings. Autonomy is the idea of a free being's self-determination, which can be understood "apart from any relations" in which it stands. The idea of independence, by contrast, is irreducibly relational. In the hope of keeping this contrast firmly in view, outside of this paragraph and one quotation from a court, the word "autonomy" does not appear in this book.

Readers familiar with Kant's writings about private law will recognize more specific traces of them here—the focus on relations, the idea of setting and pursuing purposes, the claim that each human being has the right to be beyond reproach, and the idea that rights survive their own violation. A broader Kantian perspective also shapes the project as a whole: Kant argues that a central part of interpersonal morality requires institutional instantiation in a body of positive law. This book can be read as an illustration of how this claim applies in a specific instance.

I have been thinking and writing about torts for more than two decades, and would not have started, let alone finished this book, without the advice and assistance of many people. I first became interested in tort law in conversations with my colleague Ernest Weinrib. Since then, Ernie has been a constant source of inspiration, friendship, engagement, and conversation. He will always be the *Rav* for philosophical writing about torts. Around the same time, my summer-camp and graduate school friend Ben Zipursky started law school, and we, too, began what turned out to be many decades discussing torts. I quickly learned that the law has better examples than any that philosophers could come up with—ones that are obvious and baffling in just the right combination. As my interest in the topic deepened, I decided to spend my first sabbatical at Yale Law School, where I had the opportunity to study torts with Guido Calabresi. Although I found myself disagreeing with much of what Guido had to say—beginning with his claim that you can teach someone all of tort doctrine in about twenty minutes, after which you get to the interesting policy questions—I knew I was in the presence of greatness. In addition to learning a great deal about how people respond to incentives, Guido taught me two things of life-changing importance. First, that the intellectual interest of torts is matched only by its fun as a teaching subject, and second, that you are strictly liable for anything you say in print. While at Yale I also learned much talking to Jules Coleman. I articulated my ideas about part of tort law in a 1999 book, *Equality, Responsibility, and the Law*, in the context of another series of debates. I take no position on whether the position developed here is consistent with those earlier views. Just as it appeared, I moved half of my teaching to the Faculty of Law, where I have taught torts regularly since. I am grateful to Ron Daniels, the Dean who exercised the power of eminent domain over my appointment, and to Deans Mayo Moran and Ed Iacobucci for their continuing support. I am also grateful to two of the three Philosophy Department chairs during this time—Cheryl Misak and Donald Ainslie—for their encouragement and support. My role as the third of the three chairs was less conducive to completion of this book.

I am fortunate to hold appointments in two disciplines in which research and teaching can be integrated more or less seamlessly. It has probably been a long time since a mathematician established a research program focused on topics in the first-year curriculum, but in both law and philosophy you can spend your entire career writing about the topics that you teach. I have been privileged in the extraordinarily talented and engaged students that I have taught in my torts classes. Many of the ideas and arguments developed here began as reflections on how to explain a particular case or answer a challenging question. I am grateful to my fellow torts teachers, especially Bruce Chapman, for countless conversations about cases that interested me.

I have been developing and discussing preliminary versions of this material for many years, and am grateful to all of the people who asked questions at talks that I gave or provided comments on earlier papers, and particularly to Hanoch Dagan, Avihay Dorfman, Barbara Fried, Greg Keating, Henry Richardson, and Stephen Smith for extended correspondence. I benefited from conversations with Lisa Austin, Peter Benson, Andrew Botterell, Erika Chamberlain, Abraham Drassinower, David Dyzenhaus, David Enoch, John Gardner, John Goldberg, Alon Harel, Martín Hevia, Tony Honoré, Paul Hurley, Frances Kamm, Greg Keating, Dennis Klimchuk, James Lee, Paul Miller, Mayo Moran, Sophia Moreau, James Penner, Stephen Perry, Stephen Pitel, Irit Samet, Catherine Sharkey, Henry Smith, Lionel Smith, Steve Smith, Daniel Statman,

Sandy Steele, Rob Stevens, Catherine Valcke, Stephen Waddams, Gary Watson, Arnold Weinrib, and Leif Wenar.

As the book neared completion, I got much help and support. Hanoch Dagan and Avihay Dorfman invited me to discuss parts of the book in their Private Law Theory Seminar in March 2015. Members of the law and philosophy discussion group at the University of Toronto—Alan Brudner, Bruce Chapman, Pavlos Eleftheriadis, Timothy Endicott, Chris Essert, Joanna Langille, Ronit Levine-Schnur, Larissa Katz, Michael Kessler, Hillary Nye, Hamish Stewart, Martin Stone, Malcolm Thorburn, Ernest Weinrib, Jacob Weinrib, and Ariel Zylberman—spent a term of weekly meetings discussing a draft of the manuscript. Jason Neyers and Nick Sage each sent me detailed written comments on the entire manuscript. I owe an additional debt to Jason, without whose prompting Chapters 5 and 6 might never have been written. I also received helpful comments from three readers for Harvard University Press, who turned out to be John Goldberg, Martin Stone, and Ben Zipursky. Lindsay Waters of Harvard University Press has supported the project from the start, and his assistant, Amanda Peery, was a model of helpfulness and efficiency. Zachary Al-Khatib provided excellent research assistance; Aleatha Cox assembled everything into a proper manuscript; and Hillary Nye prepared the index.

The Social Sciences and Humanities Research Council of Canada provided funding for this project.

My greatest debt is to my wife, Karen Weisman, and our children, Aviva and Noah. I wrote a book about the minimal standards governing the ways in which people can be constrained to treat each other surrounded and encouraged by much more than anyone can hope for—an endless supply of love, intelligence, good humor, and generosity of spirit.

The final text is informed by discussions first advanced in several of my earlier articles:

"Tort Law in a Liberal State," *Journal of Tort Law* 1, no. 2 (2007): 1–41.

"Civil Recourse and the Separation of Wrongs and Remedies," *Florida State Law Review* 39 (2011): 163–207.

"As if It Had Never Happened," *William & Mary Law Review* 48, no. 5 (2007): 1957–1997.

CHAPTER 1

Introduction

Retrieving the Idea of a Private Wrong

A TORT IS A PRIVATE WRONG that one private person commits against another. The aggrieved party comes before a court on his or her own initiative, seeking a remedy against the alleged wrongdoer. The factual situations that give rise to tort actions are diverse, yet familiar. A pedestrian is hit by a motorist who is texting while driving; a careless waiter spills scalding hot coffee on a customer; a physician fails to close a wound properly, or closes it, leaving an instrument in the patient's abdomen; a perfectly tame circus elephant escapes and tramples someone's home; a dam bursts; a neighbor's barking dog keeps someone awake at night; someone mistakenly enters and collects wood from somebody else's land; a stranded hiker breaks into a cabin in a storm; artworks are looted from the homes of fleeing refugees; a manufacturer calculates that an unsafe product will generate more revenue than the cost of compensating those it injures; an angry neighbor makes a noise so as to disrupt a nearby business he dislikes; a carefully researched but erroneous news report ruins someone's reputation. In each of these examples someone complains, not only of another's wrongdoing, but that she or he in particular has been wronged. The claimant comes before the court to demand a remedy, which is supposed to repair that very wrong.

1. Retrieving the Idea of a Private Wrong

Despite the familiarity of its subject matter, tort doctrine can seem puzzling from the perspective of prominent ideas in legal scholarship and moral and political philosophy. In some of the above examples, such as the hiker in the storm, or the person who mistakenly enters another's property, or the carefully researched news report that ruins someone's reputation, it looks as though a morally innocent person is legally liable. In others, one person is held liable while another, who was equally careless, is not—perhaps the pedestrian hit by the texting driver was injured just before a second, third, or fourth texting driver passed by. Tort doctrine is also puzzling because of the problems that it chooses to ignore: Although the person who suffers discomfort from sunlight reflected from a neighbor's glass roof gets a remedy,[1] the person whose hotel is rendered worthless by a shadow cast over its beach area does not;[2] the person who slips and falls gets a remedy, but someone who dies or is injured while another person stands by and does nothing has no legal complaint against that person.

The past century of legal scholarship has made tort law more, rather than less, puzzling. Oliver Wendell Holmes Jr. set the agenda for most subsequent writing about torts by arguing that the moral language of duty, right, and obligation is really just a misleading cover for concerns about consequences and social policy. For Holmes, the only real question in tort litigation is "who wins?" and that question can be answered only in a resolutely forward-looking way. He remarked that the law "abounds in moral phraseology,"[3] and nowhere does he seem to think that this is more apparent than in the law of torts. Holmes is dismissive of talk of rights and duties, characterizing the Latin maxim *sic utere tuo ut alienum non laedas*—use what is yours in a way that does not injure your neighbor—as "a benevolent yearning."[4] At best, he suggests that such fine phrases

---

1. Bank of New Zealand v. Greenwood, [1984] 1 NZLR 525.

2. Fontainebleau Hotel Corp. v. Forty-Five Twenty-Five, Inc., 114 So. 2d 357, 1959 Fla. App.

3. Oliver Wendell Holmes Jr., *The Common Law* (Boston: Little, Brown, and Co., 1881), 79.

4. Oliver Wendell Holmes Jr., "Privilege, Malice, and Intent," *Harvard Law Review* 8 (1894): 3.

actually function as a smokescreen for decisions that are made on grounds of something he calls "policy,"[5] in the face of which all juridical distinctions dissolve.

Some academics and judges have followed Holmes's lead. Guido Calabresi describes "right" as a "weasel word" behind which judges hide their policy choices;[6] Lord Denning wrote, "the truth is that . . . duty, remoteness and causation, are all devices by which the courts limit the range of liability for negligence or nuisance . . . The law has to draw a line somewhere. Ultimately it is a question of policy which we, as judges, have to decide."[7] Both Calabresi and Denning suppose that a private dispute provides a judge with a convenient (if not welcome) opportunity to make and implement broad policy judgments about more general societal problems. On this view, both the rights of the parties and the remedies awarded must be understood as instruments, available for whatever purpose officials think best. This idea that judges operate under such a general power-conferring rule[8] and struggle to disguise their choices gets much of its impetus from the supposed impossibility of taking remedies at face value.

A century of Holmes-inspired scholarship has proposed a wide range of policy purposes and postulated even more mechanisms through which the law might be seen to realize them. Often, however, what began as an explanatory enterprise becomes prescriptive or even abolitionist, when the author realizes that tort law is a wasteful or ineffective way of realizing whatever he or she initially contended was its underlying purpose.

I believe that these modes of thinking are the product of losing sight of a simple way of thinking about private wrongs, one that is both morally and legally familiar.[9] When a plaintiff brings a tort action against the

---

5. Ibid.

6. Guido Calabresi, "Concerning Cause and the Law of Torts: An Essay for Harry Kalven, Jr.," *University of Chicago Law Review* 43 (1975): 92n39. He says the same of causation in *The Costs of Accidents* (New Haven: Yale University Press, 1970), 6n8.

7. Lamb v. London Borough of Camden, [1981] QB 625 (CA).

8. I owe this formulation to Martin Stone, "Focusing the Law: What Legal Interpretation Is Not," in *Law and Interpretation: Essays in Legal Philosophy*, ed. Andrei Marmor (New York: Oxford University Press 1995), 31–97.

9. As Adolf Reinach remarks, "Philosophy begins in marveling at what seems to be obvious." Reinach, *The A Priori Foundations of the Civil Law* (1913), trans. John Crosby

defendant, the basic form of the complaint is "the defendant is not allowed to do that to me," rather than any of "the defendant is not allowed
to do that," "this can't be allowed to happen to me," or even "I demand
compensation." The plaintiff goes to court seeking a remedy, but the
ground of the remedy is what the plaintiff contends is a wrong. On this
simple and familiar picture, the point of the remedy is to make up for the
wrong; the remedy is meant as a substitute for some right that was infringed.[10] By its nature, a substitute is not an equivalent; a substitute is a
deficient version of an equivalent. The point of the substitute is to
make up for something, even if that something cannot be made up for
completely. What needs to be made up is not an object, but the plaintiff's entitlement to constrain the defendant's conduct. That is, the plaintiff's right is not extinguished by being violated.

These ideas—that a tort is a private wrong, and that the point of a tort
action is to correct or remedy a wrong—are very old. Aristotle describes
courts in such cases as doing "corrective justice," which he characterizes
in explicitly transactional terms: The point of corrective justice is to reverse a transaction. In recent decades scholars have revived this idea. Most
prominently, Ernest Weinrib has argued that any policy-based account
of tort law cannot explain the most fundamental feature of a tort action—the fact that the court is addressing a dispute between two private
parties and asks only about whether the plaintiff currently before the court
is entitled to a remedy from the defendant currently before the court.[11] The
plaintiff does not come before a court to enforce a general moral norm or
assist in the pursuit of a general public policy; the demand for a remedy
is against the very person who is alleged to have wronged that very plaintiff. Nor does the plaintiff demand to be put back in the position he or
she would have been in, in the service of a policy of seeing to it that people
have the objects of their rights. That policy would apply regardless of why

---

(Berlin: Walter de Gruyter, 2012), 9.

10. See Robert Stevens, *Torts and Rights* (Oxford: Oxford University Press, 2007),
59–91.

11. Weinrib first formulated this argument in a series of articles in the 1980s. The devel-
oped statement of his position is in *The Idea of Private Law* (Cambridge, MA: Harvard
University Press, 1995). A similar critique is developed in Jules Coleman, *Risks and Wrongs*
(New York: Cambridge University Press, 1992).

the plaintiff no longer had it. Both the dispute and its resolution are bipolar: the only issues concern the past transaction between the parties. The remedy depends on the transaction between the parties because the wrong to which it is a remedy must be understood in terms of the relation between them, not in terms of any feature particular to only one of them.

Weinrib argued that any policy purpose being pursued through tort litigation inevitably focuses exclusively on one or the other of the parties. The prominent suggestion that the point of tort liability is to encourage better behavior looks only to the effect on people not currently before the court; the defendant is of interest only to be held up as an example to influence others, and the particular plaintiff is not relevant to the inquiry. Conversely, any concern with compensation for the injured plaintiff has no explanation of why the particular defendant who wronged the plaintiff should be the one to provide it. Any combination of such purposes will at most explain why the defendant before the court should be made to pay damages to some person or organization, and why the plaintiff before the court should be entitled to receive compensation from some source, thereby failing to explain the nexus between this plaintiff and this defendant. The point of the bipolarity critique is that any instrumental account will represent this familiar and fundamental feature of a tort action as merely accidental. Working backward from this feature of a tort action, Weinrib defended the familiar pre-Holmesian thought that the point of a remedy must be understood in terms of the right the violation of which it repairs.

Corrective justice accounts have met with vigorous resistance. One response has been to suggest that the failure of instrumental accounts to explain legal doctrines and processes simply shows that those doctrines and processes should be changed.[12] A different line of objection charges that the idea that a wrong can be remedied is an illusion; what is done is done, and a court cannot change the past.[13] Still another complaint is

12. For an extreme statement of this position, see Louis Kaplow and Steven Shavell, *Fairness versus Welfare* (Cambridge, MA: Harvard University Press, 2002).

13. Scott Hershovitz wistfully formulates the point: "We cannot undo what we have done. No matter how hard we wish that we could turn back time when a trigger is pulled or

that such an account must ultimately be empty because no noninstrumental explanation is available as to why courts would take an interest in reversing or correcting some transactions but not others. Instead, it is sometimes suggested, a system of corrective justice must borrow its content from a substantive theory of which purposes and activities are most important.

2. The Main Ideas

I think that Weinrib has the better of his debate with the instrumentalist, and I share his conception of wrongs as violations of rights and remedies as substitutive. But I defend these conclusions by a different route. Rather than working backward from a tort action, my account moves in the opposite direction, starting from the moral idea that no person is in charge of another. I develop an account of that idea, and use it to generate distinctions between the different types of private wrongs, each of which, except for defamation, is organized in terms of the use of means. I provide an explanation of the familiar divisions of tort law in terms of the consistent use of means. Defamation receives a separate treatment, because it is not concerned with the use of means, but is an application of the same idea of no person being in charge of another to imputations of wrongdoing. I argue further that the normative relationship through which one person is not in charge of another continues to hold even after a wrong has been committed, and so, like Weinrib, arrive at the conclusion that the particular plaintiff recovers from the particular defendant because of the right that was violated.

Although the point of a remedy is to provide a substitute for the right violated, I have sought to avoid putting the point in terms of "correction." Despite its distinguished pedigree, talk of corrective justice has led some people to suppose that the organizing idea is exclusively remedial,[14] that

---

a driver hits a child, we cannot. The moment one person wrongs another, the wrong is part of our history, indelibly, and we must decide how to go on." See Hershovitz, "Corrective Justice for Civil Recourse Theorists," *Florida State University Law Review* 39 (2011): 117.

14. To some ears, the term "corrective" sounds irredeemably and irremediably remedial. Whether this is so of course depends on how it is understood. Weinrib's account of

it applies only in cases in which the plaintiff's loss is matched by an equivalent gain by the defendant, or that the point of the remedy is to replicate an antecedent factual situation, something that cannot be done in cases of loss, because any restoration of the plaintiff must come at the defendant's expense. But that isn't it at all. Instead, both right and remedy must be understood relationally.

I will develop this account by focusing on norms of conduct and will say almost nothing about remedies or liability until Chapter 8. Remedies are remedial, and for that reason secondary: They give continuing effect to the norms of conduct even after those norms have been violated. Ordinarily a dispute only makes it to court if one party seeks a remedy from the other. But although disputes provide the impetus for litigation, the rationale for the remedies is to be understood in terms of the norm of conduct, and applies even when the factual state of affairs cannot be restored. But, I will argue, only certain norms of conduct are capable of and require remedies in this way. I will argue that the point of a remedy is to protect what people already have: their person (understood as bodily integrity and reputation) and property. Tort law is a system that not only protects but *constitutes* each person's entitlement to use their bodies and

---

corrective justice focuses on the idea of a system of rights to person and property that survive their own violation; it is an account of remedies that is nonetheless dependent upon an account of rights considered as nonremedial. See Weinrib's *The Idea of Private Law* and *Corrective Justice* (Oxford: Oxford University Press, 2012). Others have taken the term "corrective" in other directions. Other torts scholars, including Jules Coleman and Stephen Perry, have, in the process of articulating alternatives to the economic analysis of tort law, used the term "corrective justice" to refer to what is arguably a remedial view, a view that is supposed to explain the duty of repair owed by a defendant to the plaintiff he or she injured. Jules L. Coleman, *The Practice of Principle: In Defence of a Pragmatist Approach to Legal Theory* (Oxford: Oxford University Press, 2001), 31–34. Perry, by contrast, characterizes it in terms of the correction of harms for which the tortfeasor is responsible, where that responsibility, in turn, is to be analyzed in terms of having had an adequate capacity and opportunity to avoid causing those harms. Stephen Perry, "Responsibility for Outcomes, Risk, and the Law of Torts," in *Philosophy and the Law of Torts,* ed. Gerald J. Postema (Cambridge: Cambridge University Press, 2001), 72–130. John Gardner suggests that corrective justice is the norm "that regulates (by giving a ground for) the reversal of at least some transactions." Gardner, "What Is Tort Law For? Part 1: The Place of Corrective Justice," *Law and Philosophy* 14 (2011), 10.

property as they see fit, consistent with the entitlement of others to do the same, by specifying the terms of consistent use of means.

The morality of interaction to which tort law gives effect—the idea that others must not interfere with your body, property, or reputation—rests on a few simple ideas: first, that human beings are active beings who are entitled to set and pursue their own purposes, restricted only by the like entitlement of others to do the same; second, that the rights to which this norm of interaction gives rise survive their own violation; third, that no person ever needs to clear his or her own name. These three ideas are interrelated: Your entitlement to set and pursue your own purposes, to use your body and property as you see fit, is not changed when someone violates your right, and the point of the remedy is not to return things to the antecedent factual state of affairs, but rather to uphold the wronged party's entitlement that others restrict their conduct. The right to reputation is slightly different, in that a good reputation does not figure in your setting and pursuit of your purposes. Instead, it is an application of the same idea of no person being in charge of another to imputations of wrongdoing; if another person imputes a wrong to you, you do not need to defer to the imputation; you are entitled to demand that it be established or withdrawn. The idea that no person is the superior or subordinate of another—captured in the Roman law idea that each person is *sui iuris*—includes the right to demand that anyone who alleges wrongdoing establish it. This idea underlies and organizes the law of defamation.

Rather than importing content from some more general moral or economic theory, I argue that the rights enforced by tort law are specific to the form of interaction appropriate to free beings. The restrictions governing such beings focus on the ways in which they pursue their purposes, rather than on the content of those purposes. A system of private rights is a system in which each person's uses of his or her body and property are consistent with everyone else's, and each person's reputation is fixed by what that person has done. A wrong is an action that is inconsistent with another person's right to body, property, or reputation, and a remedy restores the consistency to the extent that it is possible to do so. The chapters that follow identify the different types of inconsistency that can arise between separate persons setting and pursuing purposes.

The principal way in which inconsistency can arise is though the inappropriate use of means; the relevant norms govern the means that a person uses, rather than the ends being pursued. Using means is the only way in which a person can pursue purposes. I mean "means" to be construed in a specific way: Your means are just those things about which you are entitled to decide the ends for which they will be used. The means that you have, then, are whatever it is that you are entitled to use for setting and pursuing purposes. But although I mean to construe the idea of means broadly, at the same time, the implications of this broad construal have a narrow range: The means that you have, in the first instance, are just your body—your ability to decide what to do and to manipulate objects in space—and your property, that is, the things outside of your body that you are entitled to use for pursuing purposes.

Understood in this way, the law of torts focuses on means in three interrelated ways. First, it protects the means that each person has for setting and pursuing purposes. Second, it restricts the means that each person can use by precluding one person from using means that belong to another without that other's authorization. Third, it restricts the ways in which each person can use his or her own means, to those ways that are consistent with everyone else being able to do the same. The first and third come together in prohibiting interfering with another's means by using yours in dangerous or defective ways; the second generates the prohibition on trespasses against persons and property.

The norms governing the ways in which people use their bodies and property do not demand or even recommend particular ends; they prohibit one person from using another's body or property, and constrain the ways in which each person can use his or her own body and property in light of its effects on every other person's entitlement to use theirs. Thus, the organizing norms all govern what one person is allowed to do to another. Because I am not in charge of your body, I can neither use it for purposes you have not authorized, nor act in ways that make your rights with respect to it irrelevant to the ways in which I pursue my purposes. So I may not pursue those purposes in ways that damage or destroy your body. My conduct is subject to parallel restrictions because I am not in charge of your property—that is what it is for property to be yours. But the same structure also entails that neither of us needs to use our own bodies or property in ways that best suit the other's preferred purposes.

The familiar legal distinction between misfeasance and nonfeasance, between doing something *to* someone and failing to do something *for* that person, is a direct implication of the idea that the principal norms of tort law focus on means rather than ends. You are allowed to use your means however you see fit, and you have no obligation to use them in a way that enables your neighbor to use his or her means in the way that he or she wishes to. Misfeasance consists in using your means in a way that compromises your neighbor's means; nonfeasance is failure to use them in a way that suits your neighbor's preferred use of those means. The misfeasance/nonfeasance distinction animates familiar legal doctrines, including, prominently, the absence of a duty to rescue, but also, I shall argue, the law's treatment of cases in which one person wrongs a second, as a result of which a third person is affected but cannot recover compensation. If the defendant does not need to do anything for the plaintiff, the plaintiff has no claim that the defendant refrain from committing a wrong against some third party.

In addition to providing an explanation of why the rights protected by tort law are distinctively eligible to be remedied when violated, the same set of ideas serve to explain why legal concepts that are analytically distinct typically appear together. Discussions of rights often employ Wesley Newcomb Hohfeld's taxonomy of legal concepts, distinguishing between (1) a *claim right*, understood as a requirement that someone do or refrain from doing something, which is correlative to a duty on the part of that person; (2) a *power* to compel someone to do something, which is correlative to a liability on the part of that person; (3) a *privilege*, which is correlative to what Hohfeld calls a "no-right," that is, the fact that the other has no claim to prevent its exercise; and (4) an *immunity*, which is correlative to a disability, that is, the absence of a power.[15] Hohfeld's ambition was to bring clarity to legal scholarship and judicial practice by drawing attention to these differences. The gains in clarity are significant: The fact that I have a privilege to do something means that you cannot

---

15. See Wesley N. Hohfeld, "Some Fundamental Legal Conceptions as Applied in Judicial Reasoning," *Yale Law Journal* 23 (1913): 16–59; Hohfeld, "Fundamental Legal Conceptions as Applied in Judicial Reasoning," *Yale Law Journal* 26 (1917): 710–770.

call on the law's assistance to prevent me from doing that thing, but it does not entitle me to prevent you from doing something that would make it more difficult for me to exercise that privilege. I can only constrain your conduct if I have a claim right.

But Hohfeld's distinctions bring clarity to private law only if they are separated from a different perspective often associated with his work, according to which the justification of each legal relation is particular, and whether to associate one legal relation with another is "ultimately a question of justice and policy; and it should be considered, as such, on its merits."[16] The reference to justice and policy may seem to cover the full range of possibilities, but Hohfeld's followers have frequently supposed that the absence of logical entailment between rights, privileges, powers, and immunities requires that the justification of each legal relation be treated as entirely independent from the justification of any other legal relation. Any co-incidence of different legal relations is really just a bundle created for policy purposes, and so can be dismantled if those policies change.[17] Hohfeld's followers have gone further, often supposing that the only appropriate justification for a legal relation is consequentialist balancing of the benefits to the right (or power, privilege, or immunity) holder against the burdens thereby placed on others.[18]

On the alternative developed here, tort law's only "policy" is doing justice between private persons. You have *both* claim rights (correlative to duties on the part of others) and powers (correlative to liabilities to en-

---

16. Hohfeld, "Some Fundamental Legal Conceptions," 36.

17. The most familiar instance of this approach is the "bundle of rights" theory of property, according to which the familiar incidents of property are not unified in any way, because the apparent *in rem* nature of property is an illusion. Instead, for Hohfeld an owner's right to exclude others is an aggregate of separate personal rights as against each other person, no different from a contractual right. James Penner has argued that such an account has difficulty explaining that transmissibility of property rights: If I give or sell you my car, it does not seem that I exit indefinitely many legal relationships with others and you take them on. See James Penner, "On the Very Idea of Transmissible Rights," in *Philosophical Foundations of Property Law*, ed. James Penner and Henry E. Smith (Oxford: Oxford University Press, 2013), 244–271. For an earlier formulation of this point, published the same year that Hohfeld published the first of his articles, see Reinach, *A Priori Foundations*.

18. See Barbara Fried, *The Progressive Assault on Laissez Faire: Robert Hale and the First Law and Economics Movement* (Cambridge, MA: Harvard University Press, 1998), 52–53.

forcement on the part of others) with respect to your body and property. Although the claim right and the power can be distinguished, they come as a package: If you are entitled to constrain my conduct, I owe you a duty to conduct myself in certain ways—not entering your home without your permission, avoiding damaging your body and property through my carelessness, and so on. You also have various powers to enforce those rights—you can ask me to leave if I overstay my welcome, you can seek an injunction to make me abate a nuisance, and you can take me to court to demand damages if I violate a right.

Although these formulations might make it appear that the power is in the service of the right, both are coordinate components of a system in which no person is in charge of another; both the constraint and the power to enforce are essential to that system. It is up to you whether to enforce your right, as it must be if you are the one who determines the purposes you pursue. Moreover, the justification of the right and power does not look to benefits to you and burdens to me; it looks only to the negative relationship between us: Neither of us is in charge of the other, so each of us must restrict our conduct, but each of us is also entitled to decide whether to stand on our own rights.[19]

Remedies—most prominently damages—uphold the fundamental norms of conduct. This structure is morally familiar in some settings: If I take your coat, I need to give it back because it is still your coat; if I consume your sandwich, the reason I need to replace it is that you continue to be entitled to it, even if it has ceased to exist. And if I break your arm, I need to do what can be done to put you back in the position you would have been in if I had not done so. As a physical object, the coat survives the wrong intact, but that only makes the remedy easier to implement without modifying its basic rationale: I need to return it not because it survives as a physical object, but because your right to it does. If I destroy or consume it, the basis of the remedy is the same: I do not extinguish

19. Although right and power sometimes come apart. For example, a child has rights against others but requires an adult parent or guardian to exercise any powers in relation to those rights. Such examples do not show that rights and powers require independent or radically different justifications. The parent or guardian is supposed to exercise those powers on the child's behalf—that is, the powers accompany the rights, even when the rightholder is not competent to exercise them.

your right by violating it; instead, your right survives its own violation: I owe it to you to conduct myself in ways that are consistent with your coat, sandwich, or even your body being subject to your choice, not mine. Sometimes the remedy will be a near equivalent; in many others it will be deficient, but the best that can be done. But the best deficient substitute is still a substitute, and in each case the rationale is the same: to uphold the right that was violated.[20] I will show that the same intuitive idea covers other examples of tort liability. The point of a tort remedy is to give you back what you already had: In each case, what you have is not a physical object such as a coat, but an entitlement to constrain others in relation to that thing.

The role of a court in this account—that the plaintiff comes before a court and complains about the defendant's conduct—is secondary, but not thereby merely incidental. It is secondary because a dispute makes it to court only when one party contends that a right has been violated; at least in principle, everyone's private rights could be enjoyed consistently. Were that to happen, no case would ever make it to court. Legal institutions would still be required even in such a situation. The conceptual structure of private wrongs is abstract, and needs to be made more determinate in order to apply consistently to particulars. That determination and application must be done by institutions that can claim to be speaking (that is, exercising judgment) and acting (that is, ordering people to do things, backed by the possibility of enforcement) on behalf of everyone. Without courts, one person's say-so or enforcement of tort law's requirements would just be a different way of being in charge of others.

---

20. Including, in the limiting case, life itself; even where the rightholder is permanently unable to enforce a right, the right itself need not disappear. Legal systems have developed two distinct ways of dealing with this. The first, beginning with Lord Campbell's act of 1846 (9 & 10 Vict. c.93, "An Act for Compensating the Families of Persons Killed by Accidents") provided for survivors. The history and subsequent developments are examined in detail in Cox v. Ergo Versicherung AG, [2014] UKSC 22 (2 April 2014). Other jurisdictions quickly followed, beginning with New York in 1847. These statutes characterized the death of a family member as a wrong personal to (normally his) dependents. As such they do not suppose that the deceased's right survives its own violation. The sense in which the deceased person's own right survives its own violation is captured in statutes giving the estate the power to sue for wrongful death, beginning with Ontario Statute Amendment Act 49, Vic. c.16, s.23, amending the Trustees and Executors Act R.S.O. 1877, c.107, ss.8, 9, cited in Stephen Waddams, "Damages for Wrongful Death," *Modern Law Review* 47 (1984): 437–453.

The court's public status is also essential to its role in resolving a private dispute, for three reasons. First, unlike a private arbitrator, a court's authority to resolve a dispute does not depend on the agreement of the parties. It is available, and one party can invoke its procedures. Second, courts make authoritative determinations, binding on the parties, both about the facts alleged by the plaintiff and the law governing the dispute. Third, as a public authority, a court can order a remedy, making a binding determination of what will substitute for the right violated and, in so doing, compel the defendant to provide it and the plaintiff to accept it as sufficient. This picture of tort law is simple, and I will complicate it to varying degrees in the chapters that follow.

3. Some Contrasts: Accountability and Responsibility

Interpersonal interaction is more complicated than even the most detailed account of private wrongs. Whether you take someone to court, and, if you prevail, whether you pursue your remedy, will depend on a variety of factors extraneous to the question of how things stand between you and the person whom you believe to have wronged you. You might decide to stand on your rights because you thirst for revenge, or think it important to hold wrongdoers accountable,[21] or you might decide not to because you think forgiveness important, or because you just want to get on with

21. Stephen Darwall and Julian Darwall report that plaintiffs "are primarily interested in receiving an apology and restoring social order and respect." "Civil Recourse as Mutual Accountability," *Florida State University Law Review* 39 (2011) 40. They quote Tom R. Tyler and Hulda Thorisdottir, "A Psychological Perspective on Compensation for Harm: Examining the September 11th Victim Compensation Fund," *DePaul Law Review* 53 (2003): 355–391, who report at 361 that "the key issue on people's minds [is] moral accountability," and that "where an individual has been negligently injured, compensation is generally 'a poor substitute for . . . accountability.'" This may motivate many people, though it is in tension with the high rate of settlement for tort claims, which typically occurs without admission of liability. Theodore Eisenberg and Charlotte Lanvers find settlement rates for tort claims other than constitutional torts approaching 90 percent. "What Is the Settlement Rate and Why Should We Care?," *Journal of Empirical Legal Studies* 6 (2009): 130. They suggest that the propensity to settle a tort suit correlates with the merits of the case. If their data and analysis are reliable, plaintiffs who believe they have been wronged are satisfied with remedies rather than accountability.

your life. Perhaps you are too embarrassed to come forward with your grievance—you don't want to admit that you were *there,* or that you fell for *that*—or too proud to let something go. The law does not make a global moral assessment of whether you should stand on your rights; it leaves that question to you. Neither the person who wronged you nor a court has standing to impose any sort of all-things-considered judgment about how you should respond to a wrong against you.

More generally, when one person wrongs another, other morally salient things may also occur. A variety of virtues and vices may be on display, wrongdoers may vary in their culpability, tempers may flare and resentments simmer. Although private wrongs are often fraught with life and all of its meanings, these things are incidental to the wrong, triggered by a morality of interaction that does not depend on them. In the same way, to acknowledge the existence of other types of moral considerations does not show that every aspect of life should give expression to them: To mention some obvious examples, the genuine virtue of loyalty to friends has no place in the administration of justice, and the obligation to render services for money received does not govern public officials accepting bribes.

Two families of moral ideas figure prominently in and around the interactions that are the subject matter of private wrongs. The first of these is responsibility. What you do, including what happens as a result, can figure prominently in your understanding of your own life. Bernard Williams offers an example—a careful lorry driver who runs down a child who has darted out from between parked cars—to draw attention to the ways in which a person's life is changed, and appropriately so, by the mere fact of causing a terrible event.[22] Tony Honoré has suggested that a special form of responsibility, which he calls "outcome responsibility," is essential to our understanding of ourselves as active beings who make their own way in the world.[23] Honoré argues that this idea figures in the law's readiness to hold people responsible for things they bring about, even if the results include a significant measure of luck.

---

22. Bernard Williams, "Moral Luck," in *Moral Luck: Philosophical Papers, 1973–1980* (Cambridge: Cambridge University Press, 1982), 28.

23. Tony Honoré, *Responsibility and Fault* (Oxford: Hart, 1999), 14–16. See also Stephen Perry, "The Moral Foundations of Tort Law," *Iowa Law Review* 77 (1992): 449–514.

The second neighboring idea is second-person <u>accountability</u>. Stephen Darwall has drawn attention to the ways in which our reactive attitudes of anger and resentment both underwrite and reflect interpersonal accountability. For Darwall, the basic form of responsibility is holding someone accountable, whether it comes in the form of you asking me to get my foot off your toe, or a drill sergeant reprimanding the disobedient recruit.[24] More recently, Darwall and others have argued that the law of torts must be situated in a broader framework of reactive attitudes, and that legal proceedings be understood as a way of calling people to account.[25]

I mention both Honoré and Darwall not to dispute their accounts of these aspects of responsibility and interpersonal accountability, but because I think that however important these aspects are in other domains of life, they do not figure in an account of the moral basis of the law of private wrongs.[26] Neither outcome responsibility nor interpersonal accountability follows the distinction between misfeasance and nonfeasance, because each fits specific events into larger patterns of thought that comprehend much more than the narrow question of how things stand between the rights of two persons. Your failure to assist someone else in his or her moment of need, or being a stickler for your rights, might properly loom large in your conception of yourself as an active agent, making your way in the world, just as you might rebuke yourself for conduct that it would be inappropriate for others to criticize.[27] Conversely, your life

24. Stephen L. Darwall, *The Second-Person Standpoint: Morality, Respect, and Accountability* (Cambridge, MA: Harvard University Press, 2006).

25. Stephen Darwall and Julian Darwall, "Civil Recourse as Mutual Accountability," 17–41; Benjamin Zipursky, "Substantive Standing, Civil Recourse, and Corrective Justice," *Florida State University Law Review* 39 (2011): 299–340.

26. Someone might bring an action against another person in the hope of having the court serve as a forum of accountability, or to get an authoritative declaration with respect to a historical episode. Michael R. Marrus, "The Case of the French Railways and the Deportation of Jews in 1944," in *Holocaust and Justice: Representation and Historiography of the Holocaust in Post-War Trials,* ed. David Bankier and Dan Michman (New York: Berghahn Books, 2010), 245–264.

27. As Bernard Williams puts it, "No conception of public responsibility can match exactly an ideal of maturity because, among other reasons, to hold oneself responsible only when the public could rightfully hold one responsible is not a sign of maturity."

narrative will typically attach significance to events based on their consequences for you. If another person's negligent collision with your car makes you miss a flight that subsequently crashes, you may be thankful that you were delayed by the collision, but you still have a cause of action against the other driver.[28] Alternately, you might wrong someone else, but find yourself unable to do anything but affirm the course that your life takes as a result.[29] The place of the act in your life's narrative has no bearing on the standing of the person you wronged to demand a remedy. Moreover, whether it makes sense for others to blame or resent you for an action or omission doesn't depend only on whether you were acting within your rights; that is why others may resent you for standing too narrowly on your rights by being petty or driving a hard bargain.[30] So, too, you might be haunted by the effects of your actions on someone who had no right that you behave differently. That person might have grounds to resent you, in the absence of a legal wrong. Conversely, the law of torts properly holds people accountable for some things that others will not resent. You might find it difficult to resent the person whose misconduct made you miss that fatal flight, but that does not mean you do not have a valid claim for the damage to your car.

Williams, "Voluntary Acts and Responsible Agents," *Oxford Journal of Legal Studies* 10 (1990): 10.

28. The example is from Ernest Weinrib, "Right and Advantage in Private Law," *Cardozo Law Review* 10 (1989): 1283. Weinrib points to a similar example in Robert J. Peaslee's "Multiple Causation and Damage," *Harvard Law Review* 47 (1934): 1139–1141. R. Jay Wallace considers a parallel example in which you miss the doomed flight because I break my promise to drive you to the airport. Wallace points out that your affirmation of my promise breaking does not make it nonwrongful. See Wallace, *The View from Here* (Oxford: Oxford University Press, 2013), 99.

29. This is the point of Bernard Williams's characterization of the decision by the famous French Impressionist painter Paul Gauguin (1848–1903) to abandon his family to move to Tahiti to paint. As Williams notes, Gauguin's own affirmation of his decision does nothing to address whatever grievance his wife and children have against him. See Williams, "Moral Luck," 198.

30. See Aristotle's contrastive characterization of the "stickler for justice in the bad sense" with the equitable man who "takes less than his share though he has the law on his side." *Nicomachean Ethics* 1137, in *Complete Works of Aristotle, Volume 2: The Revised Oxford Translation,* trans. Jonathan Barnes (Princeton: Princeton University Press, 2014), 1796.

As important as other forms and forums of accountability, such as self-reproach or dressing down, may be, none of them is either necessary or sufficient for tort liability. Tort law concerns itself with another dimension of moral life, the idea that no person is in charge of another.

4. Understanding Wrongdoing

Rather than turn to ideas of responsibility or accountability to explain the "moral phraseology" about which Holmes complains, I have drawn on moral formulations that are on conspicuous display in tort judgments. So I draw attention to talk about wrongdoing, the violation of rights, the idea that a wrong must be "personal" to the plaintiff, and frequent claims that the point of a tort remedy is to restore the right that was violated.

Not all of the vocabulary is as familiar. No case lays down the proposition that no person is in charge of another, or draws the distinction between misfeasance and nonfeasance in terms of that between violating a right and failing to provide another person with a context favorable to his or her purposes. The point of this new vocabulary is to organize the domain of private wrongdoing. Courts characterize remedies in terms of the right violated, and I offer a characterization of what rights must be in order for the judicial characterization to be apt. Courts focus on rights to person and property; I offer a more abstract characterization of why this is a non-accidental set of rights to protect.

Still, it might be wondered how courts, deciding individual cases over a period of centuries, should arrive at something so systematic. That question, however, arises only if the unintelligibility of familiar moral and legal ideas of wrongdoing and its remedy is assumed from the outset. The central claims developed here—the idea of a private wrong and the idea that each person is entitled to decide what is done with his or her body or property—is a central element of ordinary moral thought, and already implicit in the plaintiff's assertion of a right in bringing a defendant before a court to demand a remedy for a wrong. The questions at the heart of familiar wrongs are no less familiar—who is entitled to decide whether I am allowed to cross your land, or touch your body, or the ways in which my actions are limited by their side effects, or what I can say about you. These ideas figure prominently in Roman law, and in different ways in such staples of legal thought and education through the nineteenth century as Blackstone's *Commentaries on the Laws of England,* where they are implicit, and Justinian's *Institutes* ("give each his own") and Hugo Grotius's *The Law of War and Peace,* where they are more explicit. The point of articulating a more general account is not to show that something radically different is going on than the participants in litigation presuppose; it is to make explicit the presuppositions of familiar ways of thinking and making demands.

In this respect the account differs from the Holmesian analysis in terms of policy and more recent economic analyses in terms of efficiency or minimizing accident costs. Those accounts necessarily suppose that the plaintiff comes before the court as a sort of private attorney-general, having been selected for the role by chance and bribed into taking it up by the prospect of damages, perhaps made more appealing by a loss recently suffered.[31] Such an approach must deny that anyone who claims to stand on his or her rights has any idea of what is actually going on. Conversely, it must insist that whether a claimant prevails depends on factors that have no connection to the explicit content of her claim.

Theoretical accounts of specific doctrinal areas of law are sometimes divided into classifications, such as historical, descriptive, prescriptive, and interpretive.[32] I do not purport to be offering a historical account here, if by that is meant an account that identifies the origins of particular features of tort doctrine. My account is not inconsistent with such a historical treatment, provided it allows for the possibility that the product of history is not just a heap of accidental results. Given the choice between the other three classes—is the account descriptive, prescriptive, or interpretive?—I am inclined to answer "yes." My object of

31. "Rational people base their decision on expectations about the future rather than regrets about the past. They let bygones be bygones." Richard Posner, *Economic Analysis of Law,* 7th ed. (Boston: Wolters Kluwer, 2007), 7. Guido Calabresi writes of providing suitable incentives to make the plaintiff in a tort action "a good private attorney-general"; Calabresi, "The Complexity of Torts," in *Exploring Tort Law,* ed. M. Stuart Madden (Cambridge: Cambridge University Press, 2005), 337.

32. See Stephen A. Smith, *Contract Theory* (New York: Oxford University Press, 2004), 4; Peter Cane, "Rights in Private Law," in *Rights and Private Law,* ed. Donal Nolan and Andrew Robertson (Oxford: Hart, 2012), 37.

inquiry is the law of torts as it has existed and continues to exist. But the inquiry is not purely descriptive: Not only do I begin from organizing assumptions that may not be explicitly stated in the materials I seek to organize; my inquiry also differs from a purely descriptive enterprise because I readily acknowledge cases that do not fit my analysis. Some of these cases, including the passage from Lord Denning I quoted above, deny that juridical concepts can be taken at face value. Another significant line of cases avoids the language of policy, but treats a tort action as raising questions of where to place an existing loss. The judges in these cases sometimes engage in a comparative exercise, preferring to place a loss on a negligent or otherwise culpable defendant rather than leaving it on the shoulders of an innocent plaintiff.[33] The results in many of these cases are decided in the same ways as a rights-based analysis would require, but other cases complement these comparative assessments with considerations of policy and reach results that a rights-based analysis would not.

I do not pretend that these cases do not exist, but I do argue that they are inconsistent with the law's organizing principles and also inconsistent with the plaintiff's claim to come before a court demanding a remedy from specific defendant. In my discussion of defamation, I consider and criticize cases that could not be legitimate applications of the structure of a defamation action. Not all speech that makes others think ill of a person is thereby defamatory. I criticize these cases as mistaken; my readiness to do so might lead some to label this a prescriptive enterprise.

But if the account is not descriptive, it is also not prescriptive in one familiar sense of that term. The prescriptions that I make are not from a standpoint outside of what is presupposed in the legal materials I seek to render intelligible. In this I depart from a standard way of characterizing prescriptive accounts. H. L. A. Hart urged the importance of a critical reflective attitude, and cautioned against what he called the "old confu-

---

33. French law operates in this way. Article 1383 of the Civil Code focuses on the duty to compensate on the part of those who cause damage through fault, specifying, "Any act whatever of man, which causes damage to another, obliges the one by whose fault it occurred, to compensate it."

sions between law and the standards appropriate to the criticism of law."[34] Hart's caution might be taken to suggest that any normative account of the law must be couched in a vocabulary that does not presuppose any distinctively legal concepts, and so must import moral ideas from elsewhere. Beginning with Bentham's characterization of natural rights as "nonsense on stilts,"[35] writers in the utilitarian tradition have claimed that concepts of right can only be given a reductive characterization, and that the only way in which a normative rule can be assessed is in terms that make no reference to anything that looks like a rule.[36] For Bentham, the external measures by which to evaluate rights were pleasure and pain; for later writers, candidates have included harm, desire satisfaction, and economic efficiency. Although I will frequently appeal to moral ideas and arguments, the law will appear as an exporter rather than importer of those ideas, because a significant part of the morality of interpersonal interaction shares with tort law the idea that each person is *sui iuris*— that no person is in charge of another's purposes.

Finally, the combination of descriptive and prescriptive elements might be thought to make this an interpretive account, the aim of which is to make the interpretive object (here, tort doctrine) "the best that it can be."[37] Yet my aim is not exclusively interpretive either, at least if interpretation is taken in the way in which it has figured in legal philosophy through the work of Ronald Dworkin. For Dworkin, to interpret is to bring "convictions about the point—the justifying purpose or goal or principle—of legal practice as a whole"[38] to bear on the particular legal question at issue, and determine a judgment based on the account that best fits and justifies the settled law. My account is not interpretive in that ambitious sense, because unlike Dworkin's enterprise, I do not suppose that the ideal case

34. H. L. A. Hart, *Essays in Jurisprudence and Philosophy* (Oxford: Clarendon Press, 1983), 11.

35. Jeremy Bentham, "Anarchical Fallacies," in *The Works of Jeremy Bentham*, vol. 2, ed. John Bowring (Edinburgh: William Tate, 1838), 914.

36. The most developed version of this form of argument is the critique of the "morality of common sense" in Henry Sidgwick, *The Methods of Ethics*, 7th ed. (London: Macmillan, 1907).

37. Ronald Dworkin, *Law's Empire* (Cambridge, MA: Harvard University Press, 1986), 77.

38. Ibid., 87.

of this exercise would be a complete Herculean determination of every actual or possible case. Instead, I hope to identify a set of relevant norms and concepts, and a way of reasoning with them, which govern the interactions between private persons. Courts are essential for their role in making these ideas apply to particulars.

To see how these three distinct ways of giving an account might be integrated, consider the following proto-account of an argument, which is descriptive, normative, and interpretive and, at the same time, none of them. The idea of an argument, in which the premises support the conclusion, is not a generalization based on the ways in which people try to convince each other of things, nor is it based on empirical evidence about which things people are most likely to find convincing. That is, the question of what is a good argument is not a question of empirical psychology. It is a normative idea. But it isn't a normative idea external to argumentation, against which actual arguments are assessed. Good arguments contrast with bad arguments, not because that they are two species of a single genus that can be identified as such in advance of any evaluation. Instead, the starting point for thinking about an argument is a good argument, one where the premises are true and provide reasons to accept the conclusion. A bad argument is a defective version of a good one.

Perhaps someone could develop a mode of evaluating arguments that is entirely external to the concept of an argument. A political speechwriter, for instance, may be more concerned with an argument's persuasiveness than its logic, or decide against making a sound argument out of concern that the audience will misunderstand it, or that it will be misappropriated by an opponent. Empirical psychology might even confirm the suspicion of the Greek sophists that bad arguments are more effective than good ones. Contemporary culture contains traces of a more general version of this result-focused mode of evaluation: Airport bookshops carry titles that suggest strategic modes of managing friendships by pursuing a mode of evaluation entirely external to friendship. Holmes, Denning, Calabresi, and many others suppose that tort law can only be analyzed in the way the sophists proposed to examine arguments, and the authors of those books look at friendships, by treating any apparent structure as a façade, and looking at each instead as a tool through which devious but gifted rhetoricians pursue other goals. My aim is to offer a different way of looking at tort law, taking its structures and doctrines at face value.

Rather than being normative in this external sense, the concepts that figure in tort law both create the private rights that tort law protects and provide the basis for remedies in case of their violation. Law presents itself as a reasoned enterprise—as the parties address the judge, and the judge addresses the parties, certain types of arguments are given, while certain other types of argument are thought to be inappropriate. Departures from what I will characterize as the predominant form of reasoning are often treated as being in need of assimilation to it. Whether something is an instance of a form of reasoning itself can be answered only within that form of reasoning. In this, tort law, as I will characterize it, emerges as a specific and in certain ways distinctive form of argumentation.

5. Synopsis

From the perspective of much recent scholarship, I will defend what may seem to be a naive view of private wrongs. Many of the chapters of this book will take their titles from things that judges have said or that have appeared in canonical discussions of private wrongs in the seventeenth through twentieth centuries. I will unashamedly maintain that the point of tort litigation is to resolve the specific dispute between the parties currently before the court, based entirely on what transpired between them. I will take at face value tort law's central focus on rights to person and property, and its identification of your person with your body and reputation, and argue that the purpose of damages is to make it as if a wrong had never happened. I will contend that the law of defamation serves to protect your own good name, and take judicial talk about duty and remoteness at face value. Prominent strands in recent writing about tort law have represented these turns of phrase as falling in various places along the continuum between useful legal fictions and outright falsehoods that obfuscate true judicial intent. My aim in appealing to these ideas is to vindicate the naive view of private wrongs.

Chapter 2, "What You Already Have, Part 1: Your Body and Property," introduces an account of private wrongs in terms of restrictions on the means that you can use in setting and pursuing your purposes. You are entitled to use your body and property for whatever purposes you see fit, but you cannot use anyone else's body or property without that person's permission, nor are you entitled to injure another person or damage another's property through unduly dangerous use of what is yours. I argue that these two constraints generate two basic forms of wrongdoing: (1) what I call use-based torts, which consist in using another person's body or property without that person's permission; and (2) what I call damage-based torts, which consist in damaging another's body or property through inappropriately dangerous use of your own body or property. Distinguishing between use and damage illustrates two distinct ways in which one person can wrong another, because they are the two ways in which one person's use of body or property is inconsistent with another's claim to use his or her body or property as he or she sees fit. Use-based wrongs are typically actionable even though they may not cause damage: If I enter your land without your permission, or perform surgery on you without your consent, I wrong you, even if my entry to your land is harmless, or the surgery benefits you. Although damage is not an element of the wrong in these cases, you are entitled to a remedy for any damage consequential on a use-based wrong against you. Damage-based torts, by contrast, are wrongful only if damage is done. I argue that damage-based torts also require some form of defective conduct on the part of the wrongdoer, but use-based torts do not.

This division into use- and damage-based torts involving bodies and property provides an incomplete taxonomy of private wrongs. Chapter 2 postpones discussion of wrongs growing out of special relationships, and it is silent on several familiar categories of tortious wrongdoing. In particular, it says nothing about defamation, and it says nothing about the cases in which an act is tortious only if actuated by malice. It may also appear to say nothing about those cases in which the law is often said to impose liability in the absence of any wrongdoing, including dangerous but worthwhile activities, such as blasting, and situations of necessity. Each of these categories requires a separate treatment, which, although consistent with the analysis developed in Chapters 1–3, is best introduced through a series of contrasts with it.

Chapter 3, "Using What You Have: Misfeasance and Nonfeasance," offers a general account of the distinction between wronging another, understood as doing something *to* someone, and failing to do something *for* that person in terms of the distinction between damage- and use-based torts. You need to restrict the side effects of the ways in which you use your means, but you do not need to use your means in the way that best suits the preferred purposes of others. Any requirement that you provide another person with a favorable context would entitle that person to determine the purposes for which you use your means. I argue that this distinction explains and unifies what are sometimes thought of as diverse cases, including the absence of a duty to rescue in tort, the bar to recovery for pure economic loss, and a variety of cases in which one person causes loss to someone by violating a duty owed to some other person. I also use the account to explain why tort law cannot be analyzed in terms of the importance of interests or transaction costs.

Chapter 4, "Wrongdoing for Which the Offender Must Pay: Negligence," is about the tort that has attracted the most scholarly attention (legal, economic, and philosophical) over the past century. Negligence is not more basic than other private wrongs, but it has shaped scholarly discussions of private wrongdoing. Clarifying its structure positions me to address cases of strict liability and malice, which can be made to seem more difficult than they are because of misunderstandings of negligence. I also use negligence as a case study to (1) develop the idea of a completed wrong, (2) characterize the nature of fault in damage-based wrongs, (3) explain the role of interpretation and the exercise of judgment in bringing abstract legal concepts to bear on particulars, and (4) explain the role of special relationships (such as an auditor advising on the soundness of a business, a dentist caring for the plaintiff's oral hygiene, or a solicitor preparing documents) that give rise to a new relationship between the parties—one that governs a subsequent transaction and entitles the plaintiff to constrain the defendant's conduct in distinctive ways.

Chapter 5, "Use What Is Yours in a Way That Does Not Injure Your Neighbor: Strict Liability"—a rough-and-ready translation of the *sic utere* maxim that Holmes dismissed as at once a benevolent yearning and a façade—takes up so-called strict liability torts, which are often said to be instances of pure liability rules, that is, liability without any wrongdoing. Paradigmatic cases include damage caused by bursting reservoirs, explosions, escaping wild animals, and the boat owner who preserves his boat in a storm by staying moored to another person's dock. As my use of the term "so-called" suggests, I argue that the idea of liability without wrongdoing is an illusion. I show how all of the relevant wrongs turn on the inconsistency of the defendant's conduct with the plaintiff's right. Many of the cases are damage-based torts, and the inconsistency is to be found in the way in which the defendant uses his or her means. In cases of necessity, the basis of the inconsistency is the defendant's use of the plaintiff's property, a use that is privileged by law because of the systematic requirements of property in land.

Chapter 6, "A Malicious Wrong in Its Strict Legal Sense: Motive and Intention in Tort Law," examines cases in which an act is wrongful because of the way in which it is performed, even though the plaintiff appears to have no general right to constrain the defendant's conduct. For example, if you require unusual quiet in your home (perhaps you are a music teacher), you cannot complain if your neighbors make noise at levels that ordinary uses of your home, such as having a family discussion, could tolerate. But if the same level of noise is made in order to interfere with your music lessons, you have a claim. I engage with some of the literature on the seemingly related doctrine of "double effect," and show that the cases in which motive figures into tort law depend, not upon any reference to the end being pursued, but rather on special characteristics of the means that are used.

Chapter 7, "What You Already Have, Part 2: Your Own Good Name," offers an account of the tort of defamation. Defamation has a bad name in many circles (and many of its traditional requirements have been abandoned in the United States) because it seems to impose an unjust burden on the person accused of making a defamatory statement. Whereas the person who complains of the statement needs only to establish that it was made, the person who made the statement must establish either that it was true or that it was made on a privileged occasion. I argue that all of the law of defamation rests on a simple moral idea: You never need to clear your own name. Anyone who alleges you have done wrong must bear the burden of proving his or her statement to be true. Moreover, I will argue that this structure animates the burden of proof in other contexts, as well as the presumption of innocence in criminal law. The law of defamation is therefore not an exception to this moral idea but its central instance, because it is the person who has been defamed who stands accused, and the accuser must make good on the accusation.

Chapter 8, "Remedies, Part 1: As if It Had Never Happened," is about damages, and develops the familiar juridical idea that the point of damages in a tort action is to make it as though the wrong had never happened. It is easy to make this familiar idea look preposterous, because payment of money will never fully replace a treasured piece of property, let alone a limb or a loved one. Despite these complaints, the organizing idea behind damages is not that the object of the wrong can always be physically repaired. Drawing on the accounts of rights developed in Chapter 2, I show that the sense in which the remedy makes it as if the wrong had never happened is not by attempting to replace the material object of a violated right, but by enforcing the violated right itself, understood as the plaintiff's entitlement to constrain the defendant's conduct. This understanding of rights reflects the deeper moral idea that rights always survive their own violation. If I take your coat (whether willfully or by mistake), it does not stop being your coat. That is why I must return it. So, too, your claim to your coat—your entitlement to constrain my conduct in relation to it—is not changed if I destroy your coat. That is why I must provide you with as near a substitute as possible. The same structure explains why, if I deprive you of means that you were using or about to use to produce further means—profits from your factory, or wages by your body—I have also deprived you of those further means, and so am liable for consequential damages.

Chapter 9, "Remedies, Part 2: Before a Court," takes up the role of the court in resolving a dispute. It engages with some recent literature that has suggested that the idea that rights survive their own violation cannot be correct because a court plays a central role in tort liability: Someone who wrongfully injures another or wrongfully uses what belongs to another does not have a duty to make up the wrong until ordered to do so by a court. Instead, the wronged party has only a power, to the exercise of which neither the court nor any other agent of the state is committed. I offer an alternative explanation of these phenomena, drawing on the idea that no private person has standing to compel anyone to address a wrong. Only public institutions can require someone to repair a wrong, for two reasons. The first is that (as explained in Chapter 4) the abstract concepts of right may be indeterminate in many cases, and so there may be no definitive answer as to what remedy the wrong requires. The second (as argued in Chapter 7) is the idea that anyone who alleges another has done wrong must do more than make a unilateral allegation: He or she must establish a claim in a public court that is capable of deciding and issuing orders on behalf of both of the parties before it.

The concluding chapter, "Horizontal and Vertical," takes up the relation between the private wrongs and the role of the state in providing for distributive justice. Rights-based accounts of private law are often mistaken for libertarian or Lockean accounts, in which the form of private law holds not only between private persons, but also between individual citizens and the state. On this sort of view, the private rights of individuals (typically the focus is on property and contract, but the same point applies in principle to torts) cannot be compromised or restricted in any way by other branches of government. Defenders of these positions thus sometimes suppose themselves to have a principled objection to any regulatory regime that might restrict the enforcement of private rights, such as workplace compensation schemes, no-fault automobile insurance, and workplace health and safety regulations. Perhaps there are principled objections to these schemes, but the account that I will develop provides no basis for them. A legal system purports to speak and act on behalf of everyone; its claim to do so depends in part on its securing the full conditions of membership on all of those over whom it exercises its authority. I argue that sometimes those conditions can only be secured through restrictions on the operation of private rights.

CHAPTER 2

What You Already Have, Part 1

Your Body and Property

IN THIS CHAPTER I develop this idea of what you already have, and the sense in which you have it, to explain two basic forms of wrongs against persons and property. In this chapter I will say almost nothing about some of the special relationships that give rise to additional duties, and so create additional potentials for private wrongs.

I wrong you only by interfering with something to which you have a right, or, as I shall put it, something you already have. You already have your person (including your body, mental capacities, and reputation) and your property. There are lots of bad things that one person can do to another that do not count as a tortious wrong: I can ruin your plans, spoil your view, block your access, lure away your customers, preempt your efforts, let you down, and stand idly by in your moment of need. Each of these truthfully describes something that I did to you. Many of them can even be characterized as losses that you suffered through my deeds. But they are not private wrongs, because I have not interfered with anything you already had.

No prior transaction between us is required for you to have the right that I refrain from touching you without your permission, or carelessly damaging your property. Instead, the rights at issue in these examples are ones that you already have, and they restrict what I may permissibly do to you. In this chapter I will focus on wrongs against bodies, broadly construed to include psychological capacities, and property.

Many writers have found the law's focus on bodies and property puzzling. How well or badly your life goes depends on many things other than the condition of your body and property, and their condition depends on many things other than the actions of other people. From a different direction, property, in particular, can be made to look suspect. The condition of your property makes less of a difference to how your life goes than the condition of your body, but the law protects property with at least as much enthusiasm as it protects bodies.[1] Many people think that property is distributed unfairly or arbitrarily, and protecting it might be thought to reinforce that arbitrariness or unfairness.

I will offer a normative framework within which the law's protection of bodies and property is central. The organizing idea is straightforward: Your body and property are just what you use in deciding what purposes to pursue. You don't ever do anything except with your body; what you can do or accomplish depends on the other things you are entitled to use. That entitlement is protected by constraints on the conduct of everyone else: Nobody else is in charge of your body or property. That is, no other person gets to determine the purposes they are used to pursue. Another person is not entitled to so much as touch your body, or enter your land, or use your chattels without your authorization. As you do things using your body and property, you also must limit the side effects of your actions, so that every other person's body and property remain available for their purposes. The same constraints apply to others. A private wrong consists in pursuing purposes in a way that is inconsistent with some other person's entitlement to do so.

Together, these ideas comprise an account of a system of private rights as a system of constraints on each person's use of his or her means. Several specific ideas require elaboration: (1) the significance of pursuing (as opposed to achieving) purposes, (2) the idea that no person is in charge of any other, (3) the sense in which your body and property are the things

---

1. In Akenzua & Anor v. Secretary of State for the Home Department, [2002] EWCA Civ 1470, Lord Justice Sedley refers in paragraph 17 to "the old reproach that the law of England and Wales was more concerned with property than with people."

through which you pursue purposes, (4) the distinction between use- and damage-based wrongs, and (5) the difference between interfering with what someone else already has, and merely using your body or property as you see fit. This fundamental distinction, which I describe in terms of the difference between wronging someone and merely failing to provide a favorable context in which that person sets and pursues purposes, is one of the organizing distinctions of tort law. Indeed, I will argue in Chapter 3 that it generates the familiar distinction between misfeasance and nonfeasance.

1. Having Means and Setting Ends

Setting purposes is not a matter of making up your mind inwardly; it is instead a matter of acting in the world, of taking up means to achieve a purpose. You can wish for things—you might think that quitting your job and writing a novel, or surfing all the great waves of the world, is the ideal life for you—but then show up at work each day, and never do anything about your dream. In such a case, you have not chosen to do these things; you have simply wished for them. Having your wishes come true is not the same as acting to achieve a purpose. By contrast, you can make something your purpose even if the prospects of achieving it are remote. Olympic sprinters can make it their purpose to win the gold medal, knowing that most will not succeed. In order to make this their purpose, they must take up means—their bodily abilities, a healthy diet, training shoes, racing spikes, and so on—that they believe will enable them to achieve it.

Most things that people make their purposes lie between these extremes. Their prospects of success are better than those of aspiring Olympians, but, like those athletes, they take means in order to achieve their purposes. By taking up those means, they determine what their purposes will be, and what will never be more than a wish.

To make something your purpose by taking up means does not require that you have some metaphysical ability to stand outside the causal order, or to repudiate all of your inclinations. The problem when someone else determines your purposes—forcing you to do something, by using your means for purposes that you have not authorized, or by destroying or damaging your means and thus making them less usable—is that they, rather than you, determine the purposes for which you can act.

The concept of using means to achieve your ends is potentially ambiguous, and the law resolves that ambiguity in a specific way. To take up means toward achieving some end sometimes involves the executing of a plan or procedure, which requires taking a series of steps. One might think that these steps constitute the means you use to pursue your end, and, depending on the particulars, that thought would be correct in at least some cases. But for embodied beings—beings that occupy space—action involves the use of means in a more prosaic sense: your body and physical objects that you can control. If you make it your end to read a book, but the room is dark, you may need to change a light bulb. Changing the light bulb is an act you perform; the means you use are the ladder, your hands, the spare bulb (or money to purchase it), and so on. For reasons that will become clear, many other things that make up the context in which you use your means are not among the means you have. Changes to the context in which you use your means may make your means useless (at least temporarily) for the specific end you seek, but leave the means intact, in the sense that they remain subject to your choice. Sometimes those changes will stop you from receiving things that you require to use your means as you see fit—one person's careless or reckless conduct might make it impossible for someone else to deliver something such as raw materials or electricity. But you have no claim that any other person uses his or her means in ways that provide you with a favorable context for another to deliver something to you.

Only beings that can set purposes, and use things—paradigmatically, their own bodies and property—to pursue those purposes, can be (and so, fail to be) in charge of anything. Only such beings are vulnerable to being wronged by having another be in charge of them or what is theirs, and they can be wronged only by other such beings. That does not mean that no other bad things can happen to a person, or that people cannot behave badly toward animals, plants, or other parts of nature. It means only that a distinctive part of morality governs ways in which persons—beings who set and pursue purposes—may treat other beings that set and pursue purposes. Its fundamental principle is that no other person is entitled to determine the purposes for which you act. A being that acts exclusively from instinct is neither in charge nor not in charge, because it does not determine the purposes for which some available means will be used; it simply uses them. (I take no position here on which, if any, non-human animals can set purposes rather than act from instinct.) Legal persons are different: They can stand in "in-charge-of" relations because they are in a position to determine how means will be used, and others can interfere with their capacity to do so.

2. Not in Charge Of

The moral idea that no person is in charge of another is both simple and familiar. It is up to you, rather than others, what purposes you pursue. That is just what it is for you to be your own person—what in Roman law was called *sui iuris*—rather than to be another person's slave, serf, or subordinate. You act in your own name, using your means to pursue purposes that you, rather than others, determine. Others may neither use those means nor deprive you of them.

The claim that you are entitled to determine your own purposes is not a claim about a special relationship in which you stand to yourself. Instead, its focus is exclusively on the relations in which you stand to others. If I use your body or property without your authorization, I determine the purposes for which they are used directly; if I wrongfully damage them, I determine the purposes for which they can be used indirectly, by narrowing the ways in which they can be used. The negative specification reflects the sense in which your rights to your body and property are negative. They consist in restrictions on what others may do in relation to your capacity to set and pursue purposes, rather than affirmative duties to assist you in your pursuits or improve or even protect your capacity to pursue purposes.

Your rights to your body and property can be characterized as a kind of authority relation, but this negative character makes them narrower than other familiar examples of authority. The police officer can order you to stay put or move on; more generally, a legal system can either require or forbid you to do various things. Your authority over your person and property is only negative: You can forbid others from doing things, and so you may permit them to do many of those things, but (absent a special relationship or a wrong requiring a remedy) you can never require another person to do anything for you. This asymmetry reflects the way in which each person's rights are members of a system of rights. You are in charge of your own body and property, but other people are in charge of their bodies and property. You lack the power to require someone to perform an affirmative act because such a power would put you in charge of that person or his or her property.[2] So you cannot require another person to do something to enable you to use what is yours in the way that best suits your preferred purposes, because you are not entitled to determine the purposes for which they use what is theirs. This restriction on your authority also figures in the nature and limits of any remedy you can demand if somebody wrongs you. You can only require that they give you back what you already have, because your entitlement to demand a remedy is just an aspect of the authority that was violated by the wrong, and goes no further than it.[3]

2.1. Some Clarifications

Your entitlement to use your means to set and pursue your own purposes is a constraint on the conduct of others. It does not depend upon the value

2. This is not to deny that children do have claims to affirmative acts against their parents and guardians, or that parents have powers in relation to their children (which must, however be exercised on behalf of those children) that adults do not ordinarily have against each other. The moral and legal dependence of children stands in sharp contrast with the moral and legal independence of adults. Young children are incapable of setting their own purposes; that is why their parents or guardians make choices for them. Children can be wronged both through unauthorized touchings and wrongful injuries (hence the requirement that a parent or guardian consent to medical procedures or participation in risky activities).

3. Recent discussions of authority, under the influence of Joseph Raz's "service conception," point to the analogies between theoretical expertise and authority, and also to the ways in which authorities serve those subject to them by enabling them to better conform to the reasons that apply to them. See, for example, Raz, "Authority, Law, and Morality," in *Ethics in the Public Domain: Essays in the Morality of Law and Politics* (Oxford: Oxford University Press, 1994), 196. The sort of authority you have over others with respect to your body and property lacks this feature. What you say goes simply because of your say-so; there is no independent fact of the matter, no reasons as to what others should do about which your decisions are a reliable indicator. Your decisions determine rather than indicate what they may do. Avihay Dorfman points out that this means that property owners have more authority than government officials. See his "Private Ownership and the Standing to Say So," *University of Toronto Law Journal* 64 (2014): 402–441.

or even content of those ends, your success in pursuing them, or the overall value of people pursuing ends. Nor does it impose requirements to protect any other person's means against the effects of nature. The core moral idea is that no person is in charge of another person's means.

(a) Pursuit, not success. Others are not required to guarantee that you succeed in achieving the ends that you have set for yourself. This point is obvious in competitive situations, but it is much more general. The idea that no person is in charge of another is just the requirement that some other person's decision to pursue a particular end does not impose a requirement on you to pursue it also. That is just what it is to be independent.

(b) Restrictions on means do not depend on the value of ends. A system of rights governing who is in charge of which means does not attend to the ends for which you might use those means. You will normally regard the ends that you pursue as worthwhile—otherwise you would not pursue them—but the constraint on the conduct of others is not generated by the value of your ends. Nor is your entitlement to determine the ends for which your means are used restricted by the value of alternative uses to which others might propose to put them. You might have a field that you wish to leave fallow, a piece of jewelry that you want to leave in a locked cabinet in your basement, or books in unopened boxes in your attic in languages that you are unable to read about topics that hold no interest for you. Others are not permitted to interfere with your choice about how you employ your property. Even if you make no use of your possessions, others are not thereby allowed to use them for purposes you have not authorized, let alone damage or destroy them.

(c) Restrictions on means do not depend on the value of intact means. The security of your means does not consist in a guarantee that those means remain in a constant condition, nor that the context in which those means are used—which is made up in part by the effects of everything else everyone else does with their means—will be suitable to your preferred use of them. As objects in the natural world, any means that you have are subject to generation and decay, so they may stop being useful, or become

more useful, with the passage of time. Many other normative regimes, legal and otherwise, might *improve* your capacity to choose by giving you additional means, or by depriving you of means that you are likely to use in a way that will eventually subvert your own capacity to choose. Economic redistribution is often defended on the grounds that it enables choice for those who benefit from it, and only restricts it slightly for those who contribute to it. Laws requiring seatbelts and prohibiting the use of certain drugs are sometimes defended on the grounds that they extend a person's global capacity to choose by limiting specific, local choices. Social insurance covering health, retirement, and unemployment seeks to protect your means against a wide range of perils. The law of torts is different. It does not augment what you have, or protect what you have against all hazards; it takes what you have as given, and protects it only against the acts of others.

(d) Restrictions on means do not depend on the more general value of people pursuing ends. The contrast between means and ends sometimes invites the thought that ends must be intrinsically valuable, and means only in-·strumentally so. A morality of means looks strange from this perspective. The claim is not that means have intrinsic or unconditional value; it is that moral principles govern their acceptable use. The vocabulary of intrinsic and instrumental value is awkward here: Its natural application is to things characterized apart from their relations to other things.[4]

2.2. Relations and Comparisons

Private rights can only be explained in relational terms: Your rights to your body and property are restrictions on the ways in which others may use

---

4. This contrast applies even if what is thought to be intrinsically valuable is two or more things standing in a specific relation. G. E. Moore's "principle of organic unity" holds that a whole may be more valuable than the value of its parts. Moore offers the example of the pleasure produced by beauty, which is more valuable than the sum of the values of the pleasure and of the beauty. Even if intrinsic value comprehends relations in this Moorean sense, the value attaches to the whole so composed, apart from any relation that it stands in to anything else. See G. E. Moore, *Principia Ethica* (1903), ed. Thomas Baldwin (Cambridge: Cambridge University Press, 1993), 78–80.

their bodies and property. These limits turn exclusively on the way in which each of you can use your means in relation to the means of others. The relations at issue do not admit of degree; they are not awkwardly expressed comparisons.[5]

The contrast between relations and comparisons is familiar in other settings. If I say that one patch of blue is brighter than another, the "relation" in which I place them is just another way of making a comparison of properties that each of them has apart from it; each is as blue and as bright as it is, apart from the other. The comparison refers to two things, but it is composed of nonrelational features of the particulars being so related. By contrast, if you tell me that one object is to the left of another, you are describing them in relational terms; neither is left or right to any degree except in terms of its relation to the other. Although "to the left of" admits of degrees—you can describe the position of a number of objects along an array—none has any degree except in relation to a specific location regarded as fixed. Unlike the example of "brighter than," the degree is derived from the relation, rather than vice versa. Again, the judgment that I am sitting across from you is relational rather than comparative, because neither of us is across or not across to any degree whatsoever, except in relation to the other. The same structure applies to uncles and aunts and nieces and nephews. Nobody is an uncle to any degree, except in relation to the children of his siblings or his spouse's siblings.

The in-charge-of relation has the same structure: Being in charge of your own body, or of some item of property, is something that can only be conceived in relation to others. To say that something is "up to you" is to say that it is not up to others; you are neither in charge nor not in charge of anything except in relation to other persons. The constraint on others' conduct is not in the service of enabling you to set and pursue your own purposes; instead, the extent of your entitlement to set and pursue

---

5. The distinction between comparisons and relations figures in Kant's argument that space is the form of outerness ("in order for me to represent them as outside one another, thus not merely as different but as in different places, the representation of space must already be their ground"). Immanuel Kant, *Critique of Pure Reason,* trans. Paul Guyer and Allen Wood (Cambridge: Cambridge University Press, 1998), 157 (A23, B38). See also Daniel Warren, "Kant and the Apriority of Space," *Philosophical Review* 107 (1998): 179–224.

your own purposes is determined in relation to the entitlement of each other person to do the same. If no person is in charge of another, then each is subject to a set of restrictions on the way he or she can use his or her body and property in relation to the others. But none of this depends on the content of the purposes for which any of these persons is using any of those things. Instead, the restrictions reconcile the independence of each person from all the others.[6]

Many contemporary discussions of specific torts overlook this distinction between relations and comparisons. For example, prominent views of negligence focus on a comparative inquiry, sometimes comparing the cost of the defendant taking a precaution to the expected cost of the plaintiff's injury, other times comparing the negligence of the defendant and the innocence of the plaintiff. Discussions of defamation sometimes speak of "balancing" the defendant's interest in freedom of expression against the plaintiff's interest in reputation. In subsequent chapters I will explain why such comparative analyses fail to capture the structure of the wrongs in question. Many of those analyses reflect a formal confusion between the existence of a wrong and its seriousness. It is natural to think that some wrongs are more serious than others, and so to suppose they have a degree. A negligently inflicted scratch is less serious than the negligently inflicted loss of a limb; trespassing into someone's yard is less serious than trespassing into his or her home; putting an unwanted hand on someone's shoulder is less serious than groping that person. All of these differences are genuine, but the differences of degree are secondary to the wrongfulness of both members of each pair. Differences of degree may be relevant to remedies, just as they may be to the extent of permissible self-help, or, in a criminal law context, to the appropriate punishment. But any such factors are relevant only in relation to a wrong, and the question of whether one person has wronged another is not one of degree.

---

6. As we shall see in Chapters 4 and 5, the role of quantitative measures in assessing due care does not entail that rights turn out to have a degree after all. Instead, quantitative measures presuppose a characterization of the place of those rights within a system of rights.

3. Your Body and Property

Your body and property[7] are protected because they are the means through which you set and pursue your own purposes. You do not have your body as a means in the way in which you have your property, but you do anything at all only by doing things with your body. The sense in which it is yours is that others are constrained in the ways in which they may deal with it; for it to be yours is for others to be constrained, for it not to be up to them which purposes you pursue.

3.1. Your Body

To describe your relationship to your own body in terms of means that you use may seem artificial: You are your body; you do not just happen to be the one who owns or occupies it. The point of including it in the means that you have is to emphasize the fact that you, rather than anyone else, are entitled to decide the purposes for which it is used. So the claim is not that you use your body in the way in which you use an item of property, because your relation to your own body is not in question: You and your body are one. Instead, the issue concerns what *others* may do in relation to your body. Your body is external to them, but they are not entitled to use or damage it, because it is not up to them which purposes you pursue, so it is not up to them which purposes your body is used to pursue. The form of the constraint on them—"This is not yours, do not interfere with it!"—is the same as the form of the constraint on them with respect to your property.

Anything you do, you do with your body. Legal systems (as well as ordinary moral thought) recognize this fact in treating wrongs against your body as wrongs against your person. Your mental and physical powers

7. I will not attempt to extend this account to what is described as "intellectual property," including copyrights, patents, and trademarks. On copyright, see Abraham Drassinower, *What's Wrong with Copying?* (Cambridge, MA.: Harvard University Press, 2015). Patents do not apply to spatially individuated objects, but rather to action types—the patent holder is entitled to exclude others from "practicing" the patent, that is, performing the series of steps described in it. As such, they are vulnerable to only one type of wrong, that of unauthorized use; act-types are abstract objects, and so cannot be damaged.

are the precondition of your setting and pursuing any purposes. Although you can fantasize about, entertain, or wish for things without moving your body, the only way you can pursue purposes is with your body. And you (your body) can also use other means, most prominently property.

Human bodies are not the only things that can be persons. Artificial persons figure prominently in sophisticated legal systems. Corporations—not just economic ones but religious institutions, universities, and charitable foundations—are legal persons, capable of setting and pursuing purposes. But although artificial persons can wrong others through the acts of their officers and employees, and their property can be damaged or destroyed, they do not have bodies.

These familiar observations do not establish that human bodies are the only natural persons. Fortunately, there is no need to establish such a claim; the claim that they are persons is neither an empirical discovery of a true nature nor a problematic hypothesis, a competitor to Descartes's doubts about whether the hats and coats he saw outside his window were conscious.[8] Careful analysis and casuistry are sometimes required to bring particulars under legal categories. On other occasions, the law can simply take up the most familiar features of human interaction. Absent some reason to doubt that living human beings are legal persons, each person's body (including mental capacities) is that through which he or she acts, and so is that which can wrong others or be wronged by them.

3.2. Your Property

The law of torts treats your body and your property in strikingly parallel ways. There are differences in the factual circumstances of certain wrongs. Your body can never be physically separated from you, making innocent trespasses and mistakes about title unlikely—it would be hard to mistake someone else's arm for your own.[9] But the two basic forms of wrongs are

---

8. René Descartes, "Meditation 2," in *Meditations on First Philosophy with Selections from the Objections and Replies,* trans. Michael Moriarty (Oxford: Oxford University Press, 2008), 23.

9. For the reverse problem, see Oliver Sacks, "The Man Who Fell out of Bed," in *The Man Who Mistook His Wife for a Hat and Other Clinical Tales* (New York: Touchstone, 1985), 55–59.

the same for bodies and property: Both can be used without authorization, and both can be wrongfully damaged. Much has been written about the vulnerability of human bodies.[10] In legal terms, however, bodies are vulnerable, not to suffering, but rather to having wrong done to them. Many of the things that can go wrong with the human body, such as infections entering through wounds or the aggravation of preexisting conditions, can also go wrong with an animal.[11] And some of them can go wrong with a building or ship.[12]

Still, it might be thought that treating property in terms of the in-charge-of relation requires more justification than does the treatment of bodies. Bodies differ in many ways; but, it might be said, they are distributed more or less equally, at least in the sense that every natural person has exactly one. In excluding others from your body, you are being your own person; but in excluding others from your property, it might be thought, you are keeping them from something they need.

Questions about the justification of private property often take place against the background of some imagined conception of public or collective property. Other questions concern capital property, and the extent to which government or collectives should play a role in the economy, and the problems both of poverty and of the concentration of income and wealth. Moral questions also arise about the acquisition of property through first possession.

Nothing so ambitious as a general justification of property is required to understand wrongs against property. All that is required is an account of how property can stand in the in-charge-of relation. Indeed, many of the moral objections to the distribution of property depend on the thought

10. Gregory Keating, "The Priority of Respect over Repair," *Legal Theory* 18 (2012): 293–337; Glanville Williams, "The Risk Principle," *Law Quarterly Review* 179 (1961): 193–197.

11. Katy Barnett and Sirko Harder, in *Remedies in Australian Private Law* (Cambridge: Cambridge University Press, 2014), 154, note the lack of clear cases on the "thin hull rule" but also the difficulty of defending the alternative. In *Causation and the Law* (Oxford: Oxford University Press 1985), 79–80, H. L. A. Hart and Tony Honoré treat the parallel as a causal principle on the grounds that both can be changed in the same ways.

12. In McColl v. Dionisatos [2002] NSWSC 276, a case involving water damage to a poorly constructed wall, Young C. J. notes that the defendant was unable to provide the court with a single case in which the doctrine was held to apply only to personal injury.

that *property* should be distributed differently—that homeless people should have homes of their own rather than shelters,[13] or that income should be distributed so that citizens have enough to make meaningful choices about how to live their own lives. That is, they rest on the thought that people have things that stand in the in-charge-of relation. This relational conception of property does not require that property be a natural right, beyond the scope of government regulation. Whether its ultimate justification is based on some idea of a natural right, or on ideas about a Humean convention or stewardship, the organizing principle of property is the same: The owner, rather than others, gets to determine the purposes for which it will be used, and other private persons are not permitted to use or damage the property without the owner's permission.[14] If a right

13. For a powerful analysis of homelessness in these terms, see Christopher Essert, "Property and Homelessness" (forthcoming).

14. This applies to both conventional and stewardship accounts of property. Hume's conventional account of property is one of the earliest and still the most powerful. Hume argues that property is the solution to a problem about the reliable availability of usable objects. The solution to the problem is to "put those goods, as far as possible, on the same footing with the fix't and constant advantages of the mind and body." The convention that does so prescribes "abstinence from the possessions of others." David Hume, *A Treatise of Human Nature,* ed. L. A. Selby-Bigge (Oxford: Clarendon Press, 1888), bk. 3, pt. 2, §2, p. 489. Hume does not use concept of a "convention" in either a game theoretic or a debunking sense. For the former, see David Lewis, *Convention: A Philosophical Study* (Cambridge, MA: Harvard University Press, 1969). For Lewis, a convention exists if each of a group of people engages in a pattern of activity because each of the others does, and exists only if the same group of people might instead have coordinated their behavior by engaging in one or more alternatives; a familiar example is the rule determining which side of the road to drive on. Hume's account of property is not conventional in this sense, because no alternative rules are available. Nor is it a debunking account; it does not regard the basic rule of property in the ways in which one might regard rules of etiquette.

The idea of property as a form of stewardship dates at least to Aquinas, and receives a clear expression in John Rawls's claim that "unless a definite agent is given responsibility for maintaining an asset and bears the responsibility and loss for not doing so, that asset tends to deteriorate. On my account the role of the institution of property is to prevent this deterioration from occurring." Rawls, *The Law of Peoples* (Cambridge, MA: Harvard University Press, 2001), 8. Just as Hume refers to "abstinence," Rawls refers to "responsibility." Both are focused on the idea of one person being in charge of a thing to the exclusion of all others. These are what are sometimes called "two-level" or "practice" accounts of property: the constitutive rule of the practice differs from its justifying purpose, but because the practice is justified, practitioners are not permitted to consult its justifying purpose diis a constraint on the conduct of others—that I am not in charge of your (or any other person's) property—then it is not my place to act on any judgments I might make about whether you or others have too much property, how it was acquired, or that you should use what you have in a way that best suits some purpose of mine. So I cannot take or use your property without your authorization, because I am not in charge of it. Further, I cannot act in ways that are inconsistent with your being in charge. So I cannot use what I have in ways that damage what is yours. Such an account is silent on the further question of what citizens, acting as a collective body through their governments, should do about the distribution of property. A public authority is entitled to restrict private rights for properly public purposes, but any entitlement to do so (or instance in which it declines to do so) does not depend on any consequentialist assessment of costs and benefits. Nor does it show that private rights are just another lever available to government in pursuit of its objectives.

4. Two Types of Wrongs: Using and Damaging

There are two basic ways in which one person can interfere with another person's means, corresponding to the familiar distinctions between torts that are intentional and those that are not. I can wrong you by using what is yours without your authorization, or I can wrong you by damaging what is yours. These may not seem to be exclusive categories. I could use what is yours and also damage it, particularly if I am using your body. Battery frequently leads to injury, but the basis of the wrong is the unauthorized touching, not the fact of injury or the intention to cause harm.[15] That is

---

rectly. For a discussion of the concept of a practice and two-level theories, see Michael Thompson, *Life and Action: Elementary Structures of Practical Thought* (Cambridge, MA: Harvard University Press, 2008), pt. 3. I raise doubts about the general success of indirect strategies in "Possession and Use," *Philosophical Foundations of Property Law,* ed. James Penner and Henry Smith (Oxford: Oxford University Press, 2013). But if a two-level account, such as Hume's or Rawls's, can be made to succeed, it justifies bringing things into the not-in-charge-of relation.

15. See Vosburg v. Putney, 50 N.W. 403, 1891, in which a twelve-year-old boy lost the use of his leg as a result of a kick from a classmate.

why batteries without damage are actionable.[16] Examples familiar to philosophers—throwing someone from a bridge to block the path of a runaway trolley,[17] or dynamiting someone to clear a path to escape from rising waters[18]—focus on the intention to cause harm, sending the analysis off in an unpromising Holmesian direction. The law of torts is a law of wrongs, not of harms. The difference between wronging you by using you or your property and wronging you by damaging those things is a difference between types of wrongs. If I injure you or damage your property while using either for a purpose you have not authorized, the damage is wrongful, though not because I intended to harm you or make injury to you or damage to your property part of my plan.[19] Outside of consensual activities, if one person intentionally injures another, the injurer is using the victim's body for an unauthorized purpose, whatever that purpose might be. Neither the damage nor the fact that it was the victim's in particular may have figured in the injurer's thoughts at all. In some cases, damage to the other person's body was the way in which the defendant tried to achieve some purpose. In such a case, the plaintiff's body is used.[20]

16. In Cardozo's words, "Every human being of adult years and sound mind has a right to determine what shall be done with his own body." Schloendorff v. Society of New York Hospital, 211 N.Y. 125, 105 N.E. 92 (1914).

17. See Phillippa Foot, "The Problem of Abortion and the Doctrine of Double Effect," *Oxford Review* 5 (1967): 5–15; Judith Jarvis Thomson, "The Trolley Problem," *Yale Law Journal* 94 (1985): 1395–1415.

18. Foot, "Problem of Abortion."

19. As suggested by Thomas Nagel in *The View from Nowhere* (Oxford: Oxford University Press, 1986), 180.

20. In a small number of cases, courts have made findings of battery or assault based on the doctrine of transferred intent, imported from the criminal law. An early English case was James v. Campbell, 5 Car. & P. 372, 172 Eng. Rep. 1015 (1832); after that it largely disappeared from English law, but was revived in Bici & Anor v. Ministry of Defence, [2004] EWHC 786 (QB) (7 April 2004). *Bici* held that an action for battery could succeed with transferred intent, but an action for assault could not, on the grounds that the fear "experienced as a consequence of the shooting would have been felt quite independently of the chosen target. Indeed, it would be quite fortuitous whether there was a chosen target or not" (¶80). In these cases, the defendant intended to inflict force on one person's body, but that intent is treated as sufficient to encompass the force inflicted on the body of another. These cases count as batteries, because the defendant intended to use another person's body. The appeal to transferred intent is a way of bringing these cases within the scope of the intentional tort of battery, but unlike more familiar instances of battery, the defendant

In other cases, the damage itself may not have been intended; I just wanted to take your canoe for a quick ride down the rapids, and thought myself fully competent to return it in perfect condition. My act would have been a wrong against you even if I had not wrapped the canoe around a rock; it would have been the same wrong if I had taken your canoe entirely by mistake, thinking it to be my own. And it would have been a wrong no matter how careful I was being with your canoe.

Use- and damage-based torts differ in kind. Discussions of John Stuart Mill's "harm principle" in the criminal law context sometimes suggest that the only acceptable rationale for prohibiting trespasses against property is that they are likely to do harm, where the harm in question can be identified independently of the specific act that causes it.[21] Whatever their fortunes might be in the criminal law,[22] such accounts face a fundamental difficulty in accounting for use-based wrongs in tort. In the case of damage-based wrongs, the defendant's conduct is of a type that typically does damage, but the law is content to wait for the damage to happen before providing the plaintiff with a remedy. Use-based torts are actionable without proof of damage, and it is no answer to an action for trespass against a person's body, land, or chattels to point out that the act ultimately provided a benefit to the plaintiff, whether in the form of an

---

did not intend to use injury to *this* person, i.e., the person who was injured. As Robert Stevens points out, these cases sit awkwardly in the law of torts, which should, as he puts it, not allow intent "in thin air" no more than it should allow negligence in thin air, that is, not toward the particular plaintiff. Stevens, *Torts and Rights* (Oxford: Oxford University Press 2007), 102. Transferred intent has been more prominent in U.S. cases; in his classic article "Transferred Intent," *Texas Law Review* 5 (1967): 650–662, William Prosser cites multiple cases, but represents the wrong of trespass in terms of intention to cause harm, and includes within the scope of transferred intent cases of consequential damages predicated on trespass, on the grounds that these are harms that were not intended. He rationalizes the cases in terms of the allocation of a loss. Narrower cases seem to adopt the principle "the intention follows the bullet," State v. Batson, 96 S.W.2d 384, 389 (Mo. 1936). See, for example, Manning v. Grimsley, 643 F.2d 20 (1st Cir. 1981).

21. Joel Feinberg, *Harm to Others: The Moral Limits of the Criminal Law* (Oxford: Oxford University Press, 1984), 31. The earliest application I have found of this idea to use-based torts is in John W. Salmond, *The Law of Torts: A Treatise Law of Liability for Civil Injuries* (London: Stevens and Haynes, 1907), 9.

22. I argue that no such account can be developed. See Arthur Ripstein, "Beyond the Harm Principle," *Philosophy and Public Affairs* 34 (2006): 215–245.

unwelcome but lifesaving blood transfusion or improvement to land or exercise for his or her horse. The law's indifference to damage suggests that something else is at issue. Nor can the damage be said to consist in having someone else use your body or property without your permission. To turn that into a head of loss or damage is to simply repackage the distinction between damage- and use-based torts, because the only thing that can set that interest back is a wrongful use.

4.1. Using

Intentional torts against bodies and property involve using something of which you are not in charge. Trespass to land is a central example, as is battery. Doctrinally, a trespass against minerals is a central case,[23] as is conversion. If I trespass on your land, I do so intentionally, because I intend to enter and stand on *this land,* even if I do not realize it is yours, and so do not intend to stand on *your* land. So, too, if I run my fingers through your hair without your authorization, I have committed trespass against your person. In both cases I am using something of which you are in charge.

Liability for familiar intentional torts against body and property is strict, and makes no reference to whether the defendant acted in a way that was attentive to the plaintiff's rights.[24] The intention is required

---

23. This line of cases was examined and upheld in Star Energy Weald Basin Limited & Anor v. Bocardo SA, [2010] UKSC 35, a case involving trespass to land for hydraulic fracking, although the Crown owned and had licensed the petroleum within it. Lord Hope noted at ¶26, however, that "as a general rule anything that can be touched or worked must be taken to belong to someone," and held that the Crown's claim to the petroleum does not deprive a landowner of rights to the rock formations that must be traversed to access it.

24. John Goldberg describes the tort of trespass as "normatively complex" because it can be done innocently yet intentionally. See John C. P. Goldberg, "The Constitutional Status of Tort Law: Due Process and the Right to a Law for the Redress of Wrongs," *Yale Law Journal* 115 (2005): 524, 597. Goldberg's claim is not that this combination is normatively problematic, only that it appears complex if it is supposed that intentional torts require an intention to do damage. See, for example, Tito v. Waddell (No. 2), [1977] Ch 106, 335; Jaggard v. Sawyer, [1995] 1 WLR 269, 282. See also Wrotham Park Estate Co. v. Parkside Homes, [1974] 1 WLR 798 at 812, 813; Livingstone v. Rawyards Coal Company, (1880) 5 App Cas 25 at 41 (Lord Blackburn). An intentional tort violates the right of the owner of the land to determine the purposes for which it is used. The fact that someone can violate

because to act intentionally is simply to take up means in order to pursue
an end. Liability is strict because someone can use something without
knowing who is in charge of it. I can set up my tent on your land without
knowing whose land it is. I may not even be reflectively aware that I am
using it—perhaps I am so tired, or setting up my tent has become so rou-
tine, that I do it without thinking about it at all. I still act intentionally,
because my intention is to use *this land* to set up my tent, *here*, that is, to
use these means (the land) to achieve this end (set up tent). The means I
use are yours rather than mine. The description under which I use the
land focuses on its usefulness for my particular purpose, rather than its
situation from the standpoint of rights. There is nothing objectionable
about my thinking in this way. The wrong is not reflective indifference
to the rights of others. It is the use of something in a way that is inconsistent with someone else being in charge of it. That question is relational,
and is not a matter of degree.[25]

The category of use-based torts includes those that fell under the old
common law writ of trespass—battery, false imprisonment, trespass to
land, and trespass to chattels, each of which is actionable without proof
of damage. That writ included a requirement of "directness," which is potentially misleading, as the distinction between use- and damage-based
torts is not between direct and indirect injury. If I carelessly stumble into
you, our contact is direct, but there is no sense in which I am using
you—I am not trying to accomplish some purpose by stumbling into
someone, and you happen to be available because nearby. If I am—the
authorities are closing in on me, and I want to slip the secret vial into
your pocket before they search me—then I didn't stumble into you at all,
I committed a battery. I can commit the tort of conversion by receiving
stolen goods, purchasing them at an auction, for example, without taking
physical possession of them, and so not dealing with them directly. So,

---

the owner's right without any realization that the land belongs to him or her means that an
intentional tort can be committed innocently.

25. In Ellis v. Loftus Iron Co., (1874) LR 10 CP 10, Lord Coleridge remarks, "It is clear
that, in determining the question of trespass or no trespass, the court cannot measure the
amount of the alleged trespass; if the defendant places a part of his foot on the plaintiff's
land unlawfully, it is in law as much a trespass as if he had walked half a mile on it."

too, I can falsely imprison you, even if I do so by remote control, luring you into a room that I then lock from the outside.[26] In cases of indirect conversion and false imprisonment, the wrong consists in use, for two reasons. First, the nature of the wrong consists in asserting control over the object of the right. In the case of conversion, I treat another person's property as my own and so as subject to my choice and not the owner's. In the case of false imprisonment, I treat you as subject to my choice; your legal right to freedom of movement is just your entitlement that others not be in charge of your body. Another person's entitlement to exclude you from his or her land is consistent with that right, but other private persons are not entitled to contain you within a restricted space. One person can falsely imprison another even if the other is physically unable to go out due to illness.[27] Second, the wrong can be completed in the absence of any damage.

4.2. Damaging

Use-based torts involve using the means of others; damage-based torts involve using your own means in a way that is inconsistent with the entitlement of others to use theirs. If I damage your property, or injure your person, I wrong you by depriving you of the use of means that were available for your pursuit of whatever purposes you set for yourself. I wrong you by depriving you of those means even if you had no plans to use them.[28]

The difference between using another's means and the side effects of using your own means generates two other familiar differences between damage-based and use-based torts. First, use-based torts are normally actionable without a showing of loss; damage-based torts are not. I wrong

26. In Herring v. Boyle, (1834) 1 Cr. M. & R. 377, 380, Bolland B. says, "There are many cases which show it is not necessary, to constitute an imprisonment, that the hand should be laid upon the person."

27. Grainger v. Hill and Another, (1838) 4 Bing NC 212, 132 E. R. 769.

28. In *The Mediana,* [1900] AC 113, Lord Halsbury remarks on the obviousness of this point: "Supposing a person took away a chair out of my room and kept it for twelve months, could anybody say you had a right to diminish the damages by showing I did not usually sit in that chair, or that there were plenty of other chairs in the room?"

you if I enter your land without your permission. If I break into your house and clean it for you, I commit a trespass to land, even if you have benefited from it.[29] So, too, if I take your horse for an unauthorized ride, even if the horse is healthier as a result; or if I perform an unauthorized medical procedure on you, even if by doing so I save your life.[30]

Second, damage-based torts involve the side effects of the defendant's use of his or her own means. Not all such side effects are actionable, only the ones that characteristically cause damage. This difference reflects the distinction between damage and use. Damage-based torts occur when separate persons pursue their separate purposes, and one, through inappropriate use of his or her means, causes damage to the other's person or property. Merely damaging the plaintiff's means is not sufficient; the defendant must have damaged those means by acting inappropriately. Inappropriate action is often termed "fault," which is most familiar in the tort of negligence, but the general rationale carries over to all torts involving personal injury or property damage without use. Anything you might do with your means has some potential side effects. Your entitlement to use your means to set and pursue your own purposes cannot be limited by the mere potential effects of your doing so on the security of the bodies and property of others.

In the tort of negligence, the requirement of "ordinary," "due," or "reasonable" care reflects the entitlement of each person to use his or her means to set his or her own purposes. Qualifiers such as "due" or "reasonable" characterize the conditions under which the defendant's doing damage to the plaintiff's body or property is consistent with each person's entitlement to use his or her means. That entitlement requires that each person be secure in his or her own means, but also that each restrict the use of those means up to the point where interference with another is either unlikely or minor. In negligence, conduct that poses only trivial risks to the person and property of others need not be moderated.[31] Those

---

29. See Susan Warren, "'Cleaning Fairy,' Accused of Breaking into Home And Cleaning It," *Huffington Post,* May 31, 2012, http://www.huffingtonpost.com/2012/05/31/susan-warren-cleaning-fairy-broke-into-home-cleaned-ohio_n_1559477.html.

30. Malette v. Shulman, 72 O.R. (2d) 417 (1990) (Ont. C.A.).

31. Bolton v. Stone, [1951] AC 850 (HL).

risks sometimes lead to injuries, but your entitlement to use your means to pursue your purposes entitles you to impose to those "background" risks. To require you to refrain from activities that carry those risks would effectively disable you from using your means at all, and would amount to requiring you to use what is yours to suit the specific purposes of others.[32]

I suggested above that your entitlement to the security of your means does not protect them against their natural vulnerability to deterioration and decay. That vulnerability is just a feature of your means as natural objects. Similarly, the law treats the ordinary "background" effects of other people's actions as just part of the natural world, because the possibility of damaging what belongs to another accompanies anything anyone might do. Only if someone acts in a way that is characteristically damaging is damage that results wrongful. In negligence cases, acting in a way that raises a significant risk of harm is characteristically damaging; in nuisance cases, interfering with another's ordinary use and enjoyment of his or her land is; in other cases, it means doing something that simply cannot be done safely. In all of these torts, it is only because one party acted in a way that would characteristically damage another's means that the damage is wrongful.

Talk about reconciling the independence of separate persons sounds superficially similar to the Holmesian idea of striking a balance between

---

32. Fraud might appear to be difficult to fit into this classification. If I deceive you, I use you in one sense of that word, but deceit and related torts are only actionable on a showing of damage, and, unlike trespass, they cannot be committed mistakenly. The wrong is completed only if the fraudster meant to deceive, and the dupe acts on the false belief that the fraud induced. So the fault element and damage requirement appear together. The right at issue is not against being lied to, but rather against being deprived of what you have through deceit. The protection of that right is a structural requirement of the system in which each person is entitled to use his or her means consistent with the entitlement of others to do the same. Getting other people to do things by deceiving them is necessarily inconsistent with separate persons pursuing their separate purposes. By contrast, saying things that turn out to be false need not be inconsistent. For the same reason, plaintiff consent is not a defense to fraud. This is not because of the seriousness of fraud (in the way in which, in the criminal law, consent is not a defense to murder), but rather a reflection of its interpersonal structure. Consensual fraud is impossible. If you consented to the deception, you weren't defrauded after all; you were just playing along.

the competing interests in one person's successful achievement of his aims and another person's interest in avoiding injury. Like the other utilitarian glosses on familiar normative ideas that Holmes brought to the center of tort theory, however, the Holmesian interpretation replaces the idea that separate persons are free to set and pursue their purposes as they see fit, with a very different idea of assigning weight to interests, and striking a "balance" between them.[33] Such an account has no choice but to attend to the particular purposes that a given defendant is pursuing, the likelihood of success in that pursuit, and the particular vulnerabilities faced by the plaintiff. It all but inevitably leads to aggregation as well—Holmes's contrast between "isolated ungeneralized wrongs" and the "incidents of certain well-known businesses"[34] extends the balancing exercise to its natural stopping point by asking about the long-term costs and benefits of ongoing activities rather than the specific transaction between the plaintiff and the defendant.

The alternative focuses instead on the capacity of each person to set and pursue his or her own purposes, whatever they might be, and accords to each person the entitlement to use his or her means as he or she sees fit, consistent with others having the same entitlement. Neither the defendant's purposes nor the plaintiff's vulnerabilities play any role in this analysis. Nor does liability reflect the idea that security takes priority over liberty, as though these were somehow always in conflict. Instead, a system in which nobody is in charge of another person's means requires everyone to limit their activity in the same ways, which protects the liberty of others *by reconciling each person's entitlement to use his or her means to set and pursue his or her own purposes.*

33. See, for example, Mark Geistfeld, "Necessity and the Logic of Strict Liability," *Issues in Legal Scholarship*, Volume 5, Issue 2 (Oct 2005): 6: "This interpersonal conflict of the liberty and security interests is mediated by the standard of care in a manner that defines unreasonable conduct for purposes of negligence liability."

34. "Our law of torts comes from the old days of isolated, ungeneralized wrongs, assaults, slanders, and the like, where the damages might be taken to lie where they fell by legal judgment. But the torts with which our courts are kept busy to-day are mainly the incidents of certain well known businesses." Oliver Wendell Holmes, "The Path of the Law," *Harvard Law Review* 10 (1897): 469.

5. Conclusion

Decades of scholarship inspired by Holmes, and later Hohfeld, has represented the law of torts as a domain of policy, one of the techniques available to someone designing a system to use in bringing about desirable outcomes. This mode of scholarship stands on two pillars. The first of these is the suggestion that the law's explicit characterization of wrongdoing makes no sense in the terms in which it presents itself. This opens up space for the further suggestion that it is merely a façade, and that something else must stand behind it. The second pillar is a positive account focused on vulnerability, harm, and loss. These nonrelational ideas are said to be the real basis of legal decisionmaking.

The only way to show that something is not merely a façade is to display the elements of its structure. In this chapter I have laid the groundwork for doing so, beginning by showing that a more general structure organizes the wrongs against bodies and property in which the law of torts takes an interest. Your body and property are protected as means, that is, as conditions of your setting and pursuing purposes, and their protection consists in restrictions on the ways in which others may set and pursue purposes. Each person is entitled to use his or her means as he or she sees fit, restricted only by others' entitlement to do the same, but nobody is entitled to use another person's means except with that person's permission. This normative structure generates an organizing distinction between two ways in which one person can wrong another's body or property, which I have characterized in terms of use- and damage-based wrongs.

CHAPTER 3

Using What You Have

Misfeasance and Nonfeasance

Tort duties restrict the ways in which each person can use his or her means; they do not require anyone to use his or her means in the way best suited to some other person's ability to use his or her means in a preferred way. You do not need to refrain from building a tower so as to give me access to sunlight.[1] So, too, I have no standing to complain if you breach your contract with another person on whom I have come to depend,[2] injure another's property that I regularly use,[3] or

---

1. Fontainebleau Hotel Corporation v. Forty-Five Twenty-Five, Inc., 114 So. 2d 357, 1959 Fla. App.

2. H. R. Moch Co. v. Rensselaer Water Co., 247 N.Y. 160, 159 N.E. 896 (1928).

3. Rickards v. Sun Oil Co., 41 A.2d 267, 269–270 (N.J. 1945); Robins Dry Dock & Repair Co. v. Flint, 275 U.S. 303 (1927); Weller v. Foot and Mouth Disease Research Institute, [1966] 1 QB 569; Cattle v. Stockton Waterworks, (1875) LR 10 QB 453. In Elliot Steam Tug Co. Ltd. v. Shipping Controller, [1922] 1 KB 127, (CA), Scrutton L. J. puts the point succinctly: "At common law there is no doubt about the position. In case of a wrong done to a chattel the common law does not recognize a person whose only rights are a contractual right to have the use or services of the chattel for purposes of making profits or gains without possession of or property in the chattel. Such a person cannot claim for injury done to his contractual right." See also 532 Madison Ave. Gourmet Foods, Inc. v. Finlandia Center, Inc., 750 N.E.2d 1097 (N.Y. 2001), in which a public sidewalk damaged by the defendant's negligence made the plaintiff's business inaccessible to customers. Such cases raise

offer products or services that my (former) customers find more attractive than what I offer. In each of these cases you have neither used nor
damaged my means; all you have done is change the world in which I
use them. I still have my (now shady) land; if you fail to provide something to someone else on whom I depend, I may now be vulnerable, but
absent some special relation between us, I am not entitled to demand
that you protect my means.[4] My customers are independent persons,
and just as I cannot compel them to favor me with their business, I cannot
compel you to refrain from making them a better offer.

I will explain these ideas in terms of the familiar legal distinction between misfeasance and nonfeasance. That distinction is most familiar in
cases in which the law declines to find that the defendant was under a duty
to assist the plaintiff; most notoriously, it figures in the common law's refusal to impose a duty of easy rescue. I will offer a broader interpretation
of the distinction, so that it will comprehend both those cases and others
that are sometimes treated as *damnum absque iniuria,* loss without wrongdoing, and others that have been described in terms of the absence of a
duty or the remoteness of the loss of which the plaintiff complains. I will
argue that all are instances of the same distinction. One person is entitled
to constrain the conduct of another only with respect to a right to body or
property. This simple idea explains why there is no duty to rescue, no
recovery for economic loss created through wrongful damage to the property of, or breach of a contract with, a third party, and no liability for de-

---

the conceptual possibility of negligently depriving the plaintiff of access to his or her property, so that he or she is no longer able to make any use of it at all, perhaps by spilling chemi-
cals so toxic that the authorities evacuate the area for an extended period. In principle such
an action could be a private wrong, as it separates the owner from his or her property. On
the facts of *Finlandia,* this wasn't established. In People Express Airlines v. Consol. Rail
Corp., 495 A.2d 107, 109 (N.J. 1985), the defendant was held liable for the plaintiff's loss of
use of a terminal due to an oil spill. The court put the point in terms of loss, rather than
being deprived of access to property.

4. Contrast Caltex Oil (Australia) Pty. Ltd. v. The Dredge "Willemstad," (1976) 136 CLR
529. The Court in *Caltex* framed the issue in terms of indeterminate liability, and concluded that because the pipeline in question had a single user, the specter posed no ob-
stacle to liability in the absence of a duty. *Caltex* was rejected by the Judicial Committee of
the Privy Council in Candlewood Navigation Corporation Ltd. v. Mitsui OSK Lines Ltd.,
(1985) 60 AR 163.

priving someone of a path across one's land. In all of these cases, the distinction is between wrongfully doing something *to* the plaintiff and failing to do something *for* the plaintiff. In the case of failure to rescue, the thing that the defendant might have done for the plaintiff is to provide assistance. In some other examples, the defendant failed to provide a conduit or path for the plaintiff to receive something from the other side of the defendant's land, but the plaintiff has no right that the defendant's land be used in that way. In still others, the defendant wronged someone other than the plaintiff, for example by destroying the bridge that the plaintiff's customers use to get to his restaurant, but the plaintiff does not have a right to constrain the conduct of the defendant with respect to the rights of anyone else. If rights are understood in relational rather than comparative terms, these are also cases in which the defendant failed to do something for the plaintiff, because, as between the two of them, refraining from committing a wrong against someone other than the plaintiff is properly understood as the failure to provide the plaintiff with a favorable context.[5]

1. Using and Damaging

The examples I have introduced involve losses that one person suffers as a result of the action or inaction of another. The distinction between misfeasance and nonfeasance is not, however, fundamentally about damage or loss. Instead, it is a reflection of the relation between norms governing the effects of one person's conduct on another's means, and norms

5. I am not the first person to note the continuity between these cases. Peter Benson, "Misfeasance as an Organizing Normative Idea in Private Law," *University of Toronto Law Journal* 60 (2010): 739–798, draws attention to them. In his discussion of civil law in the final chapter of *Torts and Rights* (Oxford: Oxford University Press, 2007), Robert Stevens considers the relation between the willingness of French law to impose a private law duty to rescue with its readiness to impose liability for pure economic loss occasioned by a wrong done to another. Benson notes that in Home Office v. Dorset Yacht, [1970] UKHL 2, [1970] AC 1004, Lord Diplock groups many of them together. In *Moch*, a case in which the plaintiff's warehouse burned down as a result of the defendant's failure to meet a contractual obligation to supply the municipality with adequate water for its fire hydrants, Cardozo J. explains the lack of liability in terms of the "time-honored" distinction between misfeasance and nonfeasance. The difficulty is that a contractual relation between two parties would "mean the involuntary assumption of a series of new relations, inescapably hooked together."

governing the use of another person's means. The central idea in all of these cases is that the plaintiff could not have a right to constrain the defendant's conduct unless he or she was entitled to determine the purposes for which the defendant uses his or her own body and property. A plaintiff could not have such a power in a system in which no person is in charge of another; the plaintiff is not entitled to determine the purposes for which the defendant's means are used.

The fact that I depend on another person's property or performance cannot give me a right against anyone other than that person. At most, I can have a contractual right as against the owner of that thing, but that contract doesn't give me any rights against anyone else with respect to that thing.[6] Absent a right, the availability of anything belonging to somebody else is just part of the context in which I use what I already have. To allow me to require you to provide me with a favorable context for my preferred purposes would make your means subject to my purposes. I have no right to your assistance or forbearance with respect to your dealings with third parties because I am not entitled to determine the purpose for which you use your means.

But if I am not entitled to constrain your conduct with respect to a third party's body or property, there is no basis for liability in these cases, because liability is based exclusively on what transpires between us. I cannot have a right against you to some third person's body or property, even if I depend on them.

These examples have the same structure when viewed from the opposite direction, focusing not on the distinction between the presence and absence of a right, but instead on whether you need my permission to do

---

6. Peter Benson makes this point by noting that the plaintiff would have no claim if the defendant were intentionally using the object, even if doing so interferes with the plaintiff's interests, and so can have no claim if he or she does so negligently. See Benson, "The Basis for Excluding Liability for Economic Loss in Tort," in *Philosophical Foundations of Tort Law,* ed. David G. Owen (New York: Oxford University Press, 1995): 427–461. Benson's formulation may seem puzzling: How is intentional use relevant? (See Nicholas McBride, "Rights and the Basis of Tort Law," in *Rights and Private Law,* ed. Donal Nolan and Andrew Robertson [Oxford: Hart, 2012], 337.) You are entitled to constrain the conduct of others with respect to something only if you are entitled to determine the purposes for which it is used. If you are not so entitled, then nobody wrongs you by using those means or making them unavailable.

any of these things. You do not need my permission to put up a structure that occupies some of the space on your land.[7] You do not need to consult me about whether to breach a contract with someone else, or damage someone else's property—I cannot give you permission to do so. Nor can I withhold permission for you to do either of these things. If I have no say about whether you do those things, I have no standing to complain if you do them. Nor do you need to check with me before offering products or services to others, or building or dismantling a structure on your own land.

The case in which you wrong nobody and the case in which you wrong someone other than me are alike in that my permitting or forbidding them is meaningless. These matters are not up to me. The distinction maps onto a contrast Bertrand Russell drew when he wrote, "Work is of two kinds: first, altering the position of matter at or near the earth's surface relatively to other such matter; second, telling other people to do so."[8] You can move around the bits of matter that comprise your means, and tell others what they may do with your means. But you have no standing to move around or tell anyone what he or she may do with any other person's means.

The most notorious instance of the distinction between misfeasance and nonfeasance is the common law's lack of a duty to rescue. At the appropriate level of generality, it is no different from the examples above: Absent a special relationship, you do not need to use your means in a way that best suits my preferred use of mine. Because this is a general structuring principle, it applies regardless of how urgent my situation is. Failing to rescue me is formally the same as failing to provide me with sunlight I need, and not only because sunlight might be what I need to survive. The same point explains the legal rule that an ultrasensitive plaintiff does not recover for foreseeable injuries. You are allowed to make a certain amount of noise, even if it will cause me great discomfort or illness, or interfere with my preferred use of my property.[9] Just as you do

---

7. Zoning regulations may impose public law requirements that change this; the relevant point concerns how things stand between the parties.

8. Bertrand Russell, "In Praise of Idleness," *Harpers Monthly Magazine*, October 1932, 553.

9. See Rogers v. Elliott, 146 Mass. 349, 15 NE 768 (1888), in which the defendant's ringing of a bell caused convulsions to the plaintiff, who was recovering from sunstroke.

not need to use your land in a way that provides a path for sunlight to mine, you do not need to organize your activities because of my un-usual need for quiet. These are all examples of your entitlement to de-termine the purposes for which your means will be used, and so to leave out my claims of need. If you do not need to consider my ends in de-ciding how to use your means, then you do not need to confer a benefit on me, no matter what is at stake, even my own life.

In these cases, the difficulty is not that the law has a policy objective that overrides the claim of need, or exhibits "philistinism,"[10] worries about opening the "floodgates" of litigation,[11] prefers the benefits of eco-nomic competition, or expects the economy as a whole to suffer no loss because others will engage in substitute transactions.[12] The rationale is

10. Oliver Wendell Holmes Jr., "Privilege, Malice, and Intent," *Harvard Law Review* 8 (1894): 4.

11. Fleming James, "Limitations on Liability for Economic Loss Caused by Negligence: A Pragmatic Appraisal," *Vanderbilt Law Review* 25 (1972): 43–44; Robert L. Rabin, "Tort Re-covery for Negligently Inflicted Economic Loss: A Reassessment," *Stanford Law Review* 37 (1985): 1513–1515. These arguments, like the reasoning in *Caltex*, above, appeal to Cardozo's reference in the *Ultramares* case to "liability in an indeterminate amount for an indetermi-nate time to an indeterminate class," but fail to note that the phrase appears as part of a *re-ductio* of basing liability on foresight alone. The passage immediately follows an explicit turn to the issue of whether the defendant owed a duty to the plaintiff. "We are brought to the question of duty, its origin and measure." Focused on that question, he continues: "If liability for negligence exists, a thoughtless slip or blunder, the failure to detect a theft or forgery beneath the cover of deceptive entries, may expose accountants to a liability in an indeterminate amount for an indeterminate time to an indeterminate class. The hazards of a business conducted on these terms are so extreme as to enkindle doubt whether a flaw may not exist in the implication of a duty that exposes to these consequences" (Ultramares v. Touche, 255 N.Y. 170, 180 [1931]). That is, Cardozo does not consider the possibility of limiting liability when a duty has been breached; he focuses instead on the question of whether the defendant owed a duty to the plaintiff. Having answered the duty question in the negative, the issue of liability does not even arise. Cardozo makes the relational structure even more clear at 190, quoting his earlier decision in *Moch*, which expressed the same cau-tion in expressly relational terms: "Undertaking to perform a service for one person does not generate rights in others. By contrast, bringing a dangerous object into circulation endangers the bodies and property of others, independently of contractual arrangements."

12. W. Bishop, "Economic Loss in Tort," *Oxford Journal of Legal Studies* 2 (1982): 1–29; William M. Landes and Richard A. Posner, *The Economic Structure of Tort Law* (Cam-bridge, MA: Harvard University Press, 1987), 251. This analysis overlooks the availability of damages for consequential economic loss in cases in which the plaintiff owns both the

much simpler: However serious these losses might be to those who suffer them, they are not cases of one person depriving another of means to which the latter has a prior right. No person could have a right in any of these cases, except by means of a contract or prescriptive easement, because any right would create in another person a duty to tailor his or her use of his or her means to the specific purposes of another. Contract generates an obligation of precisely this sort, but there is no background obligation to work for the benefit of another private person's specific purpose. To impose such an obligation would replace each person's own responsibility for his or her own life with a responsibility for the particular projects of another.

2. A Comparative Note on Misfeasance and Nonfeasance

It is often remarked that not all legal systems carry the distinction as far as the common law does, and sometimes the absence of a duty to rescue is treated as merely a peculiarity of positive law. On some understandings this peculiarity is treated as a reflection of the difficulties of enforcement, or of the special problems of drawing lines between the easy and difficult rescues in a nonarbitrary way. On others, it reflects an outdated nineteenth-century focus on rugged individualism[13] or an excessive concern for the defendant's liberty at the expense of the plaintiff's security. These accounts represent what the law treats as a distinction in kind as one of degree, suggesting that a less individualistic law might impose greater obligations of assistance. Looking more carefully at the compara-

---

restaurant and the bridge, despite the fact that those customers would also have taken their business elsewhere (a feature of these cases already noted a decade earlier by James, "Limitations on Liability," 45). The net loss is the same but is the violation of the plaintiff's own right. An alternative economic account focuses on "channeling," allowing those suffering economic loss to sue their contractual partners who suffer physical injury and so are able to claim consequential damages. Mario Rizzo, "A Theory of Economic Loss in the Law of Torts," *Journal of Legal Studies* 11 (1982): 281–310. Channeling theory fits the case law well, because it contends that you can sue only if you have a right. Its claim that the rights are assigned to enable channeling is less plausible.

13. Francis H. Bohlen, "The Moral Duty to Aid Others as a Basis of Tort Liability," *University of Pennsylvania Law Review* 56 (1908): 217, 219–220.

tive materials suggests that the basis of the distinction between misfeasance and nonfeasance is not to be found in individualism or a preference
for the defendant's liberty over the plaintiff's security.

In those countries—notably France—in which there is tort liability for
failure to rescue, the liability always follows the breach of a public law
provision requiring rescue.[14] The French Civil Code includes a general provision on causing loss through faulty conduct, and a further
general provision incorporates the criminal code, and so finds the breach
of a criminal statute is sufficient fault for liability. Thus, although the
person who is not rescued is entitled to recover damages, the recovery is
predicated on a separate level of analysis. The need for this form of in-
corporation via other legal regimes reveals how foreign the idea of simple
liability for nonfeasance is to tort law. The French approach is also distinctive in that its imposition of liability for any form of wrongdoing is
undifferentiated. Provided that there is the breach of any legal, statutory,
or contractual obligation, the wrongdoer is liable for any losses that
ensue to anyone.[15]

German law is also sometimes said to reject the distinction between
misfeasance and nonfeasance, but the situation is more complex. In
German law, liability arises only in cases in which the defendant has a
special role, or has undertaken a special relationship with the plaintiff,

14. Under French law (*Code Civil*, Art. 1382, 1383), breach of a criminal statute gives rise to
an action in tort. In the *Branly* case (Civ. 27 February 1951, D 1951, 329), the principle was
broadened to include cases in which "the act that was omitted should have been done either
by virtue of a legal, statutory or contractual obligation, or by virtue of the demand for objective
information within a profession." See Jeroen Kortmann, *Altruism in Private Law: Liability
for Nonfeasance and Negotorium Gestio* (New York: Oxford University Press, 2005), 37, 42.

15. Thus the presence of the duty to rescue in French civil law is an instance of a more
general addition of private liabilities based on duties that are not private duties. In one case
a football club recovered for its costs occasioned by the defendant's negligent killing of one
of its players. Colmar 20 avr. 1955, D. 1956 323. At the same time, such results are avoided
in other similar cases based on an analysis of causation. A similar case involving an opera
company and its tenor led to the opposite result on the grounds that the loss was indirect.
Ch. Civ. 14 nov. 1958, G. P. 1959, I.31. Both are discussed in Frederick Henry Lawson and
B. S. Markesinis, *Tortious Liability for Unintentional Harm in the Common Law and the
Civil Law* (Cambridge: Cambridge University Press 1982), 210. See also the discussion in
Stevens, *Torts and Rights,* 342–345.

or has created a hazard and fails to control it.[16] That is, liability is not for the failure to render aid, but rather for the failure to live up to the terms of a relationship into which the defendant has entered with the plaintiff. Like the liability of a common carrier for the safety of its passengers, these special relations turn on an analysis of how they are formed,[17] rather than any general supposition that the plaintiff has a right to a benefit. Provision §323c of the German Criminal Code requires easy rescues, but courts have held the duty to be owed to society as a whole, and so not to fall within the scope of tort liability for inaction.[18] Thus, it is treated in the same way as other criminal law requirements imposed as parts of systems of mandatory social cooperation. You need to move out of the way of an emergency vehicle, but the person who arrives late to the hospital, or whose house suffers greater fire damage because of your failure to move, does not have a private cause of action against you. You have failed in your civic duty, but have not committed a private wrong. The same might be said in cases in which you fail to pay your taxes and government services are cut back. Those who suffer as a result have no private claim against you, not because your contribution to their loss is hard to trace,[19] but

16. *Code civil,* arts. 1382, 1383.

17. I take this issue up in the discussion of duty in Chapter 4.

18. Cees van Dam, *European Tort Law,* 2nd ed. (Oxford: Oxford University Press, 2014), 465, describes the situation in German law this way:

> Although it is likely that the legislator intended this provision to protect individuals, the current majority opinion is that the criminal duty to provide help to someone in peril (323c StGB) does not aim to protect the person in danger or his next of kin, but only society as a whole. It is argued that it cannot reasonably be the aim of the rule that the person who did not prevent the crime or the accident is liable in the same way as the offender or the direct tortfeasor. The purport of the threat of punishment is not the warrant of individual help for the benefit of certain persons, but the citizen's duty (einstätsbürgerlicher Pflicht) to assist to preserve the public order and safety in extremely dangerous situations.

Van Dam notes that the provision's structure makes it difficult to treat the duty as correlative to a right to bodily security held by the plaintiff, because any attempt to render aid discharges it, even if unsuccessful.

19. Legal systems have developed sophisticated ways of keeping track of benefits when a legal claim is at stake. See the discussion of "identification" in Peter Birks, *An Introduction to the Law of Restitution* (Oxford: Oxford University Press, 1985), 358–375.

because your duty was owed to the public, rather than to any or all individual beneficiaries. Thus, in German law, as in the common law, there is no private cause of action for failure to rescue.

The combination of a criminal law requirement that easy rescues be undertaken with the absence of a tort duty is puzzling for any account of tort law that supposes that its function is to strike an appropriate balance between liberty and security, where each of these are understood in non-relational terms.[20] On such a view, the combination seems to grant a measure of freedom with one hand only to take it away with the other: the suggestion is that you are exempt from a tort duty to rescue because your liberty outweighs the other person's security, but in the criminal law, with the same two interests at stake, the balance tips in the opposite direction, and your freedom is outweighed. The conclusion to be drawn from this is not that there is something incoherent in the German position, but rather that the picture of legal norms as aiming to strike this sort of balance is mistaken.

3. Ease and Difficulty

The absence of a private law duty to rescue is one manifestation of the more general principle that the law of torts never requires you to use your means in a way that is best suited to another person's use of his or her own means. A duty to rescue would just be a duty to use your means to enable another person to succeed in the purpose of preserving his or her means (in this case, him- or herself). But from the formal standpoint of relations of right, the urgency of the situation is irrelevant; it is just a case of one person being under no duty to use his or her means in a way that suits the particular purposes of another.

It might be thought that an exception can be made for the case of easy rescue, on the grounds that the stakes are low for the rescuer—the rescue must be easy—and high for the person in peril. But something is easy or difficult only in relation to some other cost or opportunity. Whether measured in terms of the purposes of the potential rescuer, or in terms of some set of imagined purposes for normal or ordinary potential rescuers,

---

20. See, for example, Gregory Keating, "The Priority of Respect over Repair," *Legal Theory* 18 (2012): 318; Hanoch Dagan and Avihay Dorfman, "Just Relationships" (unpublished).

that ease/difficulty distinction is only available if some purposes are considered. A set of restrictions on the ways in which means are used contains no such dimension of comparison.

The irrelevance of ease and difficulty thus shows the continuity of the absence of a duty to rescue with familiar landmarks of tort law. A tort action must not only establish that the defendant could have foreseen that the plaintiff would suffer a loss, but also that a right has been invaded. This is so no matter how severe the loss suffered, or how trivial the cost of preventing it might have been. If I damage the bridge on which you depend, but which you do not own, you have no cause of action against me for the loss of your customers, even though anyone who gave it a moment's thought would realize that people cross bridges, and even though I was already under a duty to the bridge owner to avoid damaging it, so that giving you an additional claim against me would not prevent me from doing anything I was entitled to do. The distinction does not turn on how difficult it would be for me if you had a right; it turns instead on your entitlement to constrain my conduct, something you can do only with respect to your body and property. But if you own the bridge, I am liable for your losses, including the loss of custom, even though those losses are no more foreseeable or avoidable than they would be if you did not. The same point applies to my breach of a contract with someone other than you,[21] or failure to provide a path across my land for something on which you depend.[22] The same structure can be simplified to remove any reference to contract or property: If you stop eating bananas, mosquitoes will no longer be attracted to you as much, as a result of which I may suffer additional bites.[23] I cannot constrain you to eat bananas, even if I am severely allergic to mosquito bites.

21. H. R. Moch Co. v. Rensselaer Water Co.

22. Fontainebleau Hotel Corporation v. Forty-Five Twenty-Five, Inc.; Mayor of Bradford v. Pickles, [1895] AC 587.

23. Australian courts have sought to generate a distinctive category of vulnerability to sort through the wide range of effects of one person's conduct on others. In Perre v. Apand Pty. Ltd., [1999] HCA 36, the defendant negligently introduced infected seed potatoes into an area, as a result of which the plaintiff's fields, though not infected, were quarantined. Gaudron C. J. decided the case based on the narrow idea of depriving the plaintiffs of the use of their property, effectively treating the quarantine as an unusual mechanism. Other judges relied more heavily on *Caltex,* above.

The distinction between misfeasance and nonfeasance reflects the ir-
reducibility of the "in-charge-of" relation. You do not need to use your
means in pursuit of any end, not even the end of preserving me. That is the
sense in which I am entitled to constrain your use of your means—you may
not use your means to use mine, or use them in ways that damage mine—
but I am not in charge of you: I cannot require you to use them for the sake
of any end. These distinctions are formal, reflecting the difference between
restrictions on the manner in which means may be used and requirements
that they only be used in pursuit of my ends. The irreducibly relational notion of private right makes it impossible to raise any questions of degree.

4. Three False Paths to the Distinction

The distinction between misfeasance and nonfeasance structures the
rights of private persons to their bodies and property. I have already argued that it cannot be explained in terms of attaching priority to the defendant's freedom of choice, because the distinction applies even when
the defendant's choice is already restricted by some other obligation,
whether through the criminal law or a private law obligation to someone
other than the plaintiff. In this section I show that it cannot be explained
in terms of other morally familiar ideas.

I cannot claim to provide an exhaustive survey of every proposed characterization of the value that is supposed to be produced by "giving"
people rights that are structured by the distinction between misfeasance
and nonfeasance. What I want to do instead, as a proxy for that more exhaustive discussion, is consider some prominent forms of argument, and
explain why none of them can make sense of the distinction. It is open to
those who insist that normative principles must ultimately be concerned
about ends rather than means to say "so much the worse for the distinction between misfeasance and nonfeasance," and to propose remaking tort
law in the image of their preferred accounts. My own view is that the idea
that no person is in charge of another is normatively attractive, and cannot
be dismissed solely on the grounds that it is inconsistent with some general thesis that any justification must always appeal to some sort of end.

1. *Acts and omissions.* Moral philosophers draw attention to the distinction that ordinary moral thought draws between acts and omissions, doing

and allowing harm, or between harming someone and failing to aid that person. The prohibition of wrongful actions is said to be more stringent than that against wrongful omissions, or, alternatively, the prohibition on harming others is said to be more demanding than the obligation to render aid to those in need. This is not a book in general moral philosophy, and so I will not attempt to characterize, let alone explain or evaluate, that distinction. My aim is only to show that whatever its general importance, it cannot generate the distinction between misfeasance and nonfeasance.

There are two obstacles to aligning the act/omission distinction with the misfeasance/nonfeasance distinction. The first is that the legal distinction between misfeasance and nonfeasance is not merely a distinction of stringency; rather, the law makes the much stronger claim that no private person is under an obligation to confer a benefit on another. The ordinary moral supposition that harming someone is more serious than failing to benefit that person is a distinction of degree; it is not that there is nothing wrong with failing to benefit a person, only that harming someone is worse. The distinction between doing and allowing harm is meant to explain why certain acts are prohibited even when a greater good can be achieved.[24] Any such explanation, however, presupposes that in other circumstances it is impermissible to fail to render aid; its point is to explain the restriction. As a result, it cannot explain the legal absence of a duty to rescue; at most it could explain the wrongfulness of injuring one person in order to rescue five. Put differently, the distinction between acts and omissions is a comparative distinction, and so cannot show why omissions are not actionable.

Moreover, many familiar instances of the distinction between misfeasance and nonfeasance do not involve omissions at all, but instead acts that are not actionable. Destroying the bridge on which you depend, or the factories of people who have contracted to supply you, taking down (or erecting) a structure on my land, are all acts, not omissions. In the case of destroying the bridge, I am already prohibited from doing so; the law's distinctive claim is not that I have failed to act, or even that I have done

---

24. See, for example, Warren S. Quinn, "Actions, Intentions, and Consequences: The Doctrine of Doing and Allowing," *Philosophical Review* 98 (1989): 287–312; Frances Kamm, *Morality, Mortality,* vol. 2 (Oxford: Oxford University Press, 1996); Samuel Scheffler, "Doing and Allowing," *Ethics* 114 (2004): 215–239.

no wrong. It is that I have not wronged those who use the bridge but do not own it. That is not a claim about inaction; it is a claim about the relations in which we stand.[25] So, too, if there is a criminal law requirement to render assistance, as in German law, the criminal prohibition already imposes a demand. The exemption from tort liability does not turn on the distinction between acts and omissions.

The same point applies to Richard Epstein's suggestion that the absence of a duty to rescue reflects the fact that failure to rescue does not cause the victim's injury, loss, or death.[26] Epstein's thought is that the failure to do something is never a cause. This approach may seem promising because causation is relational; nothing is a cause except in relation to an effect, and nothing is an effect except in relation to some cause. This relational feature of causation figures in the requirement, explored in Chapter 4, that damage-based wrongs be completed. But causation alone cannot explain the distinction between misfeasance and nonfeasance; it requires the antecedent concept of a right.

Some cases of failure to rescue do map onto the distinction between causation and inaction; the bystander who does nothing does not create the peril from which the child drowns.[27] But Epstein's proposal has much greater difficulty with the other examples, such as the bridge case, which treats the owner-user of the bridge differently from the nonowner-user. In both cases you have suffered because of something I have done, but there is no serviceable concept of causation on which I cause your financial losses if you own the bridge that I carelessly destroy but do not cause them if you do not own it. The only way to get such a result is to build the distinction between misfeasance and nonfeasance into the concept of causation.[28]

25. For the same reason, I can wrong you by removing something—say, by pumping all of the air out of the building you are in; in so doing, I use my pump in a way that damages your lungs.

26. Richard Epstein, "A Theory of Strict Liability," *Journal of Legal Studies* 2 (1973):189 ff.

27. But even some of the rescue cases are difficult to fit to the action/inaction distinction; the person who dares another to do something dangerous and then stands by while the latter gets in trouble could be described as creating the peril. In Osterlind v. Hill, 160 N.E. 301 (Mass. 1928) the defendant failed to rescue the plaintiff when the canoe he had rented to him overturned.

28. Stephen Perry has suggested that Epstein's account of causation imports an idea of responsibility. See Stephen R. Perry, "Libertarianism, Entitlement, and Responsibility," *Philosophy & Public Affairs* 26 (1997): 351–396.

Aside from being cumbersome, such an approach would fail to explain the distinction. The factual effects of the defendant's conduct do not depend on legal categories, such as who owns what, but the legal effects do. In the previous examples, the restaurateur's loss of customers is among the effects of the tugboat destroying the bridge, the shadow cast by the defendant's tower causes the plaintiff's loss of custom, and the loss of the plaintiff's warehouse is a consequence of the defendant's failure to supply water to the municipality. If someone were to ask, "Why did the restaurant close?," or "Why did people stop going to the Eden Roc?," or "Why was the fire department unable to put out the fire?," the obvious answer would point to the defendant's conduct, treating the results as straightforward factual consequences of ordinary bump-and-grind causation. So although the concept of causation is relational in the right way, it is the wrong relation.

Proposals to focus on some idea of foreseeability,[29] responsibility,[30] or the capacity to control face the same obstacles: You are not responsible in tort for either all or only the foreseeable consequences of your actions. If you have no way of ascertaining where the boundary is, you are nonetheless a trespasser if you enter another person's land; you commit the tort of conversion if you receive stolen goods that you had no way of knowing to be so, and if, you move someone else's leg mistaking it for your own, you commit a battery. In damage-based torts, many foreseeable forms of damage are not actionable. If you take down (or build) a structure on your land, you can probably foresee, and avoid, blocking the light or casting the shadow on to my land. In all of these examples, the fundamental question is whether one person has a right against another. Although someone might try to construct a concept of responsibility that follows the concept of a right,[31] such an exercise would be an elaboration of a novel sense of responsibility, rather than an explanation of the concept of a right.

These difficulties reflect a much broader challenge to any attempt to explain the distinction between misfeasance and nonfeasance without

---

29. Ibid.

30. Tony Honoré, *Responsibility and Fault* (Oxford: Hart, 1999).

31. I made such an attempt in Arthur Ripstein, "Justice and Responsibility," *Canadian Journal of Law and Jurisprudence* 17 (2004): 361–386. I now regard my efforts as largely a detour.

appealing to a distinctively relational concept of a right. Such attempts are subject to a crucial ambiguity, the specifics of which I will detail below. Its broad structure, however, is straightforward: Reductive accounts of the distinction between misfeasance and nonfeasance either explain it in terms of something that really is entirely independent of the concept of a right, but then fail to account for either its structure or familiar instances. Alternatively, they account for the structure because the concept to which they seek to reduce the concept of a right actually turns out, on closer inspection, to presuppose it.

2. *Rights as protected interests.* The second strategy I will consider takes the relational feature of private rights seriously, but supposes that the rationale for imposing it in particular situations is based on an assessment of the significance of interests, which are then reprocessed into the form of relational rights.

Consider, for example, the suggestion made by John Goldberg and Benjamin Zipursky that the task of tort law is to give protection to particularly pressing interests. Their account is particularly interesting on this matter because they expressly conceive of rights in relational terms; they emphasize the ways in which tort duties always run from a particular defendant to a particular plaintiff, and argue that only the plaintiff has what they describe as "substantive standing" to make a claim in tort.[32] Yet despite recognizing the relational features of rights, their claim that relational duties are imposed by law in order to protect interests, the importance of which is specified exclusively in terms of a nonrelational idea of individual well-being, cannot explain the distinction between misfeasance and nonfeasance. They draw attention to the "plurality" of fundamentally different interests protected by tort liability.[33] Goldberg characterizes the legal concept of injury in terms of interests:

32. The distinction is first introduced in Benjamin C. Zipursky, "Rights, Wrongs, and Recourse in the Law of Torts," *Vanderbilt Law Review* 51 (1998): 1–100; and developed further in "The Moral of *MacPherson*," *University of Pennsylvania Law Review* 146 (1998): 1733–1847.

33. John C. P. Goldberg and Benjamin C. Zipursky, "Torts as Wrongs," *Texas Law Review* 88 (2010): 941. Compare Nicholas J. McBride, "Rights and the Basis of Tort Law," in Nolan and Robertson, *Rights and Private Law,* 353: "When we grant A a coercive right

Specifically, it is used to refer to a set of individual interests that the law recognizes as worthy of protection and vindication. For example, even though interference with one's interest in being free from annoyance—or in having aesthetically pleasing surroundings—might fairly be treated as a setback or harm to the victim, neither is treated by tort law as a sufficiently weighty interest to warrant recognition of duties on the part of others to refrain from or avoid interfering with that interest. If *D* acts carelessly with regard to *P*'s interest in not being annoyed so as proximately to cause *P* annoyance, *P* has no tort cause of action against *D* because the law of negligence does not regard the suffering of annoyance as the sort of harm that rises to the level of an injury, even though the annoyance is a loss or harm suffered by *P*.[34]

The vocabulary of interests and the idea that they enter the law on the basis of factors external to ideas of wrongdoing is elaborated further in a later piece.

Tortious wrongdoing always involves an interference with one of a set of individual interests that are significant enough aspects of a person's well-being to warrant the imposition of a duty on others not to interfere with the interest in certain ways, notwithstanding the liberty restriction inherent in such a duty imposition. In part out of a sense of the limitations as to what sorts of interferences and injuries are justiciable, and in part for policy considerations that have changed over time with changes in social norms and economic and political circumstances, courts and legislatures have never sought to render interferences with all such interests actionable.[35]

This insistence on protecting interests distracts from the structure of reasoning in which the putatively diverse interests figure. Interests matter

---

that B do *x*, we are saying that A's interest in B's doing *x* is so weighty that it would be right to burden B with a duty to do *x*."

34. John C. P. Goldberg, "Two Conceptions of Tort Damages: Fair v. Full Compensation," *DePaul Law Review* 55 (2006): 440n16. See also the discussion of tort law's "gallery of wrongs" in John C. P. Goldberg and Benjamin C. Zipursky, *The Oxford Introductions to U.S. Law: Torts* (New York: Oxford University Press, 2010), chap. 3.

35. Goldberg and Zipursky, "Torts as Wrongs," 944.

only if a right to body, reputation, or property already protects them, or if a special relationship obtains between the plaintiff and the defendant. In cases of special relationships, interests that would otherwise be excluded, such as prospective financial gain, may be protected. The creation of a relationship does not somehow multiply the weightiness of money in the plaintiff's well-being; it changes how things stand between the parties. That means, at a minimum, that neither nonrelational judgments about well-being nor comparative assessments of whether interests are "weighty" are the starting points for analysis.

Goldberg's example in the first quotation draws attention away from this feature of rights, by running together the question of the mode in which a legal interest is protected and the question of whether it is protected at all. The example treats negligent injury as the default mode of private wrongdoing, making it seem as though the basic question is whether an interest is serious enough to require people to look out for it. But the question of whether the law protects something is antecedent to the question of whether it attends to negligence with respect to it. The category of foreseeable damage and carelessness is not generically available, with courts deciding whether to apply it to this or that proposed interest. Instead, the question of whether the defendant was careful comes up only if the plaintiff is entitled to constrain the defendant's conduct with respect to the damaged object. That question cannot be answered in terms of an interest that is characterized without reference to a right, because interests are not constraints on the conduct of others.

The example of annoyance is misleading in another way. It introduces an interest that readers are likely to regard as trivial, and leaves out any characterization of how the annoyance comes about. The example of aesthetic surroundings is misleading in yet another way, as it looks like a busybody's interest in restricting what others do with their own property, and so is relational in the wrong direction. But neither of these captures what is distinctive about relational rights, so the fact that the interests at issue will not be "weighty" enough is overdetermined. Both are cases in which no possible right is at issue, and so provide no support for the contention that whether the law finds a right and correlative duty depends upon how weighty an interest is.

These difficulties are symptomatic of a more general difficulty with analyzing the rights protected by tort law in terms of interests: The concept of an interest is ambiguous at a crucial point. Its core difficulty can be summed up in Leif Wenar's suggestion that "the meaning of 'interest,' like butter, is semisolid. When Interest Theorists are rigorous, and freeze the concept into hedonist or objective list meaning, the concept then becomes unsuitable for analyzing rights outside those of a limited, if growing, set of natural-kind right-holders . . . But 'interest' can also be smeared across roles."[36] The core of the objection is that the concept of an interest is either too narrow to cover the wide range of cases it purports to cover, or so broad as to include interests that are most naturally described as the interest in having your right protected. Applied to the law of torts, the narrow reading appears to be unable to account for the sense that a battery is a wrong even if it benefits the victim, an unauthorized use of another's horse is a trespass to chattels even if the horse needs the exercise, and an unauthorized use of another's field is a trespass to land even if the use improves the land along some uncontroversial dimension. The alternative is the wide reading, on which the interest itself is in being in charge of your body or horse, or the plaintiff's interest in being free of certain forms of conduct by others. People certainly do have an interest in being free of unauthorized touchings and unauthorized use of their property, but—as the word "unauthorized" indicates—the interest itself cannot be characterized except by reference to the concept of a right. The interest is in being in charge of their bodies and property as against others.

The source of difficulty is that the concept of an interest is explanatorily significant only if it is analytically distinct from that which it is supposed to explain. The distinctness is easy enough to maintain if the interest is in something like bodily integrity or the physical security of an object. The difference between a broken or an unbroken leg or vase is intelligible without any reference to the concept of a right. So, too, the difference between having a headache and not having a headache is transparent without any talk about rights.

The robustness of this "frozen" concept of an interest makes it poorly suited to explaining the things that the law of torts protects. There are many frozen or freezer-ready interests, including interests in the

---

36. Leif Wenar, "The Nature of Claim-Rights," *Ethics* 123 (2013): 228.

tranquility brought about by being free of annoyance and having pleasant aesthetic surroundings, to which the law pays no attention. Absent a violation of any personal or property right, the law pays no attention to economic losses, yet ordinarily the loss of income is a serious setback to a person's well-being. Worse, even dimensions of well-being to which it does attend, such as bodily security or the condition of your property, are only protected against specific setbacks. The law of torts requires me to avoid injuring you, but it does not normally require me to take any affirmative steps to protect you from other dangers, no matter how significant or easily abated, and no matter whether those dangers are natural or created by other persons who are not in my charge. The same frozen interests—important aspects of well-being—are at issue when I injure you as when I fail to rescue you or carelessly collide with the ambulance that was rushing to assist you.[37]

In private law, the fundamental question is whether a right has been invaded; only after that threshold question has been answered does any question of the degree of the invasion arise.

Alternatively, the concept of an interest can be modified to account for these cases, but only by characterizing the interest in terms of the relation between one person's act and another's right. Tort law's prohibition on harmless wrongs might be thought to protect your interest in being the one who determines the conditions under which others touch your body or your property. That is a genuine interest, but it is not frozen in the right sense; it is an interest in standing in a certain type of relation, that is, in having a certain type of right, and so has no analytical purchase in explaining the rights at issue. The same point applies to any attempt to distinguish between an interest in being free of harm by others and an interest in being protected from harm. The distinction is important, but the concept of an interest can only be used to restate a conclusion based on a very different type of analysis—one that supposes, not that rights re-

37. In a recent piece Goldberg and Zipursky suggest that rights can be analyzed in terms of relational directives specified by the positive law, and that they can sidestep the question of whether rights are "by definition connected to certain important human interests, such as the interest in bodily integrity, dominion over property and the like." See "Rights and Responsibilities in the Law of Torts," in Nolan and Robertson, *Rights and Private Law,* 262.

flect the significance of the interests that they serve to protect, but instead one that supposes that the law of torts is fundamentally concerned with the relations in which people stand to each other, that is, something closer to a rights theory of interest than an interest theory of rights.[38]

These difficulties are the mirror image of the difficulties canvassed for accounts that focused on the defendant's action or capacity to foresee, avoid, or control the effect of his or her action on the plaintiff. Interest theories focus exclusively on the plaintiff, while foreseeability-type accounts focus exclusively on the defendant. The concept of a wrong is, however, irreducibly relational. That is why, as Weinrib noted several decades ago, the question for the law is always about the relation between the parties, the question of why this plaintiff recovers from this defendant.[39] It is not because the plaintiff's interest was set back, or the defendant could have avoided setting it back; each of these proposals considers only one of the parties in isolation from the other. Nor will simply combining the two ideas address the underlying difficulty, because any such combination will be both over- and underinclusive.

3. Transaction costs. The economic analysis of law was born with Ronald Coase's influential article "The Problem of Social Cost."[40] Coase used a classic nuisance case, *Sturges v. Bridgman,*[41] to identify a difficulty with

---

38. The failure of an interest theory of rights in this instance does not amount to a triumph of the will theory of rights, which is usually identified as its major competitor. For a will theory, a necessary condition of having a right is that the rightholder can determine whether to exercise it; to have a right is, in Hart's words, to be a "small scale sovereign." H. L. A. Hart, *Essays on Bentham: Studies in Jurisprudence and Political Theory* (Oxford: Clarendon Press, 1982), 81. Standard objections draw attention to the rights of children and to inalienable rights. I take no position here on the general debate between them. My claim is only that the rights protected by tort law cannot be explicated except through the concept of a right, understood as a standing in relation to others. That does not require any assumption about every rightholder being able to waive every right that he or she has. It only requires that rights be understood as constraints on the conduct of others, and that any power of enforcement be exercised by or on behalf of the rightholder.

39. See, generally, Ernest Weinrib, *The Idea of Private Law* (Cambridge, MA: Harvard University Press, 1995).

40. *Journal of Law and Economics* 3 (1960): 1–44.

41. Sturges v. Bridgman, (1879) 11 Ch. D. 852.

the economic idea of cost internalization. *Sturges* involved a conflict between a physician who built an examining room along the party wall on the other side of which sat the defendant confectioner's noisy mixing machines. The central holding in the case concerns whether the order in which the parties began their activities makes a difference to their respective rights; the court held that the plaintiff having come to a nuisance is no defense, on the ground that the defendant could not have acquired an easement to interfere with the plaintiff's use of his land until there was some conflict between their uses.[42] Coase reads the case differently. Picking up on a remark about the likely impact of any other holding on the construction of residential housing, he represents it as a case about efficient resource allocation, as his interest was in the (limited) impact of legal rules on economic efficiency, rather than the economic basis of those rules.[43] He uses the case to argue that if there were no transaction costs, it would not matter to whom the right was assigned; the allocation of resources would be efficient regardless. If the law gave the physician the right to prohibit vibration, then he could sell it back to the confectioner if the confectioner was willing to pay more than the expected loss in the value of the physi-

---

42. The question of whether an ongoing nuisance can provide the basis of an easement was raised, but settled only hypothetically, in *Sturges*. More recently, the same issue faced the UK Supreme Court in Coventry & Ors v. Lawrence & Anor, [2014] UKSC 13 (26 February 2014). Lord Neuberger concluded that it could, though he did not grant an easement, and conceded that there were no reported cases in which an easement had been granted. The crux of his reasons can be found in ¶34, where he writes: "Subject to questions of notice and registration, the benefit and burden of an easement run with the land, and, therefore, if a right to emit noise which would otherwise be a nuisance is an easement, it would bind successors of the grantor, whereas it is a little hard to see how that would be so if the right were not an easement. Given the property-based nature of nuisance, and given the undesirable practical consequences if the benefit and burden of the right to emit a noise would not run with the relevant land, it appears to me that both principle and policy favour the conclusion that a right to create what would otherwise be a nuisance by noise to land can be an easement." Lord Neuberger's reasoning incorporates the idea that an easement runs with the land, but it does not hew to the traditional view according to which an easement licenses the *use* of the servient tenement. Thus, it is consistent with the use/damage distinction as developed in this chapter, as it provides a basis for an easement based on damage rather than use.

43. Coase, *The Firm, the Market, and the Law* (1988), cited in Thomas W. Merrill and Henry E. Smith, "Making Coasean Property More Coasean," *Journal of Law and Economics* 54 (2011): S77–S104.

cian's income. The confectioner would be willing to pay more if and only if the price charged by the physician was less than the increase in income by continuing with the vibrating. Conversely, if the law gave the right to the confectioner, he would sell it back to the physician if and only if the physician was willing to pay more than the confectioner stood to lose by shutting off his machines. The price at which each would be willing to buy and sell would reflect exclusively the expected gains and losses, and so whichever stood to gain more would continue with his activity.

Coase acknowledges that we do not live in a world without transaction costs. Rather, he thinks that the existence of transaction costs can be used to explain and justify specific allocations of entitlements and liabilities. Appropriate assignments of entitlements will produce results that come as close as possible what the parties would have agreed to had they contracted freely.

Coase's approach has been proposed as a way of understanding many familiar instances of the distinction between misfeasance and nonfeasance. If this approach could be made to work, it would provide a radical alternative. Coase treats the physician's entitlement to constrain the confectioner as a case of one person acting on another, in the same precise sense as the vibration in the examining room.[44] If the familiar distinctions can be explained without beginning with either the concept of a right or even the concept of one person acting on another, the result would be significant indeed.

A number of writers have sought to develop Coase's organizing ideas in a selective way. In his influential work on equality of resources, Ronald Dworkin once suggested that tort law was best explained as a response to the fact that an ideal market requires what he calls a "principle of correction" for cases in which different people's uses of their fair shares of resources come into conflict.[45] Dworkin's use of the principle of correction represents contracting as the ideal solution to problems of interper-

44. Coase, "The Problem of Social Cost,": 2.

45. As he puts it, "a regulatory constraint or an article of tort law is justified under the principle of correction only if there are good grounds for supposing that the corruption of the opportunity cost test would be less with the constraint in place than it would be without it." Ronald Dworkin, *Sovereign Virtue: The Theory and Practice of Equality* (Cambridge, MA: Harvard University Press, 2002), 157; see also Dworkin, *Law's Empire* (Cambridge, MA: Harvard University Press, 1986), 295.

sonal coordination, and represents other areas of law as attempts to approximate contractual results in cases of market failure. On this view, the
distinction between misfeasance and nonfeasance is shallow; it represents
a way to approximate a contractual conclusion, and to facilitate contractual arrangements. Richard Posner has sought to explain the rule in
negligence as the rule to which parties would agree if they were able to
negotiate.[46]

More recently Henry Smith has sought to explain a central instance of
the distinction between misfeasance and nonfeasance—the right to exclude in property—in terms of transaction costs. Smith characterizes the
right to exclude as one of two organizing "strategies" in the law of property.[47] As we have seen, the in-charge-of relation is reflected in the right
to exclude, because ownership imposes a negative obligation of noninter-
ference on all others, but imposes no positive obligation of aid on owners.
Thus, nobody needs to use his or her property in the way that best suits
the preferred uses of others. Smith seeks to explain the effectiveness of
exclusion as a strategy that works because of its low information costs.
As he puts it, it is a "first cut," which "does not mean that exclusion is the
most important or 'core' value because it is not a value at all."[48] Instead,
the real value is making usable things useful; exclusion is a good strategy
because it minimizes transaction costs. Smith puts it this way: "Property
clusters complementary attributes—land's soil nutrients, moisture, building
support, or parts of everyday objects like chairs—into the parcels of real
estate or tangible and intangible objects of personal property. It then em-
ploys information hiding and limited interfaces to manage complexity.
For example, if a car is not mine, I do not need to know who owns it,
whether it is subject to a security interest or lease, etc., in order to know
not to take or damage it. When A sells the car to B, many features of A
and B are irrelevant to each other, and most are irrelevant to *in rem*
dutyholders (not to steal the car)."[49] The point of information-hiding

46. See Richard A. Posner, *The Economics of Justice* (Cambridge, MA: Harvard University Press, 1983), 62.

47. The other is "governance," that is, public direction. But even exclusion turns out to
be a delegated form of public direction.

48. Henry Smith, "Property as the Law of Things," *Harvard Law Review* 125 (2012): 1705.

49. Ibid., 1703.

and limited interfaces is that it costs ordinary people very little to figure out what they may or may not do. This focus on information costs reveals Smith's debt to Coase: If information were costless, the parties could do without property and bargain directly in the manner of Coase's physician and confectioner.

The idea common to Dworkin, Posner, and Smith is that contracting is fundamental and other legal rules such as trespass, nuisance, and negligence are somehow derivative. I want to suggest, however, that the very possibility of voluntary transactions presupposes the distinction between misfeasance and nonfeasance, and so cannot be used to explain it.

This point holds no matter how much information there is, and so no matter how fine-grained the entitlements with which people bargained. Fine-grained entitlements would still need to have the nonfeasance/misfeasance structure to them. This idea is explicit in Dworkin's presentation, where he supposes that parties can make voluntary exchanges of their shares of resources. That possibility presupposes the distinction between those ways in which you can change the world without others' permission, and those for which you must first secure the permission of some other person or persons. But that is just the distinction between misfeasance and nonfeasance.[50]

Coase's own presentation of the problem presupposes that the units around which parties bargain are government-defined permissions to perform particular actions; Smith suggests that in our actual world, it would be more true to Coase's organizing ideas to make physically individuated objects the subjects of negotiation.[51] This intramural dispute does not circumvent the need for the organizing distinction. In the same way, Dworkin's account starts with an equal distribution of resources, divided into maximally divisible units. These, too, presuppose the distinction between the things the use of which you do, and those for which you do not, require others' permission.

The idea of the world with perfect information costs can be represented in a more radical way, as one in which everything is permissible unless

---

50. I believe that the same point applies to the concept of efficiency: the question of whether a resource has gone to its most highly valued use can be answered only against the background assumption that particular people are entitled to offer or withhold it.

51. Smith, "Property as the Law of Things," 1703.

some contrary bargain is struck. Coase uses the example of a farmer whose crops are trampled by a rancher. Here, bargaining takes place only once we know who needs to pay for what. This feature is supposed to be absent in the limiting case of Coase's world, in which there are no information or transaction costs. In such a world, each person could in principle make a complete contingent contract with every other person[52] (or even possible person) governing every possible state of the world and organize their respective affairs accordingly.

This pure case of the world of perfect information is supposed to be one in which the distinction between misfeasance and nonfeasance does not apply. But it is also a world in which the distinction between voluntary and involuntary transactions does not apply.

In such a world the price at which goods or services are exchanged would factor into the amount parties would offer each other to refrain from taking goods, enslaving others, or murder, as they, too, would have to be part of the terms of the complete contingent contract on which any transaction took place. In the same way, in cases of accidental injury, the terms of any remedy would reflect the cost to the injurer of refraining from injuring. This may well be a model on which the distinction between misfeasance and nonfeasance is absent, but that absence also collapses with it the distinction between voluntary agreements and whatever else it is with which they are supposed to contrast. Perhaps there are circumstances in which the distinction between voluntary and involuntary arrangements lacks application. In the seventeenth century Hugo Grotius offered the clearest analysis of such a situation, writing that it would be impossible for wars to end in peace treaties if coerced agreements were not binding.[53] Grotius's analysis is embedded in his more general account of the nature of war, which he regards as a contest in which the competing sovereigns use force to settle the question of which one will have its way. Grotius

52. The concept of a Pareto efficient complete contingent contract is introduced in Steven Shavell, "Damage Measures for Breach of Contract," *Bell Journal of Economics* 11(1980): 466–490.

53. Hugo Grotius, *De Jure Belli et Pacis* (1625), bk. 3, chap. 19, ¶11; in English as Hugo Grotius, *The Law of War and Peace,* trans. William Whewell (Cambridge: Cambridge University Press, 1853), 410.

sensibly notes that in such a situation, any agreement necessarily takes place against the background of the threat of force.

But if this is a world in which the distinction between misfeasance and nonfeasance lacks application, more needs to be said in order to establish that the rationale for drawing the distinction in our world is that parties lack sufficient information to conduct themselves as they would in that world, in accordance with comparative threat advantage, and so must focus on rights in bodies, land, and chattels as a second-best. In Grotius's account of war, each sovereign purports to be in charge of the other; and a world in which everything is permissible unless someone offers an incentive to refrain from it is, in the same way, a world in which everyone is in charge of everyone else.

It is at best highly artificial to suggest that in the real world, nobody is in charge of anyone else, because we do not have the time or information to properly calculate threat advantage and negotiate accordingly. Something counts as a solution to a problem only if there is some deficiency in the situation characterized as the problem in need of a solution. It is difficult to see the normative interest of a world with perfect information and no normative constraints, except perhaps to follow Hobbes in insisting that it is a disaster out of which we must find our way, not an ideal that we should strive to approximate.

5. Conclusion

The law of torts protects what you already have. You have those things as means, subject to your choice and not the choice of another. Chapter 2 explained the sense in which your right to your body and property restricts the ways in which others may treat you. This chapter has explained the converse point: why your right to your body and property limits the claims that others can make against you, even if their body or property are in danger or they suffer losses through your use of what is yours.

CHAPTER 4

Wrongdoing for Which the Offender Must Pay

Negligence

IN THE CELEBRATED snail case of *Donoghue v. Stevenson,* Lord Atkin says that "liability for negligence" is "no doubt based upon a general public sentiment of moral wrongdoing for which the offender must pay."[1] In this chapter, I characterize the nature of the moral wrongdoing of which Lord Atkin speaks. I will characterize it entirely in relational terms, using it to illustrate the inconsistency of the defendant's act with the plaintiff's right.

Relational obligations are a familiar feature of both law and morality. The obligation to keep a promise or honor a contract reflects the relationship created between the parties to it; so too with relations between spouses, parents and their children, teachers and their students, and so on. People enter into those relationships, even if in some cases their entry is not entirely voluntary. The same can even be said about use-based wrongs: Although you did not want me to enter your land without your permission, I at least intended to enter it, even if I didn't know it was yours.

The relationship between negligent tortfeasor and injured party might be thought to be different. The defendant was in the process of doing

---

1. Donoghue v. Stevenson, [1932] A. C. 562 (H.L.) 564.

something else and the plaintiff was injured because the defendant was careless. In what sense is there a relationship here, over and above the fact that the defendant was careless and the plaintiff was injured as a result?

The short answer, which I will fill out in this chapter, is that your right to security of person and property must be analyzed in terms of you *already* standing in a certain type of relation to other people. As Frederick Pollock put it more than a century ago, "The duties broken by the commission of civil wrongs are fixed by law, and independent of the will of the parties."[2] As a rightholder, you are entitled to constrain other people's conduct. The existence of your right limits what others may permissibly do as they set and pursue their purposes. Every person stands in this relation to every other person; it is not that a duty is owed to the world at large, and then particularized; rather, there is an antecedent duty with respect to the body and property of each and every other person. Once this general form of relation is in view, the structure of duties of care in special relationships also comes into clearer focus.

1. The Duty of Care as a Unified Whole ("Privity of Tort")

The modern law of negligence is often dated to the early decades of the twentieth century with the American case of *MacPherson v. Buick*[3] and the English case of *Donoghue v. Stevenson*.[4] Both cases are important for their explicit formulation of a general duty of care owed by each person to each other person. I will say more about that below. The other thing for which these two cases are thought to stand is the undermining of an earlier idea of privity of contract. In both cases the plaintiff was injured by a product manufactured by a defendant with whom he or she had no contract. In *MacPherson,* the plaintiff was injured while driving an unsafe vehicle, which had been purchased from a dealer who had in turn purchased it from the manufacturer. In *Donoghue,* the contractual relation was even more indirect: the plaintiff developed gastritis as a result of consuming ginger beer that contained the remains of a decom-

2. Frederick Pollock, *The Law of Torts,* 7th ed. (London: Stevens and Sons, 1904), 3.
3. MacPherson v. Buick Motor Co., 217 N.Y. 382, 111 N.E. 1050 (1916).
4. Donoghue v. Stevenson.

posed snail, but the ginger beer had been purchased for her by a friend, who purchased it from a retailer who had in turn purchased it from the manufacturer. Each case had to overcome the precedent set by an earlier case, *Winterbottom v. Wright*,[5] in which the plaintiff complained of injury by an unsafe mail coach. The plaintiff in *Winterbottom* failed to state a cause of action: although he had claimed that the defendant manufacturer had failed in its contractual duty to provide the Royal Mail with sound coaches, he failed to show why he should recover from the breach of a contract to which he was not a party.

In both cases *Winterbottom* was distinguished on its pleadings:[6] both courts said that the plaintiff had not prevailed because he rested his case on a contractual duty owed by the defendant to somebody else. Sophisticated commentators often suggest that this is just bluster, that really the courts wanted to hide the fact that they were doing something radically new in overturning privity of contract. I take no position here on the historical question of whether amended pleadings would have enabled the plaintiff in *Winterbottom* to prevail. But Lord Macmillan's speech in *Donoghue* makes it clear that, far from repudiating the idea of privity of contract, the result is required by a correct interpretation of it. As a general matter, a stranger to a contract cannot sue on it.[7] Conversely, a contract between two persons cannot deprive any third person of a right against either of them; I cannot make a contract with somebody else to deprive you of your rights. In *Donoghue*, the fact that the defendant manufacturer had a contract with the retailer but not with the plaintiff goes only to how things stand between the two of them, and so has no bearing on the question of whether the defendant owed the plaintiff a duty. A duty owed to somebody else, or a different duty, cannot form the basis of liability in negligence. Conversely, the existence of a duty to someone else—the undertaking to provide something in a certain condition—does not generate an exemption from duties to third parties. The most important impact of Lord Macmillan's judgment is negative, showing that one

5. Winterbottom v. Wright, [1842] 152 ER 402.

6. MacPherson v. Buick Motor Co., 391; Donoghue v. Stevenson, 592, 594.

7. I put to one side questions about third-party beneficiaries specified in a contract, such as surviving spouses in a pension agreement.

person's contract with another is not sufficient to preclude duties to others, because some duties are not founded on contract. The positive argument of Lord Atkin and the parallel argument by Judge Cardozo MacPherson show the basic form of background duties presupposed by a successful negligence claim.

The innovation marked by *Donoghue* and *MacPherson* lies in the general characterization of the relevant antecedent relations. The duty requirement in the law of negligence requires each person to conduct him- or herself in a way that is consistent with other people's secure possession of their bodies and property.[8] That is, it protects what you already have— neither something that you have a prospect of acquiring, nor an interest that can be characterized apart from your entitlement that you, rather than others, determine the purposes for which your means will be used. As we shall see, that is why negligence claims require damage, understood as interference with possible use, rather than merely defective conduct. Only damage is inconsistent with the plaintiff's right.[9] The duty requirement depends on the relationship between the parties, what we might call "privity of tort."[10]

2. The Dismantling Strategies

Negligence has generated enormous academic attention. Each of its elements—duty, breach, remoteness, causation, and damage—can be iso-

8. In section 3.1.2 I will offer an account of how negligent misrepresentation can be mapped onto this model.

9. See the judgment of Lord Hoffman in Rothwell v. Chemical and Insulating Company Limited and Others, [2007] UKHL 39. As a result of exposure to asbestos, the plaintiffs developed pleural plaques, which are described as "areas of fibrous thickening of the pleural membrane which surrounds the lungs. Save in very exceptional cases, they cause no symptoms. Nor do they cause other asbestos-related diseases. But they signal the presence in the lungs and pleura of asbestos fibres which may independently cause life-threatening or fatal diseases such as asbestosis or mesothelioma." Lord Hoffman held that the plaques did not constitute an injury, distinguishing the presence of the plaques from a psychiatric illness that one of the plaintiffs developed. The development and discovery of the plaques was rather the foreseeable mechanism through which an illness could develop.

10. Robert Stevens uses this term in *Torts and Rights* (Oxford: Oxford University Press, 2008), chap. 8.

lated and presented as the normative basis of liability; conversely, each element can also be made to look irrelevant or repackaged as a disingenuous cover for some fundamentally different mode of justification or analysis. The vocabulary of "elements" entered legal analysis in the nineteenth century, replacing the perhaps even more misleading culinary vocabulary of "ingredients" of a cause of action.[11] The dismantling strategies represent negligence as a mixture, with one or more active ingredients, while reducing the other elements to the juridical equivalent of the "nonmedicinal ingredients" found in over-the-counter medications.

The difference between a whole, each of the parts of which is determined by its place in that whole, and a collection of parts, each of which is what is it apart from the whole to which it contributes, reflects the difference between an account of negligence based on the distinction between misfeasance and nonfeasance and other accounts that see a tort as an opportunity to accomplish something that matters apart from the relation between the plaintiff and the defendant.

If the distinction between misfeasance and nonfeasance is held firmly in view, negligence comes into focus as a unified whole. The plaintiff is entitled to constrain the defendant's use of his or her means. The plaintiff is not entitled to constrain the defendant's conduct simply as such; rather, the plaintiff is entitled to constrain it only in relation to the security of his or her means. So there is no space between the plaintiff's right and the defendant's duty not to injure the plaintiff through dangerous conduct, and so no way of separating out different elements so that one is morally significant and the others mere fillers.

Attempts to dismantle the tort of negligence follow a pattern. One prominent example, which I will call "the moral luck argument," supposes that a wrong acquires its legal interest because the defendant behaved badly, and concludes that the requirement of causation is arbitrary, either because it fails to treat in the same way others who behave just as badly, or because of some disproportion between the badness of the defendant's conduct and the extent of its legal consequence. Another, which I will call "solicitude for plaintiff" analysis, focuses on the plaintiff's vulnerability, and understands the occurrence of a tort as the occa-

11. These developments are traced in Simon Stern, "Legal Analysis" (unpublished).

sion for making up a loss, making the fault requirement appear puzzling. Still other accounts, to which I will refer as "pairwise comparison" accounts, focus on the court's choice between a negligent defendant and an innocent plaintiff. These accounts represent tort liability as the opportunity for a localized exercise in distributing burdens in accordance with conduct or character. For all of these accounts, there is no organizing idea of a private wrong, only a combination of bad conduct and unwanted consequences.

Both the moral luck argument and the solicitude for plaintiffs argument find expression primarily in academic commentary or in calls for tort reform or abolition.[12] By contrast, the pairwise comparison strategy has periodically found its way into case law. This argument generates skepticism about or suspicion of both duty and remoteness, and is captured in the familiar proposal that, as between a negligent defendant and an innocent plaintiff, the former should be made to bear the loss.[13] On this view, carelessness serves as a threshold for liability; if someone has behaved badly, he or she is liable for whatever harm others suffer as a result. The underlying thought is familiar in other contexts: For example, Elizabeth Anscombe, in her essay "Modern Moral Philosophy," suggests that a person is responsible for the bad consequences of anything bad that he does.[14] Hegel takes a similar position, approvingly quoting the proverb "The stone belongs to the devil when it leaves the hand that threw it."[15]

12. Patrick S. Atiyah, *Accidents, Compensation, and the Law* (London: Weidenfeld and Nicolson, 1970). See also Royal Commission to Inquire into and Report upon Workers Compensation, *Compensation for Personal Injury in New Zealand* (Wellington: Govt. Print., 1967). More recently, see Patrick S. Atiyah, *The Damages Lottery* (Oxford: Hart, 1997).

13. H. L. A. Hart and Tony Honoré, *Causation in the Law,* 2nd ed. (Oxford: Oxford University Press, 1985), 267; William Prosser "Palsgraf Revisited," *Michigan Law Review* 52 (1953): 17; W. Page Keeton et al., *Prosser and Keeton on the Law of Torts* (St. Paul, MN: West, 1984), 287. The same wording occurs in a number of cases of factual uncertainty about causation; see, for example, Sindell v. Abbott Laboratories, 607 P. 2d 924 (1980), 936, in which the court used the choice between innocent plaintiffs and negligent defendants to justify market-share liability in cases in which multiple injured plaintiffs were unable to identify which of multiple negligent defendants had caused their specific injuries. Yet the principle overstates the rationale, because it would apply in any case in which a plaintiff is unable to prove causation.

14. G. E. M. Anscombe, "Modern Moral Philosophy," *Philosophy* 33 (1958), 11.

15. G. W. F. Hegel *Elements of the Philosophy of Right* translated by H. B. Nisbet (Cambridge: Cambridge University Press, 1991) 148. (119A)

On this view, a person is responsible for the bad consequences of violating a norm.

The pairwise comparison of the negligent defendant and the innocent plaintiff has sometimes been proposed (though not necessarily under that description) as an explanation of liability without reference to any requirement that the defendant violates a right of the plaintiff. That is, the implicit suggestion is that it provides an alternative to the distinction between misfeasance and nonfeasance. A prominent example can be found in Judge Andrews's dissent in the *Palsgraf* case,[16] where he argues that the defendant's negligence in hurrying an unidentified passenger onto a train is sufficient basis for liability to those whose injuries are close enough as a matter of what he calls "practical politics."[17] On this analysis, no question arises of the relation between the defendant and the plaintiff, who was standing some distance away and was injured when some scales fell on her. Instead, Andrews urges that "everyone owes to the world at large a duty to refrain from those acts that may unreasonably threaten the safety of others."[18]

The same threshold analysis of the significance of failure to take care has led to cases and commentary in which directness has been urged as the appropriate standard for the remoteness of damage. In the *Polemis*[19] case, the English Court of Appeal held that an unforeseeable explosion was actionable because it was the direct result of negligence by the defendant's servants. Still other cases have adopted the pairwise comparison model, only to reintroduce both duty and remoteness under the head of "control devices"[20] to prevent the "floodgates" of liability from opening in situations of psychiatric injury or pure economic loss. On this view, negligence and causation both matter, but duty does not, and so, implicitly, rights do not.

16. Palsgraf v. Long Is. R. R. Co., 248 N.Y. 339.

17. Ibid., 352.

18. Ibid., 350.

19. Re Polemis & Furness, Withy & Co. Ltd., [1921] 3 KB 560. In addition to endorsing the pairwise comparison view, Hart and Honoré also endorse the result in *Polemis*, even after *Wagon Mound* rejected it (Overseas Tankship [UK] Ltd. v. The Miller Steamship Co. Pty. [The Wagon Mound No. 2], [1966] 2 WLR 877). See Hart and Honoré, *Causation and the Law*, lxvi .

20. Alcock & Ors v. Chief Constable of Yorkshire, [1992] AC 310 H.L.; John Fleming, *The Law of Torts* (Sydney: Law Book Co., 1992), 135–136.

My aim in this chapter is to present a negligence action as a unified whole. The significance of each element reflects its place in the whole. From this perspective, the puzzles about negligence do not so much require solutions as simply fail to arise. I will foreground my positive account, but the contrast with a pairwise comparison view will always be lurking in the background. It came to prominence with the doctrinal legal realism of the mid-twentieth century,[21] and its appeal has the same "making the best of a bad business" attitude toward the law.

The beginning of an answer to each of these challenges is already contained in the thought that the law of negligence protects the means that you already have against the side effects of other people's use of their means. The basic case of a damage-based tort is the case of a completed wrong, that is, the case in which one person damages what belongs to another through the use of means in ways that characteristically cause that type of damage. As always, the wrong consists in the inconsistency of the defendant's act with the plaintiff's right. Provided that the plaintiff's means survive intact, there is no inconsistency between the defendant's act and the plaintiff's right to his or her means, regardless of how badly the defendant behaves in relation to some more general standard of conduct. So, too, if the defendant injures the plaintiff in the course of using his or her means in a way that is generally consistent with the plaintiff's security of his or her means, there is loss without wrongdoing. Similarly, if the defendant is negligent toward someone other than the plaintiff and the plaintiff suffers a loss, the defendant may be negligent and the plaintiff innocent, but the defendant's conduct is not inconsistent with the plaintiff's right. Negligence always involves the realization of a specific risk to the plaintiff created by the defendant in an injury suffered by the plaintiff. The wrong is the completed act of the form

---

21. In the introduction to the first edition of his *Handbook of the Law of Torts,* William Prosser characterizes the "function of the law of torts": " 'Tort' is a term applied to a miscellaneous and more or less unconnected group of civil wrongs other than breach of contract for which a court of law will afford a remedy in the form of an action for damages. The law of torts is concerned with the compensation of losses suffered by private individuals and their legally protected interest, through conduct of others which is regarded as socially unreasonable." *Handbook of the Law of Torts* (St. Paul, MN: West, 1941), 1.

defendant-injuring-plaintiff-through-the-negligent-use-of-defendant's-means.[22]

In talking about the completed wrong as the basic unit of analysis, I do not mean to deny the fruitfulness of breaking the wrong down into elements, and I will proceed to do so below. Rather, I want to emphasize the conceptual priority of the completed sequence, because, as we saw in Chapter 3, the plaintiff's right is to be identified, not with his or her interest, but rather with the constraint on the defendant's conduct. That conduct, however, is constrained only with respect to the object of the plaintiff's right. Conversely, that right is protected only with respect to the constraint on the defendant's conduct.

To fill out these ideas, I will work my way through the elements of a negligence action. I will first look at duty and remoteness together, before characterizing the standard of care and the way in which it is immanent in the completed wrong, rather than something that exists apart from it. Along the way I will explain how social and contextual factors figure in each of the elements without swallowing or displacing them.

3. The Elements of Negligence

Standard treatments divide the law of negligence into elements: duty, standard of care, remoteness, causation, and damage. Each of these elements considers a different question about a single risk in relation to the damage of which the plaintiff complains. The risk must be realized in the form of damage or injury to the plaintiff; questions about causation and remoteness of injury apply only to a risk that has been realized. In a negligence action, no global assessment of risk is to the point; the plaintiff comes before the court complaining of something that the defendant did to her in particular, some specific risk that was realized, rather than any of the other risks that the plaintiff or the defendant posed to themselves, each other, or third parties. The complaint is not that the defendant behaved badly, or that the plaintiff was injured, but rather that the plaintiff was injured through the defendant's unduly dangerous conduct. The plaintiff's injury

---

22. I repeat the clarification that if the defendant uses some other person's means—injuring someone while driving a stolen bicycle, for example—the same analysis applies.

was the realization of the excessive risk that the defendant created to the plaintiff, which was the risk of that very type of injury.

In what follows I will go through these elements in order, drawing attention both to the single risk that is the ongoing object of attention in each of them, and to the way in which thinking of them as aspects of a unified wrong illuminates their most familiar features.

3.1. Duty and Remoteness

Both *Donoghue v. Stevenson* and *MacPherson v. Buick* are sometimes characterized as having established the irrelevance of antecedent relations between the plaintiff and the defendant to tortious liability.[23] But in fact both cases are about getting the right relationship in view. Lord Atkin formulates what he calls the law's "restricted reply" to the question "Who is my neighbour?" in terms of others "who ought reasonably to be in my contemplation." I owe a duty to "those persons who are so closely and directly affected by my act that I ought reasonably to have them in contemplation as being so affected when I am directing my mind to the acts or omissions which are called in question."[24] The emphasis on foresight might be thought to explain the basis of duty: you owe a duty to your neighbor because you can foresee his or her vulnerability. I want to suggest, however, that foreseeability has no such positive role to play. Instead, it enters as purely formal constraint: The law cannot require you to take account of something of which no account can be taken. Something unforeseeable is precisely something of which no account can be taken. The plaintiff comes before a court complaining that the defendant had a duty,

23. In "The Moral of *MacPherson*," *University of Pennsylvania Law Review*, 146 (1998): 1733–1848, John C. P. Goldberg and Benjamin C. Zipursky draw attention to both the prevalence of this interpretation and its inadequacies. A particularly striking instance of it is William Prosser's often quoted claim, "There is a duty if the court says there is a duty; the law, like the constitution, is what we make it. Duty is only a word with which we state our conclusion that there is or is not to be liability; it necessarily begs the essential question." Prosser, "Palsgraf Revisited," *Michigan Law Review* 52 (1952): 15. For a view of *Donoghue* similar to Prosser's view of *MacPherson*, see Jane Stapleton, "Duty of Care Factors: A Selection from the Judicial Menus," in *The Law of Obligations: Essays in Celebration of John Fleming*, ed. Peter Cane and Jane Stapleton (Oxford: Clarendon Press, 1998).

24. Donoghue v. Stevenson, 580.

that is, that the defendant should have taken account of the specific aspect of the plaintiff's safety that was injured. If the defendant could not have foreseen the injury suffered by the plaintiff, no sense can be attached to the claim that the defendant should have taken account of it, even if the plaintiff was foreseeable in relation to risks attendant on other things the defendant was doing. In the *Palsgraf* case, the New York Court of Appeals faced the question of whether the defendant could be liable for an injury suffered by the plaintiff when platform guards hurrying a passenger onto a moving train dislodged a package that turned out to contain fireworks. When the package exploded, scales further along the platform fell on the plaintiff, either from the concussion of the blast or from the effects of other passengers fleeing it. Writing for the majority, Judge Cardozo treated the question as exclusively concerned with duty: although the defendant's employees were negligent toward the unidentified passenger, the plaintiff was not visible to the "eye of ordinary vigilance," and thus she could not complain of having been wronged. The defendant did not, indeed could not, owe her a duty with respect to the risk that injured her, even if it owed her other duties in relation to her safety. Cardozo speaks of the "maze of contradictions" to which any other result would lead. The contradiction is just the idea of owing the duty to someone who is unforeseeable. That would be a requirement to take account (or conduct yourself as you would if you took account) of someone of whom no account can be taken. Nothing the guards could have done would qualify as vigilance for the plaintiff's safety in this case, so nothing could qualify as conforming to the duty, and thus nothing as violating it.

On this reading, then, the foreseeability of the plaintiff is a necessary condition of a duty in negligence, rather than its moral core. Lord Atkin speaks of whether the defendant "ought reasonably" to have had the plaintiff in contemplation; the restriction, like Cardozo's reference to "the eye of ordinary vigilance," underscores the question of whether the possibility of injury could guide conduct. Others can be entitled to constrain you to moderate your conduct in light of a risk to them only if something would qualify as conformity with the constraint. If nothing counts as conformity with a duty, then the duty itself is illusory. The same holds if the only thing that would count would be generalized hypervigilance—restraining yourself in light of the prospect of injury to someone, without attending to a specific risk to anyone in particular.

A parallel point applies to what English courts call "remoteness" and American courts call "proximate cause": you are liable only for reasonably foreseeable injuries, that is, the type of injury that is within the ambit of the risk that makes your conduct negligent. Just as others cannot constrain you to take account of them if there is nothing that would qualify as taking account of their safety, you can only be required to take account of a risk of which some account could be taken. Any other risks that, as it turns out, would have been prevented, were not ones with respect to which the plaintiff was entitled to constrain you. Even if your conduct was defective in relation to some other risk to the plaintiff, the plaintiff's injury was not the *realization* of a risk of you using your means too dangerously, even if it was the *result* of you using those means too dangerously.[25] If the negligence inquiry were focused on the burden to the defendant, such cases appear to create no extra burden and therefore to speak in favor of liability.[26] But the question is not whether the defendant was endangering the plaintiff, and the plaintiff suffered some injury as a result. Instead, it is always a question of whether the defendant injured the plaintiff through the very risk in relation to which the defendant's conduct was unreasonably dangerous. For example, the risk of psychiatric injury often accompanies the risk of physical injury, but the two are analytically distinct; your duty to protect others from psychiatric injury is independent of the duty to protect against physical injury, and can be breached without physical injury.[27]

25. See, for example, Doughty v. Turner Manufacturing Co. Ltd., [1964] 1 QB 518, in which the defendant's carelessness with respect to the risk of a lid splashing if it slipped into a cauldron of molten metal does not go to the unforeseeable risk that some time after its immersion, the lid caused the molten metal to erupt out of the cauldron.

26. In Jolley v. Sutton District Council, [2000] UKHL 31, the child plaintiff was injured when an abandoned boat that the defendant council had failed to remove fell on him. Lord Hoffman seems to suggest that because the defendant was under a duty to remove the boat because of the risk of a child falling through rotting planks while playing on it, no extra precaution was required to remove the risk of the boat qua heavy object that might fall if jacked up. However, he restricts this rationale to cases involving children, noting, "it has been repeatedly said in cases about children that their ingenuity in finding unexpected ways of doing mischief to themselves and others should never be underestimated."

27. In Dulieu v. White & Sons, [1901] 2 KB 669, Kennedy J. held that "nervous shock" did not require physical injury, but did not separate the risks; that distinction was made explicit in Hay or Bourhill v. Young, [1942] 2 All E.R. 396. In Dooley v. Cammell Laird,

The law focuses on the plaintiff's entitlement to constrain the defendant's conduct, not on the burden imposed by that constraint. In this, the rule of duty and remoteness in negligence is an instance of the same general structure as the distinction between misfeasance and nonfeasance. Liability to an unforeseeable person injured by an act negligent toward another, or for an unforeseeable risk to someone you put in the path of a different foreseeable risk, is not different from liability to the users of a bridge as well as its owner, or being made to compensate those you are under a public law duty to assist. None of these would restrict your sphere of action in any way that it was not already restricted; it would just cost you more after the fact. But as we saw in Chapter 3, private rights are never a function of the range of options that you have. They concern one person's entitlement to constrain another's conduct. Absent the relevant relations, no questions of degree can arise.

The formal structure of the role of foresight helps to explain the familiar distinction that courts draw between limiting the defendant's liability to foreseeable types of injury and extending liability to the full extent of the injury that results, including what may have been an unforeseeable event. In the so-called thin skull cases (and their analogues involving property, sometimes called "thin hull" cases), the plaintiff recovers for the full extent of his or her injury, because the defendant injured the plaintiff through negligence with respect to a risk of foreseeable damage. Even if the extent of the damage turns out to be greater than could have been foreseen, damage is the realization of the foreseeable risk that made that defendant's conduct negligent. Many of these cases involve wounds that become infected or cancerous. Although the plaintiff's precise vulnerabilities may not have been foreseen, some bodily injury was foreseeable; the role of intact skin in protecting a human or animal body against infection makes the consequences of its breach foreseeable.

[1951] 1 Lloyd's Rep 271, the plaintiff developed a psychiatric illness after the negligently maintained crane he was operating dropped a heavy load into the hold of a ship in which men were working. Although the men were uninjured, the operator's claim was successful: His claim against those who had failed to maintain the crane did not depend on injury to others but on the foreseeable effect on him of believing himself to be implicated, even non-negligently, in their deaths.

This negative characterization of the role of foresight makes sense of the wide range of cases in which a plaintiff is foreseeable but has no right at issue. As we saw in Chapter 3, in many nonfeasance cases the effects on people who do not hold a right would be foreseeable to anyone who gave the matter any thought: If you are a merchant and I breach a contract with you, your customers will be affected, as will be the ultimate consumers of the goods that I failed to deliver. If I damage something on which you depend but do not own, again, depending on the nature of that object, it may be perfectly foreseeable that others will use it.

In addition to the more familiar nonfeasance cases, there are cases in which the defendant's activity increases the likelihood of injury to the bodies and property of others, but courts have been reluctant to find duties in these cases. Such cases are sometimes characterized in terms of considerations of something called "policy." The implicit suggestion is that courts recoil from finding a duty because they worry about the potential long-term consequences, such as discouraging valuable activities or opening the doors to excessive liability.

I want to propose a different explanation, according to which such cases involve exercises of judgment about the application of abstract categories to particular types of fact situations. After explaining this idea in abstract terms, I will illustrate with an example, one that I concede is handpicked to cast doubt on the suggestion that courts' real concern is with protecting valuable activities: The liability of social hosts for automobile accidents caused by drivers who get drunk at the host's home while consuming their own alcohol. I doubt that courts want to encourage "BYOB" parties; instead, the only parties in which they take any interest are those before them in court, between whom they must do justice. To do so requires applying broad categories of duty to the specific social world that those parties inhabit.

3.1.1. Abstract Categories and Social Norms

As a general matter, if no person is in charge of any other, a defendant is not in charge of how others respond to conditions that he or she has created, or opportunities he or she has provided. But if this is the general structure, there are important exceptions. The pattern of those exceptions might be taken to show that a finding of liability reflects a court's attitude toward the activities of the parties, rather than any principled view about rights. Courts have held that endangering one person also endangers those who come to the rescue.[28] Other examples include a psychiatric hospital that releases a patient who then kills someone, a radio station that sponsors a car rally that leads to injury, inadequately supervised prisoners in custody who attack each other, prisoners who escape and do damage on their way, the police neglecting to warn potential victims of a rapist, and taverns providing excessive alcohol to patrons who then drive.

I want to suggest an organizing structure for these cases by distinguishing between creating a risk and providing an opportunity for others to create a risk. This distinction is related but not identical to the distinction between interfering with another person's means and failing to provide that person with a favorable context in which to use those means. The law ordinarily considers adults as independent agents, each acting in his or her own right, and the mere provision of a foreseeable opportunity for wrongdoing is not a wrong against those who are injured. This distinction is one of kind rather than degree, but requires judgment in its application, and in some cases the judgment could go either way, depending on how, precisely, the facts are characterized.

In *Home Office v. Dorset Yacht*[29] the plaintiff's boat was damaged when a group of Borstal boys used it to attempt an escape from an island where they were supposed to be under the supervision of the defendant's employees. The Borstal officers had gone to sleep for the night. As a practical matter, the plaintiffs could not recover from the escaping Borstal boys—although they may have been in Borstal detention because they had taken other people's money, they had no money of their own. The plaintiff therefore sought to recover from the Home Office, arguing that the Borstal officers owed him duty of care. The Home Office sought to avoid liability on the grounds that it was not responsible for the acts of the Borstal boys. Instead, their duties of supervision were said to be public law duties, which did not entail a private law duty to those who might be injured as a result of the failure to conform to that duty.

The defendant's argument was thus a basic nonfeasance argument: Any duty that the defendants were under was not owed to the plaintiff in par-

28. Haynes v. Harwood, [1935] 1 KB 146; Wagner v. International Railway Co., 133 NE 437 (1921); Chadwick v. British Railways Board, [1967] 1 WLR 912.

29. [1970] AC 1004, [1970] UKHL 2.

ticular, and so there was the wrong kind of relationship for recovery.[30] Lord Diplock's judgment focused on the relationship between the parties, against the background of the recognition that the duty to supervise the Borstal boys did not, as a general matter, give rise to a private law right on the part of those affected if the boys escaped. Should an escapee commit a crime halfway across the country, the Borstal officers (and thus the Home Office) could not be responsible, regardless of how negligent they had been. Analyzing other cases involving wrongs committed by those in the custody of public officers, he concluded that the relevant relationship did exist in situations in which that custody exposed a particular class of persons to danger. The risk was not that of the Borstal boys being at large—that was the subject of a public law duty—but rather of the damage they might do in the course of escaping. That risk was concentrated on those whose property might be damaged in the course of an escape, and the Borstal officers owed a duty to those people.[31]

Lord Diplock's speech illustrates the way in which general categories of misfeasance and nonfeasance can be brought to bear on classes of actions. The same pattern emerges in other cases involving the liability of public authorities. In *Jane Doe v. Toronto Police Commission*,[32] the defendant police force, seeking to catch a serial rapist, decided to carry out a "low key" investigation to avoid alerting the rapist that they were on his trail. They identified a group of likely victims in the hope of catching him,

---

30. In Lord Reid's judgment, the absence of the relevant relationship was said not to matter; implicitly adopting a version of the innocent plaintiff/negligent defendant approach, Lord Reid suggested that because the plaintiffs were foreseeable to the defendant—if Borstal boys escape, they are likely to reoffend—the only question was whether there was some reason to restrict liability, such as the ways in which it might interfere with the success of the Borstal program by causing the Borstal officers to be excessively cautious with their charges. Lord Reid concluded, "Her Majesty's officers are made of sterner stuff," and so found the defendant liable.

31. Hart and Honoré characterize the law's normal treatment of intervening actors as "breaking the causal chain" between the defendant and the plaintiff. In discussing *Dorset Yacht*, they conclude that the basis of liability is that the defendant "provided another with opportunity for doing mischief." *Causation and the Law*, 198–200.

32. Jane Doe v. Board of Commissioners of Police for the Municipality of Metropolitan Toronto et al., 39 O.R. (3d) 487 [1998] O.J. No. 2681. The case also involved constitutional issues concerning the plaintiff's right to security of the person, but these are in addition to the negligence issues.

but did not notify the victims that the police were watching them to see who would be attacked next. The plaintiff was raped at knifepoint, and sued the police. Much of the case concerned more general problems with the defendant department's investigation of rape, but a key legal issue was the concentration of the risk—the use of the victim as "bait" to capture the rapist. The case follows the same structure as *Dorset Yacht*. The public law duty to prevent crime does not give rise to a private right, and the plaintiff would not be entitled to recover simply because the police had failed to apprehend the rapist. The department's active choice of the specific means that it used was wrongful as against the plaintiff because they concentrated the existing risk on her.

Both *Dorset Yacht* and *Jane Doe* involve public officials and might be thought to be special cases as a result. But both cases turn on the absence of a general private law duty, and instead look at the way in which the defendants' defective conduct in the carrying out of their public law duties put a particular plaintiff in peril.

Many other cases involve private actors who create conditions through which third parties put the plaintiff in danger. In *Weirum v. RKO*,[33] the defendant radio station ran a contest in which prizes were awarded to the first person to physically locate one of its disc jockeys based on information broadcast over the station. Two teenage drivers, eager to win the prize, chased the disc jockey's car, and jockeying for position behind it, forced another car off the road, killing the driver. The driver's widow successfully recovered because the contest had created the danger.

Owners of taverns that serve alcohol are required to protect their patrons from each other, and, more recently, to protect others from drivers who become intoxicated on their premises. Although these obligations are in many cases imposed by statute, their basic rationale is straightforward: A tavern owner who serves too much alcohol to someone who will drive home endangers other users of the road.[34]

The availability of the category of exposing others to risk through the deeds of third parties does not, however, cover all cases. Not only does it not cover cases in which the police, had they done a better job, might have

33. Weirum v. RKO General, Inc., 15 Cal.3d 41 (1975).
34. Stewart v. Pettie, [1995] 1 S.C.R. 131, 21 D.L.R. (4th) 222.

prevented crimes from occurring, it also does not extend to cases in which the defendant's conduct merely provided an opportunity for someone else to impose a danger on the plaintiff.

In this context, consider the remarks of McLachlin CJ. in *Childs v. Desormeaux*.[35] That case involved the potential liability of the host of a "BYOB" party to a plaintiff severely injured by a guest who had consumed excessive amounts of alcohol at that party. From the standpoint of foreseeability, a social host and a tavern owner are in the same position toward the plaintiff; providing a venue for alcohol consumption increases the likelihood of drunk driving. But that question does not arise unless the defendant owes the plaintiff a duty with respect to the risk in question. The court found no duty:

> As discussed, the implication of a duty of care depends on the relationships involved. The relationship between social host and guest at a house party is part of this equation . . . The guest remains responsible for his or her conduct. Short of active implication in the creation or enhancement of the risk, a host is entitled to respect the autonomy of a guest . . . The conduct of a hostess who confiscated all guests' car keys and froze them in ice as people arrived at her party, releasing them only as she deemed appropriate, was cited to us as exemplary. This hostess was evidently prepared to make considerable incursions on the autonomy of her guests. The law of tort, however, has not yet gone so far.[36]

McLachlin CJ. also draws a contrast between a social host and a commercial establishment: "The consumption of alcohol, and the assumption of the risks of impaired judgment, is in almost all cases a personal choice and an inherently personal activity. Absent the special considerations that may apply in the commercial context, when such a choice is made by an adult, there is no reason why others should be made to bear its costs."[37] Thus, guests at social occasions are presumed to be acting independently, and, as such, the social host is not under a duty to protect

35. Childs v. Desormeaux, [2006] 1 SCR 643, 2006 SCC 18.
36. Ibid., ¶45.
37. Ibid.

third parties from the carelessness or poor judgment of those guests.[38] Even if the defendant knew or had reason to know of guests' past occasions of driving while impaired, the absence of a duty to protect one person from the acts of another renders any such knowledge irrelevant.

It is not difficult to imagine classifying the particular cases differently, either finding a duty in the case of social hosts or none for tavern owners. McLachlin CJ.'s remark that the law of torts has not yet "gone so far" acknowledges the possibility that it might one day so go, and also acknowledges that the classification of the different cases is an exercise in judgment, based on a view of social life in Canada in the twenty-first century. In that context, the defendant's act is characterized as a failure to protect the plaintiff against the acts of another, rather than as endangering the plaintiff. The possibility of classifying things more than one way does not show that there is nothing to the distinction; it shows instead that the distinction needs to be applied in a concrete context.

The suggestion that any genuine distinction would have to classify particulars rests on the supposition that the point of legal analysis must be to generate results. But the concept of duty does not work like that. It is an abstract characterization of a question about the relationship between the defendant's activity and the plaintiff's right: Was the plaintiff "so closely connected" that he or she "ought reasonably to be in the [the defendant's] contemplation"? The inquiry is distinctively legal, in that the court is charged with bringing the settled law to bear on the question before it. The phrase "bringing to bear" is open-ended; it is not that the settled law necessarily resolves the case. Instead, the role of the court is to resolve the dispute before it in light of the settled law. In many cases, the question of how things stand between the plaintiff and the defendant will require judgment, and that judgment, although general, will turn on features of the type of interaction.

3.1.2. A Note on Special Relationships

In our discussion of the distinction between misfeasance and nonfeasance as it applies to the lack of a duty to rescue, we saw that the law of tort holds

---

38. As John Goldberg and Benjamin Zipursky put it in an unpublished paper, the guests at such a party are not in the custody of their hosts in the ways in which prisoners are in the custody of their guards.

people to be under duties to aid in cases of special relationships. For example, a professional undertaking to provide special care or expert advice undertakes duties to specific persons in addition to the ordinary duty everyone has to be careful around the person and property of others. The most familiar and, to some, puzzling example of this sort is liability of those holding themselves out as experts in making recommendations with respect to specific transactions. In the New York case of *Glanzer v. Shepard,* a public weigher was held liable for the plaintiff's reliance on a representation about the weight of an order of beans on the grounds that "The defendants, acting, not casually nor as mere servants, but in the pursuit of an independent calling, weighed and certified at the order of one with the very end and aim of shaping the conduct of another. Diligence was owing, not only to him who ordered, but to him also who relied."[39] In the English case of *Hedley Byrne v. Heller,*[40] the House of Lords outlined the conditions under which an accountant or other professional giving advice would be held liable. The basis of liability is the acceptance of undertaking with respect to a specific risk. The undertaking need not be specific to the explicit making of a representation, and so therefore applies even in cases where there would otherwise be no duty. The undertaking of responsibility creates a right with respect to the specific transaction for which it is undertaken. That is why liability in such a case can potentially extend to pure economic loss that would not otherwise be actionable: If I undertake to advise you about the soundness of a company, I thereby accept responsibility for the risk of my own error.

In this, the undertaking of a duty is the mirror image of a voluntary assumption of risk as a defense.[41] If I walk alone in a dangerous neighborhood at night, I may have made it more likely that I will be attacked,

39. Glanzer v. Shepard, 135 N.E. 275 (N.Y. 1922), 238–239.

40. Hedley Byrne & Co. Ltd. v. Heller & Partners Ltd. [1964] AC 465.

41. The parallel here applies to the creation of the relationship, not to any disclaimer that the defendant might make—in *Hedley Byrne* the defendant's letter said "without responsibility." As Allan Beever points out, the disclaimer does not serve as a defense when a duty has been established; it prevents the creation of a duty. See Beever, *Rediscovering the Law of Negligence* (Oxford: Hart, 2007), 288. The burden of disclaiming lies with the person making the representation, because if the initial representation was not sufficient to create the relationship, any further affirmation of it would be subject to the same question: namely, "Yes, but did you mean to be bound?"

but an attacker cannot argue that I voluntarily assumed the risk of attack. I voluntarily assume a risk only if I accept responsibility for it in particular as against some other person in particular.[42] The availability of the defense reflects the idea that no person is in charge of another; you and I can make a private bilateral arrangement in which I take responsibility for a risk attendant on your conduct toward me, even though you would otherwise be responsible for it. Conversely, we can make a private arrangement in which I undertake responsibility for a risk attendant on my giving you advice, or to exercise some other special skill. As Lord Morris of Borth-y-Gest puts it in *Hedley Byrne*, "if someone possessed of a special skill undertakes, quite irrespective of contract, to apply that skill for the assistance of another person who relies upon such skill, a duty of care will arise. The fact that the service is to be given by means of or by the instrumentality of words can make no difference."[43] The point is not that such reliance is foreseeable or reasonable; it might be both foreseeable and reasonable for me to rely on a representation to which you have attached a disclaimer, or a published map that is not provided for the purpose of a specific transaction.[44] Unless you have undertaken a duty, the fact that I rely on you doesn't give me a right that you be careful. But if you have undertaken one, the elements of an action for negligent misrepresentation correspond to the elements of an action for negligence more generally: The making of a representation creates the relationship required for duty (the risk *to whom*); the representation with respect to a specific transaction corresponds to the question of remoteness (the risk *of what*). The plaintiff's loss or injury in reliance on the representation corresponds to

42. See Glanville Williams, *Joint Torts and Contributory Negligence* (London: Stevens and Sons, 1951), 308; and Dube v. Labar, [1986] 1 SCR 649.

43. In Spring v. Guardian Assurance, [1994] IRLR 460 HL, 502–503, Lord Goff summarizes the point: "Furthermore, although *Hedley Byrne* itself was concerned with the provision of information and advice, it is clear that the principle in the case is not so limited and extends to include the performance of other services . . . Accordingly where the plaintiff entrusts the defendant with the conduct of his affairs, in general or in particular, the defendant may be held to have assumed responsibility to the plaintiff, and the plaintiff to have relied on the defendant to exercise due skill and care, in respect of such conduct."

44. Asquith L. J. offers this example in Candler v. Crane, Christmas & Co., [1951] 2 KB 164, 194.

the causation inquiry; the question of the defendant's breach of the standard of care is the same.

Not every positive duty in another area of law involves an undertaking with respect to a specific plaintiff or class of plaintiffs.[45] Homeowners may be under a statutory duty to clear the public sidewalk in front of their homes, a public authority may be under a duty to deal with a public health issue such as West Nile virus,[46] and the police may be under a duty to prevent crime,[47] without a duty running to any particular person—not even specific individuals who are the expected beneficiaries of passable sidewalks, the absence of dangerous diseases, or protection from crime.[48] In the same way, the fact that others rely on conformity with those public law duties does not give rise to a special relationship.[49]

45. In Gorris v. Scott, (1874) LR 9 Ex 125, the defendant failed to provide pens for sheep on a ferry, as mandated by the Contagious Diseases (Animals) Act (1869). The plaintiff's animals were washed overboard, which the pens would have prevented. But the point of the statute, as its name suggests, was to prevent the spread of disease, and so it did not cover against the risk to the plaintiff of his sheep being washed overboard.

46. Eliopoulos v. Ontario, (2007) 82 O.R. (3d) 321 (C.A.).

47. Michael v. South Wales Police, [2015] UKSC 2.

48. In Lonrho Ltd. v. Shell Petroleum Co. Ltd., [1982] AC 173, Lord Diplock describes the reasoning this way: "One starts with the presumption laid down originally by Lord Tenterden C. J. in Doe d. Murray v. Bridges (1831) 1 B. & Ad. 847, 859, where he spoke of the 'general rule' that 'where an Act creates an obligation, and enforces the performance in a specified manner . . . that performance cannot be enforced in any other manner,' unless the purpose of the statute is to provide for the safety of a particular class of person and so to create 'a correlative right in those persons who may be injured by its contravention'" (citing Lord Kinnear in Butler (or Black) v. Fife Coal Co. Ltd., [1912] A.C.149, 165).

49. In the last quarter of the twentieth century, Commonwealth courts experimented with a different model of duty. Beginning with Lord Reid's judgment in *Dorset Yacht*, and developing further in Anns v. Merton London Borough Council, [1977] UKHL 4, then crossing the Atlantic to Canada in Kamloops v. Nielsen, [1984] 2 SCR 2, this analysis proceeded in two stages: The first asked whether the plaintiff's injury was foreseeable to the defendant; the second whether there was some reason of policy to rule out liability nonetheless. In Murphy v. Brentwood District Council, [1991] UKHL 2, the House of Lords rejected its previous ruling in *Anns* because of both its inconsistency with the distinction between misfeasance and nonfeasance and the ways in which it would make legal obligations nearly impossible to predict in advance. This was only the eighth occasion on which the House of Lords had overruled itself since the practice statement of 1966 empowered it to do so: see J. W. Harris, "Murphy Makes It Eight—Overruling Comes to Negligence," *Oxford Journal of Legal Studies* 11 (1991): 416–430. Other Commonwealth jurisdictions, including

3.2. Standard of Care

The law takes no notice of the susceptibility of natural objects to deterioration or decay, only of their vulnerability to wrongful damage. As a general matter, physical objects, including human bodies, change in ways that make them less usable, either for some specific purpose or in general. The law of negligence takes an interest only in wrongful changes.

The ordinary activities of careful people are just part of the context in which you have whatever it is that you have. Lord Reid calls this the "crowded conditions of modern life," and Cardozo calls it a "busy world." On either formulation, the crowd and its busyness change things as surely as does the weather. In such circumstances, people may sometimes be injured or their property damaged, but the law treats these as the particular circumstances in which you find yourself, as you must inevitably find yourself in some circumstances or others.

A departure from the ordinary risks that careful people impose on each other is negligence. The question always concerns how careful the defendant was in relation to the plaintiff, not whether the risk could be shown to be appropriate, rational, or typical from some other perspective. The fact that the defendant or third parties stood to gain through the creation of a risk is not relevant. Nor does the risk of injury that the defendant poses to him- or herself enter into the assessment of whether his or her conduct was unreasonably dangerous.[50]

Reasonable care in negligence also contrasts with ideas of unusual or non-reciprocal risk imposition. Although the legal idea of reasonable conduct can be expressed in terms of moral ideas about reciprocity,[51] it must

---

Canada, have not officially rejected it, but in Cooper v. Hobart, (2001) 206 DLR (4th) 193, the first stage was redescribed as focusing on the rights of the parties rather than on foreseeable loss, and the second was treated as a category for "residual policy considerations." In Caltex Oil v. The Dredge "Willemstad," (1976) 136 CLR, the High Court of Australia employed similar reasoning to conclude that foreseeable economic loss should be recoverable in specific situations in which policy considerations that ordinarily block it do not apply.

50. See Robert D. Cooter and Ariel Porat, "Liability Externalities and Mandatory Choices: Should Doctors Pay Less?," *Journal of Tort Law* 1 (2006): 1–25; and Ariel Porat, "Misalignments in Tort Law," *Yale Law Journal* 121 (2011): 82–140.

51. See W. M. Sibley, "The Rational versus the Reasonable," *Philosophical Review* 62 (1953): 554–560; and John Rawls, *Political Liberalism* (New York: Columbia University Press, 1993), 48–54.

not be collapsed into an idea of uniform limits on risk imposition. The point of distinguishing between normal and excessive risks is not that a system in which everyone gets to impose the same level of risk on everyone else is fair, so that anyone who imposes greater risk than that is somehow unfairly claiming a benefit or imposing a cost on others.[52] A social world in which people regularly drove while impaired or blind-folded, discharged weapons in public places, and discarded explosives without any precautions, would not be acceptable just because everyone did those things. The law works with a very different idea of reasonable risk imposition: You are entitled to impose risks on others only to the extent that those are the inevitable concomitant of people using their means. The wrongfulness of injuring others through excessive risk is that it is using your means in ways that compromise the ability of others to use theirs.

But if the rights of others require you to restrict the side effects of your activities, a system of rights must also permit you to use your means in ways in which damage to what others have is either unlikely or minor—in negligence, the point at which conduct poses only trivial risks to the person and property of others.[53] Trivial risks—the ones that Lord Reid describes as "fantastic and far-fetched"—sometimes lead to injuries. So do some "real risks" that are small enough that you may impose them on others, just as the entitlements of others mean that you must accept those risks that they impose on you. To require you to refrain from activities that carry those small risks would effectively disable you from using your means at all, requiring you to accept limits based on the mere possibility of affecting others, and so would be inconsistent with your independence.

If tort law is seen as being exclusively concerned with liability, this distinction between acceptable and unreasonable risks looks odd. Needing to pay for the damage you cause does not limit your liberty—it just sometimes makes it more expensive to exercise it. However, that is not tort law's primary concern. Instead, as we shall see in Chapter 8, the remedy follows the primary right, and the characterization of the

---

52. George P. Fletcher, "Fairness and Utility in Tort Theory," *Harvard Law Review* 85 (1972): 537–573.

53. Bolton v. Stone, [1951] AC 850 (HL).

primary rights of both the plaintiff and the defendant governs the extent to which each is entitled to use what he or she already has. Because tort liability is always predicated on wrongdoing, the only basis of liability for the realization of reasonable risks would have to rest on characterizing safe uses of means as wrongful.

Risk and likelihood of harm sound like they should be measured quantitatively, and although in one sense they are quantifiable, these quantitative factors are relevant to what is ultimately a qualitative question.[54] In the law of negligence, "too dangerous" is a qualitative judgment about the way the defendant is conducting him- or herself in relation to other people's rights to their bodies and property. Like "unreasonably dangerous," it requires a contextual judgment to apply it to particular cases. At the same time it is objective—whether something is too dangerous does not depend on whether the defendant was aware it was dangerous, or the ease or difficulty with which the danger might be reduced.

This may still sound quantitative, but the questions of degree that arise with respect to particular cases—Is driving at 50 km/h on this road safe enough?—present themselves in the context of a structured inquiry about everyone restricting the effects of their conduct on the bodies and property of others. In many cases, the particular activities will be measurable along some sort of continuum, and so may invite a puzzle about where precisely to draw the line, leading to the further thought that the members of the series must be given a sort of weight, to be measured against the weight of some other thing. This entire setup is a mistake: the question is whether you are being careful enough. That is not a question about quantities along a continuum at all, even if answering the question will sometimes require comparative judgments. The question is whether someone attending to the bodies and property of others would engage in this conduct. That subjunctive inquiry may or may not involve questions of degree along a quantitative continuum.

As we saw in Chapter 2, damage-based torts include a fault requirement, because in a system in which no person is in charge of another, each

---

54. As Ian Hacking explains, the concept of probability has two aspects: the degree of belief warranted by evidence, and the tendency of seemingly chance processes to produce stable relative frequencies. See Ian Hacking, *The Emergence of Probability* (Cambridge: Cambridge University Press, 1975).

person is entitled to use his or her means, and each must accept the inevitable side effects of other people using their means. If the defendant did not act in a way that makes injury more likely—if the risk is not unreasonable—the plaintiff's loss is not a wrong.

The differences between this way of thinking about risk and the Holmesian idea of balancing shed light on judicial characterizations of the standard of care. Rather than talking about balancing, let alone characterizing any global calculus, those characterizations border on platitudes, which are announced with great confidence. Such platitudes are not without point, however. They are not supposed to be instructions, the application of which is sufficient to decide a question. Instead, they direct the finder of fact to frame the issue in the right way, in terms of being careful.

Consider Baron Alderson's speech in *Blyth v. Birmingham:* "Negligence is the omission to do something which a reasonable man, guided upon those considerations which ordinarily regulate the conduct of human affairs, would do, or doing something which a prudent and reasonable man would not do."[55] The formulation is abstract and hypothetical, characterizing a particular type of person in terms of the factors this imagined being would consider, but the factors are described in terms of reasonableness. Someone freshly arrived from another planet might have difficulty ascertaining just what Baron Alderson had in mind; the advice seems to be most useful to those who already know how to think about what is required. But it directs people who know how to be careful to a familiar, category-based way of thinking about safety.[56] By thinking in that way, careful people (or people thinking about being careful) judge particular acts as either safe enough or too dangerous. As a result, they do not reason as people might in other contexts, thinking, for example, of the risk/reward ratio of a possible investment or shortcut down a mountainside. The difference between these ways of thinking reflects the familiar idea that nobody is in charge of anyone else: When you are

---

55. (1856) 11 Ex. Welsh. H. & G. 781, at 783.

56. Parents watching their children at a playground often makes judgments of this sort, both when they think something is too dangerous and when they roll their eyes at other parents for being overly cautious. People may disagree about how to categorize a particular action—that is why, when rights are in dispute, an authoritative body such as a judge or jury is required. The essential role of judgment does not make the process unreasoned, let alone irrational.

the one facing a risk you create, it is for you to decide whether it is worth it to you; when the risk is to someone else, it is not up to you.

The same framing of the issue is repeated in Lord Reid's speech in *Bolton v. Stone.* "It would take a good deal to make me believe that the law has departed so far from the standards which guide ordinary careful people in ordinary life"; he also speaks of "considering the matter from the point of view of safety."[57] In *Greene v. Sibly, Lindsay & Curr Co.,* Judge Cardozo similarly speaks of "ordinary prevision to be looked for in a busy world."[58]

Lord Reid's description of the negligence standard in *Bolton v. Stone* led Richard Epstein to remark, "It cannot be a point in favor of the law of negligence, either as a theoretical or administrative matter, that it demands evaluation of almost everything, but can give precise weight to almost nothing."[59] The seemingly open-ended character of this analysis, coupled with the almost endless range of contexts in which it might be thought relevant, is not, however, a symptom of vacuity or a license for judge or jury to ask what the defendant, all things considered, ought to have done.[60] Nor does it demand evaluation of almost everything, or presuppose that the factors to be considered must each have a magnitude, so that when weighed properly they would uniquely determine a result. Instead, it directs the finder of fact to frame the issue in a familiar way, and directs attention away from superficially similar inquiries that are beside the point, including those that try to balance factors outside of the transaction between the parties.

All of this is to say that the point of such formulations is to frame the riskiness of the defendant's conduct in terms of ordinary demands—the

57. Bolton v. Stone, [1951] AC 850, at 867, per Lord Reid.

58. 177 N.E. 416 (N.Y. 1931).

59. Richard A. Epstein, "A Theory of Strict Liability," *Journal of Legal Studies* 2 (1973): 151–204.

60. John Gardner suggests that when the law uses the concept of the reasonable person, it is directing the finder of fact to consider the reasons that apply in the situation, and so giving no further legal guidance: John Gardner, "The Mysterious Case of the Reasonable Person," *University of Toronto Law Journal,* 51 (2001): 273–308. At least in the case of appeals to the reasonable person in the tort of negligence, the finder of fact is directed to a proper subset of all of the reasons that might be thought to apply: Was the defendant being careful enough in light of the potential interference with the plaintiff's safety?

claim that civilized society makes on its members, the standards that guide ordinary careful people. The careless person is identified by contrast to the careful one, who is in turn characterized in terms of those very demands. The platitudes are meant to tell you *how* to think about risk, not *what* to think about it. But once you know how to think about it, the obvious thing to do is to consider the familiar examples, both as particulars and as abstract archetypes. As a result, the platitudes direct the finder of fact to think in ordinary and familiar terms.

The appeal to ideas of ordinariness reflects the way in which the law governs conduct on the basis of abstract principles, and applies them to particulars on the basis of exemplars. "Ordinary" is not a synonym for "typical"; it contrasts with "extraordinary." The reasonable person is the careful one when he or she is being careful.[61] The fact that people are often not careful does not mean that "ordinary care" permits occasional negligence. As is the case with many moral requirements, figuring out what you are supposed to do is sometimes easier than actually bringing yourself to do it. That is why the finder of fact can make a determination of negligence even if he or she would have done no better in the circumstances, and even if most people would have done no better.[62] No matter how good your theoretical account (either of some specific virtue or of how the virtues fit together), it will not tell you everything about how to apply it to particulars; any rule for classifying particulars would need a further rule to tell you how to apply it in specific cases, and so on *ad infinitum.*[63]

---

61. As Clarence Morris puts it, "Fortunately, however, most courts hold that knowledge of what men usually do is a non-conclusive aid in deciding what a particular man should have done; that the problem of negligence is not an un-factual question to be decided by invoking unworldly values." Morris, "Custom and Negligence," *Columbia Law Review* 42 (1942): 1154.

62. In *Uncommon Law,* A. P. Herbert remarks of the reasonable man that "it is a curious paradox that when two or three are gathered together in one place they will with one accord pretend an admiration for him; and, when they are gathered together in the formidable surroundings of a British jury, they are easily persuaded that they themselves are, each and generally, reasonable men." Herbert, *Uncommon Law* (London: Methuen, 1935), 4.

63. Ludwig Wittgenstein, *Philosophical Investigations,* trans. G. E. M. Anscombe (Oxford: Basil Blackwell, 1958), 80, §201; Immanuel Kant, *Critique of Pure Reason,* trans. Paul Guyer and Allen Wood (Cambridge: Cambridge University Press, 1998), 268, A133/B172.

This general point applies to the standard of care. If you want to know what it is to be careful—given that, at the most abstract level, being careful is just a matter of limiting the foreseeable side effects of your conduct on others—you ask what ordinary careful people do. The ordinary careful person serves as an exemplar, reminding people of what they expect of each other.[64] Any such characterization runs the risk of circularity, but it is difficult to see why this would be objectionable,[65] because the task is to instruct the finder of fact as to how to frame the issue. This task requires asking how the defendant was supposed to think about the situation, using familiar thoughts that were presumably available to the defendant.

It might be objected that ordinary ways of thinking about risk are filled with mistakes of reasoning. Social psychologists have performed experiments showing that ordinary people are poor calculators of probability; depending on the manner and even the order in which alternatives are presented to them, ordinary people will assign different likelihoods to outcomes.[66] In addition, experimental subjects often fail to recognize such basic rules of probability as that the conjunction of two events is necessarily less likely than either event considered on its own. Psychologists suggests that in making judgments about the likelihood of various outcomes, people ordinarily rely on heuristics, general decision rules that

64. As Adam Smith points out, prudence (and by extension, care) may be "regarded as a most respectable, and even, in some degree, as an amiable and agreeable quality, yet it never is considered as one, either of the most endearing, or of the most ennobling of the virtues. It commands a certain cold esteem, but seems not entitled to any very ardent love or admiration." See Adam Smith, *The Theory of Moral Sentiments,* ed. Knud Haakonsen (Cambridge: Cambridge University Press, 2002), 254.

65. Unless it is assumed, as some advocates of economic analysis wish to, that if they are to be intelligible at all, all tort concepts must be reducible to concepts expressible without remainder in some other vocabulary. On the nature of circularity in common law reasoning, see Martin Stone, "Legal Positivism as an Idea about Morality," *University of Toronto Law Journal* 61 (2011): 313–341.

66. Unsurprisingly, this literature rejects the distinction between misfeasance and nonfeasance, cautioning against "omission biases"—that is, differentiating between what an agent does and what he or she allows to happen. See, for example, Jonathan Baron and Ilana Ritov, "Protected Values and Omission Bias as Deontological Judgments," in *Moral Judgment and Decision Making,* ed. D. M. Bartels et al., vol. 50 of *The Psychology of Learning and Motivation,* ed. B. H. Ross (San Diego: Academic Press, 2009), 133–167.

may have served their ancestors well in the distant evolutionary past but that lead to systematic errors.

Legal scholars have suggested that these results have important implications for the law's approach to questions of risk, and have taken the results to constitute an argument in favor of replacing platitudes and commonsense ideas with more precise mathematical ideas of cost–benefit analysis.[67] In this section I will look at the most developed proposal of this form, but before doing so, and drawing attention to its failure to fit the law, I want first to note that these psychological results are relevant only to a mode of assessment that treats action-types as alike, based on the probability of a given outcome. That is, the experimental results are plainly relevant to comparative questions of degree but, as such, have no bearing on questions of ordinary care. In saying this, I do not mean to suggest that judges or juries should be sloppy in their assessment of whether something is too dangerous, or to deny that in determining whether someone was careful enough, some factors that admit of degree, such as velocity or mass, will be relevant. But none of these familiar facts collapses the question of dangerousness into a simple matter of degree. The question before the finder of fact concerns the conduct of a particular defendant on a particular occasion, and not a requirement of reducing risk to a given level, or of balancing some degree of risk against the benefits of imposing it.[68]

Much recent tort scholarship has ignored or even rejected the category-based reasoning that figures in the traditional characterizations of how

67. See, for example, Barbara H. Fried, "The Limits of a Nonconsequentialist Approach to Torts," *Legal Theory* 18 (2012): 231–262.

68. Recent work in the economic analysis of tort law has moved away from its earlier ambition of explaining the law, and put itself forward as proposing improvements to the law. Some of these arguments seek to demonstrate the incoherence of legal concepts; for instance, Fried, "Limits of a Non-Consequentialist Approach." Others simply seek to replace them; for instance, Steven Shavell, "Liability for Accidents," *Handbook of Law and Economics,* vol. 1, ed. A. Mitchell Polinsky and Steven Shavell (Amsterdam: North-Holland, 2007); see also Louis Kaplow and Steven Shavell, *Fairness versus Welfare* (Cambridge, MA: Harvard University Press, 2002). My aim here is to respond to the former, incoherence charge; I raise some doubts about the policy proposals in Arthur Ripstein, "Critical Notice: Too Much Invested to Quit," *Economics and Philosophy* 1 (2004): 185–208.

careful people conduct themselves. Instead, the standard of care is cast in terms of the question of whether a benefit to one person is worth a risk to another. Beginning with an article by Henry Terry,[69] the test of reasonable care is to be analyzed in terms of its costs and benefits. The formula developed by Learned Hand in *Carroll Towing*, a case involving an unsupervised barge, has thus become the canonical formulation for scholars, if not for courts:[70]

> The owner's duty, as in other similar situations, to provide against resulting injuries is a function of three variables: (1) The probability that she will break away; (2) the gravity of the resulting injury, if she does; (3) the burden of adequate precautions. Possibly it serves to bring this notion into relief to state it in algebraic terms: if the probability be called P; the injury, L; and the burden, B; liability depends upon whether B is less than L multiplied by P: i.e., whether $B < PL$.[71]

69. Henry T. Terry, "Negligence," *Harvard Law Review* 29 (1915), 40–50.

70. A number of writers deny that the Learned Hand formula is used by U.S. courts either for jury instructions or in deciding cases. See Benjamin C. Zipursky, "Sleight of Hand" William & Mary Law Review, 48, (2007) 1999–2041; Stephen G. Gilles, "The Invisible Hand Formula," *Virginia Law Review* 80 (1994): 1015–1054; and Richard W. Wright, "Hand, Posner, and the Myth of the 'Hand Formula,'" *Theoretical Inquiries in Law* 4 (2003): 1–132. A distinguished American torts scholar has suggested to me that its absence in jury instructions reflects administrative concerns, and assured me that at trial the defendant's lawyers introduce evidence of both injury rates and precautionary costs, and the plaintiff's lawyers present counterevidence on this question. Summarizing discussions with trial lawyers involved in defending product liability claims before juries in the United States, Gary Schwartz reaches a different conclusion: "One argument that you should almost never make is that the manufacturer deliberately included a dangerous feature in the product's design because of the high monetary cost that the manufacturer would have incurred in choosing another design. If you do argue this, you're almost certain to lose on liability, and you can expose yourself to punitive damages as well." Schwartz, "The Myth of the Ford Pinto Case," *Rutgers Law Review* 43 (1991): 1013–1068.

Some courts do explicitly adopt the Hand formula: In People Express Airlines, Inc. v. Consolidated Rail Corp., 495 A. 2d 107, (N.J. 1985), the court says, "If negligence is the failure to take precautions that cost less than the damage wrought by the ensuing accident . . . it would be unfair and socially inefficient to assign liability for harm that no reasonably-undertaken precaution could have avoided." *People Express* is striking in permitting recovery for what it characterized as pure economic loss, abandoning the distinction between misfeasance and nonfeasance in favor of cost–benefit analysis.

71. United States v. Carroll Towing Co., 159 F.2d 169, 173 (2d Cir. 1947).

Richard Posner has carried Hand's formulation further, arguing that the standard of reasonable care formulates an economic test. On Posner's understanding, the test measures whether the defendant has taken an efficient level of precautions by weighing the cost of precaution (B) against the cost of the injury (L), discounted by its likelihood (P). As Posner puts it,

> Discounting (multiplying) the cost of an accident if it occurs by the probability of occurrence yields a measure of the economic benefit to be anticipated from incurring the costs necessary to prevent the accident. The cost of prevention is what Hand meant by the burden of taking precautions against the accident. It may be the cost of installing safety equipment or otherwise making the activity safer, or the benefit forgone by curtailing or eliminating the activity. If the cost of safety measures or of curtailment—whichever cost is lower—exceeds the benefit in accident avoidance to be gained by incurring that cost, society would be better off, in economic terms, to forgo accident prevention.[72]

Posner concedes that the Hand test has "greater analytic than operational significance," attributing this to the fact that the "parties do not give the jury the information required to quantify the variables that the Hand Formula picks out as relevant."[73]

The test's analytical significance is compromised, however, by the fact that were a jury permitted to use such information (or even their intuitive sense about it), they would exceed their role by rendering irrelevant the other elements of a tort action that a plaintiff must prove. In the United States, the jury is charged with answering questions of fact, and mixed questions of fact and law, but not with answering pure questions of law. An actual application of Posner's formulation of the Learned Hand test would violate this institutional role. The question of whether, all things considered, the cost of a precaution exceeds its benefits does not depend on whether the defendant needed to look out for the plaintiff's safety, or whether the plaintiff's losses were to body or property, or merely to the

---

72. Richard Posner, "A Theory of Negligence," *Journal of Legal Studies* 1 (1972): 32.
73. McCarty v. Pheasant Run Inc., 826 F.2d 1554, 1557 (7th Cir. 1987).

prospect of future wealth. The distinctions between cases in which a duty is and is not owed, and between cases in which the plaintiff's loss is proximate or remote, are questions of law. These relational questions are antecedent to the standard of care question of how much risk the defendant imposed on the plaintiff, but they are preempted by the thoroughgoing cost–benefit analysis proposed by Posner. So is the distinction between misfeasance and nonfeasance: The same questions about the cost of the defendant doing something and the likely cost to the plaintiff of the defendant's failure to do so apply in just the same way to cases in which the action in question is doing something *for* rather than *to* another person. The same point applies to losses to third parties—those who depend upon but do not own property that the defendant damages. They suffer losses, the prevention of which would impose no burden on the defendant. In all of these cases, cost–benefit analysis operates in the same way.[74]

This difficulty is exacerbated by the suggestion that cost–benefit analysis be restricted to questions of the standard of care; if I owe you a duty in relation to a specific risk, I need to take account of your safety, not the cost to me of taking account of it. Hand himself may have been aware of this; he is in some ways an odd champion for the economic test that bears his name. In another barge case, he endorses the traditional rule of remoteness, concluding that "so long as it is an element of imposed liability that the wrongdoer shall in some degree disregard the sufferer's interests, it can only be an anomaly, and indeed vindictive, to make him responsible to those whose interests he has not disregarded. We cannot consistently lose sight of the fact that this element relates to the person injured and admits no surrogate."[75] He also understands remedies in terms of rights rather than efficiency, describing the duty to pay damages as "an obligation destined to stand in place of the plaintiff's right, and be, as nearly as possible, equivalent to him for his rights."[76] Perhaps he only meant to cast traditional ideas in mathematical terms.

---

74. See the discussion of Bishop, "Economic Loss," in Chapter 3.

75. Sinram v. Pennsylvania R. Co., 61 F.2d 767, 770 (2d Cir. 1932).

76. Learned Hand, "Restitution or Unjust Enrichment," *Harvard Law Review* 11 (1897): 256.

If so, it is not surprising that attempts to operationalize the test do not quantify risk. Instead, more traditional ideas are paraphrased in quantitative terms. In *McMahon v. Bunn-O-Matic*,[77] in which the plaintiff suffered serious burns while transferring coffee from a take-out cup to a smaller one, Easterbrook J. frames the issue of whether coffee served at 180° F is too dangerous by characterizing negligence as the "failure to take precautions that are less expensive than the net costs of accidents."[78] Although he uses the vocabulary of cost–benefit analysis, at no point does he specify or attach weights to the "expense" of the competing factors, or even identify them as competing. Instead, the entire exercise proceeds through a characterization of the nature of ordinary human life, focusing on such matters as the temperatures at which most people prepare and consume hot beverages in their homes, the temperatures at which the different flavors in coffee are best appreciated, and the law's expectation that consumers will "educate themselves about the hazards of daily life— of matches, knives, and kitchen ranges, of bones in fish, and of hot beverages—by general reading and experience, knowledge they can acquire before they enter a mini mart to buy coffee for a journey."[79] That is, the issue of whether serving coffee at ordinary coffee temperatures is safe enough is treated as a matter of whether the coffee can be used safely by the adults using it. Familiar features of social life—ordinary users of this product know about its temperature and use it anyway, having their own coffee-specific reasons for doing so, and so on—reveal that they know how to use it safely. None of this is a matter of figuring out whether there would be a loss to coffee vendors or consumers through serving it at a lower temperature; the only question is whether it endangers competent adults. The answer is that it does not because they can use it safely. The question might be different if someone served hot liquids to small children, or balanced them precariously near passersby. But in such a situation, the benefits of serving coffee at that temperature would not need to be weighed against the risk; they would count for nothing.

---

77. McMahon v. Bunn-O-Matic Corp., 150 F.3d 651 (7th Cir. 1997).

78. Ibid., 657. The McMahons brought their claim under products liability. Easterbrook J. concludes that a Hand-type test applies to product defect cases under Indiana law.

79. Ibid., 655.

Others have objected to the Learned Hand formula on the grounds that it is inconsistent with the way in which the standard of care is objective, as it would make the care required depend upon the opportunity cost to the defendant in his or her specific circumstances, and the lost income of those who might be expected to be injured.[80] Because it collapses the class of plaintiffs, type, and extent of injury into a single variable, "L," whether a precaution was required would depend on who it was that was likely to be injured, calling for different levels of care depending on the lost income of those you might injure.

Despite these difficulties, the Learned Hand test retains its hold on American legal scholarship, if not on the conduct of courts. Recurrent references to it in the academic literature reflect the Holmesian idea that the law of torts is concerned with harms rather than with wrongs. If risk is characterized in terms of the likelihood of harm, it is a short step to conclude that harm needs to be somehow balanced against other factors; the idea that it is never acceptable to create a significant risk of harm seems preposterous. Moreover, there are so many familiar examples of harms that both law and morality are prepared to tolerate, that, if you think that the entire structure of the law is based on harm-prevention, something further must discipline its operation. This is an iatrogenic symptom of legal scholarship: by focusing on harm rather than wrongdoing, cases in which the plaintiff does not recover because the defendant did not infringe any right of the plaintiff's need to be explained in some other way. But if the distinction between misfeasance and nonfeasance is kept in view, no such difficulties arise.

Nonetheless, the alternative courses of action available are sometimes relevant to the standard of care. Consider Lord Reid's remark in *Wagon Mound No. 2:* "But it does not follow that, no matter what the circumstances may be, it is justifiable to neglect a risk of such a small magnitude. A reasonable man would only neglect such a risk if he had some valid reason for doing so: e.g., that it would involve considerable expense to eliminate the risk. He would weigh the risk against the difficulty of elim-

---

80. Posner concedes this feature of the test in "Wealth Maximization and Tort Law: A Philosophical Inquiry," in *Philosophical Foundations of Tort Law,* ed. David Owen (Oxford: Oxford University Press, 1995), 110.

inating it."[81] Lord Reid's formulation suggests that the careful person will bring the level of risk even below the ordinary background risk created by the "crowded conditions of modern life," if that can be done without in any other way compromising what he or she was doing. Despite Lord Reid's reference to "weighing the risk against the difficulty of eliminating it," this is no exercise in generalized cost–benefit analysis. Instead, the point is that if a very small risk can be eliminated, a careful person will do so.

In *Wagon Mound No. 2*, the defendant's employees neglected to turn off a spigot, leading to the discharge of oil into Sydney Harbor. Their negligence was not in the service of doing or accomplishing anything else; they simply failed to do so. In such a situation, there is room for the defendant to consider whether some obvious precaution is available, and ask: "Am I missing something?" That possibility is not one that merits some ideal degree of diligence or appropriate investment of resources in investigation. Instead, it simply requires the defendant to do what careful people ordinarily do: give some thought to the safety of others. No doubt someone impressed with cost–benefit analyses could represent the issue in this way, but that shows only that it is possible to frame any decision in terms of a cost–benefit analysis.

Many of the familiar tests that courts use to determine negligence give more specific signposts of what a careful person would do. For example, tests of "industry practice" or "custom" look at what others engaged in similar activities do by way of precautions. A defendant's failure to take a standard precaution is normally sufficient to establish negligence, but taking a standard precaution does not always establish reasonable care.[82]

A similar structure figures in many applications of safety statutes to determine negligence. As we saw in Chapter 3, statutory requirements do

81. Overseas Tankship (UK) Ltd. v. The Miller Steamship Co. Pty. (The Wagon Mound No. 2), [1966] 2 WLR 877.

82. As Hand J. noted, "There are, no doubt, cases where courts seem to make the general practice of the calling the standard of proper diligence . . . in most cases reasonable prudence is in fact common prudence; but strictly it is never its measure; a whole calling may have unduly lagged in the adoption of new and available device . . . there are precautions so imperative that even their universal disregard will not excuse their omission." The T. J. Hooper v. Northern Barge Corp., 60 F.2d 737, 740 (2d Cir. 1932).

not always generate private law duties. Public law requirements of good citizenship, whether to shovel the sidewalk in front of your house or rescue those in peril, need not impose duties running to the particular people who in fact benefit from the existence and observance of those requirements. If, however, the defendant owes the plaintiff a private law duty, then the statutory specification of a safe way to do things ordinarily shows that there was a safe way to proceed.[83] In unusual circumstances in which compliance with the statute would have made things much more dangerous, failure to comply does not constitute negligence.[84]

3.3. Causation and Damage

At the beginning of this chapter I noted the prominence of luck-skepticism in scholarly treatments of negligence. The basic thought is familiar: The law of negligence is irrational, because it treats morally similar cases differently solely on the basis of what they cause, which is entirely a matter of luck. If two people are equally careless, one might injure someone and be liable for enormous damages, while the other, through good fortune, injures no one. How can the legal system treat two otherwise similar people so differently?

I have offered a general account of why the strategy of dismantling the tort of negligence goes wrong. With an account in place of the duty, remoteness, and standard of care elements in terms of a system in which no person is in charge of another, the role of causation is straightforward: Only a completed wrong is an interference with the plaintiff's right. Nobody has authority to constrain others except with respect to their body and property.

Rather than requiring you to be careful, simply as such, or as a way of revealing your inner character or concern for others, the standard of care in negligence requires you to use your means in a way that is consistent with others using theirs. That is, like the rest of tort law, it regards you as

---

83. See Martin v. Herzog, 228 N.Y. 164, 126 N.E. 814.

84. Tedla v. Ellman, 280 N.Y. 124, 19 N.E. 2d 987. Note that this is a contributory negligence case.

an active agent, and focuses on what you do in relation to others, rather than on what you do in relation to some abstract standard.

No inconsistency arises if your use of your means in a way that is potentially or probably (or even overwhelmingly likely to be) inconsistent with another's use. The availability of these modal concepts reflects the difference between inconsistency and possible or probable inconsistency. The same structure applies to use-based torts: The person who trespasses on your land, knowingly or otherwise, wrongs you, and, from the point of view of private rights, is just like other trespassers (however much they might differ along other dimensions). The relevant comparator is not the class of persons who do not know where they are; nobody has a cause of action against the person who gets lost on his or her own land, even though such a person is just as confused about location as the mistaken trespasser.

At the same time, the inconsistency between the defendant's action and the plaintiff's right arises only if the defendant's conduct was too dangerous: The norm in negligence tells you to avoid injuring others through your carelessness. It is a qualified duty of noninjury; it does not simply tell you either that you ought be careful or not to injure others, but rather instructs you not to injure them in certain ways—that is, by acting in ways that endanger the bodies and property of others. But the qualification gets its point from the wrong of negligent injury of which it is a part.

I want to close this discussion of the elements of negligence with a diagnosis of the temptation to dismantle, using the role of causation as an example. The modern debate about moral luck was inaugurated by Thomas Nagel's essay of that title.[85] Nagel notes the similarity between his concerns about moral luck and familiar forms of epistemological skepticism. Although Nagel takes this as a marker of the significance and depth of the problem, I will propose a different diagnosis. Epistemological

---

85. Thomas Nagel, "Moral Luck," in *Mortal Questions* (Cambridge: Cambridge University Press, 1979), 24–38. But the debate is much older; like so much mischief in tort scholarship, it can already be found in Holmes's claim that "an act is always a voluntary muscular contraction and nothing else. The chain of physical sequences which it sets in motion or directs to the plaintiff's harm is no part of it." Oliver Wendell Holmes, *The Common Law* (Boston: Little Brown and Co., 1881), 91.

skeptics are notoriously difficult to answer on the terms on which they set up the problem. If you limit yourself to the contents of your own mind, and exclude anything suspected of bearing any connection to the world, the connection cannot be restored. So, too, with the luck skeptic: If you start with the assumption that the failure to take a precaution is the only thing of normative significance, and exclude anything that happens once you have moved your body, the connection to any injury that results cannot be restored.

Both skeptics set things up backward. Rather than taking successful perception as the basic case of perception, and misperception as a defective version of it, the epistemological skeptic seeks something common to successful and failed perception. By representing misperception as a genuine instance of that genus, the skeptic doubts that successful perception can stand in anything but an accidental relation to the world, given the meager materials with which it has to operate.

In the same way, the luck skeptic moves from decision or bodily movement as the lowest common denominator of action to the conclusion that it is the only morally significant aspect of it. But if the moral question concerns whether one person wronged another, the basic case must be the completed action (what one person does to another), which gives that other person grounds to complain. Inadequate attention to the safety of another person's body or property is a moral defect because that person is entitled to have their means intact. By beginning with the thought that failure to take precautions is a moral defect, the skeptic then wonders why the results of that failure merit special concern.

The analogy with perception might seem incomplete, in that the basic case of wrongdoing—a completed wrong—is already a sort of defective case, because the ideal case is the one in which no wrong is done. But because the wrong is in the inconsistency between the defendant's conduct and the plaintiff's right, the fundamental unit of analysis is the right itself, that is, the relation between the plaintiff's entitlement and the defendant's conduct. Thus, the plaintiff's right explains why the defendant must be careful. The skeptical setup therefore gets things exactly backward: You need to be careful because people have rights against injury; the wrong of negligence is interfering with the right of someone else in particular, to whom you stand in the right relation. That flaw can only

be characterized in relational terms. Removing it from its relational context makes its status as a moral flaw puzzling. Consider another example
of relational duties: If I don't owe you money, my inability or even unwill-
ingness to pay if I did may reflect badly on me, but I haven't wronged you
at all. Conversely, if I do owe you money, I can only discharge my duty
by paying you, not through a series of well-meaning but unsuccessful attempts to do so. Carelessness is just the mirror image of these: Your right
is that I not injure you carelessly, not that I be careful.

4. A Note on Comparative Negligence

The law of torts includes defenses to private wrongs. Some of these, such
as voluntary assumption of risk (provided that this is construed narrowly,
so as to turn on a "bilateral exchange of terms"[86] between the plaintiff
and the defendant), conform to the bilateral structure of private wrongs
developed here. If I give you permission to enter my land, or cut my hair,
what would have been a trespass or battery becomes a visit or service performed. Having me sign a waiver at your zip-line course may relieve you
of liability for negligence; if I sign a waiver at your game farm, I relieve
you of liability for injuries I suffer at the paws of your tigers, even though
your liability as a keeper of wild animals is strict. Although there will be
difficult questions of interpretation in determining whether a particular
act qualifies as consent, or whether a waiver printed on a ski-lift ticket was
sufficient,[87] such questions involve no comparisons between the two of
us; they arise in answering a binary question.

Other defenses go exclusively to the question of whether a court will
award a remedy for what would otherwise be a wrong that the defendant
did to the plaintiff. If the plaintiff's action is brought too late, it will be
barred under a statute of limitation. The lapsing of the limitation period
does not say anything about how things stand between the parties; it

---

86. Rand J., in Car & General Insurance Corp. v. Seymour, [1956] SCR 322, 2 DLR (2d)
369, at ¶15, describes this as a "bilateral relation in which two persons are co-operating in
complementary action." In Dube v. Labar, [1986] 1 SCR 649, Estey J. describes Rand J.'s
conception of *volenti* as a "bilateral 'exchange of terms.'"

87. See, for example, Dalury v. S-K-I, Ltd., 670 A.2d 795 (Vt. 1995).

restricts the plaintiff's ability to bring an action, but does not go to the question of the transaction between the plaintiff and the defendant.[88] Illegality on the plaintiff's part (*ex turpi causa*) serves as a defense to many tort actions; like the role of a limitation period, its focus is not on how things stand between the parties but on the broader purposes of the legal system.[89]

Comparative negligence looks different from both of these; its name and appearance suggest a comparison between the conduct of the plaintiff and the conduct of the defendant.[90] If I injure you through my carelessness (or through my dangerous activity, such as keeping a tiger in my backyard), but you have put yourself into danger—perhaps you have rolled down your window as you drove past the wandering tiger,[91] or stepped out into the path of my carelessly ridden bicycle while reading your email—my liability to you is reduced. Different jurisdictions handle the defense of contributory negligence differently in its details: At common law it was a complete bar to recovery, subject to rules, such as "last clear chance," that shifted liability back to the defendant who ignored the fact that the plaintiff was not attending to his or her own safety.[92] In the past half-century, most jurisdictions have moved to a comparative negligence regime, where the damages recoverable are reduced according to the plaintiff's degree of fault.

88. I develop an account of limitation periods in terms of the systematic requirements of a system of justiciable private rights in Arthur Ripstein, "The Rule of Law and Time's Arrow," in *Private Law and the Rule of Law,* ed. Lisa Austin and Dennis Klimchuk (Oxford: Oxford University Press, 2015), 306–327.

89. In Hall v. Hebert, (1993) 101 DLR (4th) 129 (SCC), McLachlin J. makes this explicit: the concern is with the overall coherence of the law rather than the transaction between the parties.

90. Some deny that it is a defense at all, because it only reduces the quantum of damages rather than relieving the defendant of liability. See James Goudkamp, *Tort Law Defenses* (Oxford: Hart, 2013), 71; Francis Trindade et al., *The Law of Torts in Australia,* 4th ed. (Oxford: Oxford University Press, 2007), 685. I treat contributory negligence as a defense because it is something that the defendant must raise against the plaintiff. See Robert Stevens, "Should Contributory Fault Be Analogue or Digital?," *Defenses in Tort,* ed. Andrew Dyson et al. (Oxford: Hart, 2015), 247–265. I do not share Stevens's misgivings about the defense.

91. Cowles v. Balac, 83 OR (3d) 660, 2006 (ONCA).

92. Davies v. Mann, (1842) 10 M&W 546, 152 ER 588.

The comparison of the respective contributions of the plaintiff and the defendant does not turn on their causal contribution to the damage. The comparative negligence inquiry can only arise for the plaintiff's injuries to which both contributed. If wearing a seatbelt would have prevented some of my injuries but not others, the comparative analysis applies only to those that it would have prevented. That is, the loss is apportioned based on how far each of the defendant and the plaintiff departed from the relevant standard.

The defendant's conduct is relevant to a wrong against the plaintiff, but the plaintiff's conduct, no matter how defective, is not a wrong against the defendant.[93] Nor can it be brought in as part of a pairwise comparison between a negligent defendant and an innocent plaintiff. Because that is not part of the analysis of negligent wrongdoing, some other explanation is required. Again, if the point of tort liability is to promote efficient resource allocation, perhaps it could be argued that the comparative negligence regime provides plaintiffs with incentives to invest prudently in their own safety. But, once again, if that is not its point, comparative negligence can be made to look puzzling.

The puzzle is resolved if the defense is framed in terms of the nature of the wrong; the comparison arises internal to the wrongful transaction between the defendant and the plaintiff, and so internal to the relation between them. In damage-based wrongs, the plaintiff's right is always a right to constrain the defendant from damaging the plaintiff's means through excessively dangerous use of his or her own means, where the excessive danger is in relation to a specific risk. That is why duty, remoteness, the standard of care, and causation all focus on the same risk. In contributory or comparative negligence, the plaintiff's exposure of himor herself to danger is relevant only with respect to the very risk in question. Just as the negligence inquiry takes no account of the other risks that the defendant creates, so the comparative negligence inquiry takes no account of those other risks. The familiar rule of remoteness also applies to comparative negligence: If the plaintiff ended up in the wrong place at the wrong time because of risky conduct—he would not have collided with

93. See the discussion in Beever, *Rediscovering the Law of Negligence*, 343.

the falling tree had he been driving at a safe speed[94]—the injury is not within the ambit of the risk.

If the plaintiff increased the very risk through which the defendant caused the injury, the risk, and so the wrong, is their joint product. The plaintiff is still entitled to constrain the defendant in relation to that risk to his or her safety, but not to constrain the defendant with respect to the plaintiff's putting him- or herself at risk. Because the point of a tort remedy is to ensure that the plaintiff's entitlement to constrain the defendant's conduct survives its own violation, in a case in which the plaintiff's safety is restricted by his or her own contribution, the right that survives its own violation is also restricted. The question of the extent to which that restriction applies just is the question of the extent to which each of the plaintiff and the defendant created the relevant risk.

5. Conclusion

Negligence has played a central role in the past century of tort scholarship. Its doctrinal complexity and its relation to neighboring moral ideas make it fascinating; those same features make it particularly attractive to both debunking and dismantling analyses. In this chapter I have argued that, despite those attractions, the elements of a negligence action form a unified whole, each acquiring its moral significance from its place within that whole.

Its centrality has also exerted a gravitational pull on the study of other private wrongs. In Chapters 5–7, I will turn to other torts, explaining the wrongs distinctive to them and, in the process, clearing away the misconceptions about them generated by misunderstandings of negligence.

---

94. Berry v. Borough of Sugar Notch, 191 Pa. 345, 43 A 240 (Pa 1899).

CHAPTER 5

Use What Is Yours in a Way That Does Not Injure Your Neighbor

Strict Liability

I ARGUED IN CHAPTER 2 ("What You Already Have") for a distinction between two broad classes of torts against bodies and property: those that involve using another's body or property, and those that involve damaging it. I argued that use-based torts never have a fault requirement, because nobody has any entitlement to use another person's body or property for an unauthorized purpose. Nothing more than use-without-permission is required for the use to be wrongful; the act of using what belongs to another is inconsistent with that person's rights. Use-based torts are all intentional torts, simply because using something is by its nature intentional. If I enter your land without your permission, I do so intentionally—I intend to be where I am—even if I am not aware of the boundary, or am lost and would rather not be there, and so do not know it is your land. I still use it as my way of doing what I am doing, including finding my way back to where I want to be.

Damage-based torts, by contrast, include a fault requirement: The defendant's act must not only damage the plaintiff's body or property; it must also be defective because it is the kind of thing that is excessively likely to interfere with to the usability of the object of the right. Each is entitled to use his or her body and property in ways consistent with the continuing ability of others to use theirs. I argued that this entails the requirement that one person not injure or damage another's person or property through actions that are characteristically more injurious than the ordinary background risks.

In Chapter 4, I explained the nature of the fault requirement in negligence by characterizing injuriousness in terms of risk: The defendant's conduct is defective if it is more dangerous than the ordinary background level of risk that is the concomitant of a plurality of persons using what is theirs. That sort of background risk is treated no differently than the ordinary vulnerability of human bodies and property to natural degeneration and decay. Conduct more dangerous than this is potentially inconsistent with the rights of others; when such conduct ripens into injury, it is inconsistent.

By aligning the distinction between use- and damage-based torts with the distinction between torts for which there is no fault requirement and those for which there is one, I might be accused of leaving out a legally significant category, namely, those wrongs for which liability for damage caused is strict. The strictness of liability in battery, trespass, and conversion not an issue for this alignment, but familiar cases involving reservoirs,[1] wild animals,[2] and explosives might be thought to be.[3] The former examples are use-based, and I have contended that they involve no fault element and so strict liability follows. The latter examples, however, involve damage, and so the apparent absence of fault calls out for explanation. Further difficulties might be thought to attend the cases of necessity, such as *Vincent v. Lake Erie Transportation*,[4] in which the defendant is often described as having behaved faultlessly in securing its ship to the plaintiff's dock but being nonetheless liable for the damage caused by doing so.

These cases are often presented as constituting a distinctive category of strict liability torts that is governed by principles different from those that govern either use-based wrongs or negligence. They are often grouped with cases of vicarious liability, in which an employer is held liable for

1. Rylands v. Fletcher, [1868] UKHL 1, LR 3 HL 330.
2. Behrens v. Bertram Mills Circus, [1957] 2 QB 1.
3. Hay v. Cohoes, 2 N.Y.159 (1849); Spano v. Perini Corp., 240 N.E.2d 31 (N.Y. 1969).
4. 109 Minn. 456, 124 NW 221 (Minn. 1910).

the torts of his or her employee. For reasons of both conceptual economy and space, I will say very little about vicarious liability here. Despite a handful of American cases that seek to explain it in terms of the obligation of a business to bear the costs attendant upon reaping the benefits of its operations,[5] and some recent Commonwealth cases that assimilate the liability of religious organizations charged with caring for children to the creation of dangerous conditions[6]—that is, making the liability direct rather than vicarious—the main thrust of vicarious liability has been focused on what an employee does in the course of employment, that is, when acting on the employer's behalf. Unsurprisingly, ideas from the law of agency figure, as do ideas about what is and is not within the course of employment, including the celebrated distinction between "frolic" and "detour." The prominence of these ideas is unsurprising because a corporate employer can only act through its employees.[7] Questions about whether an employee was adequately supervised do not figure prominently in these cases, as they would reproduce the same structure: Whoever is supposed to be supervising the employee is also acting on behalf of the corporation, and so stands in the same juridical relation to the corporation as does the employee who committed the tort. Although vicarious liability is sometimes treated as anomalous, almost all of the cases presuppose it. People sue railroads and manufacturers because of the acts

---

5. See Ira S. Bushey & Sons v. United States, 398 F2d 167 (2d Cir. 1968); Gregory C. Keating, "Tort, Rawlsian Fairness and Regime Choice in the Law of Accidents," *Fordham Law Review* 72 (2004): 1857–1921; Jane Stapleton, *Products Liability* (Toronto: Butterworths Canada, 1994). As Robert Stevens has pointed out, over and above the lack of doctrinal fit of the details of such accounts, they have the much more general flaw of failing to be explanations of vicarious liability in particular. The possibility of loss spreading and the internalization of benefits are not specific to employer/employee relations. Stevens, *Torts and Rights* (Oxford: Oxford University Press, 2007), 259.

6. Bazley v. Curry, [1999] 2 SCR 534; Jacobi v. Griffiths, [1999] 2 SCR 570; Lister v. Hesley Hall Ltd., [2001] UKHL 22.

7. See the judgment of Iacobucci J. in London Drugs v. Kuehne and Nagel International, [1992] 3 SCR 299, in which employees were granted the benefit of a contractual limitation of liability despite not being parties to the contract. Iacobucci J. emphasized that the point of the exclusion was to cover the very sort of situation that occurred, that is, damage to the plaintiff's property in the course of the employer doing its business by directing its employees. Otherwise the limitation would have covered nothing at all.

of their employees. As always, these structuring ideas can be given effect
only through positive law, and different legal systems will develop them
differently.

Returning to the other cases of strict liability, these torts have played
a significant role in legal scholarship over the past century. Some writers
have used them to argue that, far from being anomalous, they are representative, and negligence is the anomaly.[8] Others argue that these cases
are best understood as a court-imposed licensing regime, a system of
conditional fault in which the only defect in the defendant's action is
the failure to pay,[9] or a "pay-as-you-go" scheme designed to see to it that
costs are internalized so that the sum of accident and avoidance costs is
minimized.[10] Others have urged recognizing them as a pure liability regime, perhaps modeled on statutory regimes governing unavoidable injuries due to public health measures such as vaccination.[11] Yet others
have argued that these torts represent cases of fundamental rights to which
no duty corresponds, a rights violation that has nothing to do with the

8. Richard Epstein, "A Theory of Strict Liability," *Journal of Legal Studies* 2 (1973):
151–204; Guido Calabresi and Jon T. Hirschoff, "Toward a Test for Strict Liability in
Torts," *Yale Law Journal* 81 (1972): 1055–1085; Gregory C. Keating, "Strict Liability
Wrongs," in *Philosophical Foundations of the Law of Torts,* ed. John Oberdiek (Oxford:
Oxford University Press, 2014), 292–311.

9. Robert E. Keeton, "Conditional Fault in the Law of Torts," *Harvard Law Review* 72
(1959): 401–444. Keeton intends his account to cover strict liability in general, going so far
as to suggest that the wrong in defamation is the failure to make up losses that the plaintiff
suffers through a damaged reputation. Gregory Keating defends a still stronger version of
this view in his discussion of nuisance, the "modern" law of which "embodies a morality of
responsibility for harm which should be inflicted." See Keating, "Nuisance as a Strict Liability Wrong," *Journal of Tort Law* 4 (2012): 1–44, citing Boomer v. Atlantic Cement, 257
NE 2d 870 (NY 1970). *Boomer* is the U.S. case that rejects the English rule from Shelfer v.
City of London Electric Lighting Co., (1895) 1 Ch 287 CA, which established that the
normal remedy for a nuisance is an injunction. Under the *Boomer* rule, damages license an
ongoing nuisance.

10. Calabresi and Hirschoff, "Toward a Test"; John C. P. Goldberg and Benjamin C.
Zipursky, "Torts as Wrongs," *Texas Law Review* 88 (2010): 951–952.

11. 42 USC Ch. 6A, sub Ch. XIX: Vaccines. Quebec passed similar legislation in the
wake of Lapierre v. AG (Que.), 1975 1 SCR 241: see Sante et Services Sociaux Quebec,
"Quebec's Compensation for Victims of Vaccination Program," http://www.msss.gouv.qc
.ca/sujets/santepub/vaccination/index.php?indemnisation_en.

nature of the conduct that violates it.[12] Still others have suggested that strict liability in all of its guises—even in cases of trespass to land—is problematic from the point of view of the rule of law, because it gives ordinary citizens instructions that they should not follow.[13]

Each of these proposed analyses poses a challenge both for my claim that liability is based on wrongdoing and for my alignment of the two distinctions. Licensing and conditional-fault accounts deny that there is anything defective about the defendant's conduct and treat these torts as instances of liability without wrongdoing. The idea that focuses on rights violation challenges the alignment in a more fundamental way, by supposing that a right can be individuated in terms of its object without reference to the type of act that violates it.

My aim in this chapter is to explain away these cases. In order to make out this claim, I will examine both the old English reservoir case of *Rylands v. Fletcher,* which many point to as the high water mark of strict liability, and the flagship of the conditional fault armada, *Vincent v. Lake Erie Transportation.* I will follow custom in grouping them together, though I will argue they are analytically very different. *Rylands* is a case of the realization of an excessive risk, and it can be explained on familiar principles of damage-based torts. The role of both land and contained water figures in the doctrinal details of *Rylands,* but its broad structure as a damage-based tort is apparent in the developments that have flowed from it. *Vincent,* by contrast, is a case of trespass-based liability. The defendant is liable because of his use of the plaintiff's dock; his liability in damages is predicated on that use. It raises distinctive issues not found in other cases of use-based liability because the trespass was privileged.

Rylands is often presented as a watershed in introducing the idea of liability without fault. The defendant's reservoir burst through abandoned mine shafts, flooding a neighbor's mine. In English law, *Rylands* is often said to have by now been drained of its distinctiveness into a minor category of the law of nuisance, but American scholarship remains im-

---

12. Nils Jansen works with the assumption that the only kind of defect is culpability. See Nils Jansen, "The Idea of Legal Responsibility," *Oxford Journal of Legal Studies* 34 (2014).

13. Stephen Smith, "Strict Duties and the Rule of Law," in *Private Law and the Rule of Law,* ed. Lisa Austin and Dennis Klimchuk (Oxford: Oxford University Press, 2014), 189–206.

mersed in it. I will suggest that much of the apparent distinctiveness was never really there. The defendant's reservoir was a nuisance waiting to happen; like other nuisances, it became actionable only once it happened. Nuisance is a tort particular to land; it is committed only if something leaves the defendant's land and interferes with the usefulness of the plaintiff's land. In *Rylands* the reservoir was not a nuisance; only the flooding was. This general structure can be extended to things other than uses of land that are by their nature too dangerous. They, too, do not constitute a private wrong until the peril is realized. In both types of cases, the defendant's defective conduct is inconsistent with the plaintiff's right only when injury ensues, but the defect is to be found in the danger it poses to that right.

In *Vincent*, the defendant spared its boat in a storm by keeping it moored to the plaintiff's dock, which suffered serious damage as a result. *Vincent* has attracted attention because the defendant should not have done anything differently, and so, it would seem, there is no question of wrongdoing.[14] Instead, as it is often interpreted, the payment of damages somehow licenses the deed.

The same idea of licensing sometimes flows back into analyses of *Rylands*[15] on the assumption that reservoirs are worthwhile, but must be made to pay their way. The conjunction of the idea that the defendant did nothing wrong with the idea that payment is necessary in order to license his unobjectionable deed is puzzling, which may explain the unconvincing character of many analyses of it. I shall show, however, that *Vincent* is entirely about the rights of the parties, and only incidentally about costs and benefits that are at issue. I will show that *Vincent* is a completely unexceptional case of a privilege to use another's land, the basis of which is a systematic implication of a legal order in which property is held in both immovable land and movable chattels.

Both *Rylands* and *Vincent* can be represented as "pay-as-you-go" or licensing cases, but only because any tort case whatsoever can be so represented. The possibility of representing a wrong and its remedy as a disjunctive option—avoid wrongdoing or pay—is the basis of the Holme-

14. Robert E. Keeton, "Conditional Fault."
15. See, for example, Keating, "Strict Liability Wrongs."

sian "disjunctive" account of contract law, according to which there is never a duty to keep a contract, only a disjunctive duty to either keep the contract or pay damages.[16] Indeed, Holmes makes just this point in an early article on torts, in which he insists that no wrong is done in cases of liability for bursting reservoirs, but that modern courts "hold a man liable for the escape of water from a reservoir which he has built upon his land, or for the escape of cattle, although he is not alleged to have been negligent, they do not proceed upon the ground that there is an element of culpability in making such a reservoir, or in keeping cattle, sufficient to charge the defendant as soon as a *damnum* concurs, but on the principle that it is politic to make those who go into extra-hazardous employments take the risk on their own shoulders."[17] Holmes takes this example to illustrate a more general principle: "Apart from collateral consequences, the possibility that I may have to pay the reasonable worth or market value of my neighbor's property cannot be said to amount to a penalty on conversion, much less to make it my duty not to convert it. I do not owe my butcher a duty not to buy his meat, because I must pay for it if I buy."[18] The most striking feature of this discussion is Holmes's readiness to collapse the distinction between voluntary and involuntary transactions. There are conditions in which the payment of the market value of the thing gives clear title to it and blocks any action in conversion. We have a name for those: they are called purchases. It does not follow, however, that there is no such wrong as conversion and no damages for it in cases of involuntary transactions. To be sure, Holmes does not quite come out and say that there is no such difference; his examples all turn on what he believes to be reasons of public policy that license a certain class of involuntary transactions, which he supposes to be in some way analogous to the reasons of public policy that license voluntary ones. As we shall see, it is not easy to understand what these policies might be, or how they could make an act that is inconsistent with the plaintiff's right consistent with it on the condition that money is paid. A voluntary act on the

16. Oliver Wendell Holmes Jr., *The Common Law* (Boston: Little, Brown, 1882), 299–301.

17. Oliver Wendell Holmes Jr., "The Theory of Torts," *American Law Review* 7 (1872–1873): 653.

18. Ibid., 652.

plaintiff's part can do this easily enough, because one of the plaintiff's entitlements to property is to set the terms on which others may acquire it from her.

As we will see in more detail in Chapter 8, the disjunctive analysis is conceptually unstable: The supposed equivalence between avoiding wrong and wrongdoing but paying damages is established by replacing any idea of obligation with the idea of a prediction. Whatever the merits of thinking of private law as a system of choices, this particular option cannot be made to work: If the defendant has a duty to avoid injury or pay damages, but does neither, some other legal consequence will follow. Thus we get a three-part disjunction—avoid injuring, or pay damages, or face a contempt sanction—and so on. Each step in the sequence depends on the previous ones. But the basis of liability is not the fact that the law gives the defendant an option of avoiding injury or paying damages; the basis of liability is that the defendant has wronged the plaintiff.

1. Liability without Norms?

Before turning to *Rylands* and *Vincent,* however, I will first consider the allegation that strict liability torts do not involve duties or norms of conduct at all. This philosophical argument, as I shall call it, comes in two forms. Both endorse a conclusion similar to instrumentalist accounts of strict liability, but they differ from prominent instrumentalist accounts because they do not rest on a more general skepticism about rights and duties in tort law; instead, they treat it as different from cases of fault. One version of the argument treats it as governed by rights without duties, another as involving no duties and so no rights. Nils Jansen has offered the first form of argument and Stephen Smith the second.

Jansen argues that liability is imposed in order to protect a fundamental right, but that this imposition of liability should not be mistaken for a response to a breach of a duty. On Jansen's interpretation, the key concepts for tort liability are responsibility—understood in broadly causal terms—and rights violation. The analysis is parsimonious—the person who is responsible for an injury must respond to it.[19] Jansen argues that

19. Jansen qualifies this claim by noting the centrality of the concept of a right: "Not all interference with another person's interests would give rise to a duty to make restitution; it

this insight was lost as a result of influence of seventeenth-century Dutch jurist Hugo Grotius, who, on Jansen's reading, made the basis of liability depend on fault rather than on the infringement of a right.

Jansen fails to consider, however, the possibility that the concept of a right presupposes its membership in the system of rights, understood as a system in which no person is in charge of any other, and so presupposes the notion of fault in the sense of a defect, rather than in the sense of a flaw of character on the part of the responsible agent.

As we saw in Chapter 4, the supposition that the basis of liability in negligence is some sort of flaw of the defendant's character is the source of much confusion. Not only does it generate groundless puzzles about moral luck; it invites irrelevant considerations of proportionality into discussions of thin skull cases, and draws attention away from the inconsistency of the defendant's conduct with the plaintiff's right. If fault is understood instead as a defect in the tortfeasor's conduct in relation to the plaintiff's rights, then Jansen presents a false dichotomy in suggesting that, in cases of damage-based torts, fault and rights infringement are alternative and inconsistent bases of liability. Dangerousness figures in determining whether the defendant's conduct is part of a system in which a plurality of persons are each entitled to use their body and property as they see fit. The risks that are the inevitable concomitant of people doing things are part of such a system, whereas risks in excess of that are not. Negligence consists in injuring another through excessively risky conduct, where the risk is excessive because of the likelihood of the very type of injury of which the plaintiff complains.

Steven Smith shares Jansen's view about the absence of norms of conduct in strict liability torts, but takes a less positive view of it, arguing, "From a rule-of-law perspective, strict duties are problematic because they provide misleading guidance. More concretely, the objection is that strict duties give citizens legal reasons to do things that the law clearly does not want them to do. Specifically, strict duties provide reasons for citizens to take extreme care—even to the point (as far as this is possible)

---

was always necessary that the claimant's widely conceived sphere of legal rights and legally protected interests (*dominium*) had been infringed." Jansen, "The Idea of Legal Responsibility,": 228.

of not acting at all."[20] Smith presents his objection as perfectly general, that is, as applying not only to *Vincent* and *Rylands* type cases, but also to trespass to land and defamation. In all of these cases, Smith's worry is that the law cannot be imposing standards of conduct, because it would then be telling people to restrict their activities more than it is reasonable to do. Instead, he suggests that these cases should be thought of as simple liability rules, the basis of which has nothing to do with a duty, and so nothing to do with rights.

Smith's way of setting up the problem rests on a specific conception of what it is to have a duty, according to which the point of a legal duty is to tell you what steps to take in order to comply with it. This moment-by-moment-advice conception of legal duties is rooted in the thought that law has the open-ended function of guiding people, and that the rule of law consists in providing people with information about what precisely they have most reason to do.[21] A legal duty that required you to avoid injuring unforeseeable others or to avoid unforeseeable types of injury would face a genuine problem of failing to tell you what to do—its advice would be to take account of something of which no account can be taken. As a result, nothing would count as complying (or failing to comply) with it.

That sort of guidance is different from Smith's concern in the quoted passage. Smith's thought is that the law should give you instructions that will, if followed, enable you to do exactly what you have most reason to do.[22] From this perspective, strict liability tort duties appear to be prob-

---

20. Smith, "Strict Duties," 193.

21. Smith's approach is influenced by Joseph Raz's account of legal authority, according to which the purpose of authority is to serve those subject to it by helping them comply with reasons that apply to them better than they would be able to conform if they considered those reasons directly. See Joseph Raz, *The Morality of Freedom* (Oxford: Oxford University Press, 1988). Raz is careful to leave the content of those reasons open; his theory of authority does not presuppose any specific account of what reasons there are. Developing the Razian approach in a different way, John Gardner has argued that the law of torts focuses on what he calls "reasons to succeed"—that is, that the underlying reasons require you not to wrong others, rather than to take certain steps. See Gardner, "Obligations and Outcomes in the Law of Torts," in *Relating to Responsibility: Essays in Honor of Tony Honoré on his 80th Birthday,* ed. Peter Cane and John Gardner (Oxford: Hart, 2001): 111–144.

22. More recently, Smith has backed away from some of these claims in "Duties to Try and Duties to Succeed," in *Defences in Tort,* ed. Andrew Dyson, James Goudkamp, and

lematic because they require that you exercise more care than you have reason to exercise.

In the example of use-based torts, such as trespass to land, the worry that the duty requires you to do more than you have reason to do might be glossed in terms of a concern about overinvestment in precautions. In other cases, such as the use of explosives or the keeping of wild animals, excessive caution is less obviously a problem. Perhaps Smith's worry rests on a thought about duties restricting freedom. If you own a lion or tiger, your duty to avoid injuring others might limit the range of options that you have for making use of your pet. This might seem to put you in a different position than owners of other types of property, who have a much broader range of things that they might do with what they own. If this is Smith's worry, however, it invites a straightforward response: Your right to your property constrains the ways in which others may behave, but it does not entitle you to a context in which it can be used in your most preferred way, or in which you have a wide range of possible options. You are always required to restrict your use of your means, including your property, to uses consistent with the rights of others. That means that you cannot walk your dog (or lion) on someone else's land, that you cannot fire your handgun in a public place, that you cannot ride your horse or bicycle at high speeds in most locations. Or rather, if you do these things and someone is injured, you will wrong that person. So, too, if you accept a gift of a box of nuclear waste, the rights of others mean that there is probably no place for you to store it safely. That does not make your ownership of any of these things defective in any way.

Whatever precisely is supposed to be the worry about the law asking more of you than you have reason to do, it also rests on a misunderstanding of duties of noninjury. The law tells you not to do certain things, such as using the property of others or injuring them through your dangerous conduct. It does not tell you how much to invest in safety or in avoiding inadvertently entering the land of other people. Its silence on these details does not violate any ordinary understanding of the rule of law: Its requirements remain prospective, telling you what you must not

Frederick Wilmot-Smith (Oxford: Hart 2015): 63–83.

do; it just does not tell you what you must do in order to avoid doing what you must not do. The supposition that this could not be enough ultimately reduces to the thought that wrongdoing is nonrelational, that the real question is whether the defendant conformed to a standard that can be specified without reference to the object of the plaintiff's right. Without that assumption, the worry that prospective guidance is insufficient disappears.

Recall Smith's formulation: The law should not "give citizens legal reasons to do things that the law clearly does not want them to do." Although that sounds very plausible in the abstract, it supposes that the law does not want to encourage people to do what they do not have reason to do.[23]

What the law of torts wants most—indeed, the only thing in which it takes any interest—is that people not wrong each other, that is, that they conduct themselves in ways consistent with each other's rights. The law wants you to stay off other people's land, even if it is convenient, prudent, or efficient to trespass, but it is silent on what you should do in order to avoid it. That is because the law is more generally silent on the steps you should take to avoid wronging others. Smith sees the same rule-of-law issue in cases of strict liability for trespass to land. Does the law of trespass "provide reasons for citizens to take extreme care—even to the point (as far as this is possible) of not acting at all"? Perhaps the point is that the law should not ask people to overinvest (by whatever measure) in locating the boundary of another person's land. But that cannot be quite right: As we saw in Chapter 3, the law of torts never cares about ease or

---

23. In criticizing the Holmesian idea that law is to be analyzed in terms of advice to the "bad man," H. L. A. Hart drew attention to some other characters who might be interested in what the law has to say, notably the "puzzled man" who is unsure what is legally required of him. Hart, *The Concept of Law*, 3rd ed., ed. Joseph Raz, Leslie Green, and Penelope A. Bulloch (Oxford: Oxford University Press, 2012), 40. Smith's analysis of duty presupposes a very specific version of Hart's puzzled man, someone who wants to know what, all things considered, he should do, and turns to the law seeking guidance. Whatever the benefits of the law providing such a service, it takes a further argument to reach the conclusion that the content of the law should be governed by the needs of the still puzzled man, the one who sees what is demanded of him but awaits instruction on how to go about complying with the demand. In the limiting case, the puzzled man may await further instruction as to how to go about complying with the instructions, and so on, *ad infinitum*.

difficulty, or about efficient resource allocation. If it did, it could not maintain the distinction between misfeasance and nonfeasance. Its sole concern is with the rights of others. The instruction that the law gives to the defendant is to stay off other people's property. That is clear and excellent prospective advice, even if not everyone always knows exactly what it demands in a specific circumstance.

Both Jansen and Smith offer what are supposed to be conceptual demonstrations, rather than inductive arguments from this settled case law. In what follows, I take up the leading cases that are supposed to establish that there is something distinctive about strict liability.

2. *Rylands*

Since it was decided, the literature has been inundated with analyses of *Rylands*. *Rylands* involved an action for damages after a newly excavated reservoir burst and flooded an adjacent coal mine. The case raised procedural problems; the initial pleadings suggested that the reservoir was defectively built, but the engineer and contractors were not parties to the litigation, and the owners were not involved in its construction.[24] In the years before the action was heard, a number of English reservoirs had burst with dire consequences, and legislation had been introduced requiring particular reservoir projects to set aside reserves to compensate those injured by them.[25] A. W. B. Simpson has suggested that *Rylands* was a case of a court stepping in to fill what it regarded as a legislative void. On this reading, it is a mirror image of the legislation introducing public compensation schemes for the unavoidable injuries that result from public health programs such as mandatory vaccination.[26] In those cases,

24. See A. W. B. Simpson, "Bursting Reservoirs and Victorian Tort Law: *Rylands and Horrocks v. Fletcher* (1868)," *Leading Cases in the Common Law* (Oxford: Oxford University Press 1995), 212.

25. Ibid.

26. Quebec introduced a statutory compensation scheme in the wake of Lapierre v. AG (Que.), 1975 1 SCR 241, in which the plaintiff was denied a remedy when his daughter developed encephalitis as an unavoidable result of a vaccination. Santé et Services Sociaux Quebec, "Québec's Compensation for Victims of Vaccination Program."

legislation steps in because no tort remedy is available; on Simpson's reading, tort law stepped in because there was no legislation.

Since Holmes, it has been fashionable to insist that when judges give reasons, they are dissembling and are actually concerned with pursuing social policy. This interpretive policy has been pursued with particular vigor in discussions of *Rylands,* but before dismissing the reasons given as a mere façade, it is worth sounding the stability of any structure that lies behind them. Simpson's references to what the judges would have recognized in the pleadings, and the role of Lord Cairns in other issues involving reservoirs, raise the possibility that the judges were bending available legal categories so as to solve what they regarded as a pressing social problem, but then hurried to hide their tracks. This historical possibility does not exclude the possibility that the courts meant what they said. Their references to animals and nuisances suggest that categories were already available, even if the appeal to them in this instance was a response to the perceived social problem. Indeed, the social problem might well have drawn their attention to the tendency of reservoirs to burst, and thus to the danger they pose to those downhill of them.

In terms of the structure outlined above, *Rylands* is a case of a wrong involving fault, as all damage-based torts must be. Indeed, the English House of Lords has recently characterized it as an unremarkable instance of the English law of nuisance, which regulates the conduct of neighboring landowners with respect to the ways in which they use their land, including the things they keep on it.[27] The specific facts of *Rylands* can be

27. Francis H. Bohlen characterizes it as "an incomplete nuisance, a nuisance as it were held in suspense, not of itself unlawful, and so preventable by legal process, or actionable until harm actually results from it." "The Rule in *Rylands v Fletcher,* Part III," *University of Pennsylvania Law Review* 59 (1911): 431. In Cambridge Water Co. v. Eastern Counties Leather plc., [1994] 2 AC 264 at 306, Lord Goff of Chieveley states: "It would . . . lead to a more coherent body of common law principles if the [*Rylands v. Fletcher*] rule were to be regarded essentially as an extension of the law of nuisance to cases of isolated escapes from land." See also the even stronger language in Lord Bingham's judgment in Transco plc. (formerly BG plc. and BG Transco plc.) v. Stockport Metropolitan Borough Council, [2003] UKHL 61: "The rule in *Rylands v. Fletcher* is a subspecies of nuisance, which is itself a tort based on the interference by one occupier of land with the right in or enjoyment of land by another occupier of land as such." In *Transco,* ¶39, Lord Hoffman notes that

accommodated under the law of nuisance, as can some of the conclusions that subsequent courts have drawn from it, notably its restriction to wrongs between neighboring owners or occupiers of land. Its significance is often said to be more general, and it is often held out as an alternative to fault-based liability, and so extended to cases with no connection to the use of land, such as the use of explosives. I will first situate it within the law of nuisance, in order to bring out the way in which a fault element figures in it. With the role of fault established, I will then turn to the extensions.

Nuisance requires damage in the form of interference with the plaintiff's ability to use and enjoy his or her land. Effects on the plaintiff's land that do not interfere with use and enjoyment—ones that do not prevent the plaintiff from using it to set his or her purposes—are not actionable, but if the plaintiff develops the land in a way that the defendant's ongoing activity subsequently harms it, the plaintiff still has a cause of action.[28]

In characterizing *Rylands* in terms of nuisance, I might be thought to be digging a deeper hole, because nuisance itself is frequently presented as a matter of strict liability. The law of nuisance appears to incorporate no test of reasonableness; it is no defense to argue that the defendant was unable to carry on his preferred activity in a way that did not create the nuisance in question.[29] The fact that the plaintiff does not need to establish the defendant's lack of care does not, however, show that no fault standards are in play. The question of fault is never whether the defendant tried hard enough, or even tried as hard as anyone could try, to moderate the effects on others of his or her preferred activity. So the question is not whether a factory of this kind on this scale could be made quieter or a rendering plant less smelly by the defendant's efforts; the only question is whether it is too noisy or smelly. In *Rylands* the plaintiff had already established this inconsistency by showing the dangerousness of the

---

since the Second World War there has been no reported English case in which someone has succeeded by arguing *Rylands*.

28. Sturges v. Bridgman, (1879) 11 Ch. D 852 (CA).

29. Rushmer v. Polsue & Alfieri, Limited, [1906] 1 Ch. 234, 250–251 per Cozens Hardy, L. J., aff'd [1907] AC 121.

defendant's reservoir, its "tendency to do mischief." Bursting was a pre-dictable result of its nature. If the defendant's particular use undermines the plaintiff's ability to use his or her land for ordinary purposes—as excessive smells, loud noises, and floods of water typically do—the defendant's conduct is at fault, even if he is morally blameless or doing his best. Water in a reservoir is "something . . . harmless to others so long as it is confined to his own property, but which he knows to be mischievous if it gets on his neighbour's."[30] Indeed, Baron Bramwell's dissent in the initial hearing explicitly characterized it as a nuisance: "The nuisance is not in the reservoir, but in the water escaping . . . the act was lawful, the mischievous consequence is a wrong."[31] Blackburn's favored analogies include "stenches," a clear reference to a familiar form of nuisance, and he cites as authority Lord Raymond's translation of the familiar *sic utere* principle from nuisance law.[32] *Keeping* things that are "known to be mischievous" if they escape is a species of fault of a piece with *doing* things that should be known to be dangerous: Both involve using things in ways that are potentially inconsistent with your neighbor's entitle-ment to have his or her means subject to his choice. The inconsistency is actionable only if actual, that is, if the danger or mischief materializes and the injury is within its ambit. This parallel between mischief and danger, understood in light of the locality in which the dispute arises, is explicitly articulated in Lord Moulton's discussion of "unnatural" uses in *Rickards v. Lothian:* "It is not every use to which land is put that brings into play that principle. It must be some special use bringing with it increased danger to others, and must not merely be the ordinary use of the land."[33]

The law of nuisance also follows other damage-based torts in de-manding damage rather than the risk of it. Cast in Lord Cairns's idiom of "unnatural" uses (among which he includes the keeping of cattle, so as

---

30. (1866) LR 1 Exch 265, 279 per Blackburn J.

31. (1865), 3 H & C 774 (Ex. D).

32. (1866) LR 1 Exch 265, 279 per Blackburn J.

33. [1913] AC 263, 280. Lord Moulton continues, "or such a use as is proper for the gen-eral benefit of the community." As Lord Bingham of Cornhill remarks in *Transco,* "little help is gained (and unnecessary confusion perhaps caused) by considering whether the use is proper for the general benefit of the community."

to emphasize the relevance of the propensity to *leave* the land), the person who *brings* something "unnatural" onto his or her own land does no wrong, because nuisance is a damage-based tort. There is no tort liability for carelessness as such, or for bringing unnatural things onto your own land. The defendant's reservoir is not subject to an injunction, even though the flooding is. So long as the water or wild animals stay put, a neighbor has no grounds for complaint, because her means are intact and no wrong has occurred. If an injunction is granted, it requires the defendant to abate the nuisance, that is, the interference with the plaintiff's land. Sometimes the only way to do so is to get rid of the animals, water, or factory in question. The law of nuisance is normally silent on *what* the defendant must do to abate it, so long as it is abated, just as the law of torts is more generally silent on what steps you must take to avoid wronging others. The wording of a specific injunction may instruct the defendant on precise measures to be taken, but the grounds of doing so are simply that those are taken to be the only measures that will bring the defendant's activity within the acceptable range.[34]

Turning to the particular facts of *Rylands*, then, the defendant is subject to a qualified duty of noninjury. It includes both a prohibition on damage and a qualification on that prohibition. Neither damage nor unusual activity is sufficient to commit a wrong; only damage through dangerous activity is. The defendant's reservoir was not wrongful in itself, but because it was "unnatural"[35] and "mischievous," the plaintiff was entitled to be free of injuries resulting from it. After it burst, the

34. An anticipatory, or *"quia timet"* ("because he fears") injunction is granted only where there is a near certainty of injury. In these cases, the "showing" of damage is done in advance through overwhelming evidence. Such injunctions are not granted for keeping unnatural objects on one's land, because it is normally not possible to show that it is overwhelmingly likely that they will escape and do mischief.

35. Lord Cairns's use of the term "unnatural" has created more difficulties than it has solved; it doesn't overlap perfectly with the tendency to cause mischief. The latter is relevant to the rights of the party, whereas the former is not, unless it is equivalent to the idea of the defendant bringing something dangerous onto his or her land, which is already presupposed in the plaintiff's claim in *Rylands*. It also has led to the thought that the defendant does not need to protect neighbors from naturally occurring hazards on his or her land that are likely to escape and cause damage to a neighbor's land. See Goldman v. Hargrave, [1967] ChC 645 (PC); Leakey & Ors v. National Trust, [1979] EWCA Civ 5 (31 July 1979).

plaintiff is entitled to damages to restore his property, just as any plaintiff in nuisance is entitled to damages for harm already done. An injunction is the normal remedy in nuisance[36] even though it is a "discretionary" remedy, so if the defendant fails to abate the nuisance, he is liable for contempt. Until an injunction is granted, damages for harm suffered are the remedy.

So understood, *Rylands* is no more about "strict liability" or "pay-as-you-go" than any other nuisance case is. It is simply about the entitlement of landowners to have their lands secure against the effects of other people's use of their land. Landowners have the liberty to use their land in ways that will affect their neighbors, but only up to a point. If they exceed their rightful use of their means, they are answerable for the damage that ensues. The scope of the defendant's liberty is measured by the increased likelihood of damage to others, not by the ease or difficulty of moderating that danger; the extent of the liability is measured by the damage done. The court's rejection of the defendant's claims that the reservoir could not be made any safer echoes other nuisance judgments of the same era.[37]

The early exemplars of strict liability were wild animals and water, which have been, since Roman law, paradigmatic examples of things that could be possessed only if properly captured.[38] In *Read v. J. Lyons*,[39] Viscount Simon emphasized the analytical significance of the tendency to escape. These historical examples do not show that this is always the best way of thinking about animals or water, and on at least some occasions broad classifications may seem silly.[40] But anything that cannot be

---

Donal Nolan argues that both of these cases read more like negligence cases; see Nolan, "The Distinctiveness of *Rylands v Fletcher*," *Law Quarterly Review* 121 (2005): 421–451.

36. Shelfer v. City of London Electrical Lighting Co., [1895] 1 Ch. 287 (CA).

37. Including the example of the Liverpool alkali works on which Blackburn J. expressly relies.

38. Percolating waters are described as *farae naturae*. See Chasemore v. Richards, 7 HL Cas. 349; Pierson v. Post, 3 Cai. R. 175, 2 Am. Dec. 264 (NY 1805). Percolating water is described in similar terms by Henshaw J. in Los Angeles v. Hunter, 156 Cal. 603 (Cal. 1909) at page 607: "underground wandering drops moving by gravity in any and every direction along the line of least resistance."

39. [1947] A. C. 156, 171, 172.

40. In Behrens v. Bertram Mills Circus, [1957] 2 QB 1, the plaintiffs were injured when a tame circus elephant was startled by a dog. Devlin J. wrote, "All animals *ferae naturae*, that

controlled is something that cannot be rendered safe in the way in which other objects can.

It might be objected that by focusing on features of nuisance I am able to explain *Rylands* at the cost of giving up on a variety of other familiar cases of strict liability that do not involve relations between neighboring landowners. The keeping of wild animals, blasting,[41] and other "ultrahazardous" activities such as the transport of gasoline[42] are subject to a strict liability standard in some jurisdictions: It is not open to the defendant to show that he or she took reasonable or even extraordinary care. Nor does the plaintiff face the burden of showing that the defendant failed to take adequate care. These cases cannot readily be assimilated to nuisance; other than coincidentally, they do not involve the interference by one landowner with a neighboring landowner's use of land.

These differences are important but go only to showing that the same general structure of damage-based torts applies differently in cases not involving land. In each case, the general structure is preserved: Explosions are like wild animals in their tendency to escape and the mischief that they cause if they do.[43] A nuisance makes land less usable; these other things are movable and can injure people as well as damaging land. As in the case of wild animals, perhaps it is a mistake to suppose that explosives simply cannot be controlled. I leave that question to others; the point is only that if they are thought of as something that cannot be

---

is, all animals which are not by nature harmless, such as a rabbit, or have not been tamed by man and domesticated, such as a horse, are conclusively presumed to have such a tendency, so that the scienter need not in their case be proved." A similar point applies to a German case in which the defendant was held liable for a leaking washing machine, even though the court conceded that a conscientious person would not sit and watch a two-year-old washing machine for its entire cycle. The basis of liability was exposing other people's property to danger; the characterization of the danger may have rested in part on the known features of water. Oberlandesgericht Düsseldorf [1975] Neue Juristische Wochenschrift 159, cited in Francesco Giglio, *The Foundations of Restitution for Wrongs* (Oxford: Hart, 2007).

41. Spano v. Perini, 250 NE 2d 31 (N.Y. 1969).

42. Siegler v. Kuhlman, 502 P 2d 1181—Wash: Supreme Court 1972.

43. In Scribner v. Kelley, (1862) 38 Barb 14 (N.Y.), there was no liability for an elephant that caused damage to the plaintiff's wagon when it frightened a horse; in Candler v. Smith, 79 S.E. 395 (Ga. App. 1935), the defendant avoided liability for an illness caused by the plaintiff's fright at seeing an escaped baboon. In each case, the loss was outside the ambit of the risk characteristically posed by the animal.

controlled, then they, too, cannot be made safe. If something cannot be made safe, questions about the precautions taken by the defendant are beside the point, so the plaintiff does not need to establish that the defendant's use of that thing was too dangerous.[44] So, too, the general feature of risk carries over to ultrahazardous activities: Something that is too dangerous is always too dangerous in some specific way, to some specific person. If it is too dangerous and the risk is realized, the injured party has been wronged, whether through personal injury, property damage, or interference with use and enjoyment of land.[45]

Some ultrahazardous activities such as the transport of gasoline and blasting for purposes of construction are socially useful.[46] This appears to mark a sharp contrast with cases in which the defendant has been negligent. Others are likely to criticize someone who was negligent, not only saying things of the form "You should have been more careful," but also in judging the defendant's conduct to be defective, quite apart from whether injury ensues. No such judgments are forthcoming in cases of the transport of gasoline or blasting for purposes of construction.

44. Allan Beever suggests that the absence of reported cases in which a plaintiff prevails by arguing *Rylands* reflects the fact that "As the law stands, some events (a) are actionable under the rule in *Rylands v Fletcher* and in nuisance but not in negligence. Perhaps other events (b) are actionable under the rule in *Rylands v Fletcher* and in negligence but not in nuisance. A third category of events (c) is actionable under the rule in *Rylands v Fletcher,* in nuisance, and in negligence. (There are no events that are actionable under the rule in *Rylands v Fletcher* alone.)" Beever, "Lord Hoffmann's Mouse," *New Zealand Business Law Quarterly* 10 (2004): 169.

45. In Burnie Port Authority v. General Jones Pty. Ltd., (1994) 179 CLR 520, the Australian High Court concluded on these grounds that *Rylands* should be absorbed into negligence. In "The Distinctiveness of Rylands v Fletcher," Donal Nolan objects to this absorption on the ground that the defendant can defeat an action under the rule in *Rylands* by showing intervening causes or an act of God, concluding that these apply because the tort in *Rylands*-type cases is "*causa* rather than *culpa.*" As we saw in Chapter 4, causation is always essential to a negligence action, and with narrow exceptions, a defendant in a negligence action is not responsible for an act of others; neither an act of God nor an act of a human being is within the ambit of the risk that makes conduct dangerous.

46. Gregory C. Keating, "Recovering *Rylands:* An Essay for Robert Rabin," *DePaul Law Review* 61 (2012): 543–594; John Murphy, "The Merits of *Rylands v Fletcher,*" *Oxford Journal of Legal Studies* 24 (2004): 643–669.

This difference is difficult to deny, but it needs to be contextualized. A social norm requires people engaging in dangerous activities to take steps to make those activities safer. The distinction between behaving safely and unsafely applies *within* ultrahazardous activities such as gasoline transport or blasting.[47] But unlike other commonplace activities such as agriculture, manufacturing, and transportation, any such distinction has no legal bearing in the case of ultrahazardous activities. Even the most conscientious user of explosives is doing something that is riskier than ordinary activities; more and less unsafe ways of handling explosives or keeping wild animals can be distinguished without supposing any of them safe enough. It seems peculiar to suggest that ordinary people disapprove of negligence because they regard it as too risky but that abnormal danger or ultrahazardous activity is not too risky.

In Chapter 4 we encountered arguments pointing to the disproportion between minor culpability and massive liability. Those arguments do not show what they purport to, but they rest on the correct belief that negligence can be minor but still culpable. Failure to shoulder check while operating a motor vehicle is negligent because dangerous,[48] enough to be subject to a public law regulatory prohibition, but it is less obviously blameworthy. If someone is injured through dangerous conduct, the injury is actionable because the conduct was dangerous, even if it was not blameworthy. It is only if the basis of liability is thought to be some form of moral condemnation, punishment, or sanction that it looks as though there is anything exceptional about regarding the realization of a substantial risk as wrongful.

This is not to deny that in many cases of negligence both the plaintiff and third parties are likely to think that the defendant should have been more careful, and in some cases in which courts have held liability to be strict, few would say any such thing. But this contrast does not map neatly

47. Emergency workers sometimes conduct controlled explosions when ordnance is found; sadly, not all end safely.

48. A study from 1970 reported: "In Washington, D.C., a 'good' driver viz. one without an accident within the preceding five years, commits on average, in five minutes of driving, at least nine errors of different kinds." U.S. Department of Transportation, *Automobile Insurance and Compensation Study, 1970*, pp. 177–178, quoted in Tony Honoré, *Responsibility and Fault* (Oxford: Hart, 1999), 36–37, n. 42.

onto the division between cases in which the plaintiff must prove a lack of care on the defendant's part and those in which the plaintiff has no such a burden. If your wild animal escapes and wreaks havoc, it does not seem at all out of place to be confronted with words like "What was the matter with you? What kind of person keeps a lion in the city?"[49] By contrast, when someone is momentarily distracted and loses control of a vehicle or piece of heavy equipment, people may hesitate to judge him or her harshly.

The failure of the excessive risk and culpability to line up perfectly is unsurprising: In many situations of injury and loss, the defendant's conduct might be defective on a number of different dimensions, not all of which are relevant to the law. The person who does something dangerous may display flaws of character, such as lack of attention, self-absorption, indifference, and so on. That such defects may be on display in a particular case is largely a matter of inference, but in so many cases the facts may seem to speak for themselves. Moreover, when the plaintiff must establish the defendant's lack of care, flaws in the defendant's conduct may be more conspicuous. It may be that there is more disapproval of the conduct of the person who is cavalier about obvious risks than of the one who is conscientious but still messes up. But the latter is just as liable, because, as Holmes put it, he is "no less troublesome to his neighbors."[50]

Put differently, the word "fault" does not refer to the failure to conform to a social norm of noninjuriousness, and the defendant is not held liable because of the failure to meet social expectations. Instead, in damage-based torts, fault is a defect in the defendant's conduct, namely, acting in a way that is too dangerous with respect to the type of injury suffered. If you injure another by doing something that carries a greater than background risk of injury to the person or property of others, you are liable

---

49. "What kind of person?" in the conversation imagined above is not asked in a spirit of curiosity. Those who are curious might consult the book *A Lion Called Christian: The True Story of the Remarkable Bond between Two Friends and a Lion,* by Anthony Bourke and John Rendall, with a forward by George Adamson (New York: Random House, 1971), which tells the story of two men who bought a lion at Harrods department store in London (Harrods had acquired it from a defunct zoo) and kept it in their home and furniture store in London. Later it was reintroduced to the wild.

50. Oliver Wendell Holmes Jr., *The Common Law* (Boston: Little, Brown, 1881), 108.

because you have wronged that person by interfering with what he or she already has.

In *Donoghue*, Lord Atkin suggested that liability for negligence can be treated ("as in other systems")[51] as a species of "culpa," based upon "the general public sentiment of moral wrongdoing for which the offender must pay."[52] The wrong, however, is not the wrong of failing to *attend to* the safety of others; it is the wrong of injuring another through inappropriately dangerous conduct. As I suggested in Chapter 4, the respect in which negligent conduct is defective is that it is more dangerous than is acceptable as part of a system in which everyone is entitled to use what he or she already has. The same point carries over to other damage-based torts, including the ones that are typically characterized as cases of strict liability.

Against the background of this understanding of private wrongs, the suggestion that cases like *Rylands,* or the wild animal or blasting cases, do not involve the violation of the plaintiff's right is deeply puzzling. The plaintiff's entitlement is that others use what is theirs in a way that is consistent with everyone's security in what he or she already has. The person who damages the body or property of another by engaging in activities that are more likely than ordinary activities to do so is the paradigm of someone who wrongs another. This is so regardless of how useful the defendant's conduct is, and also of whether the defendant's conduct

51. See, for example, the Quebec Civil Code, Art. 1457 (2002 c. 19 s 15), which specifies that "every person has a duty to abide by the rules of conduct which lie upon him, according to the circumstances, usage or law, so as not to cause injury to another. Where he is endowed with reason and fails in this duty, he is responsible for any injury he causes to another person by such fault and is liable to reparation for the injury, whether it be bodily, moral or material in nature." The key concept is that of "abiding" by the rules of conduct; fault consists in failing to do so, and so necessarily connotes moral blame. See St. Lawrence Cement Inc. v. Barrette, [2008] 3 SCR 392, 2008 SCC 64, ¶34-35. By contrast, what the common law would characterize as nuisance is covered in Art. 976 (1991, c 64, a 976): "Neighbours shall suffer the normal neighbourhood annoyances that are not beyond the limit of tolerance they owe each other, according to the nature or location of their land or local custom." The latter formulation turns on reciprocal restraint. For the purposes of this chapter, it is defective because inconsistent, even if the person who commits the wrong is morally innocent in doing so.

52. Donoghue v. Stevenson, [1932] UKHL 100.

is forbidden or subject to social censure independently of whether it violates a right.

3. I Could Have Told You *Vincent*

Vincent is frequently presented as an unusual case of strict liability. Sometimes it is introduced as though it is so unusual that it needs to be explained away and reconciled with the more general fault-based structure of tort law. Other times, it enters as a sort of Trojan horse, showing that the pay-as-you-go principle is just as much at home in tort law as the fault principle. It is sometimes paired with *Rylands,* with the aim of showing that other actual or recommended areas of strict liability—most notably, products liability—are a natural development of a firmly rooted legal tradition. Still other times it is treated as a case in which the defendant is required to pay the price he would have agreed to had he been able to contract with the plaintiff under less urgent conditions.[53] But in almost every case it is treated as an example of the defendant needing to pay for the damage occasioned by perfectly faultless and reasonable behavior. It also has its share of detractors who deny that its result can be squared with the rest of the law.[54] *Vincent's* friends and foes alike start with the idea that it is a case of liability without wrongdoing.[55]

53. Landes and Posner focuses on the contract the parties "would have made had they had the opportunity to negotiate." William M. Landes and Richard A. Posner, "Salvors, Finders, Good Samaritans, and Other Rescuers: An Economic Study of Law and Altruism," *Journal of Legal Studies* 7 (1978): 113n74. Jules Coleman follows Robert Keeton's focus on the "conditional fault" of receiving a benefit but not paying for it: see Coleman, *Risks and Wrongs* (Cambridge: Cambridge University Press, 1992), 282; and Keeton, "Conditional Fault."

54. Stephen D. Sugarman, "The 'Necessity' Defense and the Failure of Tort Theory: The Case against Strict Liability for Damages Caused while Exercising Self-Help in an Emergency," *Issues in Legal Scholarship* 5 (2005), Article 1; George C. Christie, "The Unwarranted Conclusions Drawn from *Vincent v. Lake Erie Transportation Co.* concerning the Defense of Necessity," *Issues in Legal Scholarship* 6 (2006): Article 7.

55. As Mark Geistfeld puts it, "The cases of necessity are so infrequent . . . Nevertheless, the doctrine has foundational importance because it involves liability without fault." Geistfeld, "Necessity and the Logic of Strict Liability," *Issues in Legal Scholarship* 5 (2005): Article 5.

Gregory Keating's treatment of *Vincent* exemplifies the temptation to treat it as an example of some broader role of strict liability.[56] Keating begins with the question of the reasonableness of the defendant's conduct. Because leaving the dock in the storm would endanger his ship, it is, he suggests, reasonable to damage the dock. Because the boat owner benefits from his use of the dock, Keating takes it to be an example of a more general form of strict liability: "*Rylands v. Fletcher* and strict liability in the law of intentional nuisance are all cut from the same cloth as *Vincent*. Strict liability in all three cases is rooted in the same idea of fairness—in the idea that the bitter should be taken with the sweet."[57]

As I have argued above, "wrong" and "fault" are not synonymous; only damage-based torts require fault, in the sense of excessive danger; trespass against another's property is wrongful no matter how careful the defendant is. The defendant's conduct in *Vincent* may be faultless, but without more, it does not follow that it is not wrongful. Nor does it follow that the defendant's conduct would be faulty if he failed to pay. Instead, the basis of liability is a legal wrong of trespass. Failure to attend to the distinction between use and damage obscures the straightforward way in which liability is consistent with a privilege.

On its facts *Vincent* is a strange candidate for the supposed importance of liability without wrongdoing. The defendant does not damage the plaintiff's dock in the process of doing something else; he damages it in the process of *using* it. *Vincent* is, at least in the first instance, a trespass case. Under Minnesota law at the time, the dock would be considered a part of the plaintiff's land, so the case is one of trespass to land.[58] Liability for damage in trespass is strict, because the defendant has no entitlement to use the plaintiff's property.

These features of *Vincent* are removed from view by two prevalent Holmesian ideas: First, that, despite its abundance of moral language, tort law is about harms rather than wrongs.[59] Unless "harm" is just an um-

---

56. Gregory C. Keating, "Property Rights and Tortious Wrong in *Vincent v. Lake Erie*," *Issues in Legal Scholarship* 5 (2005): Article 6.

57. Ibid., 7.

58. On this point see John C. P. Goldberg, Anthony J. Sebok, and Benjamin C. Zipursky, *Tort Law: Responsibilities and Redress* (New York: Aspen, 2004), 768.

59. Holmes, *The Common Law*, 79.

brella term for any violation of any legal interest—in which case Holmes's stark comment turns out to be as empty as the *sic utere* principle he dismisses as a "yearning"—harm is a distinctive candidate for the object of tort law precisely because a harm can be identified without reference to the character of the act that brought it about. I may be liable only if I was negligent in breaking your vase, but the harm in question—a broken vase—is what it is, quite apart from any question about how it broke. Once scholarly gaze is firmly fixed on harm, trespass looks like any other harmful activity, so that whatever relevance fault has in relation to harm elsewhere, it should have in relation to harm in *Vincent*. It is no surprise, then, that some defenders of negligence liability dislike *Vincent*, and those who advocate an expanded range for strict liability hope to ride in its wake.

Second, the structure of the trespass in *Vincent* is obscured further by inappropriate focus on whether the defendant's conduct was "reasonable." Reasonable care is central to the tort of negligence, because negligence is a damage-based tort, and the relevant qualification on the duty of noninjury requires potential injurers to reduce the dangers of their activities to an acceptable level. In *Vincent*, however, the question of whether to stay moored or put out in the storm is a question of the defendant's prudence, not of whether the risk to the plaintiff's dock was minimized.[60]

Rather than asking about reasonableness, the court flatly rejects the plaintiff's contention that "it was negligence to moor the boat at an exposed part of the wharf, and to continue in that position after it became apparent that the storm was to be more than usually severe." The stated reasons are not the reasonableness of preferring boat to dock, but rather that "the storm which made it unsafe was one which surpassed in violence any which might have reasonably been anticipated"—that is, that the danger to the dock was unforeseeable in what would "be considered a proper and safe place, and would undoubtedly have been such during what would be considered a very severe storm." The plaintiff's allegation of negligence fails, then, because the likelihood of damage was low enough that the failure to take steps to alleviate it could not be negligent.

---

60. The Learned Hand formula discussed in Chapter 4 for determining liability exacerbates this confusion, because it take the word "reasonable" to mean "efficient," and so entails damage without liability.

Rather than focusing on negligence, the court considered whether the ship's master had adequate grounds for believing that staying moored was the only way to save his ship, which it took to be relevant to the analysis of an incomplete privilege to trespass on the land of another. The words of the majority opinion are significant here: "The record in this case fully sustains the contention of the appellant that, in holding the vessel fast to the dock, those in charge of her exercised good judgment and prudent seamanship."[61] That finding has no bearing on the usual questions about *Vincent:* whether the defendant stood to gain more than the plaintiff would likely lose, whether he imposed a nonreciprocal risk, or whether people who act for their own gain must always indemnify those who lose as a result. If any of these putative principles are adopted, they quickly overwhelm the defendant's claim to a privilege to stay, making it irrelevant to the analysis. Indeed, they wash away the entire distinction between misfeasance and nonfeasance, because they are focused on outcomes rather than rights. The court's conclusion about "good judgment and prudent seamanship" concedes the defendant's characterization of the entire episode as a rescue operation. The court takes that characterization to show only that the plaintiff had no right to expel the defendant's boat. Again, the majority's hypothetical in which the defendant "appropriated a valuable cable lying upon the dock" speaks not in terms of damaging what belongs to another, but of using it to preserve one's own property. The hypothetical cable's owner could not have blocked the defendant's use of it, but the defendant would still need to pay for it.

The question of the defendant's prudence is put forward, then, as relevant only to his entitlement to stay put. The court makes this point through its discussion of cases in which the absence of a positive obligation to aid does not entitle someone to remove another from a position of safety into the path of danger. In *Depue v. Flatau,*[62] the plaintiff fell ill, suffering fainting spells while conducting business in the defendant's home. The negotiations did not go well, and the defendant placed the plaintiff in a cutter with a team of horses and sent him out into the Minnesota winter night. The plaintiff fainted again, fell off the cutter, and was

61. *Vincent v. Lake Erie Transportation Co.*, 458.

62. Depue v. Flatau, 100 Minn. 299, 304; 111 NWI (1907).

found in the morning nearly frozen to death. In *Ploof v. Putnam*,[63] the plaintiff attempted to moor his boat at the defendant's dock in a storm, but the defendant's representative unmoored it, as a result of which it suffered serious damage from the storm. Had the plaintiff in *Depue* not been ill, the defendant would have been entitled to ask him to leave; had the weather been better, the defendant in *Ploof* would have been entitled to send the boat out into the lake. In discussing each of these examples, the court takes it as established that the plaintiff has a right to stay put, and asks what follows from that entitlement. In *Vincent* itself, the task for the court is to explain the defendant's entitlement to stay put in a way that integrates with the plaintiff's property right in the dock but does not overwhelm it, and with it the distinction between misfeasance and nonfeasance.

Any entitlement to stay put must come from the storm itself. It is not clear whether the court accepts the claim that an emergency "suspends the ordinary rules of property,"[64] or only the defendant's more modest claim that in the circumstances the plaintiff could not force the defendant to leave. The cases the court cites are directly relevant to the latter claim (though they might be awkwardly expressed in terms of the former.) The rule that could be described as suspended in this case is the basic rule of property, the right to exclude: In an emergency, the plaintiff is not entitled to exclude the defendant from his dock. The court cites *Ploof v. Putnam* as authority for this proposition. *Ploof* is not about a general suspension of property rights, but only about the right to forcibly exclude in an emergency. The court in *Ploof*, in turn, relies on *Proctor v. Adams*,[65] a case in which one person enters another's land to retrieve property.[66]

63. Ploof v. Putnam, 81 Vt. 471, 71 A. 188 (1908).

64. In their torts casebook, Goldberg, Sebok, and Zipursky suggest that the famous sentence about suspension of property rights is a "scrivener's error," and in fact the word "If" should precede it. See Goldberg et al., *Tort Law*, 768. Their grammatical reconstruction of the sentence is plausible, and would reduce the bold claim that property rights are suspended to the paler one that if they were suspended, there would be no liability. Yet the judgment does presuppose that at least one aspect of the property right is suspended, as do the references to the other cases in which the defendant is held liable for expelling the plaintiff in bad weather.

65. 113 Mass. 376, 18 Am. Rep. 500.

66. The court also cites Mouse's Case 77 England, Rep. 1341, in which the plaintiff fails to recover from the defendant who threw his goods overboard to save his own life. *Mouse's*

If I enter your land to retrieve my own property, the rules of property aren't exactly suspended—they already contain the exemption. If a fleeing thief throws my wallet onto your lawn,[67] I may enter your land to retrieve it. My entitlement to do so has nothing to do with the reasonableness of my doing so on the particular occasion, or the fact that wallet retrieval is a low-risk activity, or even of people retrieving chattels more generally from the land of others. Instead, it has a systematic basis in the law of property.

Exclusive rights to property in land can form a mutually consistent set: Each of us is required to refrain from entering the land of others or conducting activities on our own land that interfere with the ability of others to use their land. People also have property in chattels, that is, in movable objects. In both cases the normative structure of the property right is the same: The owner has the right to exclude other private persons from using the land or chattel, and has a right that others refrain from damaging it in certain specified ways. Despite the parallel normative structure, property rights in land and in chattels do not automatically form a consistent set, because my chattel can find its way onto your land. If it does, your right to exclude me from your land would prevent me from being able to use my property, while my right to my property would prevent you from being able to use it, or even to remove it from your land. The way to render property in immovable objects consistent with property in movable objects is incomplete privilege: You can touch my

---

Case does not establish a right of necessity to preserve property; indeed, it presupposes the opposite rule. It holds that, because life is at stake, the defendant's action is not covered under the law of jettison, which demands proportionate payment from those whose property is preserved by destruction of the property of others. Thus, the law of jettison presupposes a close relative of the principle in *Vincent:* if you use another's property to preserve your own, the other must be compensated.

67. Or an animal drops it there. By contrast, I cannot give myself a privilege by *placing* my chattel on your land, because doing so in the first place would already be a trespass. In The Case of the Thorns, (1466) YB 6 Ed 4, 7a pl 18, the defendant committed a trespass when he entered the plaintiff's land to retrieve thorns that had fallen when he trimmed his hedge, but the court also held that had they arrived through no act of his, he would be permitted to enter his neighbor's land to recover them. See also the discussion in Millen v. Fawdry, (1662) Latch 119, 82 E.R. 304. The entitlement to enter another person's land to recover property is an incident of a system in which each person is free to use his or her property to set and pursue his or her purposes independently of the others. In a situation in which I use my property to generate an entitlement to enter your land, our acts are not independent.

wallet without my authorization to remove it from your land, or I can enter your land to retrieve it. The only alternative would make my wallet a *res nullius,* something that nobody could rightfully use.[68]

In this example, landowner and wallet owner each have an incomplete privilege: Landowner can remove the wallet (without damaging it or putting it in a place of danger or where it constitutes a hazard to others), and wallet owner can enter landowner's land to retrieve it. If landowner removes it and returns it to its owner, he can demand that his expenses be covered, because he is providing a benefit which wallet owner freely accepts. Wallet owner cannot compel landowner to remove it, but he can enter the land to retake possession of it. But the analysis does not turn on the fact that landowner and wallet owner are symmetrically situated; if, as on the facts of *Proctor v. Adams,* I need to cross your land in order to retrieve my property from a public beach at low tide, I am also entitled to do so.[69]

Parallel reasoning underlies the judgment in *Depue v. Flatau:* The plaintiff's own person is movable, but in order to preserve himself, that is, to have his person continue to be subject to his choice, he is entitled to stay in a location of safety.[70] In *Ploof v. Putnam,* the same principle is extended to the case where a person brings himself and his property to a location of safety. *Depue* concerns the plaintiff's own safety; *Ploof* extends to the plaintiff's vessel the right to remain in a safe place. The court does not consider the possibility that the defendant's servants might have taken the passengers off the boat and sent the empty vessel out into the storm; *Procter v. Adams* restricts a landowner's right to separate an owner from his or her movable property. If the right to exclude others from your land (including your dock) (1) does not entitle you to remove another person

---

68. In Miller v. Jackson [1977] QB 966, Lord Denning offers a different description of the law in the nineteenth century, contending that a chattel on another's land would be *res nullius.*

69. The fact that land is being used is pivotal to the analysis. As a result, it generalizes to some of the favorite examples in the literature, including the person who breaks into a cabin to save himself in a storm. It does not, however, apply to all examples: e.g., Jules Coleman's example of the person who uses another's medicine would not be covered under this analysis. See Coleman, *Risks and Wrongs,* 293.

70. In the case of a human body, the formal possibility of leaving it as *res nullius* does not arise because it cannot be physically separate from the person whose body it is.

from a place of safety into an ongoing peril, and also (2) does not allow you to separate an owner from his or her movable property, then it also (3) does not entitle you to remove the passengers from an imperiled boat and send it out into the storm.

Vincent integrates both of these to cover the case in which the defendant is entitled to keep his property subject to his choice by bringing it to a place of safety. The dock owner's general right to exclude does not carry with it the power to specifically enforce it when the plaintiff's boat is in danger. The problem is also the same; if the dock owner's property right entitles him to separate the boat from its owner, then the boat is not only likely to perish, but it is likely to perish because the dock owner's property right prevents the boat owner from bringing the boat under his control. The dock owner's right to exclude cannot entitle him to separate the boat from its owner (or owner's representative) or, what comes to the same thing, to give the owner the choice of staying on the boat as it is sent off into the storm.

The principle in the cases of displaced and endangered objects shows the sense in which the boat owner in *Vincent* has an "incomplete privilege" to commit a trespass, that is, to use the plaintiff's dock without his authorization. But it is a privilege only to use the dock to preserve his property, not to do anything further.[71]

The existence of the privilege blocks the plaintiff's entitlement to forcibly exclude the defendant, by cutting the ropes that are fixing the boat (even if they were the plaintiff's own) or pushing the boat away, or preventing the plaintiff from securing it if the cables part. Precisely because the privilege suspends the plaintiff's power to exclude, the plaintiff is not entitled to nominal damages for the defendant's entry to the plaintiff's land. Despite the suspension of the plaintiff's power to exclude, the defendant's use of the dock is nonetheless inconsistent with the plaintiff's entitlement to determine the purposes for which it will be used. That is the sense in which the privilege is incomplete.

---

71. In this, it differs from the complete privilege in cases of public necessity. If a public road is blocked due to bad weather, you are entitled to cross private property in order to get where you are going, regardless of the reason you are going there or the urgency of your getting there. You are not liable for any damage that you cause.

In both the wallet example and *Vincent,* the privilege is not consensual; the law mandates it. That mandate is not usefully modeled on a consensual transaction; the plaintiff needs to permit the defendant to use the dock, but the defendant's use of it does not thereby become one of the plaintiff's purposes. The plaintiff does not cease to be entitled to determine the purposes for which the dock is used; he just cannot do anything to enforce his right. But it does not follow that the right disappears.

On this understanding, *Vincent* is a case in which the defendant's act to preserve his property privileges his use of the plaintiff's land without the plaintiff's authorization. The defendant's purpose defines the privilege, but does not thereby become the plaintiff's purpose in a way that would cancel the plaintiff's right as against the defendant, to have his property intact. Because the defendant is using the plaintiff's land for a purpose that the plaintiff has not authorized, it is a trespass, for which no fault standard applies, so the defendant must pay for the damage he does, just as I must pay if I trample your flowers in the process of entering your land without your authorization. The defendant cannot be prevented from using the dock, but it must be returned at the end of that use in the condition in which it was prior to the use.[72]

The structure differs from that of a bailment in which one person is in possession of another's property whether by loan or involuntarily, as, for example, when a package is delivered to the wrong address. Bailees are subject to a standard of reasonable care because, although in involuntary bailments a bailor does not authorize the bailee's possession of the object, the bailee is still deemed to be keeping it on the bailor's behalf. The preservation of the object is a purpose that the bailor is deemed to have authorized as his or her own purpose; that is why the bailee's possession is not conversion. By contrast, if I use your property to retrieve or preserve my own, I am not acting for your purpose.[73]

---

72. In Munn & Co. v. M/V Sir John Crosbie, [1967] 1 Ex. Ct. R 94, the facts were substantially similar to those of *Vincent,* with one difference that the court held to be significant: in *Vincent,* the defendant's employees reattached the boat when its lines parted; in *Munn* the lines held fast. The court took this difference to be dispositive, because they interpreted the ship's master as doing nothing in the storm; the use of the dock was already complete. The question of how to individuate acts of dock use gets no answer from the category of using another's property to preserve your own, though a system of positive law must make some decision.

73. Coggs v. Bernard, (1703) 2 Ld Raym 909, 92 ER 107.

Although the privilege applies only in situations in which someone is entering another's land in order to recover or preserve a chattel, this does not constitute an exception to tort law's general indifference to the ends for which a person is acting. Instead, the analysis goes in the opposite direction: The class of cases in which your exclusion of another person would separate that person from his or her chattels is extensionally equivalent to the class of cases in which that person is acting in order to retrieve or preserve them. But the analysis is driven by the need to reconcile a landowner's right to exclude with a chattel owner's right to have the chattel subject to his or her choice, not by the owner's purpose of retrieval.

On this analysis, then, the basis of liability in this case is that the defendant's conduct is inconsistent with the plaintiff's right, even though the plaintiff is not entitled to do anything to prevent it. The damage is privileged, rather than licensed subject to a condition. Any appeal to a conditional permission would require an explanation of the source of the condition. I have proposed such an explanation. If no such account is successful, the condition remains inexplicable; if it does succeed, the idea of conditional fault repackages the result without explaining it. So there is no point in saying that the use of the dock is rendered permissible by the payment, so that if the boat owner was insolvent there would be no such permission, but provided sufficient liquidity or insurance, there is.

Vincent is sometimes described as a case of a private power of eminent domain.[74] The analysis offered here explains both why this is a mischaracterization and why it might have some initial appeal; it is a mischaracterization because the use of the plaintiff's dock is for the defendant's private purpose, and not for a public purpose. Scholars and courts disagree about how broadly the idea of a public purpose is to be construed—whether it includes acquiring land to sell to another owner who will increase the municipal tax base.[75] But preserving someone's private property is not even a candidate.

---

74. Francis H. Bohlen, "Incomplete Privilege to Inflict Intentional Invasions of Interests of Property and Personality," *Harvard Law Review* 39 (1926): 307–324.

75. Kelo v. City of New London, 545 U.S. 469 (2005).

4. Benefits and Burdens

Francis Bohlen characterized *Vincent* as a case in which "it is obviously just that he whose interests are advanced by the act should bear the cost of doing it rather than that he should be permitted to impose it upon one who derives no benefit from the act."[76] The principle to which Bohlen appeals does not generally apply in either law or morality, and he offers no account of why it should apply in the specific case. Rivalrous activities— including market competition—often have the structure of one person benefiting at another's expense, but require no indemnification. Nor can this case be isolated from those on the grounds that market competition is generally advantageous, for so, too, is salvage in a storm. Although the defendant's interests are advanced by the act, he would be liable even if his ship had been lost in spite of his efforts.

Thus the fact that the defendant benefited at the plaintiff's expense does not underwrite a more general claim that anyone who benefits from using their own means must bear the burdens that creates for another. It is not a claim about some sort of ideal matching of benefits and burdens at all. Unfortunately, many scholars have sought to elevate Bohlen's claim to a broader principle of private law. The economic version of this pro- posed principle focuses on cost internalization—those who create costs through their activities should bear them. More recently, Gregory Keating has offered a fairness-based rationale for the same set of ideas.[77]

Keating echoes Holmes's confident announcement of the transition from a world in which the injuries that occupy courts are the result of iso- lated "acts" to a world in which they are the predictable result of the re- alization of the hazards accompanying ongoing "activities."[78] Despite this change in what courts find in their dockets, a tort action still focuses on the particular transaction between a particular plaintiff and a particular defendant. If this focus on individuals is thought to belong in Holmes's catalogue of "revolting" holdovers from the time of Henry VIII,[79] it is

76. Bohlen, "Incomplete Privilege."

77. Keating, "Property Rights and Tortious Wrong."

78. Gregory C. Keating, "The Idea of Fairness in the Law of Enterprise Liability," *Mich- igan Law Review* 95 (1997): 1266–1380.

79. Oliver Wendell Holmes Jr., "The Path of the Law," *Harvard Law Review* 10, no. 8 (Mar. 25, 1897): 469.

worth noticing the substantial obstacles to any account of the relevant benefits and burdens or the parties who are to be treated fairly.

The core of the difficulty is that, as a general matter, no moral or legal principle requires those who receive benefits to bear associated burdens. No such principle of cost internalization can be found in private law. I may reap a benefit from your beautiful landscaping, in the form of a higher resale value for my neighboring house, but I do not need to help you cover your costs. You can open a business that competes with mine, without indemnifying me for the loss I suffer. You can build a tower that casts a shadow over my beach and cabana area, effectively drawing sun-seeking visitors away from my premises to yours, again, without needing to compensate me. These are all cases in which someone gets a sweet outcome, leaving others to swallow the bitterness that results.

The converse cases are just as familiar. If I damage your property, I am liable even if, as it turns out, I gain nothing from the act or activity that caused the damage. Circuses and game farms keep wild animals in order to make money, but the law does not treat them any differently from keepers of expensive exotic pets. Instead, it ignores any questions of whether they gain, or expect to, and focus only on the danger the animals pose *to others*. The same point applies to keeping unnatural bodies of water: A swimming pool or reservoir generates liability if it bursts, even though it makes my land less valuable. Transporting gasoline provides many benefits, but the same standard of liability would apply to someone who was engaged in purely recreational transport of gasoline, or to hijackers transporting stolen gasoline. The usefulness of the ordinary commercial transport of gasoline may enter into an explanation of why there is no public law prohibiting doing so, but it does not explain why transport without incident raises no issues of private rights. There are no issues in such cases because no right is violated; when a right is violated, questions of liability arise, but not otherwise. The basis of such liability is the propensity of large quantities of gasoline to explode, no matter how carefully it is transported. In this gasoline is not only like beneficial explosives used for blasting, but also like fireworks, which many jurisdictions treat as "inherently and abnormally dangerous"[80] quite apart

80. Klein v. Pyrodyne Corp., 810 P. 2d 917 (Wash. 1991).

from any inquiry into whether fireworks displays are a cooperative activity from which everyone benefits, but from which some bear a disproportionate cost.

In cases in which the defendant uses the plaintiff's property without consent, the defendant can be made to surrender his gains, to grant sweetness to the plaintiff, and swallow bitterness all on his own. If I convert your property, taking your coat home with me, I must return it to you, even though I got no benefit from my wasted effort. Or rather, the only way to squeeze a benefit out of my effort is by supposing that the relevant benefit is getting to do what I have decided to do, by having means subject to my choice. But that description deprives the idea of paying because you reap a benefit of any content, because unless the benefit is construed narrowly in terms of using what belongs to another, it fits everything anyone has done in the history of the world.

In each of these cases, the relevant questions focus on the respective rights of the parties. What the defendant stands to gain by so doing, or what similarly situated people stand to gain by so doing does not enter into the legal analysis. Once the rights of the parties are identified, any defendant who is liable can be represented as having received some benefit—most notably the benefit of getting to use his or her means to set and pursue his or her own purposes, whatever they might be. To do so, however, is to reduce talk about benefits and burdens to nothing more than a format in which claims about rights are stated.

5. Conclusion

The appearance that negligence and strict liability differ is an artifact of supposing that the negligence inquiry must be some form of cost–benefit analysis. Once that supposition is accepted, some cases—at least the transport of gasoline, if not every keeping of a reservoir, swimming pool, or wild animal—pass the test of cost–benefit analysis, and so qualify as reasonable, making the imposition of liability in such cases call out for some other explanation. In Chapter 4 we saw the difficulties with this as a representation of negligence. Here we have seen some of the ways in which the same ideas are prone to do mischief if they escape.

CHAPTER 6

A Malicious Wrong in Its Strict Legal Sense

Motive and Intention in Tort Law

I HAVE ARGUED IN PREVIOUS CHAPTERS that tort law presents itself as a doctrine concerning the means a person may use, and the side effects of those uses on others. Use-based torts involve one person using (knowingly or otherwise) something that belongs to another; the damage-based torts of negligence and nuisance concern the side effects of one person's activity on another. In both types of cases, what the defendant was trying to achieve is irrelevant; the law focuses exclusively on what the defendant was doing, either using or touching something belonging to another, or damaging something belonging to another in the course of doing something else.

In a small but significant class of cases, the law appears to focus instead on the defendant's motive, and to hold the defendant liable for a result that would attract no liability if done as a side effect of something else. My aim in this chapter is to argue that although these cases are in one way exceptional, they are finally still about the use of means, rather than ends or motives.

I will make this point through an example that raises the issues in a clear way, and only later go on to argue that it is representative of a much broader range of cases. In *Hollywood Silver Fox Farm v. Emmett*,[1] the

---

1. [1936] 2 KB 468.

defendant was in the process of building a housing estate; his neighbor, a fox farmer, had a sign that he feared would make the homes he hoped to sell less desirable. Today "Hollywood Silver Fox Farm" would probably be the name of the new subdivision, but in the early part of the last century, the defendant thought otherwise, so he asked the plaintiff to take it down. The plaintiff declined. The defendant decided to put pressure on the plaintiff. Vixens are skittish, and if they are disturbed, they will refuse to breed, miscarry, or kill their young. The defendant instructed his son to discharge firearms near the boundary between the two plots of land. Ordinarily the plaintiff's specific use of his land would count as unusually sensitive, and he would have no legal standing to complain about the level of noise the defendant created. This case seems to be different, and at least one difference is easy to identify: The defendant intended to interfere with the plaintiff.

Hollywood relies on the earlier case of *Christie v. Davey*,[2] in which the defendant was exasperated by the sound of his neighbor regularly playing and teaching music. He resorted to playing loud music of his own and banging pans against the walls when she was playing, so as to disrupt her lessons.[3] The defendant had no hope of claiming the plaintiff was creating a nuisance; the music was louder than suited his work as an engraver, but not louder than ordinary use in the locality in which the parties lived. Nonetheless, the defendant was annoyed, and took the matter into his own hands. We may assume that the volume of noise created by the defendant's shooting in *Hollywood* and the defendant's banging in *Christie* was not enough, with regard to either its volume or frequency, to qualify as an actionable interference with the ordinary use of the neighboring land. In *Christie,* North J. says, "If what has taken place had occurred between two sets of persons, both perfectly innocent, I should have taken an entirely different view of the case."[4] Nonetheless, in both cases the court found for the plaintiff. The language in *Hollywood* characterizes the nature of the wrong in the following terms: "Any right which the law gives him is qualified by the condition that it must not be exercised to the nuisance of his neighbors or of the public. If he violates

---

2. (1893) 1 Ch 316.

3. *The Spectator,* December 17, 1892, 11.

4. (1893) 1 Ch 316, 326.

that condition he commits a legal wrong, and if he does so intentionally he is guilty of 'a malicious wrong, in its strict legal sense.' "[5] The puzzle raised by this case is what exactly constitutes that strict legal sense.[6]

There are many other torts that seem to invite a similar puzzle, in which the defendant performs an act that would ordinarily be acceptable if its effects on the plaintiff were a side effect of its performance, but where the effects are made wrongful in a further and distinctive sense by some other feature of the defendant's action. Some of these cases are characterized in terms of "disinterested malice," though, as we shall see, such a characterization seems to reproduce whatever problems it is supposed to address. My main focus in developing my argument will be on cases of "malicious wrong in its strict legal sense." Nuisance cases may not be fully representative of all wrongs in which motive and intent appear to be at issue, but they bring the analytical structure out particularly clearly, because they present the malicious defendant with a chance of injuring the plaintiff without ever touching the plaintiff's person or property, and so without committing an uncontroversial wrong of trespass.

1. Do Ends Matter to Private Rights?

In order to isolate the question, and to characterize the puzzle that cases of this sort generate for an account of tort law that focuses exclusively on

5. *Hollywood*, quoting Allen v. Flood, [1898] AC 1, 102, where Lord Watson is discussing Keeble v. Hickeringill, (1707) 11 East 574, 103 ER 1127. Lord Watson continues, "The object of an act, that is, the results which will necessarily or naturally follow from the circumstances in which it is committed, may give it a wrongful character, but it ought not to be confounded with the motive of the actor. To discharge a loaded gun is, in many circumstances, a perfectly harmless proceeding; to fire it on the highway, in front of a restive horse, might be a very different matter."

6. Many cases and commentators refer to Bayley J.'s characterization of the difference between factual and legal malice in Bromage v. Prosser, (1825) 4 B & C 247, 255: "Malice in common acceptation means ill will against a person, but in its legal sense it means a wrongful act, done intentionally, without just cause or excuse." He continues, "And if I traduce a man, whether I know him or not, and whether I intend to do him an injury or not, I apprehend the law considers it as done of malice, because it is wrongful and intentional." Bayley J. makes his remark in the context of holding that the plaintiff in a defamation action does not need to establish malice on the facts, unless the defendant's comment was privileged. This characterization is specific to defamation, and does not provide an independent classification of wrongs that can be done only with factual malice.

means, I first want to introduce an unlikely pair of proposed solutions to this puzzle. One rejects the idea that tort law is concerned exclusively with the means a person uses; the other proposes that the intention to cause harm is prima facie wrongful but can be redeemed by its good consequences. I use those strange bedfellows as contrast points in explaining the general structure of tort law as a doctrine concerned exclusively with means, and then return to the cases.

In a widely discussed article, John Finnis writes: "The claim that, as good motives cannot legitimate unlawful means, so bad motives cannot delegitimate lawful means—sophistically ignores one of morality's most elementary principles and moral philosophy's most strategic themes. There is no such symmetry. One's conduct will be right only if both one's means and one's end are right; therefore one wrong-making factor will make one's choice and action wrong, and all the aspects of one's act must be rightful for the act to be right."[7] For Finnis, *Hollywood* is necessarily an easy case. The plaintiff may have had an unusual vulnerability, but the defendant's intention was to cause harm to him. As such, the defendant's action is defective. Although he was using otherwise permissible means, the defendant's illicit purpose makes his act wrongful.

Those who follow the literature of moral philosophy will be familiar with the principle to which Finnis implicitly appeals. It is a close cousin of the moral idea that often goes by the name of the "doctrine of double effect," according to which foreseen consequences of an act are less serious than intended ones, and if an agent acts to bring about a good result, he may foreseeably cause lesser harm. So in wartime, a munitions factory can be bombed, even if it is foreseeable that, given what is stored there, civilians living nearby will certainly be killed. But if the same agent is acting to bring about the harm—if he makes those same civilians his direct target—his act is defective, and so forbidden.[8]

---

7. John Finnis, "Intention in Tort Law," in *Philosophical Foundations of Tort Law,* ed. David G. Owen (Oxford: Oxford University Press, 1995), 238.

8. G. E. M. Anscombe, "Medalist's Address: Action, Intention and 'Double Effect,'" *Proceedings of the American Catholic Philosophical Association* 56 (1982): 12–25; Warren Quinn, "Actions, Intentions, and Consequences: The Doctrine of Double Effect," *Philosophy & Public Affairs* 18 (1989): 334–351. Critics of the distinction and the related "doctrine of double effect" include H. L. A. Hart, "Intention and Punishment," in *Punishment and*

For Finnis, the end for which a person acts is fundamental to the quality of the action, and the same action can change from permissible to forbidden depending on the agent's purposes. Finnis has carefully crafted views about how exactly to determine an agent's intention.[9] But ultimately those are merely questions of how to characterize the action, not of what principle governs its evaluation.

From a general orientation that is about as far removed from Finnis's as is possible, consider the view of Oliver Wendell Holmes. Malice enters Holmes's writing about tort through the doctrine of the prima facie tort. Recall that the animating thought of Holmes's broader approach to the law of torts is that it is concerned with harm rather than wrongdoing. For Holmes, the law of torts aims to prevent those harms that are both preventable and worth preventing. Any act that causes harm or characteristically causes harm is prima facie worthy of prohibition. Acts that aim to cause harm characteristically cause it: "The intentional infliction of temporal damage, or the doing of an act manifestly likely to inflict such damage and inflicting it, is actionable if done without just cause."[10] However, a prima facie tort may not merit prohibition if there are concomitant benefits from the activity in question: "I do not try to mention or to generalize all the facts which have to be taken into account; but plainly the worth of the result, or the gain from allowing the act to be done, has to be compared with the loss which it inflicts."[11] So for Holmes, "just cause" really means "social benefit." Holmes offers three examples: A man has "a right to set up shop in a small village that can support but one of the kind, although he expects and intends to ruin a deserving widow who is established there already. He has a right to build a house upon his land

---

Responsibility: Essays in the Philosophy of Law, ed. H. L. A. Hart and John Gardner (Oxford: Oxford University Press, 2008), 123; Frances Kamm, "The Doctrine of Double Effect: Reflections on Theoretical and Practical Issues," *Journal of Medicine and Philosophy* 16 (1991): 571–585; and T. M. Scanlon, *Moral Dimensions: Permissibility, Meaning, Blame* (Cambridge, MA: Harvard University Press, 2009). Scanlon argues that intention is relevant to the blameworthiness of an act, but not to its wrongfulness.

9. John Finnis, "Intention and Side Effects," in *Intention and Identity: Collected Essays,* vol. 2 (Oxford: Oxford University Press, 2011).

10. Oliver W. Holmes, "Privilege, Malice, and Intent," *Harvard Law Review* 8 (1894): 3.

11. Ibid.

in such a position as to spoil the view from a far more valuable house hard by. He has a right to give honest answers to inquiries about a servant although he intends thereby to prevent his getting a place."[12]

Holmes's analysis of the grounds of the three privileges—the benefits of economic competition, the public interest in seeing land developed rather than beautiful, and the benefits of free information—are of less significance than the structure within which these privileges are supposed to operate. That structure begins with the assumption that economic loss is objectionable, that destroying somebody's view is presumptively an actionable harm, and that failing to get a job is a loss in which the law might take an interest. From that starting point, Holmes must regard them as prima facie warranting prohibition but standing in need of justification. More surprising is that two of the three cases he considers involve malicious intent, suggesting that, despite his denunciation of moral phraseology, he supposes that the harm of being driven out of business, or not getting a position you seek, is a greater harm if occasioned by malice on the part of a business competitor or former employer.[13] Or perhaps his point is only that intended harm is more likely to ensue, and so, once again, requires a substantial justification if it is not to be prohibited.

So Holmes proposes a very different structure than Finnis, but with the same result. It is, as he puts it, prima facie wrongful to intend to inflict a loss on another person. Such prima facie wrongdoing can be justified by showing that otherwise wrongful acts should be tolerated on grounds of social policy. In the larger scheme of Holmes's categorization of wrongdoing, then, causing or intending harm are the basic categories of tort law, and both causing harm and intending to create it can be redeemed by their good consequences.

Roscoe Pound provides a helpful gloss on the general picture with which Holmes is working. Pound sees in it the "modern" view of policy replacing an earlier concern with conscience, like that expressed by Finnis: "Equity sought to prevent the unconscientious exercise of legal rights; today we seek to prevent the anti-social exercise of them. Equity

12. Ibid.

13. Holmes famously remarked, "Even a dog distinguishes between being stumbled over and being kicked." See Holmes, *The Common Law* (Boston: Little, Brown, 1882), 3.

imposed moral limitations, the law of today is imposing social limitations. It is endeavoring to delimit the individual interest better with respect to social interests and to confine the legal right to the bounds of the interest so delimited. More and more the tendency is to hold that what the law should secure is satisfaction of the owner's reasonable wants with respect to the property—that is those which consist with the like wants of his neighbors and the interests of society."[14] Pound characterizes his approach in terms of the distinction between social and antisocial exercises. Crucially, however, he sees the task as one of reconciling one person's wants with another's. This is the heart of the Holmesian approach, and serves to make malice immediately relevant, because the want for another's loss cannot "consist with the like wants" of his neighbors or the interest of society.

Before explaining my own view, I would like to spend just a moment pointing out how puzzling the idea that it is wrong to intend harm actually is, even though it is familiar. It is familiar because we all know that acting from a bad motive makes an act worse. In the criminal law, malice aforethought makes murder more serious, and more generally, willful wrongdoing is more serious than accidental wrongdoing. Parents also know that a child who deliberately breaks the rules behaves worse than one who breaks the rules because too absorbed in what he or she is doing.

The puzzle about this idea, however, is that in the criminal law context, and typically in the parenting context, bad motive aggravates what is *already* a wrong. It is trite criminal law that if the accused has a guilty mind and has not committed a prohibited act, he or she has not committed a crime. The law of attempts does not require a completed act, but it draws a fundamental distinction between attempting a crime and merely preparing to commit one, even though both require a guilty mind.

More generally, the idea that a mental state can make an otherwise acceptable act wrongful is puzzling. Let me put the point in the following way: Finnis's claim about morality's elementary principles and strategic themes draws attention to two different ways in which an act can be mor-

---

14. Roscoe Pound, *The Spirit of the Common Law* (Francestown, NH: Marshall Jones Co., 1921), 186.

ally defective. It can use the wrong means, and it can pursue the wrong end. Finnis's general claim about "morality's most elementary principles and moral philosophy's most strategic themes" is surely correct. When it comes to the question that each of us, as a moral agent, faces about what to do, two considerations bind us. The first is that we set worthwhile ends for ourselves. That is the hardest part of morality, because not all worthwhile ends can be realized in a single life. It is also difficult because there are many ends that are tempting but whose worth or lack thereof is not always obvious. But the other part of morality is making sure that we use suitable means in pursuing our ends.

But Finnis uses an undifferentiated concept of wrong, and so overlooks another of morality's most elementary principles. Whether one person wrongs another depends on what actually happens between those two people. No unilateral aspect of one of the parties changes the relation between them. No matter how malicious I am in my intention to wrong you, if circumstances do not cooperate and my attempt is a failure, I have not wronged you.

Let me fill out this thought further by noting the slightly different way in which Holmes's focus on harm overlooks it: Motive makes it into the Holmesian account because intending to harm another is exactly the kind of thing that does a lot of harm. In Pound's formulation, one man's want for another's loss cannot "consist" with the other's want to avoid the loss. Holmes's crude utilitarianism makes room for permitting such harm based on the overall benefits to third parties. But malice enters his analysis either as a reliable predictor of the tendency of a certain class of motives to be socially destructive, or alternatively as an additional harm if the plaintiff becomes aware of it. It has nothing to do with how things stand between the parties.

So Holmes's approach is in one way very different from Finnis's: Finnis focuses on the goodness of the end being pursued, Holmes on the benefits of people pursuing that type of end. But they are alike in focusing on the ends being pursued. As such, neither account has the resources to explain why the plaintiff, in particular, is in a position to complain of the defendant's bad motive. In both cases the plaintiff's claim rests on the fact that the defendant did something wicked or antisocial that happened to injure the plaintiff. As we saw in Chapters 3 and 4, the concept of a private wrong cannot be assembled out of bad behavior by the defendant that causes a loss to the plaintiff. Nobody could have a right to be free of the bad effects of another person's bad behavior. Instead, the plaintiff's complaint is that the defendant has done something to her in particular. In *Hollywood*, that is exactly the plaintiff's complaint; the case does not depend on the claim that the defendant's bad ends caused him harm.

2. Means, Not Ends

I want to suggest a different way of thinking about these issues. They pose a challenge to the approach developed in earlier chapters, if, as Finnis and Holmes seem to agree, they turn on the ends for which the defendant used his means, rather than the way in which the means were used. Cast in the most general terms, the positive account I have developed so far is that tort law articulates and protects a specific form of human interaction, a form in which each person is entitled to use his or her own means—that is, person and property—to set and pursue his or her own purposes. Tort law protects each person's security in his or her own person and property by prohibiting others from acting in ways that compromise them.

Recall the three interrelated senses in which private wrongs are concerned with means rather than ends: (1) Tort law *protects* the means that each person has for setting and pursuing his or her purposes by (2) *restricting* the means that each person can use by precluding one person from using means that *belong to another* without that other's authorization, and (3) *restricting* the ways in which each person can use his or her *own* means to those that are consistent with everyone else being able to do the same. The first and third of these prohibit interfering with what another person has by using your means in dangerous or defective ways; the second prohibits unauthorized use of another person's body or property. That is why the inquiry is purely relational. If that account is correct, then nothing outside of the relation between the parties, such as Holmes's concern for countervailing beneficial consequences, and nothing unique to one of the parties, such as Finnis's focus on the defendant's ends or Holmes's on the defendant's "malevolent motive for action, without reference to any hope of a remoter benefit to oneself to be accomplished by the intended harm to another,"[15] can be any part of the inquiry.

This very compressed restatement of the role of means in the distinction between misfeasance and nonfeasance shows us where each of Finnis and Holmes goes wrong. Their proposals violate the requirement that the defendant wrong the plaintiff, because a wrong must be characterized in terms of the relation between the two parties. Each also goes wrong in supposing that whether one person interferes with another can depend upon something other than that interference. If the defendant hasn't interfered with the plaintiff's means, then the question of *why* he so interfered cannot even be asked. Again, Holmes's concern with the prevention of harm deprives him of the ability to distinguish between willfully wronging a person and willfully failing to aid that person. And so, despite their differences, neither Finnis nor Holmes can explain why, in cases in which the defendant exhibits a bad motive, the plaintiff in particular should be the one entitled to complain, or should be entitled to damages for past losses or an injunction to prevent future harm.

I now want to argue that the key to understanding such cases begins with focusing on the idea of tort law as concerned exclusively with the use of means, and on the role of damage-based torts as focused exclusively on permissible side effects of such use. The law's focus on side effects is what generates a puzzle in a case like *Hollywood*. The plaintiff has an unusual sensitivity, but that is just to say that the plaintiff will suffer damage from effects that people ordinarily have to put up with from their neighbors. Like a neighbor who is allergic to the ordinary flowers you grow in your garden, the plaintiff has no grounds for complaint, because these are just things that everyone needs to put up with in the crowded conditions of modern life. You do not need to organize your garden in the way that best suits your neighbor's wishes. Nor do you need to restrict the ways in which you use your means to those that will yield the level of quiet that best suits your neighbor's wish to raise foxes on his farm.

15. Holmes, "Privilege, Malice, and Intent," 2

The peculiarity of *Hollywood* is that the plaintiff's complaint is not about the *side effects* of the defendant's action. The plaintiff's complaint is that they are not side effects at all. It is not that effects of the defendant's use of his means turns out to be incompatible with the plaintiff's preferred use of his; it is that the defendant is using his own means *to create* that incompatibility because the incompatibility is the means through which the defendant hopes to achieve his end. These are not merely side effects, not because they are ends, but because the defendant pursues whatever purpose he has by using the inconsistency of his activity with the plaintiff's. The defendant is entitled to ignore the plaintiff's special sensitivities, including vulnerabilities attendant on his specific use of his land, when they are pursuing their separate purposes independently of each other. In the case in which the efficacy of the defendant's act depends on the particularity of the plaintiff's use of his land, their separate pursuits are no longer independent.[16]

To say that the noises are not a side effect of the defendant's pursuit of his interdependent purposes is not to say that they are the defendant's ends, or that they are among the defendant's motives. To see this, consider a number of variants on the case: Suppose that the defendant is making the noise simply because he is angry with the plaintiff for having refused his completely reasonable and neighborly request. This would be the version of the case on which the defendant acts from what Holmes calls disinterested malice. There is no hope of gaining an economic advantage; he just wants to hurt someone he hates. Next, consider the case in which the defendant has a fox farm of his own, out of acoustic range, and hopes to raise the price of furs by reducing the supply. Finally, consider the case in which the defendant fires his gun in the hope that the plaintiff will conclude that his fox-farming days in this location are over and put his land up for sale, enabling the defendant, looking ahead to the next housing estate, to purchase it at a low price. These three variants are indistinguishable from the actual facts, both morally and legally. But if we can assign the defendant three different ends and find his act defective in the same

16. The structure is thus parallel to the structure of fraud: if I set out to induce you to do something by inducing a false belief in you, our interaction is not independent in the relevant sense.

way in each of them, then, accepting the standard distinction between means and ends to be exhaustive, the difficulty must be with his means.

Again, contrast these three cases with the case in which the defendant, rather than instructing his son to discharge firearms, simply deploys his earth-moving equipment, getting an early start on the housing development, with the exact same effect on the plaintiff, and with quiet delight in the fact that this has happened. In the earth-moving version, a court would find that the plaintiff was just unusually sensitive, and the defendant did no legal wrong to the plaintiff, regardless of what or how he happens to think about it. His ultimate end—selling houses—remains the same, and the means that he uses are unobjectionable, even though he may welcome their foreseeable impact on the plaintiff's activity. That is, it is indistinguishable from the case in which, unaware of the character of his neighbor, he makes a noise that disturbs his neighbor's vixens. If he has a right to make a certain level of noise, that right is not changed by his neighbor's request that he cease to exercise it, or by the fact that he welcomes its effect on his neighbor.

What these two triptychs of examples suggest is that the defendant's conduct is defective not in the ends that he pursues but in the means that he uses. We can change the ends without making his conduct less defective, or fix the ends and make his conduct more or less defective by changing the means.

It might be suggested that the distinction between means and ends is not exclusive, and that in this case disturbing the vixens is the defendant's "intermediate end," in something like the way that grinding coffee beans is both a means that you use toward the end of making coffee and something you accomplish along the way. There is nothing wrong with describing it that way, but it may distract attention from the distinctive nature of the "malicious wrong." The category of intermediate ends may be useful for the philosophical analysis of action, but within any such analysis it always invites a question of the form "Why are you doing that?" which might just as well be paraphrased as "Why are you using those means?" That is, talk about intermediate ends provides a way of embedding talk about someone doing something in order to do something else, but at each step the doing can also be represented as the use of means.[17] The wrong consists in using the inconsistency between the defendant's use of his means and the plaintiff's ability to use his. That is the complex of means that the defendant uses, and its use is the core of the wrong.

This complex of means can be brought into sharper focus by thinking about the idea of a side effect. Private law abstracts from the ends being pursued. In so doing, it prohibits one person from using means that belong to another; beyond that it focuses on the side effects of actions. The ends the plaintiff is pursuing are the plaintiff's own business, and the ends the defendant is pursuing are the defendant's own business; all that matters is the effect of the defendant's use of means on the plaintiff's security of means.

In a case like *Hollywood,* this picture of people restricting only the side effects of their actions doesn't seem to apply properly. This is what makes talk of purposes, of targeting, of intention, and of motive tempting in such cases but, at the same time, fundamentally misleading. The means that the defendant is using—the way in which he is achieving his purposes *whatever they might be*—is disrupting the plaintiff's specific use of the plaintiff's own means. Having made the plaintiff's specific means an issue, the defendant cannot also claim to be merely having the ordinary level of side effects on the plaintiff.

This account makes no reference to the content of any end, whether of the defendant or the plaintiff. It is not the defendant pursues a purpose that is inconsistent with purposiveness as such; it is instead that the frustration of another's use of means as a means is inconsistent with the usability of means as such. This requirement is formal in a double sense: First, it does not attend to the matter of particular choices, that is, to the specific ends being pursued by either the plaintiff or the defendant. Second, it is formal because it poses the question of whether the defendant's means are of a form that everyone could use, consistent with everyone else being entitled to use those means in the same way.

17. See the discussion in Michael Thompson, *Life and Action: Elementary Structures of Practice and Practical Thought* (Cambridge, MA: Harvard University Press, 2008), pt. 3.

An entitlement to set up an inconsistency between your use of your means and another person's use of his or her means could not be a member of system in which separate people pursue their separate purposes consistently. Its efficacy for any end depends on that incompatibility. And the one thing that cannot be enjoyed consistently by everyone is the right to stop others from using their means in the way that they wish to. The problem is not just that such an action is parasitic, but rather that the right to do so cannot be systematically enjoyed. You could not exercise such an imagined right unless it was parasitic—interfering with another person's particular use requires that other person already be doing something. But the two sets of activities cannot be exercised consistently. Frederick Pollock makes the same point in discussing *Christie v. Davey,* arguing that making noise to annoy the plaintiff "may be relevant to show that the defendant is not using his property in an ordinary and legitimate way such as good neighbours mutually tolerate."[18] Neighbors may mutually tolerate and so adjust their activities to a certain level of noise, but they cannot be required to adjust their activities to attempts to frustrate those activities. That would be equivalent to permitting one person to take charge of how another uses his or her means.

Suppose that you are walking across a public square. I do not need to move aside to provide you with a path. I can also pursue my purpose of moving from one place to another without wronging you. My coming and going as I please is consistent with your coming and going as you please. If instead I move from place to place always blocking (what was about to be) your path, I do something different—I act in a way that could not be a member of a consistent set of permissible actions.

The incoherence of the social world in which everyone sets out to frustrate the purposes of others is a normative incoherence, not a logical or factual one. In a world driven by what Lord Cooke called the "versatility of human malevolence and ingenuity,"[19] everyone would be in charge of everyone else; each person's entitlement to use his or her means would be entirely subject to the choice of others. As we have seen before, the idea that no person is in charge of another is not a claim about all of us being

18. Frederick Pollock, *The Law of Torts,* 7th ed. (London: Stevens and Sons, 1904), 400.
19. Hunter v. Canary Wharf, [1997] UKHL 14.

alike along some dimension of comparison, or all of us being allowed to do the same thing to each other. So the difficulty is the same one that faced the proposal encountered in Chapter 4, according to which the standard of care in negligence should allow people to expose each other to substantial risks, provided that everyone was allowed to do so to the same degree. But a private wrong does not consist in some people getting to do things that others do not; it consists in an act inconsistent with the requirement that no person be in charge of another.

The prohibited means in this example are means in a somewhat different sense than your body and property are your means. The characterization of their use takes place only against the background of the use of bodies and property. In such cases as *Hollywood* and *Christie,* the defendant sets up a new form of interaction, which opens up the possibility of a distinctive form of wrongdoing.

I said earlier that talk of targeting, purposes, motives, and so on is tempting in analyzing such cases. We can now see why this would be so. How would you go about determining that the defendant is using interference with the plaintiff's specific activity as his means? At least part of the answer is to be found in a broadly counterfactual test: If the plaintiff were engaged in a different activity, would the defendant do the same thing? That is a way to find out whether interfering with the plaintiff's activity is *the way in which* the defendant is pursuing his end. It is very easy to mistake this for a test about what the defendant's *end* is, because the use of the means in question carries with it internal success conditions. If the defendant has disrupted the plaintiff's music lessons, or fox breeding, then, it might truly be said that the defendant has succeeded. Such a test, too, is easily expressed in broadly counterfactual terms: Would the defendant have stopped shooting or banging if the plaintiff had gotten rid of his foxes or sign, or stopped playing the piano? But neither the possibility of such seeming success conditions nor the truth of such counterfactuals shows that interfering with the plaintiff was the defendant's end in any interesting or substantial sense, because any use of means supports similar counterfactuals and has similar internal success conditions. I have succeeded in using a knife to cut onions just in case the knife cuts through them. Otherwise I have tried, unsuccessfully, to use it. Again, I would not use my knife for slicing onions if I did not have a knife available to me, if the knife was completely blunt, if the onions were made out of metal, or if I believed any of those things to be true. Means are used only if the person using them takes them to be effective toward achieving an end. This is just the priority of having means to setting ends; you can do something by using means only when you think there is a realistic possibility that using them will enable you to do it. You can't sing if you think you have lost your voice; you can't cut if you don't think you have a suitable knife. And you can't get your neighbor to stop playing by banging on the walls if you think the walls are soundproof.

3. Some Contrasts

I have not purported to explain every case in which people have sought to appeal to motive and intention in tort law. But I should mention a few of the examples that are most frequently referred to in discussions of these matters. One of these is *Mayor of Bradford v. Pickles*,[20] in which the defendant prevented percolating water from crossing his land to reach the plaintiff's reservoir, in the hope of putting economic pressure on the plaintiff to purchase his interest. The defendant's plans were clear: He sunk shafts on his land, allegedly in order to quarry limestone, but, having sunk the shafts, he simply pumped out the water from them, piping it away from the plaintiff's reservoir.[21] Michael Taggart's book on the case reveals how the full texture of nineteenth-century urbanization and politics figured in the dispute making it to court.[22] The plaintiff's use of its own land as a reservoir plainly satisfied the sort of counterfactual test: It figured directly in the defendant's decision to sink the shaft and pump the water. If the plaintiff were using its land differently, the defendant would not have constructed his complex and expensive works. Yet the court—many of the same judges who decided *Christie v. Davey*—insisted that the plain-

20. [1895] UKHL 1.

21. A. W. B. Simpson, *Victorian Law and the Industrial Spirit* (London: Selden Society, 1995).

22. See Michael Taggart, *Private Property and Abuse of Rights in Victorian England: The Story of Edward Pickles and the Bradford Water Supply* (Oxford: Oxford University Press, 2002).

tiff had no cause of action; and the court in *Hollywood* appealed to *Christie v. Davey* and then announced that *Bradford* had no bearing on it. So the puzzle arises: Are these cases really consistent?

It might be thought that they cannot be rendered consistent. The defendant in *Bradford* sought to advance his purposes by frustrating those of the plaintiff. But the wrong in the defendant's act in *Hollywood* or *Christie* is not in frustrating another's purposes by failing to provide something to that person. That is a right that everyone could enjoy—a right to make some decisions about how to use their means based upon what they think others are likely to want to do with theirs, and using their private rights, to set the terms on which they make other things available to others. In *Bradford* itself, the defendant is unwilling to make his land available as a path for the percolating water.[23]

This short answer that *Bradford* and *Hollywood* are consistent needs filling out. The second-shortest short answer points out that nothing leaves the defendant's land in *Bradford,* and so no doctrine of the law of nuisance applies. I think that that is, finally, the correct answer, but in order to fully understand why, we must, like the defendant in *Bradford,* dig deeper. The defendant does no wrong by digging a hole on his land, because a system in which each person is entitled to use his or her own land is, thereby, also a system in which no person is permitted to either use the land of another without that other person's permission or (what comes to the same thing) require the other person to use that land in a

---

23. It matters that the water percolates rather than flowing in a defined stream, because there can be no riparian rights in percolating water. Since Roman times, percolating water, like wild animals, has been a central example of something that must be captured in order to be owned, because it cannot be possessed until it is brought under the owner's control. In Acton v. Blundell, (1843) 12 M & W 324, 152 ER 1223, the court drew attention to the discussion in Justinian's *Digest* 39, 3, *de aqua* I, §12, according to which no action could lie for interrupting the flow of water by digging on one's own field. In Chasemore v. Richards, [1859] 7 HLC 349, 372, Lord Chelmsford characterizes the right claimed by the plaintiff as "indefinite and unlimited," as it asserts a right in something that has not been acquired that would prevent others from acquiring that thing. Neither the plaintiff nor the defendant owns the water as it rains or percolates. If the defendant exercises his right to capture the water, he is entitled to set the terms on which he makes it available to the plaintiff, just as he is entitled to set the terms on which he makes the path taken by the water available for the plaintiff's specific purposes.

specific way, tailored to his or her own preferred use of neighboring land. So absent easement, contract, or statutory provision, you can have no right to a path across my land, for sunlight, or insects, or percolating water. That is why you can put up a tower even if it casts a shadow on your neighbor's land,[24] and take one down even if your neighbor's mushroom crop depends on the shade. That is why *Bradford* is unexceptional; it may be that I would find it more convenient to cut across your land, but you are free to put up a fence, even if you are not growing anything that might suffer as a result of my trampling. The defendant's motive does not enter into the analysis. Nor does the fact that the defendant's decision about how to use his or her land depends upon how he or she expects the neighbors to react. You can put up a fence because you do not want me to visit you. You can also put up a fence in the hope of enticing members of the public to pay to visit your exquisite gardens. It would be unneighborly and probably imprudent to tell your neighbors that you will block their view of your garden unless they pay you to leave it visible. But it would not be a private wrong against them; if you are entitled to do it, you are entitled to do it.

That is exactly the situation of the defendant in *Bradford:* He is deciding how to use his land based upon surrounding land use, and how he thinks it will work most to his own benefit. Such decisions could not be wrongful as a matter of law. He differs from the defendant in *Hollywood,* and *Bradford* has no bearing on *Hollywood,* precisely because everyone could decide how to use his or her own land, consistent with the right of everyone else to do the same. The defendant in *Hollywood* is not withholding a path for quiet across his land; he is using his land to produce noise to interfere with the plaintiff's activity on his land. The defendant in *Bradford* isn't interfering with the plaintiff's use of his land; the plaintiff can still use the land as a reservoir; the defendant is just using his in a way that will stop the reservoir from being replenished.

This fundamental point at issue in *Bradford* thus generates the juridical conception of market transactions; everyone is entitled to use what belongs to them in a way that does not interfere with the ability of others to do the

24. Fontainebleau Hotel Corp. v. Forty-Five Twenty-Five Inc., 114 So. 2d 357, 1959 Fla. App.

same, including deciding whether to use it in a particular way based upon how others might be expected to react. So everyone could decide how to use his or her own land in light of those expectations. That is, market relations, in which people decide what to do with their means as a way of offering others incentives, are permissible as a matter of private right.

This juridical conception of markets has nothing to do with any Holmesian contentions about the overall benefits of competition outweighing the harms that it causes; it is an implication of each person's entitlement to decide what to do with his or her property, and so to decide whether to make it available to others and on what terms. Put differently again, *Bradford* is just a nonfeasance case. *Hollywood* is a misfeasance case, and the defendant's use of the interference with his neighbor as his means involves doing something that could not, as a general matter, be done by everyone.

I began by talking about the views of Finnis and Holmes, each of whom focuses on the quality of the defendant's end in assessing the plaintiff's right. According to Finnis, malice can never be redeemed; according to Holmes, overall benefits can redeem malice. For James Barr Ames, who seeks to reconcile the two views, the defendant's selfishness becomes the factor that could justify harmful action, so that interested malice is fine but disinterested malice is actionable.[25] As Ames puts it, "the true rule, it is submitted, may be formulated as follows: The wilful causing of damage to another by a positive act, whether by one man alone, or by several acting in concert, and whether by direct action against him or indirectly by inducing a third person to exercise a lawful right, is a tort unless there was just cause for inflicting the damage; and the question whether there was or was not just cause will depend, in many cases, but not in all, upon the motive of the actor."[26] Ames's approach is taken up in the barbershop case of *Tuttle v. Buck*,[27] in which the defendant banker sponsored a rival barbershop in order to drive the plaintiff barber out of business. The court essentially adopted Ames's analysis, even though it

---

25. J. B. Ames, "How Far an Act May Be a Tort because of the Wrongful Motive of the Actor," *Harvard Law Review* 18 (1905): 411–422.
26. Ibid.
27. 119 NW 946 (Minn. 1909).

conceded that the plaintiff's contention that the defendant was motivated exclusively by malice was weak. It focused on the fact that the defendant set up "an opposition place of business, not for the sake of profit
to himself,"[28] suggesting that conduct intended to harm others can be
redeemed by the motive of profit making.[29] The court does not explain
whether this is because it is for the benefit of the defendant, or, as Holmes
would have it, because it is a form of selfishness that works to the benefit
of society in the long run. Tony Weir may be correct in his observation
that "disinterested malevolence is so rare that it is unwise to develop a
rule to combat it which can be used by a disgruntled hairdresser who
has lost his profitable local monopoly."[30] Weir puts the point as though
the situation is unusual and a legal rule to prevent it would be rife with
the danger of abuse. There is more to it than that, as I hope the above
analysis has shown. The defendant did not interfere with the plaintiff
barber's ability to use what he already had—his scissors, chair and striped
pole. Those things remained as useful as ever, except that the competing
shop offered customers a better deal.

Disinterested malevolence is a genuine vice, but whatever its frequency, it is particular to the defendant and as such has no bearing on
the plaintiff's rights. It also fails to capture what goes wrong in genuine
cases of harassment, such as *Hollywood*. No inquiry into the propriety
of the defendant's motives is required to characterize the wrong he
committed against the plaintiff. Any rule that insists that we look at
something particular to the defendant to characterize the wrong against
the plaintiff is likely to have the same problems. Indeed, I don't think
that it is entirely an accident that a view that focuses on disinterested
malice, redeemable by self-interested malice, generates a rule that lacks
application.[31]

28. Ibid., 948.

29. One consequence of this approach is that the defendant in *Hollywood* would not be
liable.

30. Tony Weir, *Economic Torts* (Oxford: Clarendon Press, 1997), 73.

31. In Eldridge v. Johndrow, 2015 UT 21, the Utah Supreme Court rejected a tort of improper motive, noting both its procedural infirmities (which made it troublingly open-ended)
and the dearth of cases in which a plaintiff succeeded in establishing an improper motive.

4. Extending the Account

Deliberate interference with a neighbor's use of his or her own land may seem an unrepresentative example on which to build a broader analysis of the role of motive in tort law. In this closing section, I want to say something, however briefly, about how the previous analysis might be extended to a broader range of cases, without purporting to actually so extend it.[32]

The first cases to which it can be extended are the broader set of economic torts. Some of the early cases, like *Hollywood,* involved a defendant who made noise to disrupt the plaintiff's activities.[33] Others involved defendants intimidating the plaintiff's customers or trading partners with threats or cannon fire.[34] As Lord Hoffman points out in *OBG Ltd. v. Allan,* driving away customers by threatening them is a special case of a more general category of unlawful means: Had the threats been carried out or the trading partners hit with the cannon, the plaintiff would have the same cause of action.[35] These cases differ from *Hollywood* because the wrong operates through third parties. The cases share an exclusive focus on the defendant's use of means, rather than the ends in the service of which they were used. An inquiry into the defendant's motives is unlikely to help the plaintiff's case, because the defendant wants to succeed in a competitive business and wants to eliminate the his rival, not capitalize on the rival's presence.

---

32. I make no attempt to extend it to tortious interference with contracts, the leading case of which is Lumley v. Gye, [1853] EWHC QB J73. The wrong in such cases is procuring breach. I take no position here on either of the important questions it raises: First, is it, as suggested by Lord Hoffman in OBG Ltd. v. Allan, [2007] UKHL 21, a form of accessory liability? Second, is intention required because of the constraint imposed on the defendant by the plaintiff's contractual arrangement with a third party—see Ernest Weinrib, "Public Law and Private Right," *University of Toronto Law Journal* 61 (2011): 191–211—or because the wrong consists in appropriation of a right, as suggested by Peter Benson, "On the Basis for Excluding Liability for Economic Loss," in *The Philosophical Foundations of Tort Law,* ed. David G. Owen (Oxford: Oxford University Press, 2008)?

33. Keeble v. Hickeringill; Carrington v. Taylor, (1809) 11 East 571; 103 ER 1126.

34. Garret v. Taylor, (1620) Cro Jac 567, 79 E.R. 485; Tarleton v. M'Gawley, (1790) 1 Peake NPC 270.

35. [2007] UKHL 21, ¶7.

The puzzle about these cases concerns the way in which the defendant's threat or injury to a third party constitutes a wrong against the plaintiff in particular.[36] In the competitive setting in which these torts arise, the wrong does not consist in the defendant depriving the plaintiff of customers, because the plaintiff does not and could not have a right to those customers. Nor does it consist in getting those customers to breach a contract with the plaintiff. Indeed, the defendant is allowed to offer inducements to them; doing so differs from the use of threats or force, not in the ends that are sought, but in the means through which those ends are pursued.

The contrast between acceptable and unacceptable inducements parallels the difference between *Hollywood* and *Bradford*. If you lower your prices or improve your products in order to attract my customers, our respective uses of our means remain consistent; it is just that if there are a fixed number of customers in our industry, your success will lead to my failure. My losses are not the mechanism of your success; both your success and my losses are the results of your innovation. Although the world may be such that we cannot both succeed in the same line of business in a limited market, our use of our respective means is consistent.

But if I make your customers unwilling to do business with you by threatening them, your inability to continue using your means is the means through which I achieve my success. Lord Hoffman puts this in terms of your failure being the "flip side" of my success: The injury was "the means of attaining [the defendant]'s desired end and not merely a foreseeable consequence of having done so." He also points out that in these torts the defendants act "to achieve the further end of securing an economic advantage to themselves."[37] The end is completely unremarkable, but the means that the defendant uses must be unavailable, because

---

36. Lord Hoffman suggests that the unlawful act must be one that is actionable by the third party, or would be but for lack of damage. In many cases of intimidation, the threat is effective, and so not carried out. In *OBG* at ¶49 Lord Hoffman also notes that the unlawful means might involve fraud without loss (citing National Phonograph Co. Ltd. v. Edison-Bell Consolidated Phonograph Co. Ltd., [1908] 1 Ch 335).

37. *OBG* at ¶134.

it could not be part of the system in which each person is entitled to use his or her means to set and pursue his or her own purposes. You, in particular, are wronged by my conduct, because my use of means is inconsistent with your use of yours—that is what gives my action its point. The wrong can only be committed intentionally because the defendant's use of his or her means takes the plaintiff's ongoing use of her means as its object. The means used by the defendant to shape the conduct of the third party must be independently unlawful because the boundary between lawful and unlawful is just the boundary between attracting someone else's customers by making them a better offer and attracting them by making them an offer they can't refuse. The wrong, then, consists in the use of means that cannot be consistently used by everyone. The plaintiff's loss is the measure of damages.

Misfeasance in a public office also requires intention; the central cases involve a public official using his or her office to injure the plaintiff.[38] In a leading case,[39] Québec Premier Maurice Duplessis canceled the liquor license of Roncarelli because he had been posting bail for Jehovah's Witnesses whom the premier had had arrested. Some have argued that misfeasance in a public office is simply a tool for enforcing public law norms.[40] The basic thrust of that argument is that only public officials can commit misfeasance in a public office, and so it is not properly private as between the parties. Further, central instances of it, such as *Roncarelli*, deprive the plaintiff of something he or she has only as a matter of public law, such as a liquor license.[41]

---

38. What have come to be called "constitutional torts," in which a plaintiff receives remedy from the state for the violation of his or her constitutional rights, share some features with misfeasance in a public office. See, for example, Bivens v. Six Unknown Named Agents of Federal Bureau of Narcotics, 403 U.S. 388 (1971) (right against unreasonable search and seizure), and Henry v. British Columbia (Attorney General), 2015 SCC 24 (right to a fair trial). However, they differ in important ways, particularly in their dependence on constitutional rights, and so lie outside the present discussion.

39. Roncarelli v. Duplessis, [1959] SCR 121.

40. E.g., Robert Stevens, *Torts and Rights* (Oxford: Oxford University Press, 2007), 243.

41. Stevens notes Lord Hobhouse's remark in Three Rivers v. Bank of England, [2004] UKHL 48, that the tort is not necessary in cases in which the plaintiff complains of the violation of an antecedent right, and concludes that denying someone the right to vote (including the earliest case, Ashby v. White, (1703) 2 Ld. Raym. 938) is not an instance of the tort.

I want to propose a different way of thinking about it: Misfeasance in a public office involves both a public law wrong and a private law wrong. The public wrong is often described in terms of an "improper purpose," but it can also be characterized in stronger terms, as the wrong of privatizing a public office, that is, of using it for a purpose other than the specific public purpose appropriate to it. The defendant takes up what are supposed to be public powers and uses them against the plaintiff, which is just to say the defendant uses those powers privately.[42] In so doing, the defendant also treats the object of those powers as private, for example, treating the withholding of a liquor license as something that is subject to his "untrammelled discretion."[43] Private rights are subject to just this sort of discretion; you can use your body and property to pursue any purpose whatsoever. Public law powers are different; an official can use them only for the purposes proper to their mandate. That means that a liquor license can be granted or withheld only in relation to the Liquor Control Act. Official discretion covers only the application of the provisions of the legislation in question.

Although misfeasance in a public office cannot be committed unless the defendant acts for what public law must regard as an improper end, the private law significance of so doing is not in the specific end that is pursued instead, but in the use of the power to pursue some other end by

---

42. In Proulx v. Quebec (Attorney General), 2001 SCC 66, Iacobucci and Binnie JJ. similarly characterized the related tort of malicious prosecution by the Crown in terms of "the misuse and abuse of the criminal process and the office of the Crown Attorney" (¶35), isolating the wrong in violation of "the prosecutor's duty not to allow the criminal process to be used as a vehicle to serve other ends" (¶43). Historically the Crown had immunity against an action in malicious prosecution, but the same structure applies when it is brought against a private person: using the criminal process for private purposes turns what is legally a public power into a private one, the use of which is wrongful.

The same structure applies to bringing a private action you believe to be without merit for purposes other than upholding the rights allegedly at issue. Lady Hale sums up the difference in Crawford Adjusters & Ors v. Sagicor General Insurance (Cayman) Ltd. & Anor (Cayman Islands), [2013] UKPC 17, ¶89: "Intentionally causing economic damage is not a tort, because that is the object of most business competition. But intentionally abusing the legal system is a different matter. That is not simply doing deals to damage the competitors' business. It is bringing claims which you know to be bad in order to do so."

43. Roncarelli v. Duplessis, 140.

injuring the plaintiff. So the difficulty is not that the premier's final ends are inappropriate; the problem is with the use of specific means—inflicting loss through use of the provincial liquor-licensing scheme—to achieve them. Indeed, Premier Duplessis appears to have had the best interests of the province of Québec in mind; he described Roncarelli's actions as a "provocation to the public order."[44]

The basis of the wrong can only be understood in terms of the relationship between the parties to it. Duplessis used powers beyond the scope for which they were conferred, so his use of them cannot be understood exclusively in terms of their public law basis. In so doing he created a new relationship between himself and Roncarelli, a relationship that lacked a basis in public law. His use of his powers counts as private only if it is for an improper purpose (as measured against legal basis of the power), but the wrongfulness does not depend on the particularity of that purpose—the improper purpose is a threshold condition for the creation of a new relationship, which is private because of the means used. Roncarelli's complaint can be understood in terms of that relationship: The use of public powers for private purposes is not a means that could be generally available. Having treated the powers conferred by the relevant legislation as generally available for pursuing goals he thought worthwhile, he made his use of them a private matter between himself and Roncarelli.[45] A public official who exercises powers illegally makes

44. See Timothy Endicott, *Administrative Law*, 3rd ed. (Oxford: Oxford University Press, 2015), 231.

45. A second branch has been added to misfeasance in a public office in recent years. Beginning with Three Rivers v. Bank of England, this branch requires recklessness with respect to illegality of the action *and* the probability of harm, rather than intention. In Akenzua & Anor v. Secretary of State for the Home Department & Anor, [2002] EWCA Civ 1470, the defendant arranged for a violent criminal to remain in the United Kingdom and be released from custody in return for his service as a police informant. The criminal went on to murder the plaintiff's decedent. The court, relying on a passage in *Three Rivers*, held that lack of good faith on the part of the defendant—which it defined broadly to include recklessness with respect to illegality—was an element. Lord Justice Simon Brown summarizes the matter at ¶30: "To commit the tort of misfeasance in a public office otherwise than by way of targeted malice, the tortfeasor must be proved to have acted with subjective reckless indifference both to the illegality of his act and as to the probability that harm will result from it." In one sense, this expansion keeps its focus on the means used—the illegal

those powers private as between the official and the person against whom they are used. Those against whom those means are used are the victims of private wrongs, as well as public ones.

5. Conclusion

The subtitle of this chapter is "Motive and Intention in Tort Law," and I seem to have said more about motive than about intention. But in fact the entire chapter has been about intention, that is, the taking up of means to achieve an end. The distinction between misfeasance and nonfeasance is just the requirement that each person restricts the means used in pursuing whatever ends he or she might have, and never a requirement that anyone either adopt or decline to adopt any end. So it is all about means, never about ends.

---

release was done in the service of overall crime prevention, a public purpose outside the mandate of the power exercised—not in order to cause injury. But the death of the plaintiff's decedent is not, in Lord Hoffman's phrase, "the means of attaining the defendant's end," but rather a consequence of the defendant's unlawful use of public power. Moreover, the unlawfulness of the defendant's acts is not related to the danger posed to the members of a class including the plaintiff. It remains to be seen whether the replacement of malice with double indifference will form a coherent doctrine in cases in which the probable harm is economic loss, or instead provide plaintiffs with a way to circumvent the lack of a duty of care in negligence actions against public officials. See the discussion of Granite Power v. Ontario, (2004) 72 OR (3d) 194 (CA), in Erika Chamberlain, "What Is the Role of Misfeasance in a Public Office in Modern Canadian Tort Law?," *Canadian Bar Review* 88 (2009): 580–605.

CHAPTER 7

What You Already Have, Part 2

Your Own Good Name

IN THIS CHAPTER I turn to the tort of defamation. It might be thought to be a difficult customer for the analysis developed in earlier chapters. In particular, your right to reputation is often thought of as a fundamental interest that you have in a different sense. In some writing, both academic and popular, reputation is viewed as a sort of asset, and defamation as a devaluing of that asset. Writers talk about the need to balance the plaintiff's interest in a good reputation against a social interest in protecting freedom of expression or a speaker's interest in free expression. More generally, you do not have your reputation in the way in which you have your body or property. Although your reputation might be useful to you (or others), your right to it is not based on the idea that others are not entitled to determine the purposes for which it is used.

My aim is to articulate the sense in which you have your reputation. Just as it is a mistake to think about property as a relation between the owner and the thing owned, so, too, it is a mistake to think about reputation as a form of self-relation. Instead, your right to reputation is an entitlement to constrain the conduct of others. Once these ideas are brought into focus, the way in which defamation fits into a system of private rights becomes transparent.[1]

Although I will discuss damages in detail in Chapter 8, defamation might be thought to require a separate analysis because of the distinctive nature of the wrong. The familiar objection that the wrong is a fact in the world that cannot be undone, or especially cannot be undone through a payment of money damages, seems especially pressing in the case of damage to reputation. How can money make this up? In what sense is the remedy the continuation of the right, or the right looked at "from the other end," or giving back what the plaintiff already had? The normal remedy in a libel action is "general damages," which are tied to the seriousness of the wrong but cannot, realistically, make up the plaintiff's loss. It is sometimes suggested that damages are meant to address the upset that the plaintiff suffers.[2] Although defamation might seem to be a particularly difficult case for the idea that the purpose of damages is to make it as if the wrong had never happened, in another sense it is an easy case, both for illustrating the general principle and for revealing the nature of its imperfect realization.

The ideal remedy for defamation would be something that made it as if the defamatory statement had never been published.[3] A retraction by the defendant is an imperfect version of this ideal remedy; a judgment by the court is a different, but also imperfect, version. The magnitude of "general" damages, keyed to the seriousness of the wrong, may go some

1. In developing my analysis, I will focus on libel, which is actionable per se, that is, without any proof of damage. Certain slanders are also actionable per se. I hope to take up the distinction between slander and libel, and the status of slanders that require proof of damage, on another occasion.

2. See the remarks of Windeyer J. in Uren v. John Fairfax & Sons, (1966) 117 CLR 118, 150: "Money and reputation are not commensurables. It seems to me that, properly speaking, a man defamed does not get compensation for his damaged reputation. He gets damages because he was injured in his reputation, that is simply because he was publicly defamed . . . Compensation is here a *solatium* rather than a monetary recompense for harm measurable in money." Yet the idea of *solatium* or consolation can be understood in two ways, one in terms of upset and the other in terms of enabling the plaintiff to get on with his or her life in changed circumstances.

3. See the essays in David Capper, ed., *Modern Defamation Law: Balancing Reputation and Free Expression* (Belfast: School of Law, Queen's University, 2012).

way toward further clearing the plaintiff's name.[4] Damages also help the plaintiff adjust to the world in which the reversal of the statement has been imperfect; special damages make up particular losses, that is, restore to the plaintiff the means that he or she would have had, had the wrong not taken place. In order to understand how the remedy can address the violated right, however, we need to focus on the right itself.

1. Overview

Defamation was considered a wrong in Roman law, one of the aspects of *iniuria*. One of the earliest English cases states its importance this way: "of such Nature is libelling, it is secret, and robs a Man of his good Name, which ought to be more precious to him than his Life."[5] In *Othello*, Shakespeare makes the same point this way:

> Who steals my purse steals trash. 'Tis something, nothing:
> 'Twas mine, 'tis his, and has been slave to thousands.
> But he that filches from me my good name
> Robs me of that which not enriches him
> And makes me poor indeed.[6]

More recently, Stewart J. in *Rosenblatt v. Baer* writes, "The right of a man to the protection of his own reputation from unjustified invasion and wrongful hurt reflects no more than our basic concept of the essential dignity and worth of every human being—a concept at the root of any de-

---

4. In Cassell v. Broome, [1972] AC 1027, Lord Hailsham suggests at 1071 that damages operate to clear the plaintiff's name in an ongoing way, "in case the libel, driven underground, emerges from its lurking place at some future date . . . to point to a sum awarded . . . [enables the plaintiff] to convince a bystander of the baselessness of the charge."

5. The Case of de Libellis famosis; or of Scandalous Libels, 5 Coke 125 (1605); David Ibbetson reports that the common law courts took jurisdiction for defamation in cases of accusations of crimes away from ecclesiastical courts in the early sixteenth century. Ibbetson, *A Historical Introduction to the Law of Obligations* (Oxford: Oxford University Press, 2001), 114.

6. Shakespeare, *Othello,* act 3, scene 3, lines 163–168.

cent system of ordered liberty."[7] Despite the appeal of the idea that reputation is beyond price, the law of defamation is often understood to consist in "balancing" the plaintiff's interest in having a good reputation against the interests of others in such things as freedom of expression.

This balancing picture invites the conclusion that the law has struck the balance in the wrong place. William Prosser captured a familiar attitude in the first edition of his *Handbook of the Law of Torts* when he wrote, "It must be confessed at the beginning that there is a great deal of the law of defamation which makes no sense. It contains anomalies and absurdities for which no legal writer has ever had a kind word, and it is a curious compound of strict liability imposed upon innocent defendants, as rigid and extreme as anything found in the law, with a blind and almost perverse refusal to compensate the plaintiff for real and very serious harm."[8] The same vocabulary of balancing appears in writings more sympathetic to the traditional law; as the Ministerial Preface to Britain's proposed *Defamation Act* (2011) puts it, "But freedom of speech does not mean that people should be able to ride roughshod over the reputations of others, and our defamation laws must therefore strike the right balance— between protection of freedom of speech on the one hand and protection of reputation on the other."[9]

In this chapter I will argue against the balancing picture, suggesting instead that the law of defamation serves to protect each person's entitlement that no other person determines his or her standing in the eyes of others. By characterizing the wrong in terms of an underlying right instead of the harm suffered, and the right in explicitly contrastive terms—"no other person"—I propose also to explain why it has the structure and distinctive defenses that it does, and explain the precise sense in which it is "at the root" of a system of ordered liberty.

7. (1966) 383 U.S. 75, 92.

8. William L. Prosser, *Handbook of the Law of Torts* (St. Paul, MN: West, 1941), 778. The same passage appears in subsequent editions, right up to W. L. Prosser and W. P. Keeton, *Prosser and Keeton on the Law of Torts,* 5th ed. (St. Paul, MN: West Group, 1984), 771–772.

9. The Rt. Hon. Kenneth Clarke QC MP, Lord Chancellor and Secretary of State for Justice, and Lord McNally, Minister of State, "Ministerial Introduction," *Draft Defamation Bill Presented to Parliament by the Lord Chancellor and Secretary of State for Justice by Command of Her Majesty,* March 2011.

The other broad theme that my discussion will bring into relief concerns the idea of tort as the system of interpersonal responsibility. I will not only argue that the right to your own good name is a right that you, in particular, have against others; I will apply to it the idea developed in earlier chapters, that the right can itself only be characterized in terms of what others may not do to you. The interest in reputation protected by the law of defamation is fundamentally juridical, not only because of the way in which the law protects it. Like the other rights that figure in tort law, it is not an interest that the law has contingently taken up and given relational form. Your right to your own good name is relational in a sense that goes beyond the mode of its protection. It is already present in the very possibility of a system of relational rights.

Several features of defamation make it difficult to assimilate to more familiar torts. Much theoretical writing about torts takes negligence as analytically paradigmatic. The two uncontroversial features of the tort of negligence are notably absent in defamation. In order for the plaintiff to succeed in a defamation action, the defendant's conduct need not have been careless or otherwise defective, and the plaintiff need not have suffered a loss through the defendant's action. Like trespass to land or battery, libel is actionable per se, that is, without a showing of loss, and can be committed regardless of how careful the defendant was being. Unlike those other torts, however, the tort of defamation appears to be a side effect of something else the defendant was doing. A battery is an unauthorized touching, a trespass to land is an unauthorized entry; in each case, the wrong consists in something that the defendant is doing to the plaintiff, or on the plaintiff's land. In defamation, by contrast, the defendant commits the wrong by making statements about the plaintiff to people other than the plaintiff.[10]

Procedurally, defamation also strikes many writers as surprising. The plaintiff need only establish that the defendant said something that would cast him or her in a negative light in the eyes of others. The plaintiff does not need to establish the falsity of the defamatory statement, that the de-

---

10. Every private wrong has a preposition: negligence, *Rylands,* and *Hollywood* are "to the plaintiff," use-based wrongs are "with the plaintiff's" or "on the plaintiff's land," and defamation is "about the plaintiff."

fendant was careless with respect to its truth, or even that the plaintiff was in any way disadvantaged through the making of the statement; the character of the statement is sufficient to make out the plaintiff's prima facie case. The burden of proof then shifts to the defendant to establish a defense. Yet these do not go to the plaintiff's conduct in the way in which such defenses as contributory negligence or voluntary assumption of risk do, or to the integrity or operation of the judicial process in the way that illegality or a statute of limitation might. Instead, they focus on other aspects of the defendant's conduct.

My aim in this chapter is to defuse the puzzlement or even bafflement generated by these differences. I will argue that defamation looks hard if you begin, as so many writers do, with a conception tort law as a law of losses, or even as the law of wrongs, where wrongs are schematized as protecting particularly weighty interests that the plaintiff has. Recent proposals to use the tort of negligence to protect the interest in reputation, or the tort of defamation to protect interests other than reputation,[11] flow naturally from the assumption that legal categories are available procedural instruments through which interests can be protected.

In so doing, I shall focus on the traditional common law of defamation, as it still survives outside the United States of America. I believe that many of the recent developments in the American law of defamation reflect the assumption that the law of defamation is a tool for protecting an interest that is intelligible entirely apart from its mode of protection.[12] The traditional doctrinal structure of defamation is seen as having no significance of its own. Once this misleading picture is in place, that doctrinal structure looks to be about as important as the material traditionally used in the handle of a hammer. If you are using a tool in order to achieve something, and discover that it has unfortunate side effects—perhaps the wooden

11. Eric Descheemaeker, "Protecting Reputation: Defamation and Negligence," *Oxford Journal of Legal Studies* 29 (2009): 603–641.

12. See, for example, Philadelphia Newspapers v. Hepps, 475 U.S. 767 (1986), as well as the Restatement (2d) of Torts §558. For another example, see *Revised Arizona Jury Instructions for Defamation,* which states that outside of cases of public figures, questions of public concern or qualified privilege, for which actual malice is required, "a common-law negligence standard applies." http://www.azbar.org/media/700258/defamation_2013.pdf.

handle gives you slivers—the thing to do is modify the tool, or replace it altogether. That is the approach that American courts have taken.

My central claim is that the law of defamation gives effect to a set of normative ideas that are *already* inherent in private law as a system of individual responsibility. Recent writing about tort law has invoked concepts of responsibility to explain the moral basis of liability.[13] That is not the sense I am proposing; my suggestion is that it is a system of responsibility in the sense that its basic doctrines are expressions of an idea that human beings are responsible agents to whom particular acts can be attributed. As a system of attribution, in turn, private law presupposes several structuring ideas. The most basic of these is the idea that any allegation of wrongdoing must be established.

I call this a structuring idea because it shapes the conduct of a legal proceeding. The burden lies with the plaintiff of establishing that the defendant has committed a wrong; if this burden is met, the defendant then has the burden of answering; if this latter burden is met, the plaintiff may have the burden of countering. The plaintiff doesn't have a burden of disproving defenses; the defendant has the burden of proving them, and so on with the plaintiff's answer.

I shall contend that this account explains each of the things that appear to be puzzling about defamation: the nature of the wrong; the requirement that a defamatory statement be "of and concerning" the plaintiff, rather than that it have foreseeably injured the plaintiff; the procedural structure in which the plaintiff need only show that the defendant has damaged her reputation, without showing any of the falsity of the defendant's claim, the defendant's lack of care with respect to its truth or falsity, or any disadvantage suffered through the defamatory claim; the shift of the burden to the defendant, and the generic types of defenses. Each of these is transparent if your right against defamation is thought

---

13. See Tony Honoré, *Responsibility and Fault* (Oxford: Oxford University Press, 1999); Stephen R. Perry, "Responsibility for Outcomes, Risk, and the Law of Torts," in *Philosophy and the Law of Torts*, ed. Gerald Postema (Cambridge: Cambridge University Press, 2001): 72–130; David Enoch, "Tort Liability and Taking Responsibility," and John C. P. Goldberg and Benjamin C. Zipursky, "Tort Law and Responsibility," both in *Philosophical Foundations of the Law of Torts*, ed. John Oberdiek (Oxford: Oxford University Press, 2014).

of as an instance of your basic right to have no wrong attributed to you that you did not do; all are baffling if the tort of defamation is thought of as a tool for protecting a nonjuridical interest.

I do not mean to deny that people in general, or particular persons on particular occasions, have an interest in being free of defamatory statements. Having others think well of you is one of the countless ways in which your life may be better, so there is a serviceable sense of the word "interest" in which you have an interest in having other people think well of you. But the law of defamation does not protect that interest. Instead, the protected interest is specifically juridical: It presupposes specifically legal concepts of reputation. It is not an interest of general importance that is protected in a restricted way; it is only protected against certain types of interference because it is, fundamentally, a right that others not do certain things to you. Its restriction to a certain class of acts is not based on any assumption about that class of acts usually setting back some interest severely. The specifically juridical character of defamation emerges both in the wrong and in the defenses available.

In order to develop my alternative account, I shall say some things, in passing, about how it is a mistake to characterize defamation in terms of an interest. My main task, however, will be to characterize the nature of the right, the violation of which gives rise to an action in defamation. I will locate this right in broader, systematic features of a legal system, and in so doing seek to show that your right to your own good name means that nobody else is entitled to besmirch it. The wrong of defamation consists in doing that. The procedural structure of defamation follows from the fact that only your deeds can determine your standing in the eyes of the community. Others who damage your reputation wrong you simply by so doing.

These formulations—nobody is entitled to besmirch your name, no other person can put you under an obligation to clear your name—may seem like circumlocutions, because they appear to locate your right in the prohibition on what others may do, rather than in a fact about you. As I have argued in earlier chapters, as a perfectly general matter, absent a special relationship, you never have a right against other private persons that they behave in ways that ensure that you be or remain in a certain condition; legal rights are always constraints on the conduct of others. Just as your right to your property is the prohibition on others using it without your authorization, so too, your right to your own good name is the restriction on the conduct of others. Only you are entitled to change your reputation because others may not.

In introducing my model, I will begin with defamatory statements that also have the structure of legal imputations: claims that someone has committed a crime or some other wrong will be paradigmatic examples. I will then extend the same structure to cover claims that you have done other things that would lower others' opinion of you. For example, the claim that you did something disgusting (albeit something that does not amount to a wrong against another human being) need not explicitly allege that you have committed a legal wrong. But it lowers your reputation in the eyes of the others, and so can be brought within the reach of defamation. I use the word "can" here deliberately; in outlining the structure of defamation, I do not mean to claim that the form is sufficient to fully determine its content. As a result, being cast in a bad light will inevitably be interpreted in part in terms of the standards prevalent in the community of which the plaintiff is a member. Your reputation resides in the opinions of others, and what those others think of as a wrong is relevant to whether someone has defamed you.

2. The Structure of Reputation: Why Reputation Is Not an Extralegal Interest

As a preliminary matter, I want to draw attention to familiar structural features of the law of defamation, and the interpretive difficulties faced by any account that would seek to explain it in terms of the protection of an interest or advantage, or to assimilate it to the law of negligence in some other way.

In setting out the difficulties with this way of thinking about defamation, my focus will be on possible interpretations of the idea that it is an interest that might be balanced against the competing interest in free expression. The organizing idea of an interest is that it can be understood, and evaluated, without any reference to its mode of protection, and that it has a degree of importance that should figure in deciding whether, or to what extent, to protect it, and to balance it against the degree of other interests. On the strategy that I mean to criticize, the mode of protection comes later in the analysis, after the interest has been analyzed and balanced against competing interests. From this perspective it would seem to be circular to identify the interest with its mode of protection.

Viewed as an instrument for protecting interests, the traditional law of defamation looks sadly deficient. Much of the difficulty comes from the extent to which the interest that people have in reputation is much less personal than the law of defamation seems to presume. On the one hand, its application is unduly restrictive; on the other, it is wildly permissive. The requirement that a defamatory statement be "of and concerning" the plaintiff makes the tort seem unduly restrictive in the interests it protects. The lives of family members are disrupted by false allegations against their spouses or children,[14] law firms lose clients because defamatory articles about senior partners are believed,[15] and investors lose money when a company in which they hold stock is criticized.[16] If reputation is viewed as an asset or benefit, these nonsuited parties have interests in the reputations of others, and it is difficult to see why it would not be protected. Indeed, in each of these examples the plaintiff is foreseeable to anyone who gives any thought to what might happen if they misspeak. Thus, if the law protects an interest in being free of disadvantages created by false beliefs that other people have, all of these plaintiffs seem to be worthy.

If reputation is thought of as an interest, it is also puzzling that the law of defamation provides no protection to professionals, whose reputation for safety or reliability is compromised as a result of wrongdoing by others.[17] In this sense, the tort of defamation seems to be too narrow, as

14. Pattison v. Gulf Bag Co., 116 La. 963, 41 So. 224 (1906); Tannenbaum v. Foerster, 648 F. Supp. 1300 (E.D. Wis. 1986); Morgan v. Hustler Magazine, Inc., 653 F. Supp. 711 (N.D. Ohio 1987); Zucker v. Rockland County, 111 A.D.2d 325, 489 N.Y.S.2d 308 (1985).

15. Cohn v. National Broadcasting Co., 414 N.Y.S.2d 906 (N.Y. App. Div. 1979) at 907–908.

16. AIDS Counseling and Testing Centers v. Group W Television, Inc., 903 F.2d 1000, 1005 (4th Cir. 1990); Dexter's Hearthside Restaurant, Inc. v. Whitehall Co., 508 N.E.2d 113 (Mass. App. Ct. 1987).

17. See, for example, Jorgensen v. Massachusetts Port Auth., 905 F.2d 515, 522 (1st Cir.1990), in which plaintiffs contended that the defendant airport authority had damaged their reputations by failing to maintain a runway, thereby causing them to be faultlessly involved in a serious accident. They sued in negligence, and introduced reputational harm as a head of damages. The court denied recovery because it held that damage to reputation

it focuses on harms suffered by a class of persons selected on the basis of something other than their vulnerability to that precise type of harm.

Second, and from the opposite direction, if the "of and concerning" requirement threatens to make liability in defamation too narrow, the structure of a defamation action threatens to make it too broad. The plaintiff does not need to even allege, let alone prove, fault on the defendant's part.

Third, like battery and trespass to land, libel is actionable per se. The plaintiff is entitled to a remedy without establishing any loss or disadvantage. So too are certain forms of slander, notably the allegation that the plaintiff has committed a crime.[18] Along this dimension, the structure of the law strikes some as unduly broad.

These three hurdles corresponded, roughly, to the elements of a negligence action. The "duty" question of to whom a duty is owed, is answered, not in terms of foreseeable loss, but instead in terms of the subject matter of the statement. As a way of protecting against loss, this seems perverse—the law ignores a serious loss, against which the defendant could easily have taken precautions. In the cases involving family members or business partners, the defendant was already under a duty to the person about whom the statement was made, and so already was legally required to avoid making the statement in question. Thus, the plaintiffs in such cases are denied a remedy even though avoiding the losses they suffered would have imposed no additional burden on the defendant.

If the analogue of the "duty" question is answered in a way that may seem unduly hostile to meritorious plaintiffs, the analogue of the "standard of care" question is answered in a way that will appear unduly hostile to diligent defendants; not merely reasonable but extreme care is not good enough. Critics of the law of negligence sometimes complain about the way in which its objective standard holds people to account for things they cannot control; such concerns pale in comparison to the strictness of liability in defamation. Questions of remoteness or proximate cause, as well as those of causation, are equally surprising from the standpoint

---

was not foreseeable. The plaintiffs had no cause of action in defamation, as the defendants had made no statement about them.

18. Clay v. Roberts, 1863 5 L.T. 897.

of negligence, because no actual loss needs to be established at all. Even those critics of the doctrine of causation in negligence, who suppose that all careless people should be treated alike, regardless of the harm that they cause, are unlikely to be happy with this feature of defamation, because of the way in which it combines with the analogues of the duty and standard-of-care questions: People who show indifference to the effects of their words on others are not subject to reproach so long as what they say is true, but others who are scrupulously careful but make an innocent mistake are held liable.

These difficulties in characterizing the wrong as the invasion of an interest reappear in the structure of remedies. As far as compensation goes, again, the traditional law of defamation seems to be both too broad and too narrow. People who suffer serious harm through misattributions, no matter how egregious, are denied a remedy if the statement was not of and concerning them; others are able to recover general damages without any showing of damage.

I mention these puzzles, not because they call the law into question, but because they suggest that if it is conceptualized as a matter of loss prevention or compensation, it makes no sense. Viewed in terms of providing prospective guidance for action or retrospective compensation for injury, the law is very difficult to grasp. The interest that it protects defies categorization except in terms of the legal structure that protects it; you have a right against being wrongly defamed.

An instrumental account could perhaps be revived as a sort of second-best solution to problems of false and harmful speech, relying perhaps on the generalization that people will be less likely to damage each other's reputations if they are hypervigilant about avoiding doing so. Any such proposal seems to make things worse rather than better for the traditional law of defamation; it seems to be vulnerable to Smith's objection from Chapter 5: It is a demand that people do more than it is reasonable to do.

Perhaps a sufficiently inventive instrumental account could explain these doctrinal structures in terms of information costs, transaction costs, or other institutional features that apply in the case of defamation but not in the case of negligence. Or perhaps it could be argued that some general interest licenses an overbroad rule to protect what is ultimately nothing more than a proxy for it,[19] or that some sort of balance must be struck between a person's interest in reputation and some other sort of interest, such as the public interest in having the truth emerge. I will not argue directly against the application of this strategy to the case of defamation. Given enough free parameters in an account, it could explain any structure at all. More detailed factual information about the likely impact of various rules on the achievement of the competing interests might resolve part of this indeterminacy. The difficulty, however, is that nobody knows any of the relevant facts. So the sense of an explanation, if there is one at all, turns on the assertion that this must be the way it works, that it must be a balance of one competing interest against another. But if the assertion is to rest on something other than speculation and the hunch that all practical reasoning must be of this form, then the explanation does not require a detailed case-by-case response, because it is not a detailed case-by-case analysis, despite its pretensions to determinacy and rigor. It is difficult to believe that if someone were interested in designing a system to minimize the costs of defamatory statements, taking account of pre-

---

19. A clear example of a proxy model can be found in Robert C. Post's characterization of the three different models of reputation that he contends have shaped the common law of defamation. The first is what Post calls a "property model." Second, Post considers what he calls the "honor" view of reputation, according to which reputation is a matter of a person's superior status. However important this idea may have been historically, Post suggests that it has no real place in a modern democracy. Third, he considers what he calls the "dignity" view of reputation, on which human dignity is understood to derive from membership in an orderly and cohesive community defined by the reciprocal observance of rules of civility. Post, "The Social Foundations of Defamation Law: Reputation and the Constitution," *California Law Review* 74 (1986): 691–742.

The difficulty of all of these accounts is not just that they fail to fit the contours of the law of defamation. More significantly, although each is introduced as an account of reputation, each is actually an account of some other good that is protected through the protection of reputation. So your own good name might be thought to merit protection because it is an asset you have, because protecting it protects the status relations in which you stand, or because protecting it enforces community cohesion and a vision of the good life. None of these is an account of what reputation is, why it would be (or even what it would mean for someone to think it) more valuable than riches or at the root of any decent system of ordered liberty, or why it is a right. Indeed, with the possible exception of the honor model, none understands reputation relationally at all, and the honor model, at least as Post glosses it, understands reputation only in terms of a comparison rather than a relation.

caution costs as well as avoidable losses, that this is the system they would
have devised.

3. Your Own Good Name

So far I have argued that the law of defamation is difficult to assimilate to
an account that focuses on the prevention of harm or loss.

The right to reputation is different from both property rights and rights
with respect to your body. Like your rights with respect to your body,
but unlike rights with respect to property, your right to your reputation
is a right to something that necessarily belongs only to you, and requires
neither acquisition by you nor conferral by another. Unlike your right
to your body, together with which it comprises your right to your person,
your right to your reputation is at the same time necessarily external to
you, residing as it does in the views of others. Because your reputation is
at once personal and external, you do not need to do anything to acquire
your own good name, but you can lose it through the actions of others.

These distinguishing features of reputation make it a right that can be
understood only in relation to the possibility of legal proceedings,[20] and
so in relation to the mechanism of its protection. The idea that an allegation of wrongdoing must be established is the organizing idea of a system
of reciprocal limits on conduct in which legally significant acts are attributed to individual human beings, and, as a concomitant to those limits, a
system of accountability.

Perhaps the most obvious and familiar instance of this idea—and, indeed, the root of much of the misunderstanding of the tort of defamation—
lies in the burden of proof in legal proceedings. In the criminal law, the
presumption of innocence works in the defendant's favor, as does the
burden placed on the Crown or State of coming forward with evidence.[21]

---

20. I do not mean to suggest that it depends on the actuality of legal proceedings; only
on their possibility. Stranded survivors after a shipwreck can do things that would count as
defaming each other, but that possibility depends upon understanding their claims in the
context of possible adjudication of their disputes.

21. See Hamish Stewart, "The Presumption of Innocence," *Criminal Law and Philosophy*
8 (2014): 407–420; Antony Duff, "Who Must Presume Whom to Be Innocent of What?,"
Netherlands Journal of Legal Philosophy 42 (2013): 170–192. Duff points to the generality of
the presumption, noting that it doesn't apply if someone declines to associate with someone

In a tort action for negligence, trespass, or conversion, the plaintiff must establish that the defendant has committed each of the elements of the tort against her.

Defamation's bad reputation as a tort flows in part from the appearance that it gives up on this basic moral idea. The plaintiff, having established merely that the defendant has defamed her, that is, said something that would tend to cast her in a bad light, thereby shifts the onus onto the defendant, because the defendant must now provide an affirmative defense.

The distinctiveness of defamation, however, does not show that it is an exception to the general presumption that a person has done no wrong; it shows instead that it gives effect to that very presumption. If I have defamed you, all that you need to establish is that I have alleged that you have done wrong. If you have established that, you do not face the further burden of needing to clear your name; it falls to me to show that the allegation is true, was not a genuine allegation, or was privileged.

I do not mean to suggest that this is anything other than the traditional way of thinking about a defamation action. Indeed, in the debates in the House of Lords leading up to the UK Defamation Act (1996), the Lord Chancellor responded to a proposed amendment to reverse the burden of proof in the following way:

> It is normally the plaintiff who is the accused and who should be presumed innocent of the defamatory charge unless the defendant can prove that he was guilty . . . The amendment would alter the whole structure of defamation law so that every hapless person against whom another chose to allege dishonesty, immorality, dishonourable conduct, incompetence and so forth would always have to prove his innocence in order to protect his reputation.[22]

Your right to your own good name protects you because it is a constitutive rule of private legal order as a system in which individual human beings are accountable for their acts. In characterizing it as a constitutive

---

he believes to be a wrongdoer, but it does "if an official deals with a citizen as if he was guilty of a crime, or if other citizens exclude him from ordinary civic amenities as being guilty (they daub his house with accusatory graffiti, or exclude him from public spaces)." Ibid., 173.

22. Baron Mackay of Clashfern, Lord Chancellor, *Hansard* HL Deb 2 Apr 1996: Column 242.

rule, I am not suggesting that it exhausts private law as a system of imputation. Instead, it structures the way in which particular standards of conduct are brought to bear on specific deeds. The prohibitions on battery, negligence, or breach of contract regulate the ways in which human beings are permitted to conduct themselves in relation to others. They determine the form of the basic rights and obligations that individuals have against each other, and the manner in which new obligations can be undertaken. These primary norms of conduct make up the law of obligations. The primary norms also generate secondary norms of repair in cases of wrongdoing.

In order to do so, however, primary norms also require the framework principle that you are accountable for what you have done. The organizing rule of imputation, presupposed by any more specific rules, is that you are not accountable for something unless you have done it. That rule is certainly morally significant—that is why the idea of a reverse onus seems so problematic. Although there is ongoing debate about the precise structure of the act requirement in the criminal law, it is widely agreed that pure status crimes are legally and morally problematic.[23] Pure status torts would be no less problematic.[24]

The moral appeal of the basic organizing rule of imputation stems from the fact that it is immanent in the very idea of interpersonal accountability. Human beings are accountable to each other, and the law gives effect to the morality of interpersonal accountability, by specifying concrete rules and procedures through which the requirements of that morality can be systematically observed and satisfied.

The law takes as its starting point the thought that, prior to performing any act, you are beyond reproach, and so have a good name as a matter of right. The only way you can lose this status is through some act that you perform. That is just to say you are not accountable for anything you have not done.

---

23. See, e.g., Robinson v. California, 370 U.S. 660 (1962) (which held that a law prohibiting addiction was unconstitutional).

24. Arguably a tort duty to rescue would be exactly that—you would be under an obligation simply in virtue of what you were in a position to do, rather than in virtue of what you had done.

An alternative starting point is conceivable, but morally suspect: You could be accountable for something that you have not done, in the manner of dystopian teen novels, or through a general system of "negative responsibility,"[25] on which you are accountable for everything that happens, and the fact that you, personally, were involved in its production is at most evidential or incidental.

The dystopian/negative responsibility alternative need not be taken to the extreme of holding you responsible for everything, or for the deeds of your ancestors, in order for its problematic status, both morally and conceptually, to be apparent. Part of what it is to hold other human beings accountable is to think of them as acting in the world, making their own way, in relation to others, and restricted primarily by the entitlements of others to act in the world. The idea that someone is born accountable to others for some deed she did not perform is deeply problematic from this perspective. Once that possibility is rejected, however, the only remaining position is the one that goes to the opposite extreme of saying that, prior to any affirmative act, you are capable of being responsible for your actions, but you have done no wrong, and stand in no legal relations except for the background ones in which every human being stands to every other. That is just to say that the burden of proof lies with anyone who imputes any legally significant deed to you.

This starting point explains the structural difference between an action in defamation and one in negligence. The plaintiff in a negligence action must establish each of the elements of the tort, because the plaintiff is the one alleging that someone else, the defendant, has committed a wrong. The burden of establishing that claim therefore lies with the plaintiff. In a defamation action, by contrast, the plaintiff's complaint is that the *defendant* has made an allegation about the plaintiff. The burden of establishing that the defendant made the claim lies with the plaintiff, as does the burden of establishing that it casts the plaintiff in a bad light, but if the plaintiff meets those burdens, the defendant avoids liability only by establishing the allegation or a privilege with respect to making it.

25. Bernard Williams, "A Critique of Utilitarianism," in *Utilitarianism: For and Against,* ed. J. J. C. Smart and Bernard Williams (Cambridge: Cambridge University Press, 1973), 95.

4. Explaining Defamation: The Nature of the Wrong

The example through which I introduced the idea of your right to be beyond reproach—the burden of proof in legal proceedings—is a specific legal proceeding. As such, they may seem unduly narrow as a model for your right to reputation. Part of what it is to have a legally protected right is for procedures to be available through which disputes about that right can be resolved. The same structure of a court specifying the precise contours of the legal rights, and resolving disputes about their application to particulars, can be brought to bear on the court's own structuring right, and thus on disputes about reputation. I now want to suggest that this is exactly what happens in a defamation action.

4.1. "Of and Concerning"

If the law of defamation were concerned with protecting an interest, it should be possible to characterize that interest apart from the means of its protection. The law of defamation fails to do this. The requirement that the defamatory statement be "of and concerning" the plaintiff shows that this concern is not with the harm that defamation does, but rather with the wrong that it is. A defamatory statement made about somebody else will foreseeably disadvantage a business associate, colleague, or family member; those foreseeably disadvantaged plaintiffs may not sue in defamation, because they have not been defamed. Like a person who relies on a piece of property, such as a bridge, owned by another, or on someone honoring a contract with a third party with whom the person does business, the person who depends on the reputation of another does not recover, because although he has been disadvantaged, he has not been wronged. Your right in defamation is not the right that others not say negative things about people that result in harm to you or are likely to do so; your right in defamation is instead the right that people not say false things about you that cast you in a negative light in the eyes of others.[26]

---

26. Someone may say something false and defamatory about you without realizing he or she is referring to you. In Hulton & Co. v. Jones, [1910] AC 20, the defendant newspaper

In this the law of defamation is parallel to other torts: Only the person who has been wronged has standing to proceed against the defendant; others who have suffered losses as a result of the defendant's wrong to someone else fail to state a cause of action.[27] More than that, your right to your own good name is necessarily yours. The defamatory statement must be of and concerning the plaintiff because the plaintiff is the one who is alleged to have done wrong, and so the only one who would need to clear his or her name if the statement was allowed to stand.[28] Nobody else is alleged to have done anything, or needs to clear his or her own name if disadvantaged, even severely, by the defamation of another. If the statement is not of and concerning you, then all that a defendant has done is change the context in which you have your reputation. In so doing, the defendant may have caused you problems,[29] or wronged others, but has not wronged you.

---

published a story about a fictitious character named Artemus Jones who engaged in various misdeeds in Paris. The story was presented in a way that made it appear to purport to be a true account. There was an actual person by that name, and he sued successfully, on the grounds that ordinary readers would take the account to refer to him. Thus it was "of and concerning" the plaintiff.

27. See the discussion of defamation in Benjamin C. Zipursky, "Rights, Wrongs, and Recourse in the Law of Torts," *Vanderbilt Law Review* 51 (1998): 1, 84.

28. Inevitably, sometimes statements will refer to more than one person with the same name. In such "reference innuendo cases" (e.g., Baturina v. Times Newspapers Ltd., [2011] EWCA Civ 308), a plaintiff may be wronged because others would reasonably take a statement to refer to him or her. Other examples include Newstead v. London Express Newspaper, [1940] 1 KB 377, 385. Although David Ibbetson traces this development of the law to "the fault element" having "ossified into two fixed defences" (*A Historical Introduction to the Law of Obligations*, 185), it can also be read as the crystallization of the right.

29. See Falkenberg v. Nationwide News Party Ltd., unreported, SC (NSW), No. 20832 [1994]. Plaintiffs complained of a *Far Side* cartoon with the caption "Graffiti in Hell" that depicted the devil glaring angrily at a wall with happy faces and other cheerful pictures beside the words "For a pleasant conversation call Satan" followed by a telephone number beginning with 555. Although 555 numbers occur frequently in popular culture because they are not assigned in the United States, they are in Australia, and the listed number turned out to be plaintiffs' phone number in their area code. They received many prank phone calls as a result, but despite their suffering, the case failed, because although the publication directed people to them, it was not of and concerning them.

4.2. Burden of Proof

The plaintiff needs only to establish that the defendant made a statement of and concerning the plaintiff that was defamatory, that is, that would tend to lower the plaintiff's standing in the opinion of others, in order to shift the onus to the defendant. The defendant's burden of showing that the statement was not defamatory follows directly from the right to your own good name. If you never need to establish or clear your name, then, the person who calls your good name into question must establish that the statement was not wrongful because some defense applies.

Placing on the defendant the burden of proving that the defamatory statement was not wrongful protects the plaintiff's entitlement to be beyond reproach. It is, at the same time, consistent with the defendant's like entitlement. The requirement that the defendant provide a defense does not require the defendant to disclaim an unsubstantiated allegation of wrongdoing; it only arises once the plaintiff has already met the burden of proof in establishing that the defendant has defamed her, that is, made a statement that lowers her in the opinion of others.

4.3. Liability without Fault

The plaintiff does not need to establish that the defendant knew or should have known the defamatory statement to be false, because the plaintiff's right to her own good name already includes the thought that no aspect of the plaintiff's entitlement ever needs to be established. The wrong does not consist in disregard of another's reputation. It consists in interference with it. Like trespass against land, liability is strict in the sense that you wrong another through a particular act, regardless of other characteristics of that type of act.

4.4. In the Opinion of Others

Your reputation consists in the opinion that others hold of you. As such, the law needs some way of characterizing what counts as what others think, what the subject matter of those thoughts must be, and what counts as damage to reputation.

Examples such as the allegation that someone has committed a wrong are analytically clear, but might be thought to be unrepresentative.

Someone can defame you without alleging that you have committed a legal wrong. The organizing analysis applies much more generally, however. Your reputation always resides in the opinions of others about you. As such, it depends on what others in your society think about you in relation to how they think about wrongdoing; for them to think ill of you is for them to think you have in some way done wrong. The relevant conception of having done wrong—and the things for which you are entitled to be beyond reproach—will extend to moral and even social wrongs. Others are not entitled to impute any of these wrongs to you. Familiar examples include the allegation that a professional is incompetent. Such an allegation need not make reference to any violation of licensing requirements to be actionable, because it already contains the suggestion that the professional has held him- or herself out as something he or she is not. The same structure can be brought to bear on a statement about something disreputable or unseemly that you have done, which does not count as a legal wrong against anyone in particular. Here, too, nobody can put you in a position of needing to clear your name in the opinions of others. These are all examples of damage done to reputation; they are not descriptions of or predictions about other disadvantage that might accrue.[30]

The structure as I have outlined it applies, in the first instance, to particular deeds. The defamatory statement, however, can also be made

---

30. The UK Defamation Act (2013), §1.1, imposes the requirement: "A statement is not defamatory unless its publication has caused or is likely to cause serious harm to the reputation of the claimant." This might seem to restrict defamation to cases in which injury to something other than reputation results. But the serious harm requirement applies only to reputation; in the Explanatory Notes to the *Act,* two grounds are identified for imposing this requirement. One of these is to prevent abuses of process. The other, more general, requirement makes explicit the focus on harm to reputation rather than any other interest. The Explanatory Notes rely on the endorsement, in Thornton v. Telegraph Media Group Ltd., [2010] EWHC 1414 (QB) (16 June 2010), of Lord Atkin's speech in Sim v. Stretch, [1936] 2 All ER 1237 at 1242, in which he summarized the requirement of serious harm in the following terms: "That juries should be free to award damages for injuries to reputation is one of the safeguards of liberty. But the protection is undermined when exhibitions of bad manners or discourtesy are placed on the same level as attacks on character, and are treated as actionable wrongs." Lord Atkin, in turn, explicitly appealed to the distinction drawn by Baron Pollock in Clay v. Roberts, 1863 5 L.T. 897, "between imputing what is merely a breach of conventional etiquette and what is illegal, mischievous or sinful." None of *Thornton, Sim, Clay,* or the UK Defamation Act (2013) entertains the possibility that defamation will be actionable only on showing of damage to something other than reputation.

about your character. There is an ongoing dispute in moral philosophy about the relative primacy of action and character in moral evaluation. The legal situation is clearer: Particular actions take primacy in legal responsibility. However, whether we suppose that character is somehow aggregated out of individual actions, or conversely, that individual actions are significant because expressions of character, many negative representations of your character are, as such, also representations of your deeds.[31] If someone disparages your character, the only way that you could clear your name would be by reference to things you have done. Indeed, it can be more difficult to answer a serious but nonspecific allegation—someone says that you are a crook—than a specific one. As a result, others can wrong you by casting your character in a bad light.

Inevitably, the particular content expressed through your right to your own good name is filled in through positive law in light of ordinary social understandings of what it is to be a proper and upright member of your community. It is also shaped by general background ideas of legality. So, for example a report that someone is a police informer or unwilling to commit certain crimes may well lower his standing if his social circle is made up of criminals. The law has treated such diminution of standing as nondefamatory.[32] Even in a social setting in which being thought a police informant or unwilling to commit crimes is considered worse than

---

31. But not all representations of character are necessarily representations of deeds: If you describe me as ungenerous, as a stickler, or selfish (except in relation to some specific role I have undertaken), you point to a defect in virtue that is less closely connected to wrongs.

32. Mawe v. Piggott, (1869) IR 4 CL 54, where a newspaper article falsely reported that the plaintiff had said he would reveal the identities of Irish Republicans, leading to their prosecution. Lawson J. said, "[Counsel for the plaintiff] argued that amongst certain classes who were either themselves criminal, or who sympathised with crime, it would expose a person to great odium to represent him as an informer or a prosecutor, or otherwise aiding in the detection of crime; that is quite true, but we cannot be called upon to adopt that standard. The very circumstances which will make a person be regarded with disfavour by the criminal classes will raise his character in the estimation of right-thinking men. We can only regard the estimation in which a man is held by society generally." The example may be troubling because of the prospect of political crimes, but the broad structure turns on the fact that the law cannot regard a reputation for law-abidingness, even a false one, as interfering with your own good name.

committing crimes, the latter is defamatory but the former not because the law will not take account of social norms that are diametrically opposed to its own operation.

The porosity of defamation to other parts of the law makes it look like an accomplice to what we now regard as objectionable attitudes, particularly toward sexuality. In one sense, that is true. Although criminalization of consensual sexual activity is deeply objectionable, it is not surprising that the law of defamation would take note of allegations that someone had committed what was, at that time, a crime, because it could not place the burden on a plaintiff of clearing his own name.

In addition to being framed in terms of the law's other commitments, this abstract structure is also porous to surrounding social understandings. One consequence is that although someone falsely praising you for acts of virtue you did not perform could (1) make it the case that you are not the one through whose action your reputation is determined, and (2) make your life much more difficult, as various people invite you to endorse their charities or products, a false allegation of virtue or heroism does not lower your standing in the opinion of others.

The fact that there is a tort of defamation but no analogous tort of "famation" shows something significant about the structure of tort law as a system of rights.[33] It is not that you have a right that other people believe

33. As Trollope notes, in a discussion of false praise of a candidate for public office, "famation" can do plenty of mischief: "No proprietor or editor was ever brought before the courts at the cost of ever so many hundred pounds,—which if things go badly may rise to several thousands,—because he had attributed all but divinity to some very poor specimen of mortality . . . But a new law of libel must be enacted before such salutary proceedings can take place" (Anthony Trollope, *The Way We Live Now* [London: Chapman and Hall, 1875], bk. 1, chap. 44, p. 280). But if "famation" in this sense is not a wrong, there are other wrongs that might operate under such a name. One of these is breach of confidence, which I mentioned briefly in Chapter 4 in my discussion of special relationships. I noted that certain special relations can be undertaken and give rise to a duty of care with respect to some aspect of the plaintiff's affairs for which the defendant has undertaken responsibility. In some cases the relevant aspect is the protection of that person's privacy: A lawyer or physician might be entrusted with someone else's secrets, and have a special role of letting that person talk about something that they do not feel comfortable sharing with a broader public. In such a relationship, a duty of confidentiality is created, and when negligent breach of that duty leads to injury, this constitutes a wrong against the plaintiff.

accurate things about you, which is compromised whenever someone speaks an untruth about you, whether that untruth raises or lowers your reputation in the eyes of others. In a relational account of rights, you could not have a right that others believe the truth about you, because, more generally, you cannot have a right to a certain state of affairs. A right is a constraint on the conduct of others. Tort law's distinction between misfeasance and nonfeasance characterizes any right that you have against another person in terms of what that person may do to you, not merely in terms of the effects of another person's actions on you. In the specific case of defamation, that person is precluded from saying something that will lower your reputation in the opinions of others. That is analytically basic, and does not reflect some further thought that you really have a right to have others believe the truth about you, which is violated when someone speaks a falsehood about what you have done. There is no tort of "famation" because you do not need to clear your name when someone falsely praises you. This is not a sociological fact about modern society; it is a juridical feature of a system of imputation and accountability. You may want to deny false praise, but you do not need to answer it.

On this understanding, the wrong of defamation cannot be characterized in terms of any concept based on agency or accuracy. To do so would be to conceptualize defamation as the wrong of causing a setback to an

---

Invasion of privacy in the absence of a special relationship—see the discussion of *Sidis* in note 75 below—is a different kind of dissemination, because it is the opposite of defamation. Whereas defamation involves circulating false information that lowers the reputation of the plaintiff in the eyes of others, invasion of privacy paradigmatically involves the circulation of true but private information. (Paradigmatically because a single statement could be both an invasion of privacy and false at the same time.) The contours of the tort of invasion of privacy are still emerging. Its relational form is straightforward: I wrong you by spreading private information about you. But the category of "private" is less determinate than the objects of other private rights. Your right to your body is the entitlement to constrain others with respect to an object that can be physically individuated; so, too, with rights to property in land and chattels. Your right to your reputation is a right to constrain others in relation to what you have done, where your deeds, once again, can be characterized using other concepts. This does not show that your right to either your body or your property or your reputation does not raise casuistical questions, only that some questions, such as whether I wrong you by depriving you of a path across my land, can be answered in exclusively spatial terms. I suspect that the right to privacy is not like this, and requires casuistry in every instance.

interest, whether it is an interest in agency, accurate representation, or "advantages and opportunities."[34] Although someone who breaks the connection between what you have done and what others think about you may put you in such a position, and thereby wrong you, breaking the connection is the mechanism of the wrong, not the wrong itself.

The law's porosity to social understandings also explains the historical prominence of what appear to be cases of defamation based on status rather than action. To allege that someone has a "loathsome disease" has long been actionable. These examples are troubling, but they show that the form of legal categories is always given effect in a concrete setting. The early loathsome-disease cases are ones in which the statement would be taken by others to suggest that the person is unfit for ordinary modes of social interaction.[35] The category of loathsome diseases was initially restricted to sexually transmitted diseases and leprosy, both of which were seen as markers of wrongdoing. The connection of sexually transmitted diseases with sin was familiar, as was the biblical representation of leprosy as a divine punishment.[36] They are thus indirect allegations of

34. Moore v. Francis et al., (1890) 121 NY 199, per Andrews J.

35. Frederick Pollock characterizes these as "contagious diseases unfitting a person for society: that is, in the modern law, venereal disease." Pollock, *The Law of Torts,* 7th ed. (London: Stevens and Sons, 1904), 241. In Grimes v. Lovel, (1698) 12 Mod 242, smallpox was excluded; the defendant had sought to escape liability because the "pox" that had been attributed to the plaintiff could have been smallpox. Holt J. rejected the application of his argument based on the meaning to be inferred from the rest of the statement, but conceded the distinction between smallpox and sexually transmitted diseases. In Le Countesse de Salops Case, (1651) 1 Benloe 155, 73 ER 1021, the imputation "she is mad" was excluded on the grounds that it is not "odious disease que vient par vice," i.e., an odious disease brought on by vice. (The Case is sometimes reported as the Countess of Shrewsbury's case, as Salops and Shrewsbury are the same town. But it is not the 1612 case considering whether a peer could be compelled to testify.) In Villers v. Monsley, (1769) 2 WILS 403, 95 ER 886, Lord Wilmot offered a different analysis, articulating defamation as statements with the effect of making someone "ridiculous, or tend[ing] to hinder mankind from associating or having intercourse with him," and professed to "see no difference between this and the cases of leprosy and plague." Later cases, including Morgan v. Lingen, (1863) 8 LT 800, treated imputations of insanity as actionable because of the tendency of others to avoid such persons, but not as an instance of a loathsome disease.

36. Taylor v. Perkins, (1607) CroJac 144, explicitly compares an allegation of leprosy to one of "the pox," i.e., a sexually transmitted disease. In the Hebrew Bible, Miriam and

wrongdoing, and so can be brought within the ambit of the general structure of defamation. Without engaging in historical conjecture, it is also
safe to say that these examples are continuous with outmoded and troubling views about the nature of disease and of sexual purity. In an age
where it is thought that certain diseases are a form of divine punishment,
the suggestion that someone has a loathsome disease is not exactly an allegation about an action, but at the same time it is not merely an allegation
of a feature having nothing to do with action. Sadly, the same point applies in the readiness of people today to blame others for certain forms
of illness.

I introduced the idea of the right to reputation by contrasting it with
what I characterized as the dystopian view on which someone could be
accountable simply in virtue of his or her birth or its circumstances. It is
important to acknowledge that there have been societies in which such
accountability has been assumed: In many, perhaps most, societies, to be
born out of wedlock was to be subject to a status-based reproach that was
not based on anything you had done, and that you could not remove.[37]

Aaron become leprous as punishment for defaming Moses (Numbers 12:1–10). See also
2 Kings 5:20–27, in which leprosy is a punishment for avarice.

37. A line of U.S. cases, originating in the South Carolina case of Eden v. Legare, 1 Bay
171 (1791), treated the imputation that a person was "of negro blood" as libel per se, on the
grounds that "if true, the party would be deprived of all civil rights." Strikingly, among the
rights of which they were deprived was the presumption of freedom: "It is true that in the
slaveholding states, a general rule of evidence has been adopted, by which every person
having negro blood, is presumed to be a slave until the contrary is proved." See Johnson v.
Brown, 4 Cranch CC 235, 13 F Cas 734 (1832). The thought that someone can occupy such
a status, let alone be born to it, has no place in a civilized legal system. Other U.S. states
had rejected it even before the abolition of slavery; see Barret v. Jarvis, 1 Ohio, 83,
Tapp. 244, (1818); McDowell v. Bowles, 8 Jones (NC) 184 (1860). In *Johnson v. Brown*, the
court conceded the disadvantages of being so labeled, but said such an imputation did not
concern a crime, a loathsome disease, or incompetence in a professional capacity. After the
Civil War, South Carolina repurposed the doctrine, drawing on a Louisiana case (despite
the fact that the case was decided under the Louisiana Civil Code) to introduce an idea of
community standards, contending that racial misidentification was actionable per se
because it "would tend to interfere seriously with the social relation of the white man to his
fellow white men." See Flood v. News & Courier Co., 50 SE 637, 639 (SC 1905). *Flood* was
followed in several other Southern states, including Arkansas, Virginia, and Oklahoma. In
one New York case, racial misidentification was held not to be slanderous per se, which was
the issue before the court, but was said in passing to be libelous: MacIntyre v. Fruchter,

People in those circumstances were thought to be unfit for at least certain forms of society.[38] Such status-based classifications are deeply troubling. That said, it is not surprising that an allegation of illegitimacy was held to be defamatory, precisely because the status was held to be something for which the person was responsible, even though he or she had done nothing.

The same porosity explains why artificial persons can be defamed, and also why no showing of special damage need be required to establish such an action. The distinctive feature of artificial persons, such as trading companies, charities, professional associations, and trade unions, is that they exist for specific purposes. Their reputation consists in working for their purposes. Since the nineteenth-century case of *South Hetton Coal Company Ltd. v. North-Eastern News Association Ltd.*,[39] English courts traditionally treated the reputation of a trading company as protected and not requiring any showing of special damage. If it were instead a financial asset, special damage would seem to be relevant. No showing is required because a trading company's reputation is not protected as a financial asset; it is protected because it is a reputation. Enabling legislation treats corporations as artificial persons, with the entitlements of natural persons, and so they are presumed to have done no wrong, and cannot be required to clear their own name. Given the nature of a trading company, its reputation will also be a financial asset. But as Lord Hope points out in *Jameel*,[40] other artificial persons may suffer other forms of

---

148 N.Y.S. 786 (Sup. Ct. 1914). *Eden* was followed in South Carolina through Bowen v. Independent Publishing Co., 230 SC 509 (1957), 96 SE 2d 564, in which the court held that the abolition of slavery and the Fourteenth Amendment to the U.S. Constitution had no bearing on the case. These cases expressly turn on the idea that the core of defamation is hurt feelings or exposure to ridicule or dislike by others, discussed below. For discussion, see Samuel Brenner, "Negro Blood in His Veins: The Development and Disappearance of the Doctrine of Defamation Per Se by Racial Misidentification in the American South," *Santa Clara Law Review* 50 (2010): 333–406.

38. Blackstone mentions loss of inheritance as an example of a disadvantage based on illegitimacy. William Blackstone, *Commentaries on the Laws of England* (London: Clarendon Press, 1765–1769), 3:124.

39. [1894] 1 QB 133.

40. Jameel and others (Respondents) v. Wall Street Journal Europe Sprl. (Appellants), [2006] UKHL 44.

loss or disadvantage; defamation of an artificial person casts doubt on its pursuit of its special purpose, whatever that purpose might be. Artificial persons differ from natural persons, to whom the law does not assign a specific purpose.

The fact that the model of reputation can be extended to artificial persons does not entail that it must be so extended. It shows only that, if they are treated as having the powers of natural persons, they presumptively do not need to clear their own names.[41] As corporations are creatures of statute, however, their entitlements are also creatures of statute, and it is within the power of a legislature to restrict them. Lord Hoffman's speech in *Jameel* urges withdrawing the extension, and the UK Defamation Act (2013) restricts actionability for trading companies to actual financial loss.[42] Nothing that I have said here about the form of defamation is sufficient to decide between these possibilities. I mention it here only to show the way the form of defamation operates.

Although the basic form of defamation, as I have described it, allows it to incorporate social understandings, it is not infinitely capacious. In particular, it does not have conceptual space for the suggestion, which periodically rears its head in the case law, according to which it is defamatory to expose someone to ridicule. The ridicule test has its origins in the remarks of Parke J. in *Parmiter v. Coupland and Another:* "A pub-

---

41. I am indebted to an unpublished paper by Aaron Farough, "Defamation, Dignity, and Damage: Extending the Presumption of Damages to Corporate Plaintiffs in Defamation Actions," for discussion of this issue.

42. The UK Defamation Act (2013), §1.2, defines harm to reputation for a trading company in financial terms. "For the purposes of this section, harm to the reputation of a body that trades for profit is not 'serious harm' unless it has caused or is likely to cause the body serious financial loss." The explanatory notes appended to the *Act* explain, "Subsection (2) reflects the fact that bodies trading for profit are already prevented from claiming damages for certain types of harm such as injury to feelings, and are in practice likely to have to show actual or likely financial loss. The requirement that this be serious is consistent with the new serious harm test in *subsection (1)*." The provision is similar to anti-SLAPP (Strategic Lawsuits Against Public Participation) legislation elsewhere, designed to prevent large corporations from suppressing criticism of them by threatening expensive defamation actions, even when those actions could not succeed. Some jurisdictions have enacted legislation permitting a suit to be thrown out at a preliminary hearing. See, for example, Texas *Civil Practice & Remedies Code* §27.001.

lication, without justification or lawful excuse, which is calculated to injure the reputation of another, by exposing him to hatred, contempt, or ridicule, is a libel."[43] Parke J.'s definition can be read narrowly, as representing ridicule as a marker for a damaged reputation, rather than as the basis of the wrong. Nonetheless, in a small group of high-profile cases, ridicule has been represented as the interest, or one of the interests, that the law of defamation protects. In *Burton v. Crowell Publishing Company*,[44] the caption "get a lift from a Camel" was in close proximity to the picture of the plaintiff that Hand J. describes as follows: "He is carrying his saddle in front of him with his right hand under the pommel and his left under the cantle; the line of the seat is about twelve inches below his waist. Over the pommel hangs a stirrup; over the seat at his middle a white girth falls loosely in such a way that it seems to be attached to the plaintiff and not to the saddle. So regarded, the photograph becomes grotesque, monstrous, and obscene; and the legends, which without undue violence can be made to match, reinforce the ribald interpretation." Hand goes on to note, "Nobody could be fatuous enough to believe any of these things . . . If the advertisement is a libel, it is such in spite of the fact that it asserts nothing whatever about the plaintiff, even by the remotest implications . . . [I]t is patently an optical illusion, and carries its correction on its face as much as though it were a verbal utterance which expressly declared that it was false." Nonetheless, he held the publication to be defamatory on the grounds that "such a caricature affects a man's reputation, if by that is meant his position in the minds of others; the association so established may be beyond repair; he may become known indefinitely as the absurd victim of this unhappy mischance."

Hand's reasoning rests on a conception of the law as deciding to protect interests that can be identified without reference to juridical concepts, and balancing these against competing factors; his contention is that the interest protected by the law of defamation is "not so much the injury to reputation, measured by the opinions of others, as the feelings, that is, the repulsion or the light esteem, which those opinions engender." For

43. [1840] Eng R 168, (1840) 6 M & W 105, (1840) 151 ER 340.
44. 82 F 2d 154 (2nd Cir. 02/10/1936).

Hand, defenses of truth or qualified privilege simply reflect the fact that the law "prefers" these to reputation.[45]

I would not want to deny that these cases are part of the settled law. At the same time, they rest on a fundamentally different conception of the wrong of defamation. If its point is to protect people from upset, it is difficult to see why that interest is not balanced more generally, subjecting it to, for example, the standard of reasonable care. Further, if the law of defamation is supposed to protect the plaintiff's self-esteem, the requirement that the defamatory statement be published to others rather than merely directed at the plaintiff becomes puzzling. Nor is it easy to understand why it has the procedural structure that it does, or why the defenses are categorial rather than engaging in a more direct balancing exercise. Prosser's complaint that there is no sense to be made of defamation may fit the inclusion of ridicule, but the rest of the traditional law fits together in a coherent way.[46]

The same point applies to the view that a publication is defamatory if it would lead people to "shun and avoid" the plaintiff: It is based on loss rather than wrong. Although defamatory statements will often lead others to shun and avoid the plaintiff, that is not the nature of the wrong, but

---

45. See also two Australian cases: Ettingshausen v. Australian Consolidated Press Ltd., (1991) 23 NSWLR 443, NSW SC., and Obermann v. ACP Publishing Pty. Ltd., [2001] NSWSC 1022 [40]. On the facts of *Ettingshausen* it is difficult to see how the defendant had exposed the plaintiff to ridicule, rather than the plaintiff having so exposed himself, as the court found the photographs to show that he had willingly posed.

46. See the discussion of these cases in the speech of Lord Justice Mullett (dissenting) in Berkoff v. Burchill & Anor, [1996] EWCA Civ 564 (31 July 1996):

> The other case is *Zbyszko v. New York American Inc.* (1930) 2239 NYS 411. A newspaper published a photograph of a particularly repulsive gorilla. Next to it appeared a photograph of the plaintiff above the caption: "Stanislaus Zbyszko, the Wrestler: Not Fundamentally Different from the Gorilla in Physique." The Statement of Claim alleged that this had caused the plaintiff to be shunned and avoided by his wife (who presumably had not noticed her husband's physique until it was pointed out to her by the newspaper) his relatives, neighbours, friends and business associates, and had injured him in his professional calling. The New York Court of Appeals held that the caption was capable of being defamatory. The case was presumably cited to us as persuasive authority. I find it singularly unpersuasive except as a demonstration of the lengths of absurdity to which an enthusiastic New York lawyer will go in pleading his case.

rather one of its consequences.[47] People may shun and avoid someone for reasons having nothing to do with reputation; if I mistakenly report that your business is likely to be the target of a terrorist attack, others might stay away from you, but I have not defamed you.[48]

Both the ridicule conception and the shun-and-avoid conception of defamation focus on losses rather than wrongs. Being an object of ridicule or shunned by others is a terrible thing to happen to a person. As

47. The leading case is Youssoupoff v. MGM, [1934] 50 TLR 581 (CA). The case is significant for two very different reasons. First, it introduced the idea that a film was actionable as libel rather than slander. Second, it introduced the idea that the tendency to "shun and avoid" the plaintiff was the wrong in defamation. Princess Irina Alexandrovna Youssoupoff of Russia argued that she had been defamed by the representation of one of the characters in the film *Rasputin and the Empress*. The film was ambiguous about whether the character was seduced or raped by Rasputin, but the court found that either allegation would lead people to avoid her. It found that, as a matter of law, to allege that someone was a rape victim was defamatory. It is not easy for us, eighty years later, to disentangle the degree to which "sexual impurity" was treated as something in which even a rape victim was complicit, and the extent to which a culture persisted in which people were held accountable for things that happened to them rather than for things that they did, or whether, indeed, there was even a sharp distinction between these two conceptions. The case appears to have involved elements of both. Leslie K. Treiger-Bar-Am, "Defamation Law in a Changing Society: The Case of Youssoupoff v. Metro-Goldwyn Mayer," *Legal Studies* 21 (2001): 291–319, suggests that Scrutton L.J.'s substitution of the word "ravished" for "raped" and his dismissal of defendant's argument that an allegation of someone having been raped is not libelous reveal a conception of being a rape victim as a stain on moral character. Surprisingly, the case broadened the range of action for sexual defamation. Until the middle of the nineteenth century, sexual slander was handled by ecclesiastical courts in England, and there was a cause of action only if the defendant attributed to the plaintiff a crime under ecclesiastical law. See Stephen Waddams, *Sexual Slander in Nineteenth-Century England: Defamation in the Ecclesiastical Courts, 1815–1855* (Toronto: University of Toronto Press, 2000).

Other aspects of the case seem to come closer to what Blackstone, in his *Commentaries* (3:123) called "*Scandalum magnatum*," i.e., an injury to a person of great dignity. At trial (during which time the princess stayed at Windsor Castle, the home of her relatives, the English royal family), much was made of her high standing in society and the expectation of purity that accompanied the status of royalty. It thus appears to be an instance of Post's "honour conception" of reputation, above. See Treiger-Bar-Am, "Defamation Law in a Changing Society," 291–292. Neither picture is appealing; both are diametrically opposed to what I have suggested is the organizing idea of the tort of defamation.

48. Brian Neill and Colin Duncan, *Duncan and Neill on Defamation*, 2nd ed., ed. B. Neill and R. Rampton (London: Butterworths, 1983), ¶7.06.

losses, however, they sit uneasily with the rest of the structure of defamation. They are categories of loss, making it puzzling why they would be
actionable per se; it is far from obvious why truth would be a defense;[49]
more significantly, it is difficult to see why loss-based liability would be
strict, or why the burden of mounting an affirmative defense would lie
with the defendant in such cases. Such losses, however painful, do not
deprive the plaintiff of something that he or she already had, namely a reputation based on what he or she had done.

5. Explaining Defamation: Defenses

Much of the puzzle about the tort of defamation is generated by the structure of defenses that surround it. If you think of negligence as the paradigmatic tort, then, as we have seen, the apparently "strict" character of
the tort of defamation can seem puzzling. But even if defamation is more
akin to a trespass than to a negligent injury, the defenses—truth, opinion,
fair comment, privilege (both absolute and qualified) and, more recently,
"responsible journalism"—look nothing like defenses to either a negligence
action or a trespass. Instead they seem to bring a completely different con-
stellation of factors into play. I now want to suggest that the standard
defenses are all implicit in the right that is at issue.

1. Truth/justification. Truth is ordinarily a complete defense to a defamation action. A true statement may lower the opinion of others about
you, and so in that sense it is defamatory. It is not wrongful as against you
because a right to your own good name is not a right that others think well
of you, but only that what others think of you depend on what you have
done, not on what someone has said you have done.[50] If the defamatory
statement is true, your bad reputation is determined by what you have done,
not by others, even if others come to know what you have done through the

---

49. Lawrence McNamara, *Reputation and Defamation* (Oxford: Oxford University
Press, 2007), 167, makes this point discussing Levi v. Milne, (1827) 4 Bing 195, 130 ER 743,
which was a case involving the publication of a doggerel poem about the "unmanly fright"
the plaintiff took at the sight of a naked woman.

50. This conceptual point is captured in the remark of Littledale J. in McPherson v. Daniels, (1829) 10 B & C 263, 272, "the law will not permit a man to recover damages in respect
of an injury to a character which he does not or ought not to possess."

speech of another. Truths can be wrongful if they invade privacy, but invading privacy is not the same as damaging a person's good name.[51]

2. *Opinion/fair comment.* The availability of fair comment as a defense also follows directly from the structure of defamation.[52] A claim of fair comment or opinion is a judgment made about the significance of something, based on a factual assertion. As such, it does not go to the question of the plaintiff's reputation, but only to the question of what to make of what the plaintiff has in fact done. That question is one about which reasonable people might disagree. More to the point, however, although an opinion will have a basis in assumed facts, it does not address the issue of fact.

If reputation is thought of as an interest or asset, the legal distinction between fact and opinion is surprising, as leading others to hold a negative opinion about someone may be just as bad for that person, or indeed even worse, either in terms of advantage or in terms of suffering, than having others believe a false allegation. When a newspaper cartoon responded to cuts to welfare payments by depicting British Colombia Minister of Social Services Bill Vander Zalm as smilingly pulling the wings off of flies, his suit failed because nobody believed the cartoon to be a depiction of an actual offense. Instead, the cartoonist used a familiar trope to represent cruelty. As such, it was an expression of opinion.[53]

Again, when Simon Singh wrote that the British Chiropractic Association recommended "bogus" treatments for children "without a jot of evidence," the Court of Appeal held that this was a statement of opinion on the grounds that he was not asserting that they recommended something believing it to be ineffective, but rather that he was opining that their grounds for believing it were worthless.[54]

---

51. See the discussion in Eric Descheemaeker, "'Veritas non est defamatio'? Truth as a Defence in the Law of Defamation," *Legal Studies* 31 (2011): 1–20. Descheemaeker argues that it is in the nature of reputation that it is based on what a person has done. He contrasts English law with civilian approaches based on the influence on the latter of Ulpian's concept of *dignitas,* which included both dignity and reputation.

52. On the development of the defense, see the cases cited in Spiller and Another v. Joseph and Others, [2010] UKSC 53, [2011] 1 All ER 947.

53. Vander Zalm v. Times Publishers, 109 DLR (3d) 531 [1980].

54. British Chiropractic Association v. Singh, [2010] EWCA Civ 350.

Hyperbole is an extreme member of the same family. It presents itself as something that does not actually interfere with a person's reputation, because it cannot credibly be taken to be a statement of fact. When Dick Cavett asked Mary McCarthy to name some overrated writers, she said of Lillian Hellman that "every word she ever wrote was a lie, including 'and' and 'the'." Hellman sued for libel.[55] She died before the case went to trial, but would almost certainly have failed because McCarthy's statement cannot be taken to be anything other than hyperbole. Neither the conjunction nor the definite article is capable of being true or false, and so neither can be lies. Indeed, it is difficult to know what would count as taking the statement at face value. If something cannot be believed, the defendant cannot have intended it to be believed. More broadly, if something is so extreme as to be unbelievable in a more familiar sense, it cannot be said to have lowered the plaintiff in the views of others, since those others would never have believed it.

Once more, such examples underscore the difference between the legal conception of reputation and the idea of it as an asset. The British Chiropractic Association[56] and Lillian Hellman may have been seriously disadvantaged by what was said about them, but their reputations were not affected.

3. Absolute privilege. Legal and parliamentary proceedings are subject to an absolute privilege; if you defame me in Parliament,[57] or in the pro-

---

55. See the account of the case and its background in Alan Ackerman, *Just Words: Lillian Hellman, Mary McCarthy, and the Failure of Public Conversation in America* (New Haven: Yale University Press, 2011).

56. "Why We Sued Simon Singh: The British Chiropractic Association Speaks," *The Guardian,* February 22, 2012, http://www.guardian.co.uk/science/blog/2012/feb/22/simon-singh-british-chiropractic-association. The BCA's president is quoted as saying, "An army of scientists, sceptics and comedians was mobilised to disgrace, degrade and demolish the chiropractic profession." The BCA also faced a 1500 percent rise in complaints.

57. This dates to the Privilege of Parliament Act 1512 Chapter 8 4 Hen 8, which specifies, "Suits against any for Bills or Speeches &c. in Parliament declared void," and is reiterated in the English Bill of Rights of 1689, which specifies, "That the freedome of speech and debates or proceedings in Parlyament ought not to be impeached or questioned in any court or place out of Parlyament." The privilege is narrow: if a member of parliament repeats a defamatory statement outside of parliament, it is not privileged. See R v. Abingdon,

cess of accusing me of a legal wrong,[58] my standing in the opinion of others may well be lowered, but you do not need to mount a defense, and I may find myself in the position of needing to clear my own name. Public proceedings may affect what others think of me, but both the carrying on of those proceedings and the reportage of them are not treated as transactions between private individuals.

Legal proceedings, particularly private actions, may seem difficult to assimilate to this picture, because both the subject matter and the outcome are exclusively between the parties before the court. But the role of the court is to provide closure to the dispute, and so it must be the forum in which allegations are made and answered. That is why the court takes control of a defamation action—if the plaintiff can establish that the defendant said something defamatory, the defendant must show the claim to be nondefamatory, true, or privileged. It is also why the plaintiff who alleges a wrong but does not prevail does not face a separate action for defamation, even though in bringing suit the plaintiff had alleged that the defendant had wronged her. The role of Parliament in managing public affairs and courts in adjudicating disputes entails that the privileges are not qualified, that is, nothing said is actionable, even if actuated by malice.[59]

4. Qualified privilege. Another basic category of justification in a defamation action is qualified privilege. Traditional examples include reference letters regarding a potential employee, communications among members of a family such as parents telling adult children about the character of potential spouses, trade union communications, business-to-business communications, communications about litigation, and medical communications. A defamatory statement is privileged if the defendant

---

(1794) 1 Esp 226 , 170 ER 337, and R v. Creevey, (1813) 1 M & S 273, 105 ER 102. The same qualification holds in the United States: Hutchinson v. Proxmire, 443 U.S. 111, (1979).

58. Watson v. McEwan, Watson v. Jones, [1905] AC 480.

59. The privilege attaching to legal proceedings might appear to be qualified by the availability of an action for malicious prosecution, in cases in which an action known to be without merit is brought out of malice. But the wrong of malicious prosecution is an independent wrong, not an answer to an assertion of privilege in a defamation action. The remedy is based on the loss inflicted on the plaintiff, through which the defendant sought to achieve his purpose; it is not actionable per se.

made it under a legal, moral, or social duty to speak truthfully about a matter. The privilege is qualified in that it does not apply if the defendant acted with malice. Unlike truth, the paradigmatic examples, such as official reports, letters of recommendation, and comments about the suitability of a potential spouse for one's child do not look exclusively to how things stand between the parties. As we will see below, there are some instances that do relate to the relationship between the parties.

In *Horrocks v. Lowe* Lord Diplock outlined its rationale:

> In all cases of qualified privilege there is some special reason of public policy why the law accords immunity from suit—the existence of some public or private duty, whether legal or moral, on the part of the maker of the defamatory statement which justifies his communicating it or of some interest of his own which he is entitled to protect by doing so. If he uses the occasion for some other reason he loses the protection of the privilege . . . The protection might, however, be illusory if the onus lay on him to prove that he was actuated solely by a sense of the relevant duty or a desire to protect the relevant interest. So he is entitled to be protected by the privilege unless some other dominant and improper motive on his part is proved. "Express malice" is the term of art descriptive of such a motive.[60]

The defense of qualified privilege needs to be situated within the structure of a libel action. As Lord Dunedin put it in *Adam v. Ward,* "Malice, which is of the essence of libel, is presumed from defamatory words. Privilege destroys that presumption. But the place of the implied malice which is gone may be taken by express malice which may be proved. It may be proved either extrinsically or intrinsically of the document, and such words in the document are apt as evidence."[61] On this under-

---

60. [1975] AC 135, 149.

61. Adam v. Ward, [1917] AC 309, 334. In Hill v. Church of Scientology of Toronto, [1995] 2 SCR 1130, Corey J. explained the traditional rule at ¶144: "The legal effect of the defence of qualified privilege is to rebut the inference, which normally arises from the publication of defamatory words, that they were spoken with malice. Where the occasion is shown to be privileged, the *bona fides* of the defendant is presumed and the defendant is free to publish, with impunity, remarks which may be defamatory and untrue about the plaintiff. However, the privilege is not absolute and can be defeated if the dominant motive for publishing the statement is actual or express malice."

standing, then, just as the defense of truth defeats one element of libel, the defense of privilege defeats another, but can in turn be defeated by an express showing of malice.

If malice is "the essence" of libel, its essential nature emerges only in the context of privilege, and discussion of malice is usually confined to that context. For purposes of defeating qualified privilege, the plaintiff can show that the defendant knowingly said something false, or was reckless or indifferent to its truth or falsity. The intention to harm the plaintiff through the statement will also establish malice. These may seem to be very different criteria, and with the exception of the intention to harm, none may seem to obviously match the ordinary sense of the word "malice" as spite or ill will.[62] But the concept of malice is continuous with the one we encountered in Chapter 6: Damaging the plaintiff's reputation is the means through which the defendant achieves some other end, whatever that end might be.

Malice does not need to be established, because any time anyone publishes a negative statement about someone, he or she does so to communicate something that damages that person's reputation. That is the (presumed) point of speech: to get those listening or reading to believe something. If the thing I intend others to believe is that you have done wrong, then I intended to defame you. Defaming you doesn't need to be the end for which I speak; I intend to defame you because saying something that casts you in a bad light is the means I use for whatever I hope to achieve though my statement. If the statement casts you in a bad light, I am thereby presumed—that is, must prove the contrary—to have intended to besmirch your good name.[63] That is the sense in which defamation is an intentional tort.

62. These differences lead Elspeth Reid to suggest that malice does no independent work in defamation. See Reid, "'That Unhappy Expression': Malice at the Margins," in *Tort Law: Challenging Orthodoxy*, ed. Stephen G. A. Pitel et al. (Oxford: Hart, 2013), 442–445. The distinction between the two senses of "malice" is introduced by Bayley J.'s discussion of privileged communication in Bromage v. Prosser, (1825) 4 B & C 247, 255: "Malice in common acceptation means ill will against a person, but in its legal sense it means a wrongful act, done intentionally, without just cause or excuse." By "just cause or excuse," Bayley J. means what is now called a privilege.

63. Paul Mitchell traces the history of the requirement (and presumption) of malice in "Malice in Defamation," *Law Quarterly Review* 114 (1998): 639–664, and "Duties, Interests,

As we have seen in earlier chapters, the wrong in tort is always a matter of the inconsistency of the defendant's conduct with the plaintiff's right, not its blameworthiness on any other dimension. Some cases of trespass or negligence may be blameworthy, and others not, but the nature of the wrong is always based on its inconsistency with the plaintiff's right.

Just as the defense of truth defeats the presumed falsity of the defamatory statement, the defense of privilege defeats another presumption: It refutes the presumption of malice by showing that it was not an attack in this specific sense. The defense is that the defendant was doing something else that the legal system either requires or necessarily permits the defendant to do.

The structure is transparent in cases in which the defendant was under a legal duty. The law cannot both require you to do something and treat your doing of that very thing as a wrong.

It might be thought that rather than restricting the plaintiff's ability to prevail in a defamation action, the tension between the plaintiff's right to reputation and the defendant's legally recognized duty owed to another person should be reconciled in the opposite direction, by placing the defendant under a qualified *duty*, to give an honest report without damaging the plaintiff's reputation. But this alternative reconciliation of duty and right cannot be made out. You could not be under an affirmative duty to speak frankly subject to the qualification that nothing said turns out to be false. You would still be under a duty and be liable for something

---

and Motives: Privileged Occasions in Defamation," *Oxford Journal of Legal Studies* 18 (1998): 381–406. He draws attention to Lord Tenterden C. J.'s appeal in Haire v. Wilson, (1829) 9 B & C 643, 645 "The Judge ought not to have left it as a question to the jury, whether the defendant intended to injure the plaintiff, for every man must be presumed to intend the natural and ordinary consequences of his own act. If the Judge thought the tendency of the publication injurious to the plaintiff, he ought to have told the jury it was actionable." He also notes that the phrase "calculated to injure" stands in for the same set of ideas in the early cases. See "Malice in Defamation," 642. Mitchell takes this to illustrate what he characterizes as "historical accident," but it could also be described as the recognition of the structure of a defamation action: The defendant is presumed to have meant what he or she said, and so therefore to have said something damaging the plaintiff's reputation, meaning to be believed and thus intending to defame the plaintiff. Therefore the defendant must prove the truth of the defamation or that it was privileged.

done in fulfillment of that duty. Absent a duty, you have the option of saying nothing; when you have a duty, you lose that option.

Still, it might be thought that no relationship between two parties should have any bearing on the rights of a third. If I owe you a contractual duty to deliver goods on an appointed date, I am not allowed to trespass on the land of others or physically injure them in the process of delivery, or to convert their property to acquire raw materials needed for producing the goods. The duty is between you and me, and does nothing to defeat the rights of third parties. Indeed, as we saw in our discussion of the doctrine of privity in *Winterbottom v. Wright* and *Donoghue v. Stevenson,* this is just the mirror image of the principle that a stranger cannot sue on a contract: Two people cannot change the rights of a third by making a contract, either in the third party's favor, or to compromise the third party's rights.[64] It might be thought that the same point should apply here: Why would that defendant's duty to a third party restrict the plaintiff's right to his or her own good name?

The answer goes to the structure of defamation and its requirement that the defamatory statement be "of and concerning" the plaintiff. To establish the defense of qualified privilege, the duty must be owed to the person to whom the defamatory statement was made, and it must be a duty to give an honest opinion to that person about the plaintiff. Such a duty can only be discharged by giving an honest opinion about the plaintiff. That is, the plaintiff's reputation is the subject matter of the duty.

If the plaintiff can establish that the defendant's statement was motivated by actual malice, the statement falls outside the scope of the duty: If you say something you believe to be false, or are indifferent to its falsity, you aren't discharging your duty all; you are just taking the opportunity to make the plaintiff look bad by saying something negative about someone in the expectation that others will believe you.[65]

The content of the legal duty is sensitive to the full legal context in which it arises. In recent years legislation has restricted the exercise of, and so the content of, what at common law were understood to be legal duties. Employment law restricts the content of letters of reference for

---

64. See the judgment of Lord Macmillan in Donoghue v. Stevenson, [1932] AC 562.
65. Clark v. Molyneux, (1877) 3 QBD, 246, per Brett, L. J.

former employees,[66] and human rights and related legislation may restrict the scope within which public officials may make honest reports of suspected misconduct.[67] The legal importance of these changes should not be taken to show that the balance between competing interests has somehow shifted; it shows instead that the permissible exercise of the legally recognized duty is subject to public law constraints.

Qualified privilege also extends to social duties, including reporting professional misconduct to the relevant body,[68] as well as to reports of suspected incompetence by public officials.[69] The animating principle is that there is a social duty to do these things, even in the absence of a legal duty. The same structure applies: Only reports to the relevant authorities are privileged. It extends further, to include such things as warning a child about the perceived difficulties of a potential spouse. Here, once more, the law's porosity to (shifting) social understandings leads it to attach significance to expectations about a broader range of obligations.

The expansion from legal duties, which are required simply in order to make the legal system as a whole speak with a single voice, to moral and even social duties raises the question of whether the law should, or could, recognize all social duties, or, if not, the principle upon which they are selected. Here, as elsewhere, the law is permeable to social understandings. The basis (but not anything amounting to a rule) on which moral and social duties are recognized is that they, too, are just part of a system in which people enjoy their rights, in part by exercising them in ways that fulfill widely understood moral and social obligations. Some social obligations, such as reporting professional incompetence or reporting a crime, fall into this category. Even if no punishment or liability attaches to the failure to report a crime, the law will not allow a legal con-

---

66. Reid, in "'That Unhappy Expression,'" discusses Spring v. Guardian Assurance, [1995] AC 296, which she notes is a negligence rather than a defamation case. Such cases do not show that reputation is properly protected by torts other than defamation, or that qualified privilege should be defeated by negligence; they show instead that a set of facts can fall under more than one legal category.

67. Clift v. Slough Borough Council, [2010] EWCA Civ 1711. The plaintiff was placed on a "register of violent persons," which was circulated more broadly than the Human Rights Act was held to permit, thus exceeding the privilege.

68. Couper v. Balfour, 1913, SC 492 at 501 (Ct. of Sess.).

69. Adam v. Ward, [1917] AC 309.

sequence to attach to reporting one. At the same time, the privilege is qualified; malicious accusations are actionable.

Lord Diplock also mentions cases in which the defendant has an interest in speaking frankly about a matter. His remarks involve a defamatory statement at a meeting of a town council, where the interest is in participating in political affairs. Other cases involve the protection of financial interests or, more prominently, the protection of reputation. In *Adam v. Ward,* the otherwise defamatory remarks were made in defense of the reputation of a third person closely connected with the defendant.[70] More recently, the UK Defamation Act (2013) has extended qualified privilege to peer-reviewed scientific and academic publications, subject to the qualification that the statement be made without malice.[71]

5. Public figures and legal proceedings. Much of the literature on freedom of expression contends that unwanted speech is the "price" that "we" must "pay" for freedom. Beginning with *New York Times v. Sullivan,*[72] a line of American cases has abandoned the traditional doctrinal structure of defamation in the service of protecting public debate. This form of analysis is always problematic: If it is a price that "we" as a society must pay, why is payment exacted from some but not others?[73] Its difficulties are particularly apparent in the case of defamation, because the particular person who was defamed "pays" for the general social benefit of free

70. Ibid., AC 309, 334. See also Laughton v. The Honourable and Right Reverend The Lord Bishop of Sodor and Man, (1872) LR 4 PC 495, in which the defendant Bishop responded to allegations made against him at a meeting of his Convocation by describing the plaintiff as "employing arguments and language not ordinarily used by any man of high professional repute when pleading before a common jury or a Parish vestry," being a "wicked man," and of violating the Ninth Commandment by "being guilty of the sin of bearing false witness against his neighbour." The Judicial Privy Council regarded his statement as privileged because spoken in self-defense, and held that, although they were "undoubtedly beyond what was necessary for self-defense," their excess was not sufficient to establish malice.

71. UK Defamation Act (2013), §6.

72. 376 U.S. 254 (1964). *Sullivan* was about a public official's performance of his duties, and the same result could arguably have been reached under the converse of the absolute privilege attaching to parliamentary proceedings, along the lines developed by Lord Keith of Kinkel in Derbyshire County Council v. Times Newspapers, [1993] AC 534.

73. See Frederick Schauer, "Uncoupling Free Speech," *Columbia Law Review* 92 (1992): 1321–1357.

expression. More to the point, it is the wrong way to analyze the situation. At common law, legal and parliamentary proceedings were never actionable on grounds of defamation; the conducting of public business is not a private matter between individuals. I want to suggest that this provides the correct model for thinking through the relation between freedom of expression and the right against defamation. Legal and Parliamentary proceedings are not protected because of a concern for the "chilling" effect of restrictions on investigation or debate; they are properly protected because participants in them are charged with acting in a public capacity rather than a private one. No doubt such an understanding is open to abuse, as is any public trust. Officials often use their official roles for private purposes, and the torts of misfeasance in a public office and abuse of privilege are supposed to protect against private wrongs committed by public officials. This is not the place to consider whether it is an adequate response to such wrongs; my point, for now, is only that someone acting in a public capacity is not necessarily appropriately assessed in terms of the categories of private law.

The converse point also holds: A public official acting in an official capacity does not, as such, have a right to his own good name.[74] Of course, should the public official leave office, his prospects for lucrative post-office employment, whether as a lobbyist, as a director of large corporations, or as counsel or rainmaker of a major law firm, may be compromised. That is, in terms of what happens to him, the difference between what is said of him as a public official and what is said of him as a private person may be of no real significance. If his reputation is viewed as an asset or advantage, it is just as vulnerable, regardless of the capacity in which he acts. It is, however, *damnum absque iniuria*.

The American law on public figures in defamation has expanded in parallel to the American law of privacy on public figures,[75] identifying as

74. Nor does a public authority. See *Derbyshire County Council*.

75. Justice Marshall's dissent in Rosenbloom v. Metromedia, 403 U.S. 29 (1971), gives two examples: in Kelley v. Post Publishing Co., 327 Mass. 275, 98 N.E. 2d 286 (1951), the publication of a picture of the body of the plaintiff's daughter immediately after her death in an automobile accident was held to be protected, and the publication of the details of the somewhat peculiar behavior of a former child prodigy, who had a passion for obscurity, was found to involve a matter of public concern in Sidis v. F-R Pub. Corp., 113 F.2d 806

a public figure anyone in whom a wide range of people take an interest.[76] This difficulty comes directly out of thinking of reputation as an interest to be balanced against competing interests. If enough people are interested in something, then the plaintiff's interest is bound to be outweighed. This holds also, on this understanding, with the plaintiff's interest in reputation. Even if widespread curiosity cannot be measured with precision, the U.S. approach conceptualizes widespread interest as a proxy for weighty interests, which it proposes to balance against rights.[77]

(CA2 1940). Another example is Time, Inc., Appellant, v. James J. Hill, 385 U.S. 374 (1967), which imposed an actual malice standard on an article about the plaintiff because it was ostensibly about a play loosely based on an actual incident.

76. For a discussion of the transition in the wake of *New York Times v. Sullivan,* see Frederick Schauer, "Public Figures," *William & Mary Law Review* 25 (1984): 905–935. In *Rosenbloom v. Metromedia,* 44, Brennan J. collapsed the distinction entirely, writing, "In that circumstance, we think the time has come forthrightly to announce that the determinant whether the First Amendment applies to state libel actions is whether the utterance involved concerns an issue of public or general concern." The United States moved away from this extreme position in Gertz v. Robert Welch, 418 U.S. 323 (1974), though it did so only on the assumption that both fault and falsity must be proven by the plaintiff.

77. The U.S. Supreme Court's extension of the burden of proving falsity to the plaintiff in private defamation actions on "issues of public concern" in Philadelphia Newspapers v. Hepps, 475 U.S. 767 (1986), essentially eliminates the central instance of each person's right to his or her own good name. Your right to be beyond reproach is paradigmatically your right to be presumed by others not to be a wrongdoer. Based on the holding in *Hepps,* the question of whether you have committed a crime is by its nature an "issue of public concern." On the particulars of the case—the defendant newspaper had alleged that the plaintiff and his company had bribed public officials—there was a further public interest, at least potentially, in the fact about those public officials. So it might be thought that the public concern was not with whether the defendant had done wrong, but rather with whether the public officials had. On this reading, the role of the press in policing the behavior of public officials and informing the public about their misconduct might be thought to license collateral damage to the reputations of private citizens. The opinion itself in *Hepps* does not even note this distinction. If it is drawn, however, the case becomes more, rather than less, puzzling. In place of an analysis of the right to reputation as an essential element of any system of ordered liberty, it turns out that the right is something to be balanced against long-term effects. Like some other U.S. Supreme Court discussions of unwelcome speech as the price to be paid for free expression, the court is prepared to allow those costs to fall on people other than the beneficiaries and, indeed, to tolerate the violation of private rights as though it were simply an unwelcome disadvantage.

6. Responsible journalism. In recent decades English and Canadian courts have introduced a new defense of responsible journalism. Although the defense is still developing, its general structure is to permit the press to defend against a libel action by establishing that the libelous statement was made in the context of a responsible report on a matter of public concern, and that the journalist made appropriate efforts to make sure that the statement was true. In *Jameel,* Lord Hoffman characterizes it as "a different jurisprudential creature from the traditional form of privilege from which it sprang,"[78] as it privileges material rather than the occasion on which it is published. At the same time, the jurisprudential difference brings it closer to the idea that legal and parliamentary proceedings are subject to an absolute privilege, rather than balancing any sort of public interest against the plaintiff's interest in reputation. Cases such as *Jameel* in England and *Quan v. Cusson*[79] in Canada are most fruitfully framed in terms of a conception of the distinctive role of the press as a sort of "fourth estate"—that is, as a guardian of the public nature of a democratic society. As the other three estates that existed when Burke coined the phrase have merged into one, the role of the press has become more important.[80] That is the reason it receives protection, and the type of protection its members receive is that of a public official.

The two stages of the test as developed in *Reynolds v. Times Newspapers Ltd.,*[81] *Jameel,* and, in Canada, *Grant v. Torstar*[82] and *Cusson*[83] serve jointly to determine that the journalist was acting within a properly public mandate. The first is, as Lord Hoffman notes, purely a question of law: Is this a topic of genuine public concern? Lord Bingham captures the point this way: "The necessary pre-condition of reliance on quali-

78. Jameel and others (Respondents) v. Wall Street Journal Europe Sprl. (Appellants), [2006] UKHL 44, ¶46. Lord Hoffman adopts the wording of Baron Phillips of Worth Matravers MR in Loutchansky v. Times Newspapers Ltd., (Nos. 2–5) [2002] QB 783.

79. Quan v. Cusson, [2009] 3 SCR 712.

80. "Burke said there were Three Estates in Parliament; but, in the Reporters' Gallery yonder, there sat a Fourth Estate more important far than they all." Thomas Carlyle, *Heroes and Hero Worship* (London: Chapman and Hall, 1840), 194. The other three were the Lords Spiritual, the Lords Temporal, and the Commons.

81. [2001] 2 AC 127.

82. [2009] 3 SCR 640.

83. *Quan v. Cusson.*

fied privilege in this context is that the matter published should be one of public interest. In the present case the subject matter of the article complained of was of undoubted public interest. But that is not always, perhaps not usually, so. It has been repeatedly and rightly said that what engages the interest of the public may not be material which engages the public interest."[84] Second, if the statement is made in the context of a discussion that is of public concern, the standard of review is a familiar one from administrative law: First, was there a rational connection between this statement and the discussion of a topic of public concern, and second, does the defendant's action pass the sort of reasonableness review that falls under the exercise of ordinary statutory powers? The power here is not statutory; however, the press enjoys a protected position because of its role in a free and democratic society. The multistep test introduced by Lord Nicholls in *Reynolds* frames the inquiry against the background assumption that well-informed citizens in a democracy must have access to information that is generally reliable and gathered in reliable ways. As a result, irresponsible activities by journalists do not fall within the protected role of journalism.

On this interpretation, then, the organizing idea behind the "responsible journalism" defense is that it is properly available only with respect to properly public activities of properly public figures. Lord Bingham's reminder of the distinction between what "engages the interest of the public" and what "engages the public interest" is fundamental. The defense conceives the role of the press in a democracy as a form of public oversight of the exercise of official power.[85] To say of an official acting in a public capacity that he or she has failed to do his or her job is not a personal defamation, but rather a criticism of conduct in the office.

Two small clarifications are required here. I do not mean to deny that these public law ideas may, in a particular case, end up removing protection of a particular person's reputation. Just as the protection of parliamentary proceedings may leave someone in the position of needing to clear his or her name because of something that appears in the pages

---

84. *Jameel*, 96.

85. "While the subject of the Ottawa Citizen articles was not political in the narrow sense, the articles touched on matters close to the core of the public's legitimate concern with the integrity of its public service." *Quan v. Cusson*, ¶31, per McLachlin C. J.

of *Hansard,* so, too, the defense of responsible journalism may leave
someone in a position of needing to clear his or her name because of something that appears in the pages of something with a wider readership.
Indeed, the availability of a defense guarantees that reputation receives
less protection than it would if the defense were not available.

My claim, then, is not that the availability of the defense makes no difference to reputation; if it made no difference, it could not serve as a
defense. Instead, my claim is that no recourse to the concepts of balancing figure in drawing the distinction between public and private.
Rather than being a matter of balancing, the distinction is category-based.
It is not that the degree of setback to reputation and the degree of setback
to the efficiency of political processes are weighed against each other,
either in the particular case or in general. The privilege that attaches to
parliamentary proceedings does not need to be understood as the result
of a balance between, on the one hand, the plaintiff's interest in a good
reputation, and, on the other, the public's interest in probing parliamentary debate. The adamantine rule that attaches absolute privilege to
parliamentary proceedings reflects the role of public law in a civilized
society. That is why it preempts a private defamation action, rather than
outweighing it; the basis of the distinction is not that one interest carries
infinite weight and so outweighs the other. It is instead that the relevant
form of reasoning for public proceedings must be public law.

The public legal character of parliamentary proceedings means that a
private citizen whose reputation is besmirched through something said
in Parliament will have no recourse through the courts. The defense of
responsible journalism, as I have suggested it be understood, is narrower,
and so properly focuses only on the conduct of public business.

Nor is it exactly the same as other forms of qualified privilege. The key
difference is that the distinctive social role it attaches to the press—the
analogue of a legal, moral, or social duty—already includes a requirement
of responsible conduct. As Lord Hoffman puts it in *Jameel,* "There is no
question of the privilege being defeated by proof of malice because the
propriety of the conduct of the defendant is built into the conditions under
which the material is privileged."[86] A journalist needs to check his or her

86. *Jameel,* ¶46.

sources diligently in order to be acting within the role at all.[87] By contrast, the traditional duties of qualified privilege require you to say what you think, and impose no demand of diligence. If you are reporting a crime, your job is to report what you think happened, *not* to investigate what actually happened. A responsible journalist's job is different.

These differences are important, and they are likely to make it difficult to formulate legal tests of responsible journalism. But no appeal to the ideas about balancing will shed any light on either the difference or the difficulties. The question of whether the defendant was engaged in responsible journalism on a topic of public concern does not depend on the likely effects of a finding of liability on third parties who are thinking of commenting on other topics that may or may not be of public concern.

Indeed, if narrowly understood, the defense requires the prior public law classification of something as a public office, but then operates in a way that can be expressed through purely private law concepts, by saying that with respect to the conduct of a public office, the defamatory statement is not of and concerning the individual who fills the office, but instead concerns the conduct of the office itself.

The second is a much more general point: The concept of what is properly public is clear in abstraction and often subject to dispute concretely. Resolution and precise demarcation, like so much else with regard to questions of right, can only take place through the development of positive law. The account of defamation developed here is an account of the relevant form of reasoning and, like all other parts of private law, is partially indeterminate in the absence of legal institutions. This point applies not just with respect to the question of the person to whom a duty is owed in negligence, or whether injury is within the risk of dangerous conduct, or whether a particular claim is or is not of and concerning a particular plaintiff. It applies also to the development of defenses, including the emerging defense of responsible journalism. That is among the most pressing reasons a legal order is required if people are to enjoy their rights.

---

87. Thus, contrary to Eric Descheemaeker's suggestion in "Protecting Reputation," the defense does not introduce an element of negligence or fault into qualified privilege. Instead, the scope of the duty is specified by the role that it characterizes—in particular, investigation. That is why an unsubstantiated report of an allegation by an unknown source is irresponsible.

The details of the application of these administrative and indeed constitutional ideas in the application of the defense are in part still under development. It is thus too soon to tell the precise form they will take. However, developments so far do not mark a fundamental departure from the basic structure of the tort of defamation, and, most significantly, understanding them requires no recourse to any idea of "balancing" freedom of expression against security of reputation.

6. Conclusion

I have argued that the traditional law of defamation has a coherent internal structure, and further, that this internal structure reflects the organizing ideas of private law as a whole. The doctrinal structure of an action in defamation reflects the right that is at issue. Rather than an interest in having others think well of you, or believe the truth about you, the right is a right that others not put you in a position of needing to clear your name. This structure explains what many regard as surprising features of the law of defamation, and also explains the standard defenses to it, and the conceptual space within which novel defenses could arise.

Like trespass to land and battery, libel is actionable per se, without showing of either damage or fault. Some writers have tried to explain torts that are actionable per se in terms of the fundamental importance of certain interests, or, coming from a seemingly different direction, as imperfect proxies for interests in cases of imperfect knowledge. Reflecting on the law of libel sheds light on the law's own resources for explaining wrongs that are actionable per se. In each case the idea that you, rather than others, are in charge of something explains it. Your right against battery is your right that nobody else gets to decide what happens to your body; your right to reputation is your right that nobody else gets to make your reputation. Rather than a right protecting an interest, the interest is constituted by the right that protects it.

CHAPTER 8

Remedies, Part 1

As If It Had Never Happened

Law students are usually told that the purpose of damages is to make it as if a wrong had never happened. As Lord Blackburn put it in *Livingstone v. Rawyards Coal Co.*, the point of damages is to put the plaintiff "in the same position as he would have been in if he had not sustained the wrong."[1] Although torts professors are good at telling students about this feature of the law, it is the source of much academic perplexity. Money cannot really make serious losses go away, and it seems a cruel joke to say that money can make a seriously injured person "whole." Worse still, if money could make an injured person whole, it seems that injuring someone and then paying is just as good as not injuring at all.

My aim in this chapter is to redeem the commonsense idea that damages really do make it as if a wrong had never happened. I do so by focusing on the normative structure of private rights to person and property. As I explained in earlier chapters, such rights are best understood in terms of an entitlement to have certain means subject to your choice, as against others. Others are not entitled to determine the specific purposes for which your means are used, or to damage your means in ways

---

1. (1880) 5 App Cas 25, 39 (Lord Blackburn).

that make them less usable. Although wrongdoing can cause a factual loss, it does not change the normative situation: These rights survive their own violation. The basic idea is straightforward: A wrongdoer cannot render a right irrelevant simply by violating it. Instead the plaintiff is entitled to constrain the defendant's conduct both before and after the defendant commits a wrong. If the defendant acts contrary to the constraint, the constraint survives in a new form as a remedy. As Peter Birks once put it, the remedy is just "the right looked at from the other end."[2] Because the object of the constraint is your having those means subject to your choice, the only way to make the constraint survive is to give you substitute means—means that, from the standpoint of your ability to set and pursue purposes, come as close as possible to what you would have had if the wrong had never happened. I will then show how money, as the closest thing to an all-purpose means, can be understood as restoring to the wronged party the means he or she is entitled to.

In this chapter I will leave out the important issue of how a claim is processed. Recent writers, most prominently John Goldberg and Benjamin Zipursky, have drawn attention to the ways in which the law of torts does not simply give effect to the underlying rights, but rather processes them by giving the plaintiff a power to proceed against the defendant. Goldberg and Zipursky insist that focusing on this dimension of what they call "civil recourse" shows that although the law of torts is fundamentally a law of wrongs rather than losses, nonetheless, at the remedial stage, the court neither gives effect to nor upholds the right that has been violated. As I shall explain in Chapter 9, these aspects of the way in which a tort claim is processed are important, and show, in particular, that recourse is indeed civil, because any remedy must be authorized by law and determined through a court's procedures. It does not, however, show that the tort remedy is anything other than remedial.

1. Rights and Remedies: The Disjunctive Objection

There is a familiar way of thinking about the law of private remedies, both loss-based and gain-based, according to which the purpose of a remedy

---

2. Peter Birks, "Definition and Division: A Meditation on Institutes 3.13," in *The Classification of Obligations,* ed. Peter Birks (Oxford: Clarendon Press, 1997), 24.

between two private parties is to make it as though the wrong in question had never occurred. So, for example, in the most familiar case of compensatory damages, the defendant is made to repair the plaintiff's loss, so that the plaintiff will be in the situation in which she would have been, if the defendant had not wronged her. In the equally important, if less familiar, context of wrongs that involve using rather than damaging what belongs to the plaintiff, the defendant is liable even if the plaintiff suffers no loss. In one important class of cases, the defendant is liable for depriving the plaintiff of the use of something that the plaintiff did not in fact (and may not have even been in a position to) use. The basis of liability is the deprivation of something to which the plaintiff had a right. In another class of cases, the defendant gains a benefit, which, in calculating damages, is represented as a detriment to the plaintiff.

The supposed difficulties are almost as familiar as the view itself: First of all, a sum of money, even a huge sum of money, does not really make it as though someone has not suffered terrible bodily injury, or lost a loved family member.[3] Personal injuries are not fungible, and so no amount of money can make them go away. In cases of property damage, if the injurer is made to compensate the victim, it may be that, from the point of view of the victim, it is as though things had never happened, but, it might be said, it is hardly so from the point of view of the injurer, who is left worse off as a result. So, the argument continues, we cannot undo the harm, we can only transfer it, and the cost of making the transfer exacerbates the problem.

These problems feed into the Holmesian thought that the law's "moral phraseology"[4] cannot be taken at face value—that old-fashioned talk

---

3. Stephen Smith writes, "More importantly, even the sums of money that courts currently require wrongdoers to pay—sums that often appear far greater than what even the most upstanding individuals would think themselves morally obliged to pay—cannot make the world as if the wrong never happened. No sum of money can make it as if a rape or assault or the loss of a loved one never happened." Smith, "Duties, Damages and Liabilities," *Harvard Law Review* 125 (2012): 1753.

This complaint is echoed by Scott Hershovitz, who writes, "We can never restore things to just the way they were, and all too often, we cannot restore them at all." Hershovitz, "Tort as a Substitute for Revenge," in *Philosophical Foundations of Tort Law*, ed. John Oberidiek (Oxford: Oxford University Press, 2014), 93.

4. See Oliver Wendell Holmes Jr., *The Common Law* (Boston: Little, Brown, 1882), 58.

about making the plaintiff "whole" or making it as though a wrong had never happened is a sort of smokescreen to disguise the difficult questions of social policy that judges are forced to confront.

In addition to these difficulties, it is sometimes said that the suggestion that damages make it as if the wrong had not happened renders wrong-doing irrelevant to the analysis of a tort action. The reasoning goes roughly like this: If damages are an adequate substitute, then both the plaintiff and the legal system should be indifferent between the situation in which the defendant wrongs the plaintiff and pays damages and the situation in which the defendant does not wrong the plaintiff. This idea, first introduced into private law theory with Holmes's suggestion that the duty in contract is not, in fact, a duty to perform, but rather a disjunctive duty to either perform or pay damages, has led to many discussions of what has come to be called "efficient breach," in which the law permits a promisor to breach a promise provided that the promisor pays damages to the promisee. From this it is concluded that there is no duty to perform a contract.[5] Holmes's friend William James argued that abstract ideas needed to be explained in terms of their "cash value" in experience.[6] The disjunctive theory is a literal application of this idea to the concept of duty, treating legal duties as pieces of advice to Holmes's "bad man" who wants only to know what will happen to him if he ignores his legal obligations.[7]

The same point might be extended to torts: If the remedy is sufficient to make it as if the wrong had never occurred, then so the thought continues, the plaintiff's right must be disjunctive in the same way.[8] But this,

---

5. Oliver Wendell Holmes Jr., "The Path of the Law," *Harvard Law Review* 10 (1897): 462. Frederick Pollock pointed out one difficulty almost immediately, in a letter to Holmes dated September 17, 1897: If Holmes's analysis was correct, "how can it be wrong to procure a man to break his contract, which would then be only procuring him to fix his lawful election in one way rather than another?" See *The Pollock-Holmes Letters: Correspondence of Sir Frederick Pollock and Mr. Justice Holmes, 1874–1932,* vol. 1, ed. Mark DeWolfe Howe (Cambridge: Cambridge University Press, 2015), 80.

6. William James, *Pragmatism* (Indianapolis: Hackett, 1981), 36. See the discussion of Holmes as a "fellow traveller" of James and C. S. Peirce in Cheryl Misak, *The American Pragmatists* (Oxford: Oxford University Press, 2013), 77–80.

7. Holmes, "Path of the Law."

8. A number of writers who do not regard themselves as Holmesians endorse this view: Peter Cane, in *Atiyah's Accidents, Compensation, and the Law,* 8th ed. (Cambridge: Cam-

it is urged, stands in tension with the idea, both etymological and normative, that torts are wrongs, and therefore also with the idea that the defendant is liable to the plaintiff because the defendant wronged the plaintiff. Benjamin Zipursky makes this point explicitly in terms of the Holmesian disjunctive account of contract; Zipursky's suggestion is that if the remedy is the continuation of the duty in tort, then wrongdoing and its repair is an option available to defendants. From this he concludes that the idea that damages serve to make it as if a wrong had never happened effaces the category of wrong and is "a variation on the reductive instrumentalist's mistaken conception of tort rules as liability rules."[9]

Stephen Smith makes essentially the same argument:

> Under the duty option, the wrongfulness of the defendant's act ceases to have significance, so far as litigation is concerned. If the only available judicial response to a civil wrong is to try to induce rights infringers to comply with their post-infringement moral duties, then so far as litigation is concerned, civil wrongs are just another category of duty-creating events. The fact that a wrong has occurred is no different from the fact that the defendant promised to pay a sum of money or received money by mistake. If the law adopts the duty option, then in every case where a court makes an award, damages or not damages, it would be doing the same thing: in every case, the court would be attempting to ensure that something that ought to have happened in the past happens in the future. The fact that in one case the duty arises from a wrong and in the other from a non-wrong would be legally irrelevant. A claim to enforce a contractual debt and a claim for damages become indistinguishable: they are both just claims to enforce existing duties to pay money.[10]

---

bridge University Press, 2013), writes, 'To say that a person owes a duty of care in a particular situation means (*and means only*) that the person will be liable for causing damage by negligence in that situation" (76). Nicholas McBride lists a number of other examples in his "Duties of Care—Do They Really Exist?" *Oxford Journal of Legal Studies* 24 (2004): 417–441. McBride characterizes this as the "cynical view," which he contrasts with what he calls the "idealistic view" that he defends.

9. Benjamin C. Zipursky, "Rights, Wrongs, and Recourse in the Law of Torts," *Vanderbilt Law Review* 51 (1998): 74.

10. Stephen Smith, "Duties, Liabilities, and Damages," *Harvard Law Review* 125 (2012): 1752.

The solution to all of these problems can be found in other ideas that are both as familiar and unpopular as the problems themselves: the legal distinction between harm and wrongdoing, and the dependence of remedies on primary rights. Most of this chapter will focus on explaining the sense in which rights survive their own violation, but to set the background against which that explanation will proceed, I will first say something about the disjunctive objection. Although it looks significant, it is incoherent. The argument that is supposed to dissolve base talk of rights into the gold of policy and prediction faces the difficulty of every other alkahest: It dissolves the vessel that was supposed to contain it.

The disjunctive objection sets up the supposed problem about the idea that rights survive their own violation by introducing an apparatus that is perfectly general in its incapacity to represent anything as a wrong or as prohibited. As Cardozo remarked in another context, this consequence may "enkindle doubt whether a flaw may not exist in the implication."[11] As with Cardozo's remark, the point is not that it would be bad policy to treat duties as disjunctive, but rather that any account of duty on which it turns out that there are no duties must have set up the problem in the wrong way.

The disjunctive objection eliminates the category of duty because it rests on a series of illicit inferences: first the reduction of two related imperatives, one of which is supposed to underwrite the other ("If you do A, you must do C," *because* "You must not do A") to a material conditional ("If A, then C"), which is subsequently transposed into a disjunction ("not-A or C").

That Holmes would be happy with such a reduction comes as no surprise, given his embrace of a predictive theory of law formulated in terms of advice to the so-called "bad man." If you want to predict what will happen, the law can indeed be represented as a system of choices. The Holmesian bad man wants to know what various possibilities will cost; he wants a flow chart so he can decide when to do what the law requires and when to ignore its requirements, because from the bad man's perspective, there are no requirements, only predicted consequences.[12] This

---

11. Ultramares v. Touche 174 N.E. 441 (1932).

12. The Holmesian advice to the bad man is actually less robust than this, because at each later stage the likelihood of enforcement may decline, depending on such matters as

dispensability is perfectly general, because the *rationale* for the enforcement of the remedy is of no interest from the predictive standpoint. The Holmesian flow chart displays options without rationales; at no point does a consequence follow because of a breach.

The same generality in the Holmesian approach permits the characterization of any other analysis of liability—including the suggestions made elsewhere by Zipursky and Smith, according to which remedies serve to replace revenge, hold wrongdoers to account, or denounce wrongdoing[13]—in the same disjunctive terms: "If you injure another, you will be liable to recourse" is equivalent to the option set, "Don't injure, or accept the plaintiff's recourse."[14] As this generality shows, the Holmesian account does not actually raise a specific problem for the idea that rights survive their own violation; by representing the law of wrongs as a system of choices or prices, it simply denies that there is such thing as a wrong.

That is why it cannot provide a coherent analysis of private law duties as having the disjunctive "perform or pay" structure that Holmes proposes. To do so is internally inconsistent. Having reduced an imperative to a conditional, and then a disjunction, it goes on to represent the resulting disjunction as the imperative "You must either perform your contract or pay damages," or, in the case of tort, "You must avoid wronging others or pay damages." But this disjunctive duty faces the same problem: If the defendant neither performs nor pays, whatever further results would follow would have to be added as yet another disjunct: "Perform or pay or face a contempt sanction." The fact that a lawyer advising a client, bad or otherwise, could represent the situation through a disjunction or series of imbedded conditionals is beside the point. The disjuncts form an

---

the plaintiff's ability to make out a case, the costs of litigation as opposed to the losses incurred through the wrong, the likelihood of detection, and competing uses for public resources. Thus, even in the cases of the simple disjunctive duty—perform or pay—the empirical equivalence is imperfect.

13. I take these up in Chapter 9.

14. Goldberg and Zipursky rightly insist on the imperatival nature of duty (see John C. P. Goldberg and Benjamin C. Zipursky, "Seeing Tort Law from the Internal Point of View: Holmes and Hart on Legal Duties," *Fordham Law Review* 75 [2006]: 1582), and would presumably also regard a court order granting a remedy as an imperative. Having done so, they cannot deny other accounts the modal resources to which they legitimately help themselves.

ordered sequence: At each stage, the liability to a result follows from the failure to do what is required at the previous one. The primary duty is primary, the remedial duty secondary, the contempt sanction tertiary, and so on. You must not wrong another because of that person's rights, and if you wrong another you are liable in damages because of the wrong you committed, and so on.

Smith's claim about the indistinguishability of rights and remedies faces the same difficulty as Holmes's. Any response that is conditional on a breach of duty, including the imposition of a liability that is entirely distinct from the duty, can be repackaged to generate a perspective from which conformity to the duty and breach combined with response are interchangeable. The idea that the defendant is liable because the defendant wronged the plaintiff can be made to look irrelevant by treating the relation of dependence as one of equivalence. In his eagerness to distance remedies from wrongs, Smith commits himself to an account on which something happens to a wrongdoer in the event that a relational duty is breached, but the plaintiff has no residual claim against the defendant. The fact that this defendant owed the plaintiff a duty is on his view just the raw material on which subsequent procedures operate.

Perhaps the appeal of the disjunctive objection comes from the thought that to qualify as a wrong, something must be so serious that nothing can ever address it—that although you can repair a damaged object, if a wrong could be repaired, it wouldn't be a wrong. This seems overstated in many tort actions involving property damage, and in civilian legal systems, such as the German Civil Code, even the Holmesian idea of the efficient breach of contracts is expressly repudiated.[15] Yet the same repudiation is accompanied by repeated statements of the claim that the injured right lives on in the form of a remedy. The same point applies in the case of an injunction if the defendant commits a nuisance or ongoing trespass: The injunction is supposed to put a stop to the wrong, but that does not mean that wrongdoing followed by injunction is just as good as no wrongdoing at all. The thought that something can be repaired does not mean that

---

15. Bürgerliches Gesetzbuch (BGB) [Civil Code] §241(1). See the discussion in Basil Markesinis, Hannes Unberath, and Angus Johnston, *The German Law of Contract*, 2nd ed. (Oxford: Hart, 2006), 299.

damage and repair is just as good; it means that whatever can be done to repair a wrong must be done because it is a wrong that requires repair.

Other familiar objections to the idea that rights survive their own violation get some of their vigor from the thought that shapes the disjunctive objection: Because repair is almost always imperfect, it is necessarily inadequate, and so must have some other point. That is why I suggested that the other objections really rest on the disjunctive. But as I shall now explain, once we understand the sense in which a right survives its own violation, we see also why none of these objections comes to anything.

2. How Rights Survive Their Own Violation

Chapter 2 developed the commonplace of legal analysis that not all harms are wrongs, and not all wrongs are harms. If I cut across your lawn without your consent, I commit a trespass against you, even though any harm that I do to you will normally be in the *de minimis* range. I wrong you nonetheless, even if it is not worth your while to do anything about it. These cases illustrate the sense in which the law is concerned with wrongs rather than harms: You could come up with a description of a harm that is suffered in these cases only by depriving the concept of a harm of any analytical purchase, by appealing to some such thing as the harm of another entering your land without your permission. It is also a commonplace of private law that not all harms are wrongful. It you lure customers away from my business, you harm me, but as a matter of legal doctrine, you do not wrong me. Again, if you damage property on which I depend, but to which I have no legal right, you harm me without wronging me. I have no legal grounds for complaint. And if you injure me or damage my property while doing something that did not pose a significant or foreseeable risk to me, or that injures me in an unforeseeable way, you do not wrong me, even if you have behaved very badly in relation to other people or other risks to me. It is equally a commonplace that private law remedies follow rights: The plaintiff in a tort action comes before a court claiming that the defendant has wronged her, and seeking a remedy to address that wrong. None of the puzzles arise if these basic ideas stay in focus.[16]

16. The misunderstandings that arise once people move away from these familiar ideas are not inconsequential, for they have come to carry weight outside of the Academy as well

If the commonsense idea is to be redeemed as an interpretation of the law of damages, exactly what *has* happened and how things would stand if it *hadn't* happened must be specified. I will argue that we can understand the idea to which damages give expression by focusing on the idea of a wrong, and so on the idea that damages serve to make it as though the wrong had never happened.

The claim that damages serve to make it as if a wrong had never happened is not a factual prediction about the effects of a payment of damages. Instead, it is a normative claim about the relation between wrongdoing and repair. Private law enforces the rights that private persons have against each other. Those are not rights against harm, as such, but rather rights against injuries brought about in certain specified ways. The rights in question cannot be identified apart from a specification of the wrongs that would violate them.

I will also offer an interpretation of the word "it" in the phrase "as if it had never happened." It is easy to make familiar and intuitive ideas baffling by turning them into claims about states of affairs rather than rights. If I wrongfully damage your bicycle, the law does not take a direct interest in the fact that you no longer have a bicycle and call on me to provide you with a new one or otherwise make up your loss. Instead, as we saw in Chapter 2, your right is the constraint on my conduct, the prohibition on my doing certain things to you. My duty to repair the wrong is also to be understood in terms of the right: I still need to conduct myself in a way that is consistent with your entitlement to be the one who determines any purposes for which the object of the right is used. In many familiar cases

---

as within it. For example, the Virginia tort reform statute sets a flat cap for medical malpractice damages. See, e.g., Etheridge v. Medical Center Hospitals, 237 Va. 87, 376 S.E.2d 525 (1989), and Pulliam v. Coastal Emergency Service, 257 Va. 1, 509 S.E.2d 307 (1999), which upheld the damages cap as consistent with the Virginia and U.S. Constitutions. See also Colin M. Gourley et al. v. Nebraska Methodist Health System, Inc., et al., 265 Neb. 918, which upheld Nebraska Revised Statute §44-2825 (1) (reissue 1998) of the Nebraska Hospital-Medical Liability Act, which limits recoverable damages in medical malpractice actions to $1,250,000.

If damages are a tool for shaping conduct, or for granting satisfaction to angry victims, flat caps make sense. If, however, they are the vindication of preexisting rights, and serve to make it as though the violation of those rights had never happened, their measure must always be that to which the plaintiff had a right.

of damage-based wrongs, such as negligence and nuisance, the only way to address the wrong is to address the factual loss. But in cases of trespass you are entitled to a remedy without having suffered a factual loss. The object of the right is to be restored to your choice to the extent that it is possible to do so, even if you had no plans to use it. If you did have plans to use it, both the object of the right and whatever gains you would have realized through the execution of those plans must be restored.

The organizing idea, then, is that for you to have a right as against me is for you to be entitled to constrain my conduct with respect to that right. As we saw, in the case of your right to property and your right to bodily integrity, the basic form of your right is that how others may deal with your person and property is not up to them. That is, neither the uses to which your person and property are put nor their continued availability for your use are up to them. Once we see this, however, it becomes apparent that if that is what your right is, then, if the right is violated, the sense in which the right survives its own violation is precisely that you remain entitled to control the conduct of others with respect to the object of the right. If I deprive you of the entitlement to determine the use of some piece of property, either by damaging the property or by using it without your authorization, I wrong you. If this is the basic form of a proprietary wrong, and if your right survives its own violation—that is, if the fact that I have used or interfered with your property does not mean that you are not, after all, entitled to constrain my conduct in relation to it—then what survives is your continuing entitlement as against me to control it. It survives, however, in modified form, in the form of your entitlement to have me do something that brings the object or a substitute under your control to the extent that it is possible to do so. The modification reflects the ways in which I have changed the normative situation: Your antecedent right was *in rem,* that is, it held against all others. By interfering with the object of your right, I changed the situation as between the two of us, so the surviving form of your right as against me is *in personam,* that is, it holds only against me. I must then provide you with a substitute to which you will have an *in rem* right.

There has been a good deal of confusion about how losses (and, in certain cases, gains) are significant to measuring the violation of a right, much of it generated by the fact that harms and losses have a magnitude in a way that neither obligations nor wrongs consisting in the violation of those obligations do. The criminal law might punish theft below $1,000 less severely than it punishes theft above $1,000, but it is artificial to say that there is somehow a different *obligation* to respect property depending on whether it is worth more or less than $1,000. It is no less artificial to imagine the magnitude of the resulting injury determines which right has been violated.[17] Fortunately, my analysis does not depend on anything so unintuitive. The *nature* of a wrong does not depend on its magnitude at all. The obligation is to avoid violating the rights of another. Your entitlement to security of person and property constrains the activities of others in exactly the same way, regardless of the actual magnitude of a particular injury. Although the *obligation* makes no reference to a magnitude, a wrong in violation of that obligation will always have a magnitude, and can only be addressed by the transfer of powers of choice equivalent in magnitude.

This talk about what does and does not have a magnitude is a way of rendering precise the familiar legal distinction between the type of damage and the extent of damage. In a negligence action, the plaintiff must first establish that the type of injury complained of was foreseeable to the defendant. As we saw in Chapter 4, this reflects the more general requirement that the law only places the defendant under a duty to take account of that of which account can be taken; unforeseeable things are just those things of which it is not possible to take account. The plaintiff does not need to establish that the extent of his or her injury was foreseeable; instead, the possibility of foresight is a threshold requirement. If the type of injury is foreseeable, then the defendant is liable for the full extent of that type of injury.

These cases are sometimes thought to be difficult to reconcile with the cases involving the plaintiffs with unusual sensitivities, but in fact they are expressions of exactly the same principle: If the defendant's conduct is not unreasonably dangerous to his or her neighbors, the defendant does not need to do anything to reduce its residual risks, even if it is known that there are people who will be injured by it. In both cases, whether the

17. Hence the entire moral luck literature about negligence considered in Chapter 4.

plaintiff recovers depends upon whether the plaintiff was entitled to constrain the defendant's conduct; if the plaintiff was so entitled, he or she recovers for the full extent of losses, because the entitlement was to prevent the defendant from interfering with what the plaintiff already had. As such, it operates independently of any questions about the costs of restoring what the plaintiff had if it is damaged.

3. Rights Survive Wrongs, Part 1: Damage and Loss

If someone deprives you of your means, they deprive you of part of your ability to choose how to use them to set and pursue your own purposes. In so doing, however, they do not deprive you of your entitlement as against them, to be in charge of those means. This is particularly obvious in the case of theft. Suppose you have a car, and I steal it. Who does the car now belong to? There is one sense in which someone might be prepared to say that it now belongs to me, if I am in physical possession of it. But as between the two of us,[18] the law is not interested in that question; it is interested instead in the question of who has a right to it. The answer to that question is that it belongs to you. My depriving you of it does not make it stop belonging to you. That is why the law can compel me to give it back, and can compel me to do so even if I took it as a result of a completely innocent mistake.

Now suppose that I deprive you of it in a different way—rather than taking it, I damage or destroy it. If I damage it, you are in the same position as you would be in if I took it or destroyed it: You would no longer be factually in charge of the car you are entitled to have. The law of damages makes it as though my wrong against you had never happened, by requiring that I give you back the thing you were entitled to have, that is, a car with those features *as against me.*

If I destroy the car, I cannot literally give it back. What I can do is give you back substitute means, that is, I can give you a sum of money equivalent to the replacement cost of the car. Not only does that sum of money put you in a position where you can go out and purchase the car if you

---

18. In relation to other legal inquiries, I will have superior title to some third person who comes along and damages or takes the car.

like. It also enables you to liquidate your interest in the car if you so choose. The law of damages views your means as available for pursuing your purposes, both directly, by using them to accomplish particular purposes, as when you use your car to drive to visit friends, or indirectly, as when you sell your car in order to buy new appliances for your kitchen. When you had the car in the first place, you could have sold it, and used the proceeds for other purposes; by compelling me to give you that amount of money, the law compels me to put you back in the position you would have been in—you can either acquire another car, or do something else. You are entitled to constrain me to restore your ability to pursue your purposes to what it would have been if I had not wronged you, to make it as if it had never happened.

Examples involving wrongs against property are potentially misleading, because the most straightforward way to restore the right—your entitlement to constrain my conduct—is by restoring the object of the right, either by directly giving it back or by restoring the object to its earlier condition. This feature of property may lead to the impression that what survives is the object of the right or some fungible replacement of it, an idea that fits, at most, a proper subset of cases of property damage. But even in the case of property, the thing (as such) is not what is at issue; your right, understood as a constraint against me, is what survives. If I take your coat, I have to give it back, not because it is a coat, but because it is yours—because you are entitled to constrain my conduct. You are entitled (as against me) to have the means in question at your disposal; you are in charge of them, so I am not entitled to use or damage them. As a result, the content of my obligation, both before and after the wrong, is: "Act in such a way as to leave the plaintiff secure in what he or she already has." If I fail to so act, my obligation does not disappear.

I will go through each of the parts of this analysis in more detail: what it is to be deprived of your means; how a right to them survives the deprivation; how money reverses the deprivation, thereby restoring the right that you had. I will begin with damage-based wrongs such as negligence, but then move on to consider use-based wrongs. I will assume the role of wrongdoer, and you of the plaintiff. As I work through the analysis, I will take it that you have established all of the traditional elements of negligence analysis, and the only remaining question concerns damages.

At no point in the analysis will I focus on what happens to *my* holdings in the process of making it as though you had never been wronged. A natural misunderstanding leads people to suppose that where there is a net loss that must either lie where it falls or be shifted to some other person, the only issue is where to place it. On the account I will defend, the "allocation" of a "burden" is a result of the analysis, not its subject matter. Just as an ordinary negligence action is structured by the question of whether the defendant owed the plaintiff a duty to avoid injuring her in that way, whether the defendant breached that duty, and whether the injury the plaintiff suffered fell within the ambit of the defendant's duty, so the analysis of whether the defendant must pay for the plaintiff's loss depends upon the same set of questions: Did the defendant wrongfully deprive the plaintiff of something to which she had a right? The law of damages requires a remedial transaction so that the net effect of the involuntary transaction and the compelled transaction is to make it as though, as against the defendant, the plaintiff is still in charge of her means. The defendant will often end up with a loss, because the effect of the remedy is to make it as though the defendant had never wronged the plaintiff. The point is to restore, not the antecedent distribution, but rather the plaintiff's antecedent right against the defendant. The idea that the defendant has wronged the plaintiff, and, with it, the concomitant idea that the plaintiff has a right as against the defendant, can be understood only in terms of the relation between the two of them.

3.1. Being Deprived of Your Means

As we saw in Chapter 2, which means are yours is a matter of your legal relations to other persons. *Your* means are the ones that you are in charge of as against others: You can use them without seeking permission from others, and others may not use or interfere with them without your permission.

3.2. Rights Survive Wrongs

If I deprive you of something to which you have a right, I wrong you. The very idea that I could do that to you depends on the fact that by wronging you I do not extinguish your right. Just as the person who steals or converts the property of another does not acquire good title in the object because the original owner retains it, so the person who damages or destroys means belonging to another does not extinguish the other's right to those means. The normative situation is unchanged, because a person can lose a right to something only through a voluntary act (and not always even that way). An involuntary transaction in which someone else takes, damages, or destroys something that is yours doesn't change your rights.

If I break your vase, all you have are shards. But you have a right as against me to the intact vase. Only deeds to which you are a party can change your private rights; a deed of which you are simply the victim cannot. It is a datable event in the history of the world, but one that is entirely without normative significance. However lamentable its factual effects may be, the point of the remedy is to see to it that it has no effects on the rightful relations between the parties.

Rights survive their own violation because they are one person's entitlement to constrain the conduct of others. If I could unilaterally dissolve your entitlement to constrain my conduct, there would be no sense in which you were entitled to constrain it. If I violate that constraint, it is not merely that the rule, considered as an abstract entity prohibiting my action, survives, in the way in which, for example, the speed limit is not changed by my driving faster than I am supposed to, or the rules of chess are not changed by my moving my rook diagonally. Rights also survive their own violation differently than authority relations do: If I ignore the police officer's instruction to move on, she doesn't lose her authority to tell me what to do. Private rights survive their own violation in a more robust sense: The relationship between us, your authority over me with respect to the object of the right, remains intact. I do not get to either determine the uses for which your property will be used or render it unusable. If I do either of these things, your continuing authority with respect to my use or damage of your property entitles you to compel me to give you back what you already had.

Examples involving taking or damaging property might be thought to make things too easy; the suggestion that you could have a right to something that no longer exists might seem more puzzling. The idea that your right survives the wrong against it underscores the fact that the entitlement to damages does not depend on anything other than the underlying constraint on another person's conduct. The counterintuitive nature of the formulation is merely verbal: If I owe you $100, due last Thursday, but failed to pay, my obligation does not disappear. I still owe you the money, even if, as it turns out, I have not earned it yet, and so it does not yet exist. In both cases, making me pay simply provides a substitute for the underlying obligation that I breached. So too, if I contract to deliver one thousand bushels of next year's crop of wheat—you have a right to it, even though it does not yet exist. In neither case is it a way of achieving something else that, through some remarkable coincidence, is most effectively achieved by my giving you means equivalent to what you were already entitled to. Instead, both the *basis* of your right to repair and its *content* derive from the primary right I invaded. You are entitled to be made whole because I have interfered with your right to your means; you are entitled to equivalent means because the right I violated was to those very means.

The sense in which your right survives is distinctive; it follows from the nature of private rights as constraints on the conduct of others, rather than as a general feature of what happens when someone does wrong. John Gardner has recently defended an account on which corrective justice is a perfectly general principle calling for the reversal of wrongful acts.[19] Gardner argues that the violation of a primary duty gives rise to a secondary duty of repair, which is a different duty, which reflects not the survival of an underlying right, but rather the survival of the reasons that gave rise to the duty that was breached.[20] For Gardner, an obligation is, as he puts it, "discharged" by its breach, by which he does not mean it is

19. John Gardner, "What Is Tort Law For? Part 1: The Place of Corrective Justice," *Law and Philosophy* 30 (2011): 1–50. In a similar vein, Jules Coleman has argued that tort law is a matter of corrective justice, charged with repairing a wrong as between two persons, but he also maintains that the concept of a wrong is merely a placeholder, requiring some independent analysis and defense. Coleman compares the principle of corrective justice to the retributive principle in criminal law, arguing that each principle of redress requires some independent account of primary norms of conduct, but is compatible with a wide range of such accounts. See Jules L. Coleman, *The Practice of Principle: In Defence of a Pragmatist Approach to Legal Theory* (Oxford: Oxford University Press, 2001), 32–33.

20. Gardner endorses Joseph Raz's interest theory of rights, according to which saying that someone is a rightholder is to say that some aspect of his or her interests provides sufficient reason for imposing duties on others. See Joseph Raz, "Legal Rights," *Oxford*

satisfied, but rather that the particular act demanded by it is no longer available. Instead, the reasons for the obligation survive. As he puts it, "Once the time for performance of a primary obligation is past, so that it can no longer be performed, one can often nevertheless still contribute to satisfaction of some or all of the reasons that added up to make the action obligatory. Those reasons, not having been satisfied by performance of the primary obligation, are still with us awaiting satisfaction and since they cannot now be satisfied by performance of that obligation, they call for satisfaction in some other way."[21] Gardner's formulation is meant to leave open the question of the content of the duties enforced by tort law, and is in that way more open to a plurality of different duties than the account developed here.

Gardner's claim that reasons continue is not required to explain the distinctive sense in which rights do. Reasons, at least as they are often described in the literature, are different from rights. Gardner speaks of them as "pros and cons" of action, which are "added up" to make that action obligatory.[22] If I have failed to conform to an applicable reason that is still "available for conformity," says Gardner, it still "counts for something."[23] Reasons that survive in this broad sense may or may not preserve the relation between tortfeasor and victim. The pros and cons that added up before the wrong may add up differently, and may now recommend different actions.

The sense in which rights survive their own violation is narrower. If I violate your private right, you in particular have a distinctive entitlement to demand that I give you back what you already had. Neither you nor anyone else has the standing to do so in other cases in which I fail to do

---

Journal of Legal Studies 4 (1981): 1–21. On this view, rights figure in an intermediate level of practical reasoning; reasons are the fundamental level.

21. Gardner, "What Is Tort Law For? Part 1," 39–40.

22. John Gardner and Timothy Macklem, "Reasons," in *Oxford Handbook of Jurisprudence and Legal Philosophy,* ed. Jules L. Coleman et al. (Oxford: Oxford University Press, 2004). Other writers propose similar theories: Derek Parfit, for example, characterizes a reason as something that "counts in favour" of an action. Parfit, *On What Matters,* vol. 1 (Oxford: Oxford University Press, 2011), 31. See also T. M. Scanlon, *Being Realistic about Reasons* (Oxford: Oxford University Press, 2014).

23. "What Is Tort Law For? Part 1," 33.

what I have a reason, or even a duty to which you have no correlative right, to do. You can remind me to take my medicine or change my tires, but you cannot demand that I do so. The distinctiveness of your claim to constrain me follows from the way in which I wronged you. You are not simply holding me to the reasons that apply to me; you are exercising the surviving form of the very right against you that I violated. That is why you can constrain my conduct, but others—such as people who depended on the availability of you or your property—might also legitimately complain about my indifference to their interests, and hold me accountable in various informal ways, while cannot demand anything. Conversely, I cannot constrain you, either before or after the fact, to act on whatever reasons you had to assist me, or to use what is yours in the ways that best suit me. Nor can I require that you act on whatever reasons there might be to refrain from standing on your rights. As against me, it is up to you whether to act on them, even if you will come to regret doing so. I might resent you; I might even demand an apology. But I cannot compel you to stand down.

I do not mean to deny that the distinctive way in which private rights survive their own violation can be characterized in the vocabulary of reasons. My point is only that the relational account begins with a characterization of the distinctiveness of both rights and remedies, which explains why private rights survive their own violation in the form that they do.

3.3. Give Them Back

If someone takes your means, the way to correct the wrong is by giving them back. If the means no longer exist, then in order for you to be given what is yours, you need to receive equivalent means. I probably can't put your vase back together again, and even if I could, the most I could give you is a repaired vase, not an intact one. Your right is to have the means you had a right to all along.

In cases in which one person accidentally injures another, the way to set things right is to focus on the injury. The injurer must repair the injury; that is, to use the language introduced earlier, the injurer must provide the injured party with means equivalent to those that were lost through the injury. If you can show that there are uses to which you would have put your body or property for earning money, I have deprived you of the further means that you would have acquired, had I not wronged you. As a result, those further means are part of what you already had.

3.4. Money

Money is something that can be used only by being exchanged. It is also an almost universal means, in that it can be exchanged for (almost) any other means. Although few people would be indifferent between being free of injury and being injured and receiving compensation, adequate compensation can provide the plaintiff with means that go as far as possible toward having equivalent means. The claim is not that life can be just as enjoyable, or easy. Compensation does not aspire to make up a welfare loss so that the plaintiff is indifferent between noninjury and injury plus compensation.[24] My sentimental attachment to my property, and my experiential connection to my body, aren't things that can be replaced, so they cannot be compensated.[25]

Compensatory damages give you back the means you had, however imperfectly. Your happiness, considered as such, is not among the means you use to set and pursue your purposes, even if your mental health is something you use in that way. That is why someone who negligently or intentionally makes you unhappy without injuring your person or prop-

---

24. In *Anarchy, State, and Utopia* (New York: Basic Books, 1974), Robert Nozick offers an account of compensation something like the Holmesian account: Nozick contends that the point of compensation is to put the injured party on the same welfare level as he or she would have been on if not for the wrong. See also John C. P. Goldberg and Benjamin C. Zipursky, "Civil Recourse Revisited," *Florida State University Law Review* 39 (2011): 368–371, which focuses on making up welfare losses. But if remedies are cast in terms of equivalent welfare, then they really are just as good as not being wronged, because, on standard analyses, a rational person would be indifferent between alternative sources of the same level of welfare. Such an approach would also require reducing damages for personal injuries in light of the widely discussed ability of people to adapt successfully to disabilities, so that they report no loss in welfare. See Peter Ubel et al., "Misimagining the Unimaginable: The Disability Paradox and Health Care Decision Making," *Health Psychology* 24 (2005): S60.

25. See Bruce Chapman, "Wrongdoing, Welfare and Damages: Corrective Justice and the Right to Recover for Non-Pecuniary Loss," in *Philosophical Foundations of Tort Law*, ed. David G. Owen (Oxford: Clarendon Press, 1995), 409.

erty is not liable, even if you are more successful at whatever you do when you are happy, but someone who negligently or intentionally causes you to develop a psychiatric illness wrongs you.[26]

In the first instance, your entitlement to your person and property does not depend on the particular purposes you pursue with it. If I negligently destroy a box of philosophy books that sat in your basement, you are entitled to their replacement cost even if you had forgotten you had them and purchased new copies, lost interest in the subject, or forgotten (or never knew) how to read the languages in which they were written.

3.5. Consequential Damages

Consequential damages are just a further application of the same set of ideas. They are a further application, because your entitlement to your person and property does not depend on your intention or ability to use them in any particular way. Consequential damages focus on how you would have used the means to which you have a right. One of the things you can use your means to do is produce more means. If I deprive you of means you could have used, I thereby deprive you of the further means you could have generated. The precise quantity you could have generated with them may be uncertain, so that some discount factor may apply. But the core idea is the same: I have deprived you of means to which you would have had a right.

If I wrongfully damage or destroy your car, it is easy for a court to determine what would make it as if the wrong had never happened. There is a functioning market in used cars, so the court can determine exactly what it would take to get a car of the same color, model, mileage, and condition. In other cases no replacement will be available; in cases of bodily injury, a prosthesis may not be available, and even if one is, it will not fully make up the loss. The difficulty of replacement makes the court's task much more difficult, precisely because your body is so closely connected to your capacity to set and pursue your own purposes that it is limited by

---

26. But if you require counseling to regain your focus as the result of a wrong, you recover the cost of it, because the wrong deprived you of the most important thing you have, the ability to decide how to use what you have.

bodily injury. If you lose a toe through my wrong, your ability to achieve the various purposes to which you in fact aspire may remain largely unchanged.[27] If so, you will have no claim to consequential damages. You are still entitled to damages for the loss of the toe, precisely because your right as against others to bodily integrity entails that it is up to you rather than anyone else what to do with your toe, even if through most of your life you decide to do nothing with it. Because there is no market in replacement toes, the precise quantum of damages will be nominal, not in the sense that it is small, but rather because it requires a decision by a competent court, based on some conception of the typical case.

3.6. A Further Illustration: Duplicative Causation

I want to illustrate these general points by focusing on a series of familiar puzzles about duplicative causation in torts. The puzzles arise in those cases in which the defendant behaves negligently toward the plaintiff, or commits a nuisance interfering with a property right the plaintiff has, but some other factor, human or otherwise, produces or would have produced the same injury. Ordinarily the burden lies with the plaintiff to show that, were it not for the defendant's wrong, the plaintiff would not have been injured. In these cases, the plaintiffs face a special difficulty, because the duplicative cause seems to show that she would have been injured anyway. A favorite example is *Corey v. Havener*,[28] in which the two defendants drove their motorized tricycles on opposite sides of the plaintiff's carriage. The noise startled the plaintiff's horse, as a result of which the plaintiff was injured. The two defendants are not each allowed to avoid liability by pointing out that the other one would have startled the horse and caused the plaintiff's injury.

The result seems obvious, but the source of the obviousness is not. Some contend that the causation is significant for reasons of administrative convenience, and where the ordinary standards of proof fail, some other convenient way of providing injurers with appropriate incentives,

---

27. Then again, it may compromise your ability to walk or run. Whether it does depends on your feet and other factors, but its wrongfulness does not depend on either of these things.

28. 65 NE 69 (Mass. SJC 1902).

or of guaranteeing compensation to injured parties, must take priority. Again, some have offered broadly moralistic explanations, according to which there is something wrong with the way in which each of the parties is able to point to the other that requires that we change our basic understanding of causation and its relevance in these cases.

A focus on administrative convenience or incentives simply disregards the significance of the transaction between the parties, and singles out the defendant to pay the plaintiff for some unrelated reason. The moralistic explanation fares no better, because it is also unable to preserve the relation between the two parties: The plaintiff recovers in the two-wrongdoers case because of the relation between the wrongdoers, to which the plaintiff seems to be little more than a bystander, what Cardozo might have called a "vicarious beneficiary" of the distaste a court rightly has for wrongdoers' claim of advantage from each other.

Two leading English causation cases point to a better resolution of these problems. In the first of these, *Baker v. Willoughby*,[29] the defendant's negligent driving injured the plaintiff, who sued for the income he would have lost because an injury to his leg prevented him from working at his normal job. Before the case went to trial, the plaintiff was the victim of an unrelated robbery attempt, during which he suffered further damage to the injured leg. The defendant sought to avoid liability for the plaintiff's lost income after the robbery, on the grounds that he would have been unable to work anyway. The House of Lords rejected the argument. In the second case, *Jobling v. Associated Dairy*,[30] the plaintiff suffered a back injury that limited his ability to work. Before trial it was discovered that he was suffering from an unrelated spinal disease, which would have made him unable to work. The defendant sought to avoid liability for the plaintiff's lost income on the grounds that he would have been unable to work anyway. The House of Lords accepted the defendant's argument, and insisted that it was consistent with the holding in *Baker*.[31]

---

29. [1970] A.C. 467 (H.L.).

30. [1982] A.C. 794 (H.L.).

31. American courts largely parallel the approach outlined in *Baker*. See David A. Fischer, "Successive Causes and the Enigma of Duplicated Harm," *Tennessee Law Review* 66 (1999): 1127–1166, citing cases at 1129n6. See also American Law Institute, *Restatement*

This combination of results may seem puzzling, because in each case it seems that it can truly be said that the plaintiff would have suffered the loss anyway, so that the defendant did not cause it. The difference that distinguishes the two cases is that the second cause in *Baker* was tortious. Yet it is not a problem of the two wrongdoers each being able to point at each other. The result would be the same if the robber had dropped out of sight, and so there was nobody at whom the first injurer could point.

In *Jobling*, Lord Keith of Kinkel declined to formulate "a precise juristic basis" for distinguishing supervening torts from supervening illnesses, noting only that it might be said that a supervening tort is "not one of the ordinary vicissitudes of life, or that it is too remote a possibility to be taken into account, or that it can properly be disregarded because it carries its own remedy. None of these formulations, however, is entirely satisfactory."[32]

If rights survive wrongs, however, there is a simple and straightforward explanation of why the wrongdoer can point to a subsequent natural event but cannot point to a subsequent tort. The plaintiff's entitlement is to have his means *free* of wrongdoing by others. That is the basic principle of damages under which the plaintiff recovers from the defendant for his loss. The defendant can say that the plaintiff would have lost what he had to natural causes, because the plaintiff has no entitlements in relation to natural causes. As we saw in Chapter 2, everything the plaintiff has is subject to natural deterioration, because all material objects are subject to such deterioration. Thus, the defendant can appeal to the fact that what the plaintiff had would have been less useful in any variety of ways, due to natural wear and tear or surprising natural accidents. The plaintiff's right against the defendant is a right to constrain the defendant's conduct in relation to the means the plaintiff would have had, that is, those means that are subject to natural deterioration. The plaintiff's entitlement is to means against which no wrongs have been committed.

Although the first tortfeasor cannot reduce liability by pointing to subsequent tortfeasors, a second tortfeasor can reduce liability by pointing

---

(Third) of Torts: Liability for Physical Harm (Final Draft), at §26, "Factual Cause," cmt. k, "Preemptive Causes and Duplicative Factors," and the *Restatement (Second) of Torts*, §924, cmt. 3 (1965).

32. *Jobling v. Associated Dairy*, 815–816.

to earlier ones. The second tortfeasor can truly say that the plaintiff had already lost some of her means. The asymmetry follows from the fact that the principle that rights survive wrongs applies as between any plaintiff/ defendant pair, rather than somehow surviving apart from a particular transaction between the parties. If the plaintiff is already injured, the second defendant deprives the plaintiff only of what the plaintiff still had, because the sense in which the plaintiff's right against the first defendant survived was just in the sense of the plaintiff's entitlement to damages from the first defendant. The subsequent defendant has not interfered with it, so the plaintiff only has a claim against the second defendant for those means with which that defendant interfered.

In the case of simultaneous torts, including *Corey* itself, each defendant is liable because the only respect in which either one can point to the other is as a subsequent wrongdoer. The defendant cannot say that the plaintiff's horse already was startled, but only that it would have been startled anyway—that is, that the plaintiff would have been wronged anyway. That is exactly the claim that the plaintiff's right does not survive wrongdoing, and so is not available.

4. Rights Survive Wrongs, Part 2: Gain-Based Damages

A use-based wrong consists in the use of the object of the plaintiff's right for purposes he or she has not authorized. The law cannot undo the fact of the defendant's use of it, but it can treat it as if it were the plaintiff's own use, by requiring the defendant to disgorge his gains. At the highest level of abstraction, it is as if the wrong had never happened: The plaintiff's property is used to create additional means for the plaintiff. Those new means are then subject to the plaintiff's choice as against the defendant.[33]

It is natural to ask whether these remedies are usefully conceived as making it as though a wrong had never happened. In some cases the defendant is made to account for profits earned by use of the plaintiff's property, even if the plaintiff was not in a position to realize those profits.[34]

---

33. If the wrong is intentional in a more robust sense, and the defendant willfully wrongs the plaintiff—for example, if I set out to use your property for my own purposes—I may be denied an offset for expenses that I incurred in making those gains.

34. Edwards v. Lee's Administrator, 265 Ky. 418 (1936).

In others, the defendant is made to pay the fair value of the benefit received. Courts often use puzzling formulae to express these ideas: In the
old "waiver of tort" cases, the basis for the plaintiff's recovery was that
the defendant must be taken to have been acting as the plaintiff's agent,
and so the defendant must pay over the benefits of that agency to the
principal, that is, the plaintiff. In another, more recent line of cases, the
defendant has been held liable for depriving the plaintiff of the opportunity to bargain over the former's use of the latter's right. Both of these
formulations have struck many readers as artificial, even fictitious (in the
pejorative rather than legal sense of that term).

Despite their artificiality, these formulations can be rendered intelligible by focusing on the plaintiff's right that is at issue. The cases all turn
on one person's unauthorized use of another's property, typically, though
not exclusively, through conversion or related torts such as trespass to
minerals. Your right to your property is the right to determine the purposes for which it will be used, and so, as against others, you are entitled
to the usefulness of your property. That is why, if somebody damages your
property so that you are unable to use it, you are entitled to the profits
you would have gained during the period that it was unusable. Conversely,
if someone else uses it without your authorization, you are entitled to the
profits of that use also, because all uses of your property are yours. That
does not mean that the other person who uses it is using it as your agent,
or that you entered into a hypothetical contract with that person. These
imagined alternative transactions serve, not as analyses of the wrong, but
as measures of what is already established as a wrong. They can so function even if it is known as a matter of fact that the plaintiff would never
have come to terms with the defendant, but instead would have rejected
the proposal out of hand. It is not that the defendant did wrong by taking
it upon him- or herself to be the plaintiff's agent, or by entering into a bargain. The defendant did neither of these things; that is the wrong of unauthorized use of another person's property. These other models show
what it is that the plaintiff had as against the defendant, with respect to
which the defendant did wrong.

Not every use of another's body or property produces a gain for the defendant. Some produce a loss for the plaintiff, in which case the plaintiff
is entitled to be put back where she would have been, if the use had never

happened. That is the result if my cattle wander onto your land and flatten your crops. Coase's famous claim that harms are the reciprocal effects of ongoing activities[35] is true but beside the point: Your *claim* to damages in trespass is based, not on the harm I cause you, but on the fact that I use your land for a purpose you have not authorized. The relationship of trespass is not reciprocal: I have used your land, but you have not used mine. Because I have wronged you, you are entitled to be put back in the situation you would have been in if the wrong had never happened. The harm you suffered only appears as the magnitude of the means of which my trespass deprived you.[36]

The measure of damages depends on the plaintiff's decision. If I wrongfully convert your property, whether you sue for my gains or for your losses will ordinarily depend on your assessment of their relative magnitude. Giving you this power is not an exception to the idea that rights survive their own violation, because it is just that very idea. The property with which I interfered is still yours, and you are the one who gets to decide which of its uses—my actual use or your use that I prevented—is the relevant one.

5. Aggravated and Punitive Damages

My main focus has been on compensatory damages, the aim of which is to put the plaintiff back in the position that he or she would have been in had the wrong not occurred. Such an account can be expanded to include other categories of damages, including aggravated damages, in circumstances in which the defendant's conduct was wrongful as against the plaintiff in a particularly high-handed way. They reflect something additional that the defendant did to the plaintiff in the course of violating the plaintiff's right. Awarding damages in aggravating circumstances is

---

35. R. H. Coase, "The Problem of Social Cost," *Journal of Law and Economics* 3 (1960): 1–44.

36. Some trespasses produce neither gains nor losses. In such cases the plaintiff is entitled to "nominal" damages, that is, damages that articulate the nature of the wrong without quantifying it. Such damages are nominal by name, but not by nature, because they are based on the existence of a wrong. As Lord Halsbury remarks in The Mediana, [1900] A.C. 113, 116, the term "nominal damages" does not necessarily mean "small damages."

consistent with a model on which the point is to make it as though the wrong had not occurred, insofar as those damages are meant to go to the nature of the wrong. Where the aggravating factor is not mere indifference to the plaintiff's right but outright hostility to it, the extent of the aggravation cannot be quantified by asking about potential substitutes or near-substitutes.

Punitive damages are quite different: Their operation in Commonwealth jurisdictions is severely limited. They are much more prominent in U.S. cases. In some situations they correspond more nearly to aggravated damages. In *Jacque v. Steenberg Homes, Inc.*,[37] the plaintiffs had refused to grant the defendant permission to cut across their land to deliver a mobile home to a neighboring lot, even after the defendant offered to pay. The defendant proceeded to cut across anyway, positioning a trailer to block the Jacques' view of what they were doing, so as to save itself considerable expense that would have been involved in using instead a steep snow-covered road. The Wisconsin Supreme Court, characterizing Steenberg as displaying "indifference and a reckless disregard for the law, and for the rights of others," as well as taking an "arrogant stance," "egregious" and as having "acted deviously," upheld a jury verdict of $1 in nominal damages for the trespass, and reinstated an award of $100,000 in punitive damages against the company. These can be understood as aggravated rather than punitive damages.[38]

Other cases of punitive damages can be understood as gain-based. In the leading English case of *Cassell & Co. v. Broome*,[39] the defendant publisher published a book it knew to be libelous on the grounds that the ensuing controversy would increase sales. In awarding punitive damages, the court keyed them to the benefit the defendant calculated to gain

---

37. 563 N.W.2d 154 (Wis. 1997). For detailed discussion of *Jacque*, see Thomas W. Merrill and Henry E. Smith, "The Morality of Property," *William & Mary Law Review* 48 (2007): 1849–1895.

38. The court also appealed to the deterrent effect, the disgorgement of the amount the defendant hoped to save through the trespass, and the incentive of plaintiffs wronged in this way to bring suit. The first and third of these do not involve the plaintiff's right, but only effects on third parties; the second is an aspect of the plaintiff's right.

39. [1972] AC 1027.

through the wrong, and so those damages can be understood as gain-based rather than punitive.[40]

Other cases in which punitive damages have been awarded, particularly in the United States, focus primarily or even exclusively on their deterrent effect, determining the appropriate quantum of such damages based on what would be necessary to deter like conduct in the future.[41] The account offered here has no resources for explaining such decisions, because they treat a damage award, not as a remedy for a wrong that the defendant did to the plaintiff, but instead as a policy lever to provide incentives to parties not before the court.[42] The inability to explain such awards is not, however, a limitation of the account, but rather the vindication of it: The practice of U.S. courts with regard to punitive damages gives up on the idea that a tort is a private wrong.

6. Conclusion

Explanatory and interpretive tort theory developed in the wake of legal realism in American law schools in the middle part of the twentieth century. One of its residues was a broad conception of what it is to be properly tough-minded and focused on the facts. One aspect of this residual tough-mindedness was a readiness to assume, almost by default

40. The same analysis applies to the popular narrative about the punitive damage award in Grimshaw v. Ford Motor Company, 119 Cal.App. 3d 757 (1981). On this telling, an internal memo indicated that Ford had decided to install in its Pinto model gas tanks that were prone to explosion on impact, based on a calculation of the comparative costs of safer tanks, the number of injuries likely to result, and the damages it expected to pay per incident. On this view, the punitive damages were keyed to the gain Ford hoped to realize from the unsafe vehicle. Gary Schwartz points out that the story contains some errors: The memo in question used figures supplied by the NHTSA (to which the memo was submitted) for the cost of a life lost, and concerned the costs of rollover protection for the entire U.S. auto industry, not Pinto gas tanks, and it was not admitted into evidence at the trial. But the general thrust is correct, and the plaintiffs' counsel paraphrased Ford CEO Lee Iacocca as saying, "$2000 and 2000 pounds. Tear it out. Let them die." See Gary Schwartz, "The Myth of the Ford Pinto Case," *Rutgers Law Review* 43 (1991): 1045.

41. BMW of North America, Inc. v. Gore (94-896), 517 U.S. 559 (1996).

42. See Ernest J. Weinrib, "Punishment and Disgorgement as Contract Remedies," *Chicago-Kent Law Review* 78 (2003): 55-103.

from the lack of a suitably tough-minded alternative, that the law of torts *must be* concerned with reducing harm. Harm and loss are real events in the world in a way that rights and duties might be thought not to be. Holmes's statement is characteristic: "The general purpose of the law of torts is to secure a man indemnity against certain forms of harm to person, reputation, or estate, at the hands of his neighbors, not because they are wrong, but because they are harms."[43] Familiar types of harm can be identified without reference to how they come about, so once harm is in view, it is a short step to the conclusion that the familiar landscape of legal doctrine is comprised of a series of tools designed to prevent or reduce unwelcome outcomes. From these premises, it is almost inevitable that law would be understood as an instrument, to be understood and evaluated in terms of its actual reduction of the target outcomes.

Half a century ago, ideas that are now prominent in torts scholarship might have been charged with failure to mean anything. But the broader assumption that tort law must have some sort of function, that it must be called to account for its success or failure at delivering some set of goods that can be specified without reference to the concept of a right—be they harm prevention, wealth maximization, or civil peace and the sublation of the desire for revenge—keeps reasserting itself.

Instrumentalism seems less inevitable once the focus is shifted from harms to wrongs. The ordinary and familiar ways of thinking and talking about wrongs and remedies do make sense. Damages aim to make it as if a wrong had never happened. The example of damages also reveals a broader point: With respect to the supposed lessons of supposedly sophisticated talk about the "purposes" of law, and the related urge to unmask or otherwise discipline legal language, we can carry on in our old ways as if none of this had ever happened.

43. Oliver Wendell Holmes Jr., *The Common Law* (London: MacMillan, 1882), 149.

CHAPTER 9

Remedies, Part 2

Before a Court

I HAVE ARGUED that rights survive their own violation, and that remedies can be understood as the continuation of those rights. In earlier chapters I have said something about the way in which legal institutions are required to make the requirements determinate, and how they incorporate social understandings and expectations in so doing. In this chapter I take up a different role for legal institutions: fashioning and ordering remedies. I explain this distinctive role in dialogue with a prominent objection to the idea that rights survive their own violation, which has come to be associated with what is called "civil recourse." Civil recourse theory has received its most prominent development in writings by John Goldberg and Benjamin Zipursky, but Stephen Smith has also made significant contributions to its development.

The core objection of civil recourse theorists to corrective justice theory has two interrelated elements: first, that the idea that rights survive their own violation cannot explain the essential role of the plaintiff in initiating a tort action; second, that it cannot explain why a remedy must be ordered by a court. Taken together, the elements are supposed to show that although a private wrong is the occasion of the court ordering a remedy, the basis of the remedy must be something other than the right.

The core objection seldom travels alone; it is usually accompanied by ancillary arguments, many of which are supposed to buttress the central argument about the essential role of the court by showing that the idea that rights survive their own violation can explain at most a small subset of the wrongs and remedies addressed by the law of torts. This objection sometimes keeps company with the claim that the past cannot be changed, and with the disjunctive objection, both of which were considered in Chapter 8, and with the claim, examined in Chapter 5, that strict liability torts involve liability without wrongdoing. My aim in this chapter is to show that the civil recourse objection does no better than any of these arguments. I will argue that the supposedly factual and doctrinal evidence adduced in developing the core objection presupposes the idea that rights survive their own violation. Things only look otherwise if legal norms are understood as specific instructions.[1] I will also examine, briefly, the alternative accounts of the point of tort remedy that are variously suggested by Goldberg and Zipursky and the account proposed by Smith.

Goldberg and Zipursky introduce their account as a critique of corrective justice theories of tort law. Unfortunately, that term has come to stand for many different things, and although some views whose defenders characterize them as accounts of corrective justice may be vulnerable to parts of their critique, I hope to simply bypass the distractions of considering all of those alternatives.[2]

Goldberg and Zipursky acknowledge the importance of the corrective justice critique of economic and other instrumental approaches to law.

---

1. I will mention only in passing Goldberg and Zipursky's other allegations, such as the charge that talk about rights surviving their own violation fails to display proper "independence from metaphysically rich notions" and "is committed to the existence of a legal order not of human creation." See Benjamin C. Zipursky, "Pragmatic Conceptualism," *Legal Theory* 6 (2000): 470. In the same article he substitutes for the metaphysics he seeks to avoid a vocabulary borrowed from bodily activity and games of skill, appealing repeatedly to the concept of a practice, and the practitioners' "grasp" of "moves" within it. Unfortunately, each of these ideas is ambiguous between an empirical regularity in a group's behavior and an idea of normative ordering. The former sheds no light on the law; the latter presupposes what Zipursky finds objectionably metaphysical.

2. See Chapter 1.

That critique, as formulated initially by Weinrib and Coleman,[3] argues in its broadest form that economic analysis is one-sided in a way that makes it unable to explain the most basic and familiar features of tort law. By focusing only on the question of what incentives will lead defendants to take the appropriate level of precaution, economic analysis is unable to explain why the plaintiff, in particular, should be the one who recovers those damages, and equally unable to explain why the measure of those damages should be the plaintiff's injury. Accounts that focus on compensation, instead of or in addition to deterrence, introduce the plaintiff into their analysis, but face a different version of the same difficulty. In addition to being unable to explain why the plaintiff, in particular, should be the one charged with policing the defendant's conduct, they double their difficulties by also being unable to explain why the defendant, in particular, should be the one charged with compensating the plaintiff.

1. The Separation of Wrongs and Remedies

Goldberg and Zipursky argue that the law of torts is in the first instance a law of wrongs; this plaintiff recovers from this defendant because this is the defendant (in particular) who has wronged this very plaintiff (in particular). But they deny that a remedy is a way of giving effect to the right that was violated; instead, they describe it as an "avenue of recourse" provided by the law to the plaintiff.[4] Their acceptance of the bipolarity critique of instrumental accounts of tort law provides the framework within which they are able to represent tort as a law of wrongs. It also pro-

3. Weinrib developed the critique in a series of articles in the 1980s, and in *The Idea of Private Law* (Cambridge, MA: Harvard University Press, 1995). A similar critique is developed in Jules Coleman, *Risks and Wrongs* (New York: Cambridge University Press, 1992).

4. Zipursky, "Philosophy of Private Law," in *The Oxford Handbook of Jurisprudence and Philosophy of Law,* ed. J. Coleman and S. Shapiro (Oxford: Oxford University Press, 2002), 623. Other writers seeking to develop the same theme include Andrew S. Gold, "The Taxonomy of Civil Recourse," *Florida State University Law Review* 39 (2011): 65–83; Scott Hershovitz, "Tort as a Substitute for Revenge," in *Philosophical Foundations of the Law of Torts,* ed. John Oberdiek (Oxford: Oxford University Press, 2014); Nathan Oman, "The Honor of Private Law," *Fordham Law Review* 80 (2011): 31–71; Jason Solomon, "Civil Recourse as Social Equality," *Florida State University Law Review* 39 (2011): 243–272.

vides the grounds on which they seek to explain why a particular plain-tiff is entitled to proceed against a defendant if and only if that is the very defendant who wronged that plaintiff. Only the person who is wronged has a claim to recourse.

Rather than seeing a remedy as the continuation of the plaintiff's right, however, they characterize it in terms of responsive conduct. Because the defendant has done something to the plaintiff, in return the plaintiff gets to do something to the defendant.[5] This, they contend, makes a tort ac-tion "a civilized alternative to vengeance—civil recourse for the plaintiff, which is appropriately channeled through and cabined by law."[6] They have offered a variety of explanations of the need for recourse. One line of argument points to social motivations that lead people to become angry (or worse) when they believe themselves to have been wronged. For Zi-pursky and Goldberg, the tort system channels these feelings of having been "aggrieved or injured,"[7] bringing procedure to bear on the anger. It thus provides a substitute for revenge. In some places they suggest that tort law is a result of a kind of Lockean social contract, in which the state, having prohibited private vengeance, must, in fairness to those to whom it is denied, provide them with an alternative avenue of recourse.[8] If this substitution of process for feeling is to succeed, the court must award rem-edies on the basis of something other than restoring that of which the aggrieved plaintiff was deprived. Recourse is "civil" both in the fact that it is subject to procedures and in the fact that it is not barbaric. In this process, "make whole" damages are at most a "default."[9] The court is not doing justice between the parties; understanding tort as a law of re-

---

5. As Robert Stevens has pointed out, this is a general feature of private remedies, and so fails to differentiate tort from contract and unjust enrichment. See Stevens, "Private Rights and Public Wrongs," in *Unraveling Tort and Crime,* ed. Matthew Dyson (Cambridge: Cambridge University Press, 2014), 119.

6. John C. P. Goldberg and Benjamin C. Zipursky, "Seeing Tort Law from the Internal Point of View: Holmes and Hart on Legal Duties," *Fordham Law Review* 75 (2006): 1581.

7. John C. P. Goldberg and Benjamin C. Zipursky, "Torts as Wrongs," *Texas Law Review* 88 (2010): 943.

8. Benjamin C. Zipursky, "Rights, Wrongs, and Recourse," *Vanderbilt Law Review* 51 (1998): 86; Zipursky, "The Philosophy of Private Law."

9. John C. P. Goldberg and Benjamin C. Zipursky, "Tort Law and Responsibility," in Oberdiek, *Philosophical Foundations of the Law of Torts.* In "Two Conceptions of Tort

course rather than one of right ineluctably leads to the diversity of remedies.

> But it is also to appreciate and accept that successful tort plaintiffs will sometimes be entitled to something more than "justice" demands or even permits, at least if justice is understood as the achievement of a just distribution of gains and losses as between tortfeasor and victim. Here, the most obvious example is the eggshell plaintiff, who may stand to recover a huge amount of compensation from a minimally culpable defendant. It is questionable whether justice is being done in such cases, but our tort system authorizes this sort of outcome because tort law is not a scheme for restoring a normative equilibrium as between doer and sufferer. It is, for better and worse, a law for the redress of private wrongs.[10]

As we saw in Chapter 8, the eggshell plaintiff's recovery is a reflection of his or her right: A wrongdoer is responsible for the full extent of the injury he or she wrongfully caused, because, had it not been for the defendant's wrong, the plaintiff would have had an intact skull and all that followed from it. The point also applies to Smith's remark in discussing a similar example. He claims that the point of damages cannot be to give effect to a plaintiff's antecedent right, because a court will sometimes order a defendant to pay more than even the "morally upstanding" defendant would consider himself obligated to pay.[11] Perhaps Smith is correct that morally upstanding defendants would find themselves unmoved by the rights of those they have injured, so long as their culpability was low. Because the idea that rights survive their own violation is supposed to explain the plaintiff's entitlement to call on the court to *compel* the defendant to make it as if the wrong had never happened, it offers neither an account nor an analysis of what a morally upstanding defendant would suppose he or she ought to do in the absence of a court. The upstanding defendant's reflection on his or her duties, like the degree of his

---

Damages: Fair v. Full Compensation," *DePaul Law Review* 55 (2006): 444, Goldberg characterizes it as a "guideline."

10. "Seeing Tort Law from the Internal Point of View," 1581.

11. Stephen Smith, "Why Courts Make Orders (and What This Tells Us about Damages)," *Current Legal Problems* 64 (2011): 77.

or her culpability, is nonrelational, even if the subject of the reflection is what the defendant did to the plaintiff. The relation is primary; if the defendant injured the plaintiff through conduct that was too dangerous, his or her culpability—the degree of his or her indifference to the plaintiff's safety—is derivative. The same point applies to the plaintiff's attitude toward the defendant; the plaintiff's degree of anger, resentment, or thirst for revenge is nonrelational. The wrong that the defendant did to the plaintiff must drive the analysis, not the attitude that it does, would, or should generate in either party.

More generally, the idea that a legal process is a substitute for something like revenge is ambiguous between empirical and normative ideas. As a piece of political sociology, the thought that people will put up with being deprived of their right to revenge only if they get what they regard as an acceptable substitute does poorly even by the low standards of armchair speculation. Aside from occasional asides in defamation cases about the cause of action for defamation having arisen to reduce the incidence of dueling, whatever historical and armchair evidence might be marshaled has more than "a whiff of the premodern."[12] So understood, it seems at best relevant to an argument for doing away with tort law as an obsolete institution, not unlike Holmes's attempt to show "that this liability also had its root in the passion of revenge, and to point out the changes by which it reached its present form."[13]

Understood instead as a normative argument that those denied the power of private revenge are "in fairness" "entitled" to a substitute, the account does no better. Fairness requires those who prohibit others from doing something to provide a substitute only if those others were entitled to do the prohibited thing. The state does not owe would-be murderers, thieves, and vandals compensation for restricting them; vigilantes are different from murderers, thieves, and vandals only if they are entitled to exact revenge. Moreover, the normative claim presupposes some version of the thesis it seeks to deny, that is, that a person who is deprived of some-

12. Arthur Applbaum, *Ethics for Adversaries* (Princeton: Princeton University Press, 2000), 47.

13. Oliver Wendell Holmes Jr., *The Common Law* (Boston: Little, Brown, 1882), 5.

thing to which he or she has a right is entitled to a remedy that comes as close as possible to a substitute for the object of that right.[14]

2. Powers and the Plaintiff's Initiative

The idea that tort law enforces social norms and provides an alternative to revenge is supposed to provide a superior explanation of the role of a court. In denying that a tort remedy does justice, Goldberg and Zipursky mean to both draw attention to the apparent disproportion between wrong and remedy and, at the same time, show that if tort law were indeed concerned with doing justice, the plaintiff's bringing an action would not figure in its deliberations. Thus, they argue, "the notion of 'corrective justice' is at least partially teleological. The assertion that corrective justice is done carries with it an implication that the state of affairs in which the defendant pays the verdict is in an important sense an improvement on the state of affairs in which there is no tort claim brought or the verdict is never paid."[15] If corrective justice were concerned with achieving or restoring a pattern of holdings, then it would, indeed, be a mystery why litigation is initiated by the plaintiff rather than the state. If upholding justice is the state's responsibility, why leave any judicial matter to a plaintiff's initiative? As Zipursky remarks, "A right of action is a privilege

14. In recent writing, Zipursky and Goldberg have sought to distance themselves from the idea that civil recourse is a substitute for private revenge, and have begun to develop an alternative. See their "Civil Recourse Revisited," *Florida State University Law Review* 39 (2011): 341–371. In a companion piece, "Substantive Standing, Civil Recourse, and Corrective Justice," *Florida State University Law Review* 39 (2011): 299–340, Zipursky focuses on social norms governing interpersonal relationships, which typically permit a person who has been wronged to hold the wrongdoer to account. He suggests that the law of tort is an institutionalized version of this, made available to provide recourse between strangers, thereby upholding each person's status as a social equal. Zipursky also compares seeking recourse to the use of defensive or self-restorative force. To date these ideas are not articulated in enough detail to assess their consistency with the idea that a right survives its own violation. On their face, they appear to be entirely consistent with it: You can only defend or restore what is already yours. Perhaps the thought is that you defend or restore your status as a rightholder, rather than the object of the specific right that was violated. If so, some explanation would be required of why that status survives its own violation, but rights to the more specific things, with respect to which you can be wronged, do not.

15. Goldberg and Zipursky, "Civil Recourse Revisited," 370.

and a power, and the state is not committed to the normative desirability of its exercise, only to the right to have it."[16]

The thought here is that if tort represented the principle of corrective justice, the defendant would be under an enforceable duty to repair his or her wrongs, quite apart from the plaintiff's power to demand a remedy. If justice requires that a wrong be undone, then it would not be up to the victim of the wrong to decide whether to initiate proceedings against the wrongdoer; the state would step in to enforce the plaintiff's right, in something like the way in which some criminal fraud prosecutions require that the fraudster repay his or her dupes, without making the repayment conditional on any act on the part of the dupes. Other criminal statutes impose similar requirements, which follow directly from conviction and require no action on the part of the plaintiff.[17] That is not, however, how the law of torts works; it gives the aggrieved plaintiff only a power to proceed against a wrongdoer, the exercise of which is left entirely to the plaintiff's discretion.

Goldberg and Zipursky are certainly right to draw attention to the fact that the plaintiff alone has the power to compel the defendant to appear before a court, and if the plaintiff prevails, to repair the wrong. From this they conclude that the defendant is not under any legal duty to repair the wrong. If the defendant was under such a duty, it would be within the purview of the state (or, for that matter, almost anyone) to enforce compliance with it. Instead, courts "empower individuals to obtain an avenue of recourse against other private parties."[18]

16. Benjamin C. Zipursky, "Civil Recourse, not Corrective Justice," *Georgia Law Review* 91 (2003): 741.

17. Zipursky gives the example of In Re: Drexel Burnham Lambert Group Inc., 995 F.2d 1 138, 1141 (2d Cir. 1993), "in which Michael Milken agreed to establish a civil restitution fund with the SEC in conjunction with his guilty plea on charges of securities fraud." See Zipursky, "Civil Recourse, not Corrective Justice," 719. This is a more general feature of some criminal code provisions; see, for example, 18 U.S. Code §3663A *Mandatory Restitution to Victims of Certain Crimes,* which mandates restitution in cases of crimes of violence, crimes against property, and tampering with medical or consumer products "in which an identifiable victim or victims has suffered a physical injury or pecuniary loss."

18. Zipursky, "Civil Recourse, not Corrective Justice," 765.

3. The Role of the Court

These mysteries, however, are entirely of the critics' own making. It is a general feature of *every* private right that "the state is not committed to the normative desirability of its exercise, only to the right to have it."[19] Within this structure, it is not merely unsurprising, but inevitable, that the plaintiff alone is entitled to decide whether or not to stand on his or her rights in cases of wrongdoing. That is a general feature of a right as between private parties; the rightholder determines whether to enforce it.[20] If a right survives its own violation, the bearer of the surviving right is the one who is entitled to decide whether to exercise it, just as he or she was entitled to decide whether to exercise the primary right. So the power has its basis in the plaintiff's right against the defendant.[21] If I am in your home, and you tell me to leave, I have to do as you say—it is up to you. The state takes no position on whether you should exercise your power; that, too, is entirely up to you. This remains the case even if I should leave—I have overstayed my welcome, or am making you or your other guests uncomfortable. It lies with you to do something about it. The state normally leaves it to you to decide whether to assert your claim that I moderate my conduct in light of your safety. It will permit you to sign a waiver relieving me of liability if you are injured as you ride in my river raft or tour my lion farm.

The same point applies to other private rights: If you and I have a contract, you can relieve me of the duty to perform. If I breach the contract, you then get to decide whether to seek judgment against me. If the court

19. Ibid., 741.

20. In Jewish law, excluding others from your property requires the exercise of a power: If you do not keep me off, I can enter your land and plant trees. But if you tell me not to, I must not, or if you ask me to leave, I must. That does not mean that your power to exclude me is something altogether different from your right; it means instead that it is incumbent on you to exercise it. See Benny Porat, "Property and Exclusivity: Two Visions, Two Traditions" in *American Journal of Comparative Law* (forthcoming). This latter structure is the structure of remedies in the common law; it is not that you have no right against the person who wronged you, but only that it is incumbent on you to exercise it.

21. Goldberg and Zipursky contend, in "Civil Recourse Revisited," that the plaintiff has a right only against the state: "The political (and constitutional) right of the plaintiff to the state-facilitated private power is correlative to a state duty to provide such a power" (362).

decides in your favor, it is up to you whether to enforce the judgment. The state therefore gives you a power and a privilege, but then stands to the side as you decide whether to exercise them.

So, too, in cases of completed wrongs, the state will not step in to resolve a private dispute unless and until the plaintiff initiates it. In a private dispute, the court conceives of its role as passive: The plaintiff must convince it to do something, and it takes no position on matters that are not before it. A court neither seeks that disputes be aired publicly nor demands that they be resolved. Thus it is no surprise that the action must take place at the plaintiff's initiative. As a plaintiff, you have a "privilege and a power," because it is always up to you to decide whether to stand on your rights.

The parties are free to negotiate whatever resolution they regard as satisfactory, or simply to let the matter drop; the court concerns itself not with negotiation but with arbitration. If I defraud you, you are entitled to demand compensation, but you might think it more important to forgive, or you might be too embarrassed that you fell for a such a ridiculous scam that you don't want to be reminded, or have others learn, of your gullibility.

In waiting for the plaintiff's initiative, the state behaves differently than a criminal court that orders restitution for victims of crime. Yet even here, the contrast is not as sharp as Goldberg and Zipursky suggest: In a criminal prosecution for which the penalty includes a requirement of restitution, the *court* also does not "stand ready to restore a normative equilibrium." Instead, the court awaits the action of the prosecution. If the accused is convicted or enters a guilty plea, the court then applies the statutorily required penalty, which may include an order of restitution. The role of a court in a legal system that separates legislative, executive, and judicial power is to resolve disputes on the terms on which they present themselves.

Volumes of political philosophy could be written about the nature of the exercise of public power by the court in resolving disputes, but a few sentences are sufficient here. The court's power to resolve disputes is required in a system in which everyone is supposed to enjoy their private rights and rights survive their own violation. If the plaintiff is not in charge of the defendant, then the plaintiff's allegation that the defendant has violated some right of the plaintiff's is just that—an allegation—until a third party with authority over *both* the plaintiff and the defendant has resolved the dispute on its merits. That does not mean that there are no obvious cases; instead it is part of what it is to live in a legal system, that the plaintiff cannot exercise his or her power—cannot compel the defendant to make it as if the wrong had never happened—except by enlisting a court, that is, a body competent to make binding determinations and orders. Only a court can be entitled to do these things, because, as we saw in Chapter 7, the defendant is entitled to demand that the plaintiff prove the wrong before anything is done about it.

A court is also needed for another reason. In some cases the existence of the wrong needs to be established; in others its extent will be in dispute. The plaintiff's right survives in an incomplete form, and requires a court with the authority to impose a resolution on both parties to determine its existence and contours. But even in uncontroversial cases—for instance, where a defendant has willfully destroyed a piece of the plaintiff's property that is easy to replace—the defendant is still entitled to refuse to do anything until the plaintiff has established the wrong. Morally, it would sometimes be better if the defendant did not stand on his or her rights. But the possibility of a defendant contesting a claim in order to wear down the plaintiff should not distract attention from the structuring role of the requirement that any imputation of wrongdoing be established. This requirement is a feature of legal proceedings more generally; as we saw in Chapter 7, the law of defamation is a reflection of, rather than an exception to, this structure. It also figures in the criminal trial; the presumption of innocence does not reflect the disproportion in resources that the state and the accused each have, but instead the accused person's right against being held to have done wrong without it having been established.

On this interpretation, then, the basic idea of a relational right surviving its own violation in the form of a remedy[22] requires institutions to adjudicate disputes and order remedies designed to give effect to the antecedent rights. The point comes up when rights are in dispute, but it

---

22. The right may survive in ways other than a remedy. For example, without going to court you can physically reclaim a chattel from someone who has converted it.

reflects a more general requirement that rights be upheld by a public authority entitled to decide on behalf of everyone, including both parties to a dispute. This structure manifests itself even in cases in which the law permits self-help; the question of whether the circumstances warrant it is subject to review, even in cases of self-defense.[23] This is just the requirement that disputes be resolved in accordance with law; the court sits as arbiter because the court's task is to apply the law to particulars on behalf of everyone.

The norms that require the court to resolve the dispute also shape the court's own processes—in particular, requiring that the plaintiff establish each of the elements of the wrong. This, in turn, shapes the content of the plaintiff's surviving right: It survives as established in accordance with the court's procedures and presumptions, that is, if and only if the plaintiff establishes each of the elements of the wrong.

This unavoidable layering of norms governing the operation of a court on top of the norms governing the conduct of the defendant sometimes leaves courts in what they regard as a quandary. For example, courts often wrestle with issues of factual uncertainty about causation in negligence. The court's task is to see to it that rights survive their own violation, and, at the same time, to resolve disputes in accordance with the fundamental assumption that the burden of establishing wrongdoing lies with those who allege it. In cases of factual uncertainty about causation, both those involving multiple negligent defendants, such as hunters shooting in the plaintiff's direction, only one of whom caused the plaintiff's injury,[24] and those involving alternate, non-negligent causes,[25] courts have dealt with this tension by inferring causation without requiring that the plaintiff exclude competing causes.[26] In *McGhee v. National Coal Board,* Lord

---

23. See Malcolm Thorburn, "Justifications, Powers, and Authority," *Yale Law Journal* 117 (2008): 1070–1130.

24. Summers v. Tice, 33 Cal. 2d 80, 199 P 2d 1 (1948); Cook v. Lewis, [1951] 1 SCR 830.

25. McGhee v. National Coal Board, [1973] 1 WLR 1 (HL).

26. As Ernest Weinrib has pointed out in "Causal Uncertainty," *Oxford Journal of Legal Studies,* Volume 34, (2015), the cases are structurally very different; the hunters are both negligent, and both contributed to the factual uncertainty by discharging their weapons simultaneously. In *McGhee,* the defendant created the risk and failed to take required steps to alleviate it; the "innocent" dust acquires its innocence from the assumption that showers

Simon expresses the concern that to require the plaintiff to establish causation in such a case would place the defendants "under a duty which they could, in the present state of medical knowledge, with impunity ignore."[27] The duty is imposed because of the heightened risk of injury. The defendant in *McGhee* failed to provide showers, to protect those who worked in its kilns from developing dermatitis from exposure to brick dust. The plaintiff was unable to establish that the dermatitis was not caused by exposure while working in the kilns, and so could not show that the failure to provide showers caused his injury. Lord Simon's point is that the plaintiff's right would not survive its own violation if it could be violated in circumstances where uncertainty made it impossible for it to ever generate a remedy.

I do not purport to offer a detailed analysis of those cases; I mention them here only to underscore the role of the court in giving effect to rights. The law treats issues of causation as questions of fact; its assumption is that there is a fact of the matter as to which of the negligent hunters caused the plaintiff's injury, or of whether the brick dust that caused the plaintiff's dermatitis was a result of the defendant's failure to provide showers, or was instead the "innocent" brick dust that would have come into contact with the plaintiff's skin while he was at work. The task of the court, however, is not to accurately discover or approximate a result that can be characterized without any reference to its procedures; its role instead is to resolve the dispute on its merits, consistent with the rights of both the plaintiff and the defendant. That is what it is for a dispute to be resolved in accordance with law.[28]

---

were provided. Whether it is negligent to operate a brick kiln depends on what is done to alleviate risks attendant on it; it is non-negligent only if showers are provided. If the showers would have reduced the risk to an acceptable level, but the operation of kilns without showers posed a significant risk, the court has no difficulty making an inference of fact that a significant risk was more likely to have caused the dermatitis than a minor one. As Weinrib puts it, "Relieving the plaintiff of the need to prove the specific effect of the breach of duty prevents the defendant from taking advantage of an uncertainty that is entirely the product of the interplay of the components of his own activity." Weinrib, "Causal Uncertainty," 2.

27. *McGhee v. National Coal Board*, 6.

28. In an earlier article, co-authored with Benjamin Zipursky, "Corrective Justice in an Age of Mass Torts," in *Philosophy and the Law of Torts*, ed. Gerald J. Postema (Cambridge: Cambridge University Press, 2001), I took a slightly different position, which I now view as

4. Smith's Argument from Orders

Stephen Smith has offered a different but related account of the distinctive role of courts in remedies. Goldberg and Zipursky focus on the role of plaintiffs in bringing an action before a court; Smith focuses on the form of remedies. His central claim is that if a remedy were the surviving form of a right, courts would issue only declarations rather than orders. Smith distinguishes between what he calls "replicative" orders, such as injunctions, decrees of specific performance, and orders to pay an agreed sum, and what he characterizes as "creative orders," among which he includes orders of damages. A replicative order tells the defendant what he or she already was under a duty to do. A creative order creates a new duty, rather than simply giving effect to one that is already in place.[29] Smith puts this point in terms of the different ways in which orders figure in practical reasoning:

> Though related in important ways to both rules and sanctions, orders are a distinct legal phenomenon. Orders are similar to rules in that they are meant to guide behaviour, but they differ from rules in that they do not invoke a claim to moral guidance. Orders are meant to motivate by their practical, not moral, authority. Viewed from another perspective, orders are similar to sanctions in that they are used for the purpose of bringing about a specific, tangible result, for example the transfer of money or property. Unlike sanctions, however, orders seek to bring about such results by enlisting the assistance of defendants. In short, orders are basically commands.[30]

Smith suggests that the correct model for damages orders is criminal sentencing. If you park in a restricted zone, or let your dog go off leash in a prohibited zone, you are liable to pay a fine. "In Montreal, there is a bylaw stipulating that citizens are liable to be fined a minimum of $300 if they allow their dogs to run unleashed. But there is no rule stipulating that if

---

relying too heavily on the thought that the role of the court was to bring about a correct result, the correctness of which could be specified without reference to its operations.

29. Zipursky makes this point in "Civil Recourse, not Corrective Justice," 720, arguing that in the case of tortious wrongdoing, the duty has not yet "ripened."

30. Smith, "Why Courts Make Orders," 86.

citizens allow their dogs to run unleashed, they should send the city a check for $300. Errant dog owners have no legal or even moral duty to pay the city prior to being ordered to do so." It is not that you have a duty to pay a fine, of which the court merely reminds you; it tells you to do something, and if, for whatever reason, it fails to tell you, you do not have to do it. Smith suggests that the same point applies in the case of orders of damages: You do not have a duty to pay damages if you tortiously injure another person. Only if the other person brings you before a court, and successfully establishes each of the elements of the tort will the court order you to pay. Only then are you under a duty to pay. Thus, rights do not survive their own violation; once a wrong is completed, a separate set of concepts comes into operation. As Smith puts it, "Like orders to pay fines, their importance lies fundamentally not in what they do, but in what they represent. And what damage awards represent is the law's recognition that the plaintiff was wronged by the defendant. Damage awards are the law's way of vindicating—not enforcing—the plaintiff's rights."[31] Smith makes this point in the potentially misleading vocabulary of pre-existing moral duties, making it sound as though legal duties are a court's best guess as to what a person ought to do, all things considered. This picture seems plausible enough with respect to duties against using and damaging other people's bodies and property and the duty to keep your dog leashed or to park only in designated locations. I leave to another occasion the question of whether this is, in general, the most helpful way of thinking about legal duties.[32] The plausibility of such examples highlights the contrast with the payment of a fine, and Smith's strategy is to

31. Stephen A. Smith, "Duties, Liabilities, and Damages," *Harvard Law Review* 125 (2012): 1728.

32. Smith's account rests on a version of Joseph Raz's influential account of legal authority, according to which a legal system claims to issue directives that enable citizens to do better at complying with the reasons that apply to them independently of those directives. Raz's theory has been the subject of a great deal of discussion and criticism, and I will not rehearse that debate here, or even take a position on it. I will note, however, that it is not likely to assist Smith in drawing the distinction between wrongs and remedies. As noted in Chapter 8, John Gardner works from similar premises to argue that reasons continue to apply when the agent fails to do what they require, and that a remedy is just the continuation of those reasons. On Gardner's version of the Razian account of authority, the court's exercise of authority consists in specifying the action that is most in conformity with the

carry some of that plausibility over to the contrast with damages. The contrast, however, is misleading. The payment of a fine stands in no systematic relation to illegal parking or off-leash dogs; it can be understood either as some version of incentive or pricing mechanism[33] or, alternatively, as a penalty attaching to the fact of disobedience. The court orders the fine, in accordance with a schedule of payments. The municipal code regulating parking or off-leash dogs is one thing, and the schedule of penalties another. In this sense, the order to pay a fine is "creative" in Smith's preferred sense, as not only its content but also its grounds are entirely different from those of the norm the violation of which prompted the order. Paying the fine does not keep roadways clear or protect letter carriers from dog bites.

Smith's analogy with fines combines two issues that are worth separating. The first is the content of the court's order, and the second its normative basis. The content of the court's order is different in the specific act it requires; it calls on the defendant to do something different from what the primary duty required. But this contrast is only significant if both norms of conduct and orders are thought of as instructions, telling you to do or refrain from performing some specific action. Both the dog-leash bylaw and a fine for its violation fit the model of instructions.

Smith moves from this observation about the different actions required by each party to the very different claim that because the wrong and the legal response to it require different actions, they must also have different rationales. This may well be true in the case of fines, even if it is not well expressed in terms of a contrast between what fines "do" and what they "represent." The rationale for a fine is that the person who committed the infraction broke the law, and the content of the infraction, on Smith's model, is just the raw material on which the scheme of penalties operates.

In the case of a remedy for a private wrong, however, a different action may be required without a difference in their rationales. If you ask why you need to pay *this* fine, the most a court can do is direct you to the rel-

---

reasons that apply to the agent. So both the duty that was breached and the remedy are exactly alike in being legal specifications of the reasons that apply to the person.

33. See Robert Cooter, "Prices and Sanctions," *Columbia Law Review* 84 (1984): 1523–1560.

evant bylaw and its schedule of fines. But if you ask why you have been ordered to pay damages in the specific amount ordered, the answer will be in terms of the factors that properly enter into the court's deliberations about whether you wronged the plaintiff. That is, the content of the order is determined by the content of the right violated.

Smith supports his analysis by adducing two pieces of what he presents as empirical evidence about the ways in which common law courts operate. First, a defendant can neither reduce nor avoid liability by showing that he or she paid money to the plaintiff, unless that payment was part of a settlement of the claim.[34] Smith reasons that if there was a duty to pay damages, any payment ought to be able to discharge it without any intervention by a court. Second, in ordinary circumstances a defendant would be unable to comply with a pretrial duty to pay damages, because its existence and its magnitude may be unknown until the case is tried. As Smith puts it, the facts "are in the victim's hands."[35] Nor are these instances of unripe or inchoate duties; Smith contends that a duty with which the defendant could not voluntarily comply makes nonsense of the very idea of a duty.

5. Vindicating Rights

In place of a focus on the continuation of a duty, Smith suggests that the purpose of damages is to vindicate rights. Indeed, he draws attention to various forms of nonpecuniary damages, mentioning "nominal damages, damages for pain and suffering, aggravated damages, punitive damages, and many instances of damage awards made under human rights legislation. Less obvious examples include damages for things like the nondelivery, loss, or destruction of goods where the sum awarded is quantified not by the actual loss suffered but by an objective measure, such as market value. In all these cases, the damage award is most naturally understood as attempting to place a value directly on the right qua right."[36] Smith's suggestion about how to understand these cases is put

34. Smith, "Duties, Liabilities, and Damages," 1741.
35. Ibid., 1743.
36. Ibid., 1756.

forward as an alternative to the idea that rights survive their own violation, but on closer inspection it turns out to presuppose it. Consider first the exception to prepayment that Smith carves out by reference to settlements. If damages awards represent "the law's recognition that the plaintiff was wronged by the defendant" and are its "way of vindicating—not enforcing—the plaintiff's rights," it is surprising that the plaintiff should be in a position to exempt the defendant from the law's vindictive impulse. How can you settle a claim if you have no claim until a court orders a remedy? If the remedy is the continuation of the right, however, the plaintiff is entitled to constrain the defendant's conduct and the two of them can negotiate a settlement acceptable to both. That transaction differs from other instances in which a defendant transfers money to a plaintiff precisely in that it is the exercise of the plaintiff's right.[37]

The same point applies to Smith's suggestion that the measure of damages is the "right qua right." This is easiest to see in the cases in which an objective measure is introduced (however this might contrast with "actual loss suffered"[38]): The defendant is required to provide the plaintiff with a substitute for that of which the plaintiff was deprived. The substitute is measured by market value, that is, replacement cost. In the other cases the attempt to place a value directly on a right is indeed a way of vindicating the right, but upholding the right to the extent that it is possible to do so is the most straightforward way of vindicating it.

37. An outstanding tort claim may underwrite a claim in contribution or serve as a juristic reason to block an action in unjust enrichment, even if the statute of limitations has expired on the original tort action. See the discussion in Ernest J. Weinrib, "Civil Recourse and Corrective Justice," *Florida State University Law Review* 39 (2011): 286. Weinrib points out that this principle dates from Lord Mansfield's speech in Moses v. Macferlan, (1760) 97 Eng. Rep. 676 (K.B.) 680–681; 2 Burr. 1005, 1012–1013, which says that an action for unjust enrichment "does not lie for money paid by the plaintiff, which is claimed of him as payable in point of honor and honesty, although it could not have been recovered from him by any course of law; as in payment of a debt barred by the Statute of Limitations, because in all these cases, the defendant may retain it with a safe conscience, though by positive law he was barred from recovering."

38. Perhaps Smith is representing losses in terms of welfare. But if the plaintiff's right against the defendant is to have specific means subject to his or her choice, equivalent means will ordinarily be the measure of the plaintiff's loss.

Smith offers a further analogy with retributive theories of punishment, suggesting that an order of damages is a form of censure and is normally tied to the magnitude of the wrong done as a way of communicating the defendant's responsibility for it.[39]

Like other expressive theories, this proposal invites a familiar response, suggested by T. M. Scanlon: Why not say it instead with flowers, or better, with weeds?[40] Smith's expressive account occupies an unstable position between instrumental accounts that treat the relation between the plaintiff and the defendant as merely incidental, and the idea that the point of the remedy is to make it as if the wrong had never happened. If the point is to communicate something, why does the court go to the trouble of estimating the plaintiff's actual loss and consequential damages? Why not follow through on the analogy with a fine, and have the remedy keyed perfectly to the degree of the censure-worthiness of the defendant's conduct (or how a morally upstanding citizen would feel) but flow into the public purse to be used for any number of public purposes? For that matter, why not follow through on the analogy with the fine completely, and replace the remedy with a fine? Smith suggests that fines provide recognition and expression of wrongdoing, and that is why courts order people to pay them, even though, absent the order, they have no duty.

This may seem to be moving too quickly. Scanlon's response invites a familiar rejoinder: Actions often speak louder than words.[41] Helping a friend in need says more about how much you value the friendship than

39. Smith, "Why Courts Make Orders," 84.

40. T. M. Scanlon Jr., "The Significance of Choice," in *The Tanner Lectures on Human Values* 7 (1986): 214.

41. This thought figures prominently in Scott Hershovitz's essay "Tort as a Substitute for Revenge" as an explanation of why something must be done rather than merely said about the wrong. This commonplace observation may well be true of a pairwise comparison between requiring payment and merely announcing that the defendant did wrong. But why suppose that the only options are compelling the defendant to do something for the plaintiff, and publishing a notice in the town square? Why not require the defendant to pay a large fine, or, to use one of Hershovitz's recurring examples, invite the plaintiff to spit on the defendant? (Hershovitz introduces his account with a discussion of Alcorn v. Mitchell, 63 Ill. 553 (1872), a case in which the plaintiff brought an action because the defendant spat on him, and argues that this sort of showing of contempt is paradigmatic of tortious wrongdoing.)

endless verbal affirmations of how close you are. Economists have sought to generalize this point, developing an elaborate account of the way in which signals are most effective if costly. The basic thought is that rational agents will invest in things that their intended audience will take to correlate with the things that the audience cares about. A classic example involves acquiring educational credentials to convince employers to hire you. Again, the principals of a company about to make a public stock offering will retain a significant portion of the stock to signal to potential investors their confidence in the company. Such signals can only work if they are expensive; they are credible because a rational agent would hold on to a large amount stock only if genuinely confident in its quality. So, too, it might be thought, the readiness to impose a penalty on a tortfeasor is a way of expressing public disapproval of the wrong.

No such analogy can be made to work here, however. The remedy does nothing to display defendant's sincerity. The state is not bearing a cost to express something either because the wrongdoer is made to bear it. Nor will it help to suggest that the wrongdoer, by bearing the cost, is being made to express something. The rational agency model of the expressive role of action depends upon the assumption that the expense is being borne because of the high degree of confidence with which an actor believes something. Here economic signaling theory and commonsense views of sincerity in expression converge. If something is expressed in response to an order, it is not expressed either credibly or sincerely. The natural response to such compelled expression is captured in the expression "You're just saying that." Perhaps that is why expressive theories of punishment typically seek to distinguish between fines and true punishments. Although the relevant legal officials must order both, fines do not express the state's view by making *it* bear a cost, because the state collects something. This is not to say that there could not be some other expressive dimension in ordering someone to pay a fine or damages. The point is that any expressive dimension supervenes on the requirement itself.[42]

---

42. It is not clear how this proposal is consistent with Smith's objection to the idea that a right survives as a remedy, which, he said, would have the implication that courts should simply make declarations rather than giving orders. If the point of a tort remedy is to ex-

The dependence of expression on the continuing right also provides a response to what Goldberg and Zipursky and Smith regard as an objection to the claim that a court resolving a private dispute seeks to do justice, that is, the disproportion between the extent of liability and the defendant's degree of fault. Goldberg and Zipursky put this in terms of doing "more than justice requires," and Smith in terms of the "morally upstanding citizen." If the point of a tort remedy is to express something, but setting things right between the parties is not part of its point, the choice of expressive media that do not track what Goldberg and Zipursky think of as justice and Smith as the view of the morally upstanding citizen is puzzling. What possible expressive purpose could be served by this alleged disproportion?

In the same way, if the point of damages is to channel and civilize the plaintiff's reactive attitudes, why give the plaintiff more by way of damages than could be justly demanded in light of the seriousness of the wrong? Why not condition damages on the defendant's degree of fault? Indeed, why limit recovery to those whose rights were violated, rather than extending it to those negatively affected by the wrongdoing of others, as they, too, may be just as angry? And, as has sometimes been suggested, if the point of the legal proceeding is to provide a forum for accountability,[43] why is that accountability measured by the right violated, rather than the defendant's culpability, or the appropriateness of the reactive emotions of those affected by it? All of these further effects of a legal proceeding may well be worthwhile, but private litigation does a terrible job of realizing any of them.

I do not mean to deny that there is an important expressive dimension to many aspects of the law's operation;[44] the point is that, outside of spe-

---

press something, then it would appear that the ordering of a remedy is just an indirect way of making a declaration after all.

43. See, for example, Stephen Darwall and Julian Darwall, "Civil Recourse as Mutual Accountability," *Florida State University Law Review* 39 (2011): 117–141.

44. Communicative and expressive theories have been increasingly prominent in legal scholarship in recent decades. Everything from punishment through antidiscrimination law to minimum wage laws and rent control have been explained in terms of their expressive function. See the discussion in Elizabeth S. Anderson and Richard H. Pildes, "Expressive Theories of Law: A Restatement," *University of Pennsylvania Law Review* 148

cial circumstances, ways of treating people express what they do because of the ways in which those people are treated. So, for example, the problem with discrimination is the way in which people are treated, not what this says about either those who so treat them or those who are so treated;[45] if a public official acts for an illicit purpose, that the act expresses that purpose is not a further wrong over and above the wrongfulness of acting for that purpose.

The same point applies, with even more force, in the case of the payment of damages. Placing a demand on the defendant keyed to what that defendant has done to the plaintiff recognizes the wrong and communicates its nature because the remedy recognizes or communicates that the defendant is responsible *to the plaintiff for the precise wrong that the defendant did to the plaintiff.* Damages are awarded in recognition of the seriousness of the wrong and the need to remedy it. But then it seems much simpler to say that the defendant is liable because the defendant wronged the plaintiff, but in so doing did not extinguish the plaintiff's right. Characterizing the transaction in terms of expression is just a detour on the way to a more straightforward explanation exclusively in terms of the plaintiff's surviving claim against the defendant.

This is not to say that the court is not essential to the process. The plaintiff does not simply enforce a right, but rather comes before court seeking a remedy; as such, the defendant can rightly demand that the plaintiff prove the wrong. The plaintiff's power, and the concomitant legal distinction made by Smith between enforcing a right and claiming a remedy, is just a reflection of the defendant's more general entitlement. The space between the defendant's wrong and the plaintiff's right to re-

---

(2000): 1503–1575. Anderson and Pildes focus on the effects that legal norms have through their expressive content, pointing out that "communications can expressively harm people by creating or changing the social relationships in which the addressees stand to the communicator" (1528). The expressive legal remedies that Anderson and Pildes discuss are all constitutional, and all operate by having the state express them. They do not provide what Smith would need, namely, that forcing people to do things for which there is no other rationale (since he has ruled out rights enforcement) is an appropriate way of communicating condemnation.

45. Sophia Moreau, "What Is Discrimination?," *Philosophy & Public Affairs* 38, no. 2 (2010): 177–178.

pair is thus a reflection of the more general structuring features of private rights.[46]

6. The Role of a Court and the Nature of a Right

Far from drawing proper attention to the role of a court, both Goldberg and Zipursky's civil recourse theory and Smith's development of it make courts puzzling institutions. They then strain to find some other role for the courts, if they are to explain the features of the legal system to which they draw attention. Although their arguments are cast in doctrinal terms, focusing on what purport to be the empirical operations of the law, Goldberg and Zipursky, as well as Smith, depend on understanding rules as instructions, and focus only on their action-guiding features. If someone fails to follow the instructions, those instructions are silent on what to do. Instructions about how to treat other people are one thing; instructions about what to do in the event of a wrong are another. Part of the issue here is a technical one about the ways in which legal duties are individuated. If a duty specifies a specific action, then the specific duty cannot survive its own violation, though the reasons for the duty can.[47] Hohfeld thought that legal relations must been viewed as atoms, each in need of its own justification on grounds of justice and policy.[48] Goldberg, Zipursky, and Smith seem to presuppose something even stronger—that the reasons or grounds for the remedy must be fundamentally different from the reasons for the right, the violation of which it is supposed to

46. To assign primacy to the court's expressive role is to give up on the bipolarity critique of economic analysis. Civil recourse theory can retain the idea that a particular plaintiff recovers from the defendant who injured him or her in one sense—the defendant's wronging of the plaintiff is the occasion of revenge, expression, or accountability—but cannot explain why these roles are reserved for the plaintiff. The plaintiff seems like the most obvious candidate, but once the idea of righting a wrong is rejected, the obviousness seems misplaced, just as it does for economic analysis.

47. John Gardner, "What Is Tort Law For? Part 1: The Place of Corrective Justice," *Law and Philosophy* 30 (2011): 1–50.

48. See Wesley N. Hohfeld, "Some Fundamental Legal Conceptions as Applied in Judicial Reasoning," *Yale Law Journal* 23 (1913): 36.

remedy. No analysis of the individuation of duties could possibly establish or even be relevant to this claim.

The difficulty for the civil recourse account is that the things that courts do, and the questions that they ask in seeking to assess damages, are not merely defective realizations of these other putative purposes; they bear no relation to them whatsoever. Asking about the extent of the plaintiff's injury, and whether it was within the ambit of the defendant's wrong, makes sense only if the basis of liability is what the plaintiff already had.

Once the role of a court in resolving a tort claim is clarified, there is no need for the elaborate explanations proposed by Goldberg, Zipursky, and Smith. The point of damages is not to express something, and the point of empowering plaintiffs is not to compensate them for the loss that they suffer by being prohibited from engaging in acts of private revenge, or to enable them to defend themselves after the fact of a wrong. Expressive accounts cannot explain why the specific plaintiff gets to recover from a specific defendant.

7. Conclusion

When a court seeks to determine whether a defendant owed a plaintiff a duty, or when a finder of fact seeks to determine whether a defendant exercised reasonable care, the question at issue enters into a chain of reasoning, the conclusion of which will be a finding that the defendant did or did not wrong the plaintiff, on the basis of which a finding is made regarding liability. An adequate account of this reasoning must make each of the elements of the determination of liability potentially relevant to the conclusion in support of which it is argued. Civil recourse theory is attentive to this point in its characterization of torts as wrongs, but abandons it in its treatment of remedies. The claim to recourse when a plaintiff is wronged can be part of the same conceptual account that begins with the concept of a right underlying the allegation of a wrong—it can be the conclusion of a set of inferences in which the right is a basic premise—only if the remedy itself stands in inferential, rather than merely psychological or causal, relations to the underlying duties.

Wittgenstein is reported to have asked Elizabeth Anscombe, "Why do people say that it was natural to think that the sun went round the earth rather than that the earth turned on its axis?" When told that it was "because it looked as if the sun went round the earth," he asked, "What would it have looked like if it had looked as if the earth turned on its axis?"[49] All of the facts about legal processes to which defenders of civil recourse draw attention are just what tort law would look like if remedies turned on the axis of rights. A system in which no person is in charge of another requires courts to take charge of disputes.

49. G. E. M. Anscombe, *An Introduction to Wittgenstein's Tractatus* (Cambridge: Cambridge University Press, 1959), 91.

CHAPTER 10

Conclusion

Horizontal and Vertical

COURTS ARE FUNDAMENTALLY public institutions: They claim to act on behalf of both parties to a dispute. Unlike a private arbitrator hired by two people to resolve the dispute, a court claims a more general jurisdiction. If you allege that I have wronged you, you do not need to convince me to submit our dispute to a public court; all you need to do is serve me with papers. If I refuse to respond to your charges, then if you successfully state a cause of action, your claim will succeed, and the court will order a remedy against me.

In this concluding chapter, I broaden the discussion to the relation between private wrongs and distinctively public institutions. In recent political philosophy, a focus on private wrongdoing and rights with respect to property has been associated primarily with libertarians, who suppose that the legitimate purposes of the state are restricted to enforcing private rights.[1] No part of the argument of this book rests on any such assumption. Indeed, those who suppose that relations between the individual and the state must be modeled on relations between private persons (and any powers exercised by the state traced to some benefit

---

1. Most prominently, Robert Nozick, *Anarchy, State, and Utopia* (New York: Basic Books, 1974).

provided in consideration of payment received) make the mirror image of the mistake that the Holmesian instrumentalist makes in imagining tort law to be a tool in the service of public purposes. If the Holmesian instrumentalist sees the relation between the state and its citizens as combining that between a benefactor and its passive beneficiaries and that of a taskmaster and its vassals, the libertarian sees the relation between the state and each of its citizens as that between a service provider and its customers. Neither is attractive or persuasive as a model of the relation between the modern state and its citizens.

A better way of thinking about the relation between the state and its citizens focuses on the role of the state as providing the background conditions for a social world of which everyone is a full member. Legal doctrine and courts are among those conditions, but do not exhaust them. A state's obligation and entitlement to set up institutions for making, applying, and enforcing law also depends on its standing in the right relation to those over whom such power is exercised: To be entitled to act on behalf of everyone, it must stand in the right relation to each citizen over whom it exercises power. This vertical relationship is different in kind from the horizontal relations between private persons that are governed by the principle that no person is in charge of another.

Fulfilling these conditions has at least two dimensions. The first of these is seeing to it that everyone has enough to avoid falling into extreme dependence on others. In *The Social Contract,* Rousseau wrote that "no citizen be so very rich that he can buy another, and none so poor that he is compelled to sell himself."[2] Different writers have offered different characterizations of just what this requires—the economic resources, education, and protection against disastrous outcomes such as disease and serious injury. The second dimension is the provision of a robust public sphere, and proper conditions for participation in it, through which a society can give meaningful answers to these questions in a way that is consistent with those answers being everyone's answers. A court resolving a private dispute purports to speak from such a public standpoint; a robust public sphere underwrites its claim to do so.

---

2. Jean Jacques Rousseau, *"The Social Contract" and Other Later Political Writings,* trans. V. Gourevitch (Cambridge: Cambridge University Press, 1997), bk. 2, chap. 11, p. 78.

This understanding of the role of a state stands in sharp contrast with the idea of a "welfare state": The state does not aim to make people happy, make transactions efficient, or see to it that resources are used by those who value them the most. Instead, it protects and provides for the ability of individual citizens to make what they will of their own lives, and, more generally, enables them to each enjoy their private rights in a way that is consistent with the ability of others to do the same, and to participate in the operation and oversight of public institutions. The state only has standing to do anything if it is doing so on behalf of all citizens.

Contemporary states do not always do as good a job as they should of guaranteeing adequate rights and opportunities to private citizens. Nor do they always do as good a job as they should of acting only for public purposes rather than private ones. The perspective from which these flaws show up, however, is not one of maximizing overall welfare, but instead, the public responsibility to guarantee citizens adequate rights and opportunities.

If the state is charged with providing citizens with the conditions of full membership, its ability to do so will require further powers that no private person can have. Beyond the entitlement to make laws and adjudicate and impose binding resolution on private disputes, the state must also have the power to tax, that is, to compel citizens to contribute to the costs of maintaining its essential programs. The power to tax is consistent with the right that each of us has to his or her own body and property. Those rights mean that your entitlement to set and pursue your own purposes is not subordinated to the private purposes of others. As we saw in our discussion of misfeasance in a public office, that same entitlement protects you against public officials using their offices for illegitimate purposes. The wrongfulness of their doing so does not show that public officials operate improperly when they act within their mandates. Indeed, the very possibility of a wrong of misfeasance in a public office turns on the fact that there are distinctively public purposes, and public officials charged with achieving them. Creating and sustaining a social world in which no person is in charge of another—in which interpersonal cooperation is voluntary—requires mandatory cooperation in providing the necessary institutions and resources to achieve these public purposes.

The fact that the state can make such demands on private citizens does not show that the private rights citizens have against each other are somehow granted by the state as a way of serving public purposes. Instead, providing people with the conditions of full membership in society is a matter of what John Rawls once described as "background justice," that is, providing conditions for free persons to set and pursue their own purposes. Rawls identifies the need for institutions of background justice with the tendency of individual transactions to erode the background conditions necessary for everyone to be a full participant in society.[3] The specifics of Rawls's formulation need not concern us; the essential point is that its requirements arise independently of the justice of transactions. Private transactions cannot guarantee full membership, precisely because private transactions do not presuppose any specific ends.

Conversely, the idea of background justice presupposes what could be called "foreground justice," that is, the system in which cooperation is voluntary rather than mandatory, in which the purposes pursued are determined by individuals. The requirement of background justice does not show that foreground justice is an illusion; indeed, the role of background justice is not as a complete determination of who has what. Instead, it gets its point from the idea that people are free to set and pursue their own purposes, and provides them with adequate means to do so. That is, the foreground justice with which background justice contrasts supposes that individual citizens are in charge of themselves, rather than each person being provided with social shares in the service of seeing to it that there is still more background justice.[4] A liberal state is not charged with pro-

---

3. John Rawls, *Political Liberalism* (New York: Columbia University Press, 1993), 267.

4. A focus on background justice thus contrasts with at least one prominent strand in Ronald Dworkin's scheme of "equality of resources." For Dworkin, the point of private rights, especially rights against private wrongdoing, is to enable a better measure of comparative distributive shares. He writes that "a regulatory constraint or article of tort law is justified under the principle of correction only if there are good grounds for supposing that the corruption of the opportunity-cost test would be less with the constraint in place than without it." Dworkin, *Sovereign Virtue* (Cambridge, MA: Harvard University Press, 2000), 157. Unsurprisingly, Dworkin sees continuities between his approach and the economic analysis of law, and, as we saw in Chapter 3, appeals to Coasean ideas about transaction costs. I describe this as one strand because Dworkin also speaks of "a division of responsibility" between society and the individual. See "Ronald Dworkin Replies," in *Dworkin and His Critics*, ed. Justine Burley (Oxford: Blackwell, 2004), 391n18. Other writers who have sought to develop Dworkin's distinction between choices and circumstances, most prominently G. A. Cohen, are explicit in treating transactions as irrelevant to

viding education, health care, and economic support to those in need in
order to better enable citizens to contribute to bringing about some outcome; it provides them to enable them both to pursue their own purposes
and to participate as they see fit in the public sphere.

The state's power to compel citizens to support its broader activities
takes many forms. Taxation is the most visible of these, but small-scale
forms of conscription through the imposition of affirmative obligations
are also familiar. In Chapter 3 we encountered a number of examples,
ranging from the German criminal law statute requiring passersby to
render aid to those in peril to the duty to move out of the way of emergency
vehicles. These requirements are parts of a system of mandatory cooperation, designed to protect people from dreadful outcomes, and so to
enable them to continue to be members of society. As public law requirements, they do not give rise to any private right, because the affirmative
obligation to render assistance is part of a public system of cooperation.
Sometimes conscription is more direct, as when vacationers are required
to assist in fighting a forest fire or building a dike to prevent a flood. Robert
Nozick once compared taxation to forced labor; these examples serve as
reminders that both can be acceptable for proper public purposes.[5]

A third mode of public provision is mandatory participation in schemes
of public insurance, such as publicly funded or mandated pension
plans, health or employment insurance, and workplace safety insurance
schemes.[6] The last of these is sometimes represented as an alternative to
tort law, a different way of achieving the same things.[7] That cannot be
quite right. Like the characterization of such systems as "no-fault com-

---

justice. Cohen identifies justice with the removal of the effects of luck, rather than with the
modern idea of individual freedom and equal citizenship.

5. Nozick, *Anarchy, State, and Utopia,* 169.

6. This marks another contrast with Dworkin's account, which models redistributive
programs on the amount of private insurance that individuals would purchase in an ideal
auction in which each person had an equal share of resources. See *Sovereign Virtue,* 105.
That is not its point at all; mandatory cooperation is not a solution to the failure of foreground justice to deliver appropriate quantities of privately valued goods; it is the provision of background justice.

7. See, for example, David Enoch, "Tort Liability and Taking Responsibility," in *Philosophical Foundations of the Law of Torts,* ed. John Oberdiek (Oxford: Oxford University
Press, 2014).

pensation," such a description misrepresents the contrast with the idea of a private wrong. Tort law is not a system of fault-based compensation, or a tool for pursuing the goals of compensation, deterrence, or sanction. It is a system of private rights that survive their own violation. Workplace compensation schemes, by contrast, are systems of public provision of insurance against outcomes that will be disastrous for most people on whom they befall. Such systems do not require a showing of fault (or any other element of a private wrong, not even that the injury be the act of another person), because the basis of the compensation is the outcome, not the violation of a right. Injuries occasioned through wrongdoing are treated the same as any other injury arising in the course of employment. Likewise, the source of the compensation need not be the injurer. The basis of recovery is not wrongdoing, and there may not be a wrongdoer.

Most jurisdictions that have implemented such systems have abolished the private right of action to make the implementation work more smoothly, both bureaucratically and politically. Employers are more likely to accept mandatory premiums if they are spared tort liability. This example shows a different way of securing resources for public provision: a combination of mandatory contributions with the abolition of private rights of action.[8]

---

8. A more thoroughgoing version of the same approach has been adopted in New Zealand. Beginning with the Woodhouse report, *Compensation for Personal Injury in New Zealand* (Wellington: Government Printer, 1967), New Zealand adopted an Accident Compensation Scheme, based on perceived defects of tort law. Each of these was articulated in terms of what were said to be the goals of tort liability, which were identified in terms of compensation and proportionality to the defendant's fault, and the deterrence of unwanted conduct. By treating tort law as a defective system of accident compensation and deterrence, the Woodhouse report treated the tort system and accident compensation scheme as competitors, and chose the latter. I will not rehearse the misunderstandings of the nature of private wrongs with which the Woodhouse report worked. In a 2008 review, a number of benefits were cited for the Accident Compensation Commission, including, among other things, support to the adventure tourism business in that country. Abolishing the action for personal injury spares tour operators of the risk of liability and protects vacationers by giving them compensation rather than requiring them to sign away all of their rights. Price Waterhouse Cooper, *Accident Compensation Corporation, New Zealand Scheme Review*, March 2008. Suppose this is a legitimate policy objective for the New Zealand government (an issue on which I take no stand here) on the grounds that it will develop the economy and create both employment and badly needed tax revenue. Perhaps a more narrowly crafted exemption would have been a better idea, but it is within the state's proper authority

Some automobile insurance systems operate in similar ways, requiring motorists to carry first-party insurance for damage to their own vehicles. I take no position here on whether these are wise as a matter of public policy, or rather instances of the sort of "regulatory capture" of which social choice theorists complain.[9] If they serve legitimate public purposes of providing for background justice, and the restriction on the operation of private rights is the only way in which they can be realistically implemented, they are legitimate. They are not alternatives to tort liability, in the sense of being alternative mechanisms for securing a common result,[10] but rather systems of mandatory social insurance. It is not surprising that they classify particular incidents differently and do not attend to fault or wrongdoing.

The acceptability of such compromises does not mean they are not compromises, or that private rights are merely instruments of public policy. Instead, it shows that the provision of background justice may be achieved through limitations on the enforcement of private rights. This is hardly surprising: In the context of defamation we saw that parliamentary proceedings are subject to absolute privilege, and that under the *Reynolds* privilege, responsible journalism provides a complete defense to an action in defamation. In these cases, restrictions on the operation of private causes of action protect institutions fundamental to the proper functioning of the public sphere. The restriction of the defamed person's right to his or her own good name may be acceptable, but is still the compromise of a right.

Social insurance for accidental injury and loss looks different from the privilege that protects the public sphere in defamation. The scheme pro-

---

to make such determinations. In such a situation, the abolition of what would have been a private right of action can be treated as the legitimate exercise of public power without supposing, as the original Woodhouse report seemed to suggest, that private rights of action are irrational and pointless as a perfectly general matter.

9. See George Stigler, "The Theory of Economic Regulation," *Bell Journal of Economic and Management Science* 2 (Spring 1971): 3–21.

10. Casebooks used for the teaching of torts in the United States frequently have sections on "alternatives to tort law." In some instances, the section becomes the entire book. See, for example, Marc A. Franklin, Robert L. Rabin, and Michael D. Green, *Tort Law and Alternatives: Cases and Materials,* 9th ed. (New York: Foundation Press, 2011).

vides something to those who have been wronged (which it also provides to others who suffer similar losses without wrongs); the person who is defamed in parliament gets nothing. But that difference reflects a difference in the aspect of the public sphere that is being protected. The point of parliamentary and *Reynolds* privilege in defamation is to protect the public sphere; the point of mandatory insurance schemes is to protect individual citizens from outcomes that would be disastrous for them from the perspective of their ability to participate fully in social life. To provide such protection, those schemes must not distinguish between wrongs and other occasions of compensation within their scope. This, in turn, reflects the fact that they do not treat compensation as a remedy, because it does not represent the survival of a right.

The liberal state's status as a legal order requires that it both secure each person's horizontal rights against other private persons and that it provide the conditions under which it acts on behalf of everyone. Sometimes both requirements cannot be fully satisfied in a specific case. But if the restriction on the operation of private rights can be justified by the demands of background justice, that does not mean that they count for nothing or that nothing is lost through the restriction.

The argument of this book has developed the moral idea that no person is in charge of another to illuminate the familiar categories of private wrongdoing: the fundamental distinction between misfeasance and nonfeasance, the idea that damages are a substitute for the object of a violated right, and the role of a court in giving effect to private rights. For those interested in background justice, it also provided an account of the moral structure of foreground justice. Private rights and norms of conduct reconcile the responsibilities that separate persons each have for their own lives. I have not attempted to show that instrumentalist accounts that aspire to reduce tort law to some other state activity have misunderstood its true meaning or essence. My anti-reductive aspirations are more humble: I have tried to show that tort law does not need to have a function in order to have a point.

Index